Lecture Notes in Computer Science 2257

Edited by G. Goos, J. Hartmanis, and J. van Leeuwen

Springer

Berlin
Heidelberg
New York
Barcelona
Hong Kong
London
Milan
Paris
Tokyo

Shriram Krishnamurthi
C.R. Ramakrishnan (Eds.)

Practical Aspects of Declarative Languages

4th International Symposium, PADL 2002
Portland, OR, USA, January 19-20, 2002
Proceedings

 Springer

Series Editors

Gerhard Goos, Karlsruhe University, Germany
Juris Hartmanis, Cornell University, NY, USA
Jan van Leeuwen, Utrecht University, The Netherlands

Volume Editors

Shriram Krishnamurthi
Brown University, Computer Science Department
Box 1910, Providence, RI 02912, USA
E-mail: sk@cs.brown.edu

C.R. Ramakrishnan
SUNY at Stony Brook, Department of Computer Science
Stony Brook, NY 11794-4400, USA
E-mail: cram@cs.sunysb.edu

Cataloging-in-Publication Data applied for

Die Deutsche Bibliothek - CIP-Einheitsaufnahme

Practical aspects of declarative languages : 4th international symposium ;
proceedings / PADL 2002, Portland, OR, USA, January 19 - 20, 2002. Shriram
Krishnamurthi ; C. R. Ramakrishnan (ed.). - Berlin ; Heidelberg ; New York ;
Barcelona ; Hong Kong ; London ; Milan ; Paris ; Tokyo : Springer, 2002
  (Lecture notes in computer science ; Vol. 2257)
  ISBN 3-540-43092-X

CR Subject Classification (1998):D.3, D.1, F.3, D.2

ISSN 0302-9743
ISBN 3-540-43092-X Springer-Verlag Berlin Heidelberg New York

Springer-Verlag Berlin Heidelberg New York
a member of BertelsmannSpringer Science+Business Media GmbH

http://www.springer.de

© Springer-Verlag Berlin Heidelberg 2002

Typesetting: Camera-ready by author, data conversion by DA-TeX Gerd Blumenstein
Printed on acid-free paper   SPIN 10846034   06/3142   5 4 3 2 1 0

Preface

Declarative languages build on sound theoretical bases to provide attractive frameworks for application development. These languages have been successfully applied to a wide variety of real-world situations including database management, active networks, software engineering, and decision-support systems.

New developments in theory and implementation expose fresh opportunities. At the same time, the application of declarative languages to novel problems raises numerous interesting research issues. These well-known questions include scalability, language extensions for application deployment, and programming environments. Thus, applications drive the progress in the theory and implementation of declarative systems, and in turn benefit from this progress.

The International Symposium on Practical Applications of Declarative Languages (PADL) provides a forum for researchers, practitioners, and implementors of declarative languages to exchange ideas on current and novel application areas and on the requirements for effective use of declarative systems. The fourth PADL symposium was held in Portland, Oregon, on January 19 and 20, 2002.

Thirty-seven papers were submitted in response to the call for papers. Each paper was reviewed by at least three referees. Eighteen papers were selected for presentation at the symposium. The symposium included invited talks by Veronica Dahl (Simon Fraser University) on "How to Talk to Your Computer so that It Will Listen"; Catherine Meadows (Naval Research Laboratory) on "Using a Declarative Language to Build an Experimental Analysis Tool"; and J. Strother Moore (University of Texas-Austin) on "Single-Threaded Objects in ACL2". Every member of the program committee went the extra mile to give constructive, detailed feedback on submitted papers. Additional reviewers were brought in to help the program committee evaluate the submissions. We gratefully acknowledge their service.

This workshop was co-located with the ACM Symposium on Principles of Programming Languages (POPL 2002). It was sponsored by COMPULOG AMERICAS, a network of research groups dedicated to promoting research in logic programming and related areas, by the Association for Logic Programming (ALP), the ACM, and the European Association for Programming Languages and Systems (EAPLS). We also thank Brown University, SUNY at Stony Brook, and the University of Texas at Dallas for generously making their resources available for the organization of the symposium. The support of many individuals was crucial to the success of the symposium. We thank John Launchbury (POPL general chair) and Kelly Atkinson (Conference Secretary) for general organizational help. We thank Gopal Gupta, the conference chair, for coordinating the organization of the symposium. We also thank Paul Graunke, who helped us develop and manage the software used to submit and review papers, and Samik Basu, who assisted in putting the final proceedings together.

November 2001

Shriram Krishnamurthi
C. R. Ramakrishnan

Program Committee

Referees

Table of Contents

Invited Talks

Using a Declarative Language to Build an Experimental Analysis Tool 1
Catherine Meadows

How to Talk to Your Computer so that It Will Listen 3
Veronica Dahl

Single-Threaded Objects in ACL2 9
Robert S. Boyer and J. Strother Moore

Regular Papers

Modeling Engineering Structures with Constrained Objects 28
Bharat Jayaraman and Pallavi Tambay

Compiler Construction in Higher Order Logic Programming 47
Chuck C. Liang

Declarative Programming and Clinical Medicine
(On the Use of Gisela in the MedView Project) 64
Olof Torgersson

Semantics-Based Filtering: Logic Programming's Killer App? 82
*Gopal Gupta, Hai-Feng Guo, Arthur I. Karshmer, Enrico Pontelli,
Juan Raymundo Iglesias, Desh Ranjan, Brook Milligan, Nayana Datta,
Omar El Khatib, Mohammed Noamany, and Xinhong Zhou*

Linear Scan Register Allocation in a High-Performance Erlang Compiler .. 101
Erik Johansson and Konstantinos Sagonas

Compiling Embedded Programs to Byte Code 120
Morten Rhiger

Typed Combinators for Generic Traversal 137
Ralf Lämmel and Joost Visser

Event-Driven FRP 155
Zhanyong Wan, Walid Taha, and Paul Hudak

Adding Apples and Oranges 173
Martin Erwig and Margaret Burnett

WASH/CGI: Server-Side Web Scripting
with Sessions and Typed, Compositional Forms 192
Peter Thiemann

A Better XML Parser through Functional Programming 209
Oleg Kiselyov

Functional Approach to Texture Generation 225
Jerzy Karczmarczuk

Abstract Interpretation over Non-deterministic Finite Tree Automata
for Set-Based Analysis of Logic Programs 243
John P. Gallagher and Germán Puebla

A High-Level Generic Interface to External Programming Languages
for ECLiPSe 262
Kish Shen, Joachim Schimpf, Stefano Novello, and Josh Singer

A Debugging Scheme for Declarative Equation
Based Modeling Languages 280
Peter Bunus and Peter Fritzson

Segment Order Preserving and Generational Garbage Collection
for Prolog 299
Ruben Vandeginste, Konstantinos Sagonas, and Bart Demoen

Exploiting Efficient Control and Data Structures in Logic Programs 318
Rong Yang and Steve Gregory

Suspending and Resuming Computations in Engines for SLG Evaluation .. 332
Luís F. Castro, Terrance Swift, and David S. Warren

Author Index 351

Using a Declarative Language to Build an Experimental Analysis Tool

Catherine Meadows

Naval Research Laboratory, Code 5543
Washington, DC 20375, USA

Abstract. In this paper we give a brief summary of our experience in using a declarative language, Prolog, to develop an experimental formal analysis tool, the NRL Protocol Analyzer, which was updated and modified over the years to incorporate new theories and techniques. We discuss the benefits of using such an approach, and also some of the downsides....

The application of formal methods to cryptographic protocol analysis is now an established field. The types of assumptions that need to be made, and the techniques for automatically proving properties of cryptographic protocols, are well known, at least for a certain subclass of problems. However, when we began working on this problem in the late 80's, this was definitely not the case. Only a few tools, such as Millen's Interrogator [6], and a few algorithms, such as those devised by Dolev, Even, and Karp, [1], existed. Although these could be used as a basis for my research, it was unclear where we would ultimately wind up. Thus, we needed to ability to build a tool that could be rapidly reconfigured to incorporate new techniques and models, and that updated over (possibly) over a long period of time.

The earliest version of the Analyzer [2] consisted of a simply of a state generation tool. The user specified a state, and the Analyzer would use equational unification to generate all states that immediately preceded it. The search strategy was largely guided by the user, and was input by hand. This was very tedious, but allowed me to collect data that could be used to build the next version of the Analyzer.

The second version of the Analyzer allowed some automatic guidance of the search. In particular, it was possible to write and then use the Analyzer to prove inductive lemmas that put conditions on infinite classes of states. The search could then automatically avoid states that were unreachable according to the lemmas. However, it was up to the user to figure out what lemmas needed to be proved.

As we continued to use the Analyzer, it was found that many of the lemmas obeyed certain canonical forms. This made it easier to automate the generation as well as the proof of lemmas. Thus, the current version of the Analyzer, although it still requires some input from the user, generates most lemmas automatically [3]. It also proves a much greater variety of lemmas than it did before, and supports

S. Krishnamurthi, C. R. Ramakrishnan (Eds.): PADL 2002, LNCS 2257, pp. 1–2, 2002.

a higher-level and more flexible specification language than earlier versions. The most up-to-date description of the Analyzer is given in [4].

Throughout this process, we found the use of a declarative language such as Prolog a great boon. The ease of writing and reading such programs made it easier to update the Analyzer incrementally, over long periods of time, and even with long periods of inactivity. On the other hand, we found that many of the special tricks that can be used to improve Prolog's performance worked against this, and as a result we intended to avoid this after a while. Because of this, and because of other design decisions that we made in order to make this incremental modification easier (the use of generate-and-test as a theorem proving strategy, for example), there are a number of cryptographic protocol analysis tools designed with more specialized applications in mind that outperform the Analyzer. However, we believe that the Analyzer is still one of the most flexible tools around, and it has been used in the analysis of more complex protocols (see for example [4,5]) than almost any other tool. Moreover, many of the newer tools make use of techniques that were pioneered by the NRL Protocol Analyzer.

In summary, we would definitely recommend declarative programming as a rapid prototyping tool, especially one which is expected to undergo major changes as a project progresses. On the downside, the very techniques that would improve such a program's performance appear to mitigate against its usefulness for rapid prototyping by making the program more opaque. However, this is a tradeoff that one might expect.

References

1. D. Dolev, S. Even, and R. Karp. On the Security of Ping-Pong Protocols. *Information and Control*, pages 57–68, 1982. 1
2. C. Meadows. A system for the specification and verification of key management protocols. In *Proceedings of the 1991 IEEE Symposium in Research in Security and Privacy*. IEEE Computer Society Press, May 1991. 1
3. Catherine Meadows. Language generation and verification in the NRL protocol analyzer. In *Proceedings of the 9th Computer Security Foundations Workshop*. IEEE Computer Society Press, 1996. 1
4. Catherine Meadows. Analysis of the Internet Key Exchange protocol using the NRL Protocol Analyzer. In *Proceedings of the 1999 IEEE Symposium on Security and Privacy*. IEEE Computer Society Press, 1999. 2
5. Catherine Meadows. Experiences in the formal analyzer of the GDOI protocol. In *Proceedings of Verlassliche IT-Systeme 2001 - Sicherheit in komplexen IT-Infrastrukturen*, 2001. 2
6. J. K. Millen. The interrogator: A tool for cryptographic protocol security. In *Proc. 1984 Symp. Security and Privacy*, pages 134–141. IEEE Computer Society Press, 1984. 1

How to Talk to Your Computer
so that It Will Listen
Extended Abstract

Veronica Dahl

Logic and Functional Programming Group, Computing Sciences Department
Simon Fraser University, Burnaby, B.C. V5A 1S6, Canada
veronica@cs.sfu.ca

1 Introduction

Currently, many developments revolutionize computing sciences: the maturing of logic programming/grammars, allowing us to communicate with computers in more human and higher level terms than ever before; the World Wide Web; and the possibility of speaking to computers through affordable software such as Naturally Speaking or Microsoft Speech Agent.

The time is ripe to try to integrate these developments, with the final aim of making speech itself the programming language of choice. This article discusses shorter term, more attainable objectives along the route to that final goal, from the perspective of our own personal research interests.

2 Research Directions

Interesting results have recently been obtained in the areas of natural language processing, virtual worlds, internet programming and mining, robotics, deductive knowledge bases, and the combination of these.

Such results indicate good promise for the following shorter term research directions:

1. Automatic creation and consultation of knowledge bases through natural language: We are developing a prototype system that will automatically initialize, update and query a database from speech commands, as well as generate spoken answers, based on initial results reported in [5]. This research branch partially addresses the need of integrating software for speech recognition, speech synthesis, and Artificial Intelligence programs. For the language component, we mainly rely on the grammatical form of Assumptive Logic Programming [34,10,9,14,6,30]. We shall also adapt our deductive database methodologies [17,13] to the task, and integrate them with our abductive reasoning methodologies for syntactic error recovery [2] and for exception handling [19]. We shall also incorporate our treatment of ellipsis and sentence coordination [12,7,15] into Assumption Grammar form, along

S. Krishnamurthi, C. R. Ramakrishnan (Eds.): PADL 2002, LNCS 2257, pp. 3–8, 2002.

the lines sketched in [34], to allow users as natural a dialogue with the computer as possible. This whole line of research is a milestone towards a longer term, more ambitious objective: programming through natural language.

2. Driving Robots through speech: This research branch was explored in a preliminary form in collaboration with Universite de Nice, for the high level routing of mini-robots [8,33] whose lower level operations were commanded in C. Possible applications include endowing robots with language understanding capabilities, including virtual robots (robots that move and execute commands in a visual world), such as explored in preliminary form with Andrea Schiel and Paul Tarau (Generating Internet-based Animations through NL controlled Partial Order Planners- SFU Internal report). Other exisiting prototypes of language-driven robots include the pet dog AIBO developed by Frédéric Kaplan at Sony CSL, Paris, and the Japanese robot of Dr Mizoguchi's team, which offers wine at social gatherings.

3. High level tools for accessing and interacting with the internet, aiming at endowing the web, that fantastic but often frustrating reservoir of knowledge, with intelligent communication capabilities such as:

   – Providing multilingual access to virtual worlds over the internet. A prototype system, LogiMOO [32] accepts interactions in various languages, translates each to a controlled English based interlingua (along the lines sketched in [11,31,21]), and reacts in the language of origin. Among the possible applications, those to distance learning have been outlined in [22], as well as those to robotics [8,33]

   – Knowledge extraction from internet documents. This branch of research, studied in [35,36], can be combined with the automatic creation of knowledge bases branch in order to produce domain-specific knowledge bases or concept classifications from web documents.

   Of particular interest for 3) is our recent research on code migration [26,23], [28,29], higher level internet tools [25,24], and resource discovery [35,36].

4. Automatic creation of taxonomies: This branch of our research is based on linguistic work [4] and has application to the two previous objectives as well as for instance to molecular biology, medical and forestry applications, etc. Our methodologies for type hierarchies will also be useful re. line of research 1), since an underlying ontology must be gleaned from the user's natural language specifications.

3   Related Work

The intersection between logic programming and the internet is a very new but rapidly growing field. Recent logic programming conferences typically include workshops or tutorials on the subject, and the journal Theory and Practice of Logic Programming has recently put out a special issue on this theme. A useful classification in terms of client-based systems, server-side systems, and peer-to-peer systems is given in [20]. Depending on the site where (most of) the processing happens, most systems fall into either client-side or server-side systems, while peer-to-peer systems (such as our own [11]) tend to have fully symmetric interaction capabilities, and use abstractions such as message passing or blackboards, while retaining the Internet as their underlying communication layer. This allows them to implement multi-agent systems, where all participants must communicate on equal terms, bypassing the intrinsic asymmetry of the client/server model. The most natural incarnation of peer-to-peer systems is the metaphor of communicating Virtual Worlds. The only system we know of which uses logic programming for virtual world simulation is our own system LogiMOO [32,11,31], although many sophisticated web-based applications and tools have been implemented in CP/CLP languages. A very large number of research projects have recently started on mobile computations and mobile agent programming. Among the most promising developments are Luca Cardelli's Oblique project at Digital, mobile agent applications, and IBM Japan's aglets (`http://www.trl.ibm.co.jp/aglets`). Database interfacing through spoken language has been little explored, possibly because speech analysis and synthesis software is relatively new and not as advanced as it should be for truly practical uses. Written text, however, has long been used for database consultation [3] and for database updates (e.g. [16]). There is increasing interest from industry in the spoken language field. However, putting all the pieces of the puzzle together will require careful crafting. Within the logic-based database field, developments such as the uses of Inductive Logic Programming to automate the construction of natural language interfaces to database queries [37] could prove most valuable.

4 Expected Benefits

Providing more human like communication with computers and with the Internet might help bridge the gap between the humanistic and the formal sciences, towards an overall more balanced world. Linguistics, being the most formalized of the humanistic sciences, holds fascinating promise when interacting with Computing Sciences.

Speech-driven database creation and consultation and robot control or programming might give some relief from computer use related health problems (tendonitis; eye, neck and back strain, Carpal Tunnel Syndrome...) that the present typing/screen based model of computer use entails. Our proposed higher level tools for internet access and interaction will add a degree of intelligent communication to the web, that fantastic but frustratingly unimaginative repository of world knowledge; and our multilingual virtual worlds will hopefully remove geographic and language barriers, perhaps contributing to enhance understanding and cooperation among the people of this world.

Acknowledgements

Thanks are due to my collaborators in the various projects here described: Pablo Accuosto, Jamie Andrews, Joao Balsa, Koen De Boschere, Andrew Fall, Jia Wei

Han, Yan Nong Huang, Renwei Li, Luis Moniz Pereira, Lidia Moreno, Manuel Palomar, Gabriel Pereira Lopes, Stephen Rochefort, Andrea Schiel, Marius Scurtescu, Paul Tarau, Marie-Claude Thomas, Kimberly Voll, Tom Yeh, and Osmar Zaiane. Special thanks go to Paul Graunke for formatting the text. This research was made possible by NSERC research grant 611024 and NSERC Equipment grant 31-613183.

References

1. J. Andrews, V. Dahl, and P. Tarau. Continuation logic programming: Theory and practice. In *ILPS'95 Workshop on Operational and Denotational Semantics of Logic Programs*, November 1995.
2. J. Balsa, V. Dahl, and J. G. Pereira Lopes. Datalog grammars for abductive syntactic error diagnosis and repair. In *Natural Language Understanding and Logic Programming Workshop*, 1995. 3
3. V. Dahl. On database systems development through logic. In *ACM Transactions on Database Systems*, volume 7(1), pages 102–123, March 1982. 5
4. V. Dahl. Incomplete types for logic databases. In *Applied Mathematics Letters*, volume 4(3), pages 25–28, 1991. 4
5. V. Dahl. From speech to knowledge. In M. T.Pazienza, editor, *Information Extraction: towards scalable, adaptable systems*, volume 1714, pages 49–75. Springer-Verlag, 1999. LNAI (Lecture Notes in Artificial Intelligence). 3
6. V. Dahl, A. Fall, S. Rochefort, and P. Tarau. Hypothetical reasoning framework for natural language processing. In *8th IEEE International Conference on Tools with Artificial Intelligence*, November 1996. 3
7. V. Dahl, A. Fall, and P. Tarau. Resolving co-specification in contexts. In *IJCAI'95 Workshop on Context in Language*, July 1995. 3
8. V. Dahl, A. Fall, and M. C. Thomas. Driving robots through natural language. In *IEEE International Conference on Systems, Man and Cybernetics*, pages 1904–1908, 1995. 4
9. V. Dahl and P. Tarau. From assumptions to meaning. In *Canadian Artificial Intelligence*, volume 42, Spring 1998. 3
10. V. Dahl, P. Tarau, P. Accuosto, S. Rochefort, and M. Scurtescu. Assumption grammars for knowledge-based systems. In *Informatica, Special Issue on Natural Language Processing and Agent Systems*, volume 22(4), pages 435–444, December 1998. (previous version in: Proc. NLDB'97, Vancouver, June 1997). 3
11. V. Dahl, P. Tarau, P. Accuosto, S. Rochefort, and M. Scurtescu. A spanish interface to LogiMOO—towards multilingual virtual worlds. In *Informatica*, volume 2, June 1999. (previous version in: Proc. International Workshop on Spanish Natural Language Processing and Language Technologies, Santa Fe, New Mexico, July 1997). 4, 5
12. V. Dahl, P. Tarau, and J. Andrews. Extending datalog grammars. In *Workshop on Natural Language and Databases (NLDB'95)*, June 1995. 3
13. V. Dahl, P. Tarau, and Y. N. Huang. Datalog grammars. In *Joint Conference on Declarative Programming*, pages 19–22, September 1994. 3
14. V. Dahl, P. Tarau, and R. Li. Assumption grammars for natural language processing. In Lee Naish, editor, *Fourteenth International Conference on Logic Programming*, pages 256–270. MIT Press, 1997. 3

15. V. Dahl, P. Tarau, L. Moreno, and M. Palomar. Treating coordination through datalog grammars. In *COMPULOGNET/ELSNET/EAGLES Workshop on Computational Logic for Natural Language Processing*, pages 1–17, April 1995. 3

16. James Davison. A natural language interface for performing database updates. In *ICDE*, pages 69–76, 1984. 5

17. Y. N. Huang, V. Dahl, and J. Han. Rule updates in logic databases: A meta programming approach. In *3rd International Pacific Rim Conference on Artificial Intelligence,*, August 1994. 3

18. Y. N. Huang, V. Dahl, and J. W. Han. Fact updates in logic databases. In *Int. Journal of Software Engineering and Knowledge Engineering*, volume 5(3), pages 467–491, 1995.

19. R. Li, V. Dahl, L. Moniz Pereira, and M. Scurtescu. Dealing with exceptions in textual databases. In *NLDB*, June 1997. 3

20. S. W. Loke. *Adding Logic Programming Behaviour to the World Wide Web*. PhD thesis, University of Melbourne, 1998. 4

21. S. Rochefort, V. Dahl, and P. Tarau. Controlling virtual worlds through extensible natural language. In *AAAI Symposium Series "Natural Language Processing for the World Wide Web"*, March 1997. 4

22. S. Rochefort, V. Dahl, and P. Tarau. A virtual environment for collaborative learning. In *World Multiconference on Systemics, Cybernetics and Informatics (SCI'98) and 4th International Conference on Information Systems Analysis and Synthesis (ISAS'98)*, volume 4, pages 413–416, 1998. 4

23. P. Tarau and V. Dahl. Code migration with first order continuations. In *Joint Declarative Programming Conference AGP98,*, July 1998. 4

24. P. Tarau and V. Dahl. A coordination logic for agent programming in virtual worlds. In W. Conen and G. Neumann, editors, *Coordination Technology for Collaborative Applications - Organizations, Processes, and Agents*. Springer-Verlag, 1998. 4

25. P. Tarau and V. Dahl. A logic programming infrastructure for internet programming. In M. J. Wooldridge and M. Veloso, editors, *Artificial Intelligence Today— Recent Trends and Developments*, pages 431–456. Springer-Verlag, 1999. LNAI 1600. 4

26. P. Tarau and V. Dahl. High level networking with mobile code and first order and continuations. In *Theory and Practice of Logic Programming*. Cambridge University Press, March 2001. (This is the new and sole official journal of the Association of Logic Programming). 4

27. P. Tarau, V. Dahl, and K. De Boschere. A logic programming approach to coordination in virtual worlds. In *Workshop on Coordination languages, models, systems in the Software Technology Track of the Hawaii International Conference on System Sciences (HICSS-31)*, 1997.

28. P. Tarau, V. Dahl, and K. De Boschere. A logic programming infrastructure for remote execution, mobile code and agents. In *Post ICLP Workshop on Logic Programming and Multi Agents*, July 1997. 4

29. P. Tarau, V. Dahl, and K. De Bosschere. Remote execution, mobile code and agents in binprolog. In *Electronic Proc. Logic Programming Workshop in conjunction with the 6th International World Wide Web Conference*, pages 7–11, April 1997. 4

30. P. Tarau, V. Dahl, and A. Fall. Backtrackable state with linear affine implication and assumption grammars. In J. Jaffar and R. Yap, editors, *Concurrency and parallelism, Programming, Networking, and Security*, pages 53–64. Springer Verlag, 1996. Lecture Notes in Computer Science 1179. 3

31. P. Tarau, V. Dahl, S. Rochefort, and K. De Bosschere. LogiMOO: a multi-user virtual world with agents and natural language programming. In S. Pemberton, editor, *CHI*, pages 323–324, 1997. 4, 5

32. P. Tarau, K. De Bosschere, V. Dahl, and S. Rochefort. LogiMOO: An extensible multi-user virtual world with natural language control. In *Logic Programming Journal*, volume 38(3), pages 331–353, March 1999. 4, 5

33. M. C. Thomas, V. Dahl, and A. Fall. Logic planning in robotics. In *IEEE International Conference on Systems, Man and Cybernetics*, pages 2951–2955, 1995. 4

34. K. Voll, T. Yeh, and V. Dahl. An assumptive logic programming methodology for parsing. In *12th Int'l Conference on Tools with Artificial Intelligence*, pages 11–17, 2000. 3, 4

35. O. R. Zaiane, A. Fall, S. Rochefort, V. Dahl, and P. Tarau. Concept-based retrieval using controlled natural language. In *NLDB*, June 1997. 4

36. O. R. Zaiane, A. Fall, S. Rochefort, V. Dahl, and P. Tarau. On-line resource discovery using natural language. In *RIAO, Computer-Assisted Searching on the Internet*, pages 336–355, June 1997. 4

37. J. M. Zelle and R. J. Mooney. Learning to parse database queries using inductive logic programming. In *Thirteenth National Conference on Artificial Inteligence*, pages 1050–1055, 1996. 5

Single-Threaded Objects in ACL2

Robert S. Boyer and J. Strother Moore

Department of Computer Sciences, University of Texas at Austin
Taylor Hall 2.124, Austin, Texas 78712, USA
{boyer,moore}@cs.utexas.edu

Abstract. ACL2 is a first-order applicative programming language based on Common Lisp. It is also a mathematical logic for which a mechanical theorem-prover has been implemented in the style of the Boyer-Moore theorem prover. The ACL2 system is used primarily in the modeling and verification of computer hardware and software, where the executability of the language allows models to be used as prototype designs or "simulators." To support efficient execution of certain kinds of models, especially models of microprocessors, ACL2 provides "single-threaded objects," structures with the usual "copy on write" applicative semantics but for which writes are implemented destructively. Syntactic restrictions insure consistency between the formal semantics and the implementation. The design of single-threaded objects has been influenced both by the need to make execution efficient and the need to make proofs about them simple. We discuss the issues.

1   Background

"ACL2" stands for "A Computational Logic for Applicative Common Lisp." We use the name both for a mathematical logic based on applicative Common Lisp [15] and for a mechanized theorem proving system for that logic developed by Matt Kaufmann and author Moore. ACL2 is closely related to the Boyer-Moore Nqthm logic and system and its interactive enhancement [2,3]. ACL2's primary use is in modeling microprocessors and proving theorems about those models. The key reason we abandoned the Nqthm logic and adopted applicative Common Lisp is that the latter can produce extremely efficient runtime code. Execution efficiency is important because our microprocessor models are often run as simulators.

In ACL2, a single-threaded object is a structure whose use is syntactically restricted so as to guarantee that there is exactly one reference to the structure. An example of a single-threaded object is the "current state" in a microprocessor model. The fact that only one reference to the object exists allows updates to the structure to be performed destructively even though the axiomatized semantics of update is "copy on write."

This work is thus addressing the classic problem of how to implement updates efficiently in an applicative setting. In that sense, our work is akin to that of [14,8,17,18]. Indeed, Schmidt introduced the term "single threaded"

S. Krishnamurthi, C. R. Ramakrishnan (Eds.): PADL 2002, LNCS 2257, pp. 9–27, 2002.
© Springer-Verlag Berlin Heidelberg 2002

in [14]. [18] contains a good survey of the most popular alternative in applicative languages, Haskell's "monads". But ACL2 is unusual among purely applicative programming languages in that it is focused as much on using the language as a specification language and on mechanically produced proofs as on execution efficiency. We find that these other concerns influenced our treatment of single-threaded objects. We do not regard the addition of single-threaded as objects as having changed the logic but rather just restricted its executable subset for efficiency reasons. The unrestricted logic is available for specification and proof.

The ACL2 theorem prover is used primarily in hardware and software verification. See [9] for many industrial case studies.

One of the main reasons ACL2 has found industrial application is that it is both a logic and an efficient applicative programming language. Once a formal model is created it is possible to test it on concrete examples and to prove properties of it.

Typically, the state of a microprocessor is modeled as an n-tuple containing fields representing memories of various kinds. Here we will imagine a state, MS, to be a triple containing a "next instruction counter" and two memories, one used for read/write and the other used to hold "execute-only" programs. The "state-transition" function, here called step, is a Lisp function that creates the next state from a given state, usually as a function of the "next instruction" indicated by the program counter and memory. The machine's fetch-execute cycle is then modeled by the simple recursive function

```
(defun run (MS  n)
  (if (zp  n)
      MS
    (run (step MS) (-  n 1))))
```

This Lisp command defines the function run so that, when applied to MS and n, it successively steps MS n times and returns the final result. In Lisp, the application of run to MS and n is written (run MS n) instead of run(MS,n).

We might define step so that it fetches the next instruction from MS and then "does" that instruction to MS,

```
(defun step (MS)
  (do-inst (next-inst MS) MS))
```

where the function next-inst fetches the instruction indicated by the next instruction counter and do-inst is defined as a case statement that invokes the appropriate transition function depending on the opcode of the next instruction.

```
(defun do-inst (inst MS)
  (case (op-code inst)
    (LOAD           (execute-LOAD inst MS))
    (STORE          (execute-STORE inst MS))
    (ADD            (execute-ADD inst MS))
    (GOTO           (execute-GOTO inst MS))
    ...
    (otherwise MS)))
```

Each instruction modeled, e.g., ADD, has a logical counterpart that specifies the transition, e.g., execute-ADD. Here is one such definition:

```
(defun execute-ADD (inst MS)
  (let ((a₁ (arg1 inst))
        (a₂ (arg2 inst)))
    (update-nic (+ 1 (nic MS))
                (update-memi  a₁
                             (+ (memi   a₁ MS)
                                (memi   a₂ MS))
                             MS))))
```

Here we are imagining that an ADD instruction has a "2-address" format. In the definition above we bind the variables a_1 and a_2 to the two addresses from which the instruction is to get its operands. We then construct a new state from *MS* by two "sequential" (i.e., nested) updates. The first (innermost) replaces the contents of memory location a_1 by the sum of contents of memory locations a_1 and a_2. The second update increments the next instruction counter, nic, by one. The program component of the state *MS* is unchanged.[1]

Suppose states are represented as triples and the memory component of a state *MS* is (nth 1 MS), i.e., the 1st element of the triple. Suppose that the memory is itself represented as a linear list. Then memi and update-memi are defined as shown below.

```
(defun memi (i MS)
  (nth   i (nth 1 MS)))
(defun update-memi (i   v MS)
  (update-nth 1
              (update-nth   i   v (nth 1 MS))
              MS))
```

where (nth n x) is the nth element (0-based) of the list x and (update-nth n v x) copies the list x, replacing the nth element with v. The definition of the latter is

```
(defun update-nth (n   v   x)
  (cond ((zp   n) (cons   v (cdr   x)))
        (t (cons (car   x)
                 (update-nth (1-   n)   v (cdr   x))))))
```

Thus, for example, (update-nth 3 'G '(A B C D E)) is equal to (A B C G E).

In principle, given a concrete microprocessor state and a particular number of steps to take we can compute the final state. This just requires executing run and the above subroutines on the concrete data. But if we actually implement

---

[1] Machines of commercial interest often have more complicated instruction semantics, e.g., the +-expression might be replaced by (mod (+ (memi a_1 MS) (memi a_2 MS)) (expt 2 32)), but this example is suggestive of the essential character of such models.

memi and `update-memi` as shown above, the time taken to execute memory reads and writes in our model is linear in the address. In addition, because the formal semantics of `update-nth` is "copy on write," storage (in an amount proportional to the address) is allocated on memory writes.

But inspection of the nest of functions starting with `run` and proceeding through `step` to the individual semantic functions like `execute-ADD`, reveals that we could in principle do this computation by destructively re-using the representation of the initial state, provided we never needed the top-level state again. If `update-memi` were implemented destructively, modifying the existing representation of the current state to obtain the next one, no harm would come because in the functions above no function references the "old" state after any update to any part of it. This is a syntactic property of the definitions and depends, in part, on order of evaluation.

This observation has led us to incorporate into ACL2 the notion of a user-defined *single-threaded object*. Such an object is a structure, possibly containing linear lists accessed positionally and usually quite large. Accessor functions, such as `nic` and `memi`, are provided, as are update functions, such as `update-nic` and `update-memi`. The axiomatic descriptions of the functions are as indicated by the definitions of `memi` and `update-memi` above. This permits us to state and prove properties of functions using the single-threaded object. However, syntactic restrictions are enforced that insure that it is sufficient to allocate only one "live" copy of the object. Updates are performed destructively on the live object. The syntactic restrictions — which actually require that we make minor changes to some of the definitions above — insure that no well-formed code executed on the live object can detect the difference between the axiomatic and implemented semantics of updates.

2   Introduction to ACL2

ACL2 is both the name of an applicative programming language and a theorem proving system for it. ACL2 is largely the work of Matt Kaufmann and Moore, building on work by Boyer and Moore. A general introduction to ACL2 may be found in [10].

2.1   The Logic

The kernel of the ACL2 logic consists of a syntax, some rules of inference, and some axioms. The kernel logic is given precisely in [11]. The logic supported by the mechanized ACL2 system is an extension of the kernel logic.

The kernel syntax describes terms composed of variables, constants, and function symbols applied to fixed numbers of argument terms. Thus, (* x (fact n)) is a term that might be written as $x \times n!$ in more traditional syntactic systems. After introducing Lisp-like terms, the kernel logic introduces the notion of "formulas" composed of equalities between terms and the usual propositional connectives. The kernel language is first order and quantifier free.

The ACL2 axioms describe the properties of certain Common Lisp primitives. For example,

Axioms.

$x = y \rightarrow$ (equal x y) = t
$x \neq y \rightarrow$ (equal x y) = nil
$x =$nil $\rightarrow$ (if x y z) = z
$x \neq$nil $\rightarrow$ (if x y z) = y

The expression (cond (p_0 x_0) ... (p_n x_n) (t x_{n+1})) is just an abbreviation for (if p_1 x_1 ... (if p_n x_n x_{n+1})...). Using the function symbols equal and if we "embed" propositional calculus and equality into the term language of the logic and generally write terms instead of formulas.

The kernel logic includes axioms that characterize the primitive functions for constructing and manipulating certain Common Lisp numbers, characters, strings, symbols, and ordered pairs.

Of special importance here, besides equal and if, are cons, car, and cdr, which, respectively, construct a new ordered pair and return the left and right components of such a pair. The predicate consp "recognizes" cons-pairs by returning one of the symbols t or nil according to whether its argument is a cons pair.

The rules of inference are those for propositional calculus with equality, instantiation, an induction principle and extension principles allowing for the definition of new total recursive functions, new constant symbols, new "symbol packages," and the declaration of the "current package" (used to support possibly overlapping name spaces). Our extension principles specify conditions under which the proposed extensions are admissible. For example, recursive definitions must be proved to terminate. The admissibility requirements insure the consistency of the resulting extensions.

For example, here is the definition of the previously mentioned function nth.

```
(defun nth (n    x)
   (cond ((zp    n) (car    x))
           (t (nth (-    n 1) (cdr    x)))))
```

The predicate zp is true if its argument is either 0 or not a natural number. Thus nth effectively "coerces" n to be a natural, by using zp as the "test against 0." All values of n other than natural numbers are treated as though they were 0. Termination of the recursion above is easy: when the recursive branch is taken, n is a non-0 natural number and the function decreases it in the recursion.

The logic supported by the ACL2 theorem prover is somewhat richer than the kernel logic sketched above.

2.2   The Relation to Common Lisp

Logically speaking, all ACL2 functions are total, but not all Common Lisp functions are total. For example, in Common Lisp, cdr is defined to be the right component of a `cons` pair and to be `nil` on the symbol `nil`. But ACL2 has the axiom

(consp x) = nil → (cdr x) = nil

Thus, in both ACL2 and Common Lisp, (cdr nil) is nil. But according to the axiom above, in ACL2 (cdr 23) is nil while in Common Lisp it is undefined and might signal an error or behave in some erratic or arbitrary way.

Our "completion" of Common Lisp makes the task of writing a theorem prover for it simpler, because the language is untyped and the axioms are strong enough to let us reduce to a constant any variable-free expression involving recursively defined functions in the primitives.

But only certain ACL2 expressions have their axiomatically described values under Common Lisp. The expressions in question are ones in which each function, f, is applied only to arguments within the domain prescribed for f by the Common Lisp specification [15]. The formalization of this notion of "prescribed domain" of a function is ACL2's notion of *guard*, a formula that describes the intended inputs to the function.

The guard for `nth`, above, requires that n be a natural number and x be a linear list or "true list". A linear list is a binary tree whose rightmost tip is `nil`. ACL2 uses an extension of Common Lisp's `declare` statement to allow the user to annotate definitions with their guards. Here is the definition of `nth` with its guard:

```
(defun nth (n  x)
  (declare (xargs :guard (and (integerp  n)
                              (<= 0  n)
                              (true-listp  x))))
  (cond ((zp  n) (car  x))
        (t (nth (-  n 1) (cdr  x)))))
```

A guard may be any ACL2 formula in the formal parameters of the function. Often guards are type-like and the system supports the use of Common Lisp's `type` declaration in conjunction with guards declared as above.

We say a function is *Common Lisp compliant* if, when its guard is satisfied by the function's inputs, the guards of all subroutines are satisfied by their inputs. The process of verifying that a function is Common Lisp compliant is called *guard verification*. Since ACL2 has a mechanical theorem prover associated with it, guard verification is elegantly implemented. Formulas expressing the conditions above are generated and handed over to the theorem prover for proof. Roughly speaking, in the definition of a function f there is a *guard conjecture* for each occurrence of a call of a subroutine g. The guard conjecture says "if the formal parameters of f satisfy the guard for f and the tests governing this call of g are true, then the actuals of the call of g satisfy the guard of g."

If an ACL2 function is Common Lisp compliant then any execution of it on inputs satisfying its guard is correctly calculated by executing the function in Common Lisp.

When the user submits an admissible function definition to ACL2, two functions are actually defined in the underlying Common Lisp. The first definition is called the *raw definition* and corresponds to what the user actually typed. The second is the *completed definition*. This definition is obtained from the given one by replacing all function names by the names of their completed counterparts as per the ACL2 axioms.

When the user submits a form to be evaluated, the system runs the guards on the form and if they are satisfied, the form is evaluated in Common Lisp, i.e., the faster, raw definitions are run. Otherwise, the slower, completed form is evaluated. Note that the guard is irrelevant to the logical meaning of a function; it only affects the efficiency with which ACL2 can compute the value of the function. If a large system of definitions has been proved to be Common Lisp compliant and some function in that system is called, e.g., to simulate a test run of a microprocessor, then the guard of that top-level function call is tested once and all subsequent execution is of fast, raw code.

Because of guards, calls of compliant ACL2 functions can be replaced by raw Lisp that is more efficient than their logical definitions suggest.

Nth, as shown above, is Common Lisp compliant. On inputs satisfying its guard, the compiled code repeatedly decrements n and cdrs x until $n = 0$ and then returns the car of x. We will use nth often in this paper.

2.3   About the Theorem Prover

The ACL2 theorem prover is an improved and extended descendent of the Boyer-Moore theorem prover, NQTHM, [2,3]. ACL2 presents itself to the user as a read-eval-print loop. In addition to the typical commands of defining functions and evaluating forms, ACL2 permits the user to pose theorems to be proved. The theorem prover is fully automatic but its behavior is determined, in part, by its state, which is in turn affected by the theorems it has already proved. We regard the theorem prover as interactive: it is led to the proofs of complicated theorems by the user, who formulates appropriate intermediate results to prove first. These results are designed by the user to lead the system to the proof of the main result.

Here is some sample input to the theorem prover:

```
(defthm nth-update-nth
        (equal (nth  i  (update-nth  j  v  x))
               (if (equal (nfix  i) (nfix  j))
                   v
                   (nth  i  x)))))
```

This form directs the system to prove the above formula and then build it in as a rewrite rule with the name **nth-update-nth**.

Consider the theorem above. It is an equality and the left-hand side is the term denoting the ith element in the result of updating x so that its jth element is v. The right-hand side tells us what that element is. The expression (nfix i) "coerces" i to a natural: if i is a natural number, (nfix i) is identically i;

otherwise, it is 0. If i and j are the same (when coerced to natural numbers), the answer is v; otherwise, the answer is the ith element of x.

If we think of the update as a destructive operation on x, then this theorem relates the ith element *after* the update to the ith element *before* the update. But update is not destructive; x does not change. We are dealing with a logic here, not a programming language.

Logically speaking, there is no "before" or "after.". There is no such "event" as the "updating of x." Instead, the logical expressions x and (update-nth j v x) both denote objects and the theorem relates the ith element of the object denoted by the first to the ith element of the object denoted by the second.

The ACL2 theorem prover proves **nth-update-nth** automatically, by induction on i and the structure of the list x. Once proved, the theorem is built into ACL2's simplifier as a rewrite rule.

ACL2 is available without fee from the ACL2 home page, http://www.cs.-utexas.edu/users/moore/acl2. Five megabytes of hypertext documentation can be browsed there. The documentation can be downloaded with the ACL2 sources.

3   Single-Threaded Objects

In ACL2, a "single-threaded object" is a data structure whose use is so syntactically restricted that only one instance of the object need ever exist and its fields can be updated by destructive assignments.

From the logical perspective, a single-threaded object is an ordinary ACL2 object, e.g., composed of integers, symbols and conses. Logically speaking, ordinary ACL2 functions are defined to allow the user to "access" and "update" its fields. Logically speaking, when fields in the object, *obj*, are "updated" with new values, a new object, *obj'*, is constructed.

But by syntactic means we insure that after an updated version of the object is created there are no more references to the "old" object, *obj*. Then we can create *obj'* by destructively modifying the memory locations involved in the representation of *obj*. The syntactic means is pretty simple but draconian: the only reference to *obj* is in the variable named *OBJ*, where that is a "name" for the object introduced when the original instance was created.

The consequences of this simple rule are far-reaching and require some getting used to. For example, if *OBJ* has been declared as a single-threaded object name, then:

– *OBJ* is a top-level global variable that contains the current object, *obj*.
– If a function uses the formal parameter *OBJ*, the only "actual expression" that can be passed into that slot is *OBJ*; thus, such functions can only operate on the current object. Note that since the formal parameters of a function must be distinct, this rule prevents a single-threaded object being passed into a function in two or more argument positions, eliminating the possibility of aliasing.
– The accessors and updaters have a formal parameter named *OBJ*, thus, those functions can only be applied to the current object.

- The ACL2 primitives, such as `cons`, `car` and `cdr`, may not be applied to the variable *OBJ*. Thus, for example, *OBJ* may not be consed into a list (which would create another pointer to it) or accessed or copied via "unapproved" means.
- The updaters return a "new *OBJ* object", i.e., *obj'*; thus, when an updater is called, the only variable which can hold its result is *OBJ*.
- If a function calls an *OBJ* updater, it must return *OBJ*.
- When a top-level expression involving *OBJ* returns an *OBJ* object, that object becomes the new current value of *OBJ*.

To avoid dependence on the left-to-right order of evaluation in Common Lisp, we impose another rule

- When a non-top-level expression returns an *OBJ* object, the result must be bound to the local variable named *OBJ* (rather than passed as an actual to a function with a formal parameter named *OBJ*).

Consider the term (`f` (`smash` *OBJ*) (`g` *OBJ*)), where `smash` is a function that takes *obj* as input and returns a modified version of it, *obj'*. Observe that `f` has two arguments and that both actuals mention *OBJ*. Logically speaking, the two occurrences of the variable *OBJ* refer to the same object, *obj*, which is, of course, the value of *OBJ* "before" the modification. But with Lisp's left-to-right order of evaluation and our surreptitious destructive modification of *obj* to produce *obj'*, the Lisp evaluation of this expression would apply `g` to *obj'*. Hence, the rule above disallows this term and requires us to write

```
(let ((OBJ (smash OBJ)))
  (f OBJ (g OBJ))).
```

If we mean to apply `g` to *obj* instead of *obj'* we must write

```
(let* ((v (g OBJ))
       (OBJ (smash OBJ)))
  (f OBJ  v)).
```

Note that `f` must return *OBJ* for these expressions to be legal under our rules.

In ACL2, (`let` ((v_1 x_1) ... (v_n x_n)) *body*), where the v_i are distinct variable symbols and the x_i and *body* are terms, is logically equivalent to the term obtained by simultaneously and uniformly replacing the v_i by the corresponding x_i, i.e., $body_{[v_1 \leftarrow x_1, ..., v_n \leftarrow x_n]}$. The raw implementation of `let` binds the variables to the values of the terms and then evaluates the body in the extended binding environment. Because ACL2 is applicative, these two "meanings" of the expression are equivalent. Lisp's `let*` construct is similar but does sequential assignments (nested substitutions).

The above restrictions on the use of single-threaded objects are enforced by the ACL2 syntax checker. When a form is submitted to the read-eval-print loop, the terms in it are checked for well-formedness. This includes, for example, the expansion of macros, the check that functions are defined and the check that function calls are given the correct number of arguments.

To enforce the syntactic rules on single-threaded objects, we must know the "signature" of every function symbol. For example, `memi` is known to take an "ordinary" argument and a single-threaded object of type *MS* as input and to yield an ordinary object as the single result. This is written ((memi * *MS*) ⇒ *). The signature of `update-memi` is ((update-memi * * *MS*) ⇒ *MS*). The signature of `cons` is ((cons * *) ⇒ *). Thus, the syntax checker is able to insure such things as that *MS* is passed into the second argument of `memi`, that *MS* is passed into the third argument of `update-memi`, and that *MS* is *not* passed into the second argument of `update-memi` or into either argument of `cons`. The last restriction prevents single-threaded objects from being referenced by other objects. The syntax checker also uses signatures to insure that the result of `update-memi` is immediately `let`-bound or else returned as the final answer.

ACL2 supports "multi-valued" functions, i.e., functions that return a vector of results. The rules above are generalized to handle such functions.

The ACL2 read-eval-print loop does not allow the use of any global variable except single-threaded objects. For example, while (car '(a b c)) is allowed, (car *x*) is not, because in our applicative setting there is no binding environment assigning a value to *x*. We make an exception for single-threaded object names. If *MS*, for example, is a single-threaded object, and `fn` is a function which expects *MS* as its only argument, then (fn *MS*) is a legal top-level form. If the signature of `fn` indicates that (fn *MS*) returns an updated copy of *MS*, then that value becomes the new "current" *MS* after the evaluation. According to our rules above, `fn` must return an updated *MS* if `fn` (or any of its subfunctions) updates *MS*. We illustrate these restrictions in the next section.

What makes ACL2 different from other functional languages supporting such operations (e.g., Haskell's "monads" [17] and Clean's "uniqueness type system" [1]) is that ACL2 also implements an explicit axiomatic semantics so that theorems can be proved about them. In particular, the syntactic restrictions noted above are enforced only when single-threaded objects are used in function definitions (which might be executed outside of the ACL2 read-eval-print loop in Common Lisp). The accessor and update functions for single-threaded objects may be used without restriction in formulas to be proved. Since function evaluation is sometimes necessary during proofs, ACL2 must be able to evaluate these functions on logical constants representing the object, even when the constant is not "the current object." Thus, ACL2 supports both the efficient von Neumann semantics and the clean applicative semantics, and uses the first in contexts where execution speed is paramount and the second during proofs.

4   An Example

We describe our implementation of single-threaded objects largely by example. For simplicity, we do not model a microprocessor state here, but rather a much simpler structure containing a "pointer" and a small memory. The following command to the ACL2 read-eval-print loop defines a new single-threaded object named *MS*. The name "defstobj" comes from the phrase "define single-threaded object."

```
(defstobj MS
  (ptr :type (integer 0 *) :initially 0)
  (mem :type (array t (5)) :initially nil))
```

This constructs a single-threaded object named *MS* with two fields. The first, named ptr, contains a positive integer and is initially 0. The second, named mem, is a list of five arbitrary (i.e., of Common Lisp type t) objects, indexed sequentially from 0 through 4. Initially mem contains five occurrences of nil.

Logically speaking, the top-level global value of the variable symbol *MS* is now (0 (nil nil nil nil nil)).[2]

The defstobj command above introduces several function definitions. These definitions extend the logic to include the corresponding axioms and they extend the underlying Common Lisp to include the completed versions of these axiomatic definitions. The completed definitions, recall, are used by ACL2 when it must apply a logically defined function outside of its guarded domain. After making these extensions, defstobj introduces raw definitions for the functions. These definitions are destructive and will be discussed after we have clearly described the intended semantics.

The axiomatic definition of the "recognizer" for *MS* objects is

```
(defun msp (MS)
  (declare (xargs :guard t))
  (and (true-listp MS)
       (= (length MS) 2)
       (ptrp (nth 0 MS))
       (memp (nth 1 MS))))
```

The sub-functions ptrp and memp are defined as informally sketched above, to check that their arguments are, respectively, a positive integer and a list of five objects.

The accessor and updater for the ptr field are

```
(defun ptr (MS)
  (declare (xargs :guard (msp MS)))
  (nth 0 MS))
(defun update-ptr (v MS)
  (declare (xargs :guard
                  (and (and (integerp v) (<= 0 v))
                       (msp MS))))
  (update-nth 0 v MS))
```

---

[2] If the ACL2 user were to print the value of the variable *MS*, the result is displayed as <ms>. Single-threaded objects are generally so large that it is counterproductive to display their values and yet by the nature of our syntactic conventions it is necessary that functions return such values.

Note that the guard ensures that we do not run the raw code (shown later) unless *MS* satisfies `msp` and, in the case of the updater, v is a positive integer.

We do not provide the user with an accessor or updater for the `mem` field. Instead, we provide an accessor and updater for the elements of that field. This allows us to implement the contents of the field itself as a (non-applicative) Common Lisp array without exposing that implementation decision. The two functions provided are

```
(defun memi (i MS)
  (declare (xargs :guard
                  (and (integerp i)
                       (<= 0 i)
                       (< i 5)
                       (msp MS))))
  (nth i (nth 1 MS)))
(defun update-memi (i v MS)
  (declare (xargs :guard
                  (and (integerp i)
                       (<= 0 i)
                       (< i 5)
                       (msp MS))))
  (update-nth 1
              (update-nth i v (nth 1 MS))
              MS))
```

Note that these names have an "i" suffix to remind the reader that they access and update elements of the `mem` component of *MS*, not the component itself.

So much for the axiomatic semantics of the new functions.

The initial value of the *MS* object is not `(0 (nil nil nil nil nil))` but a Common Lisp object outside the applicative domain of the ACL2 logic by virtue of the use of destructively modified arrays. The initial value is `(#(0) #(NIL NIL NIL NIL NIL))`. The hash marks are Common Lisp's notation for arrays. The two arrays serve two purposes. They will be destructively modified to update the current *MS* object and they sometimes allow us to avoid "boxing," the allocation of additional storage to represent runtime type tags. A pointer to this initial value is stored in the Lisp constant symbol named `*the-live-ms*`, which is not directly accessible to the ACL2 user. However, when the user evaluates a top-level ACL2 form containing the global variable *MS*, that variable is given the value of `*the-live-ms*`.

`Defstobj` introduces efficient raw definitions for these functions. We show below the raw definitions for `memi` and `update-memi`.[3] This is legal Common Lisp, but not within the applicative ACL2 subset.

---

[3] The definitions introduced actually contain heavy use of Common Lisp `declare` and `the` forms so the compiler will produce more efficient code.

```
(defun memi (i MS)
  (cond
   ((eq MS *the-live-ms*)
    (aref (car (cdr MS))  i))
   (t (nth  i (nth 1 MS)))))
(defun update-memi (i  v MS)
  (cond
   ((eq MS *the-live-ms*)
    (cond
     (*wormholep* (wormhole-er 'update-memi (list  i  v MS)))
     (t (setf (aref (car (cdr MS))  i)
              v)
        MS)))
   (t (update-nth 1 (update-nth  i  v (nth 1 MS)) MS)))))
```

Observe that when `memi` is applied to the "live" instance of *MS* it does an array access, `aref`, to get the appropriate element. When `update-memi` is used to update the `mem` field of the live instance of *MS*, it does so destructively. The clause dealing with "wormholes" has to do with an interactive environment in which ACL2 does not allow single-threaded objects to be altered and is not germane here. When the functions are applied to values that are not the "live" one, they behave as per the axiomatic definitions.[4]

Finally, `defstobj` gives these functions signatures that indicate that they traffic in single-threaded objects. For example, the signature of `memi` is `((memi * MS) ⇒ *)` and that of `update-memi` is `((update-memi * * MS) ⇒ MS)`. Thus, both functions *must* be passed the current *MS* (in the appropriate argument position) when they are called. Furthermore, the output of `update-memi` *must* be either returned or bound to the `let` variable named *MS*.

Suppose that the `defstobj` above has just been admitted (i.e., evaluated successfully). Here is a sequence of interactions with the read-eval-print loop. The "ACL2 !>" is the ACL2 prompt.

```
ACL2 !>MS
<ms>
ACL2 !>(ptr MS)
0
ACL2 !>(update-ptr 3 MS)
<ms>
ACL2 !>(ptr MS)
3
```

---

[4] These functions may be applied to "non-live" values by the theorem prover itself. In the course of proving a theorem about (`update-memi` i v MS) it is possible that the three variables get instantiated to constants and ACL2 will run the definition of `update-memi` to reduce the expression to a constant. If the particular values satisfy the guard on `update-memi`, the raw definition is run, even though the particular value of *MS* may not be the live one.

```
ACL2 !>(memi 2 MS)
NIL
ACL2 !>(update-memi 2 'abc MS)
<ms>
ACL2 !>(memi 2 MS)
ABC
```

The live version of *MS* is printed simply as `<ms>`. Case and font are irrelevant here.

The following theorem is proved immediately (provided **nth-update-nth** has been proved).

```
(defthm memi-update-memi
   (equal (memi  i (update-memi  j  v  x))
          (if (equal (nfix  i) (nfix  j))  v (memi  i  x))))
```

There are several noteworthy points about this theorem. First, it uses the variable x where the single-threaded object *MS* might have been expected. Our syntactic restrictions apply only to functions to be executed in Common Lisp, not to logical formulas to be proved as theorems. It is often necessary to break the single-threaded rules simply to state the desired properties of functions that manipulate these objects. For example, one might wish to pose a conjecture that relates components of the state before and after a change. Secondly, the theorem has no hypotheses restricting its use to (`msp` x) or legal i, j, and v. Those restrictions are reflected in the guards to the functions, not their logical meanings. The upshot of this is that powerful general theorems can often be proved — theorems without hypotheses which may encumber their subsequent use by the automatic theorem prover. However, to use the single-threaded objects in the most efficient way – i.e., to gain access to the raw code produced for them – they must be applied to their intended domains. When functions are defined in terms of `memi`, `update-memi`, and the other single-threaded primitives here, those functions should be proved to be Common Lisp compliant to gain maximal efficiency.

5   Using Single-Threaded Objects

To illustrate the use of single-threaded objects, we use the *MS* object to implement a ring buffer. We wish to define (`insert` x *MS*) so that it writes x to the `mem` location indicated by `ptr` and increments the pointer. Logically speaking we mean

```
(defun insert (x MS)
   (update-ptr (inc (ptr MS))
               (update-memi (ptr MS)  x MS)))
```

where `inc` increments its argument modulo 5. However, this violates our syntactic rules because the output of `update-memi` is not immediately `let`-bound to the variable *MS*. In addition, we have found it desirable to require the user to declare explicitly the intention to use single-threaded objects. (Otherwise, the raw definition produced by an acceptable defun would be dependent on whether its formals had been defined to be single-threaded objects. This would open the user to the possibility that the inclusion of another user's library into a session would change effect of legal definitions.) The following definition of insert is legal in our system, provided *MS* has been introduced as above.

```
(defun insert (x MS)
  (declare (xargs :stobjs (MS)))
  (let ((MS (update-memi (ptr MS)  x MS)))
    (update-ptr (inc (ptr MS)) MS)))
```

Logically, this definition is provably equivalent to the earlier one, but, we think, makes the sequencing more explicit. Finally, the user may define define a macro to produce a nest of let-bindings of the variable *MS*. We call that macro "sequentially" below. With such a macro we could write the defun above as

```
(defun insert (x MS)
  (declare (xargs :stobjs (MS)))
  (sequentially
   (update-memi (ptr MS)  x MS)
   (update-ptr (inc (ptr MS)) MS)))
```

Suppose then that we have the initial *MS* (with ptr 0 and mem consisting of five nils). If we execute the following

```
(sequentially
 (insert 'A MS)
 (insert 'B MS)
 (insert 'C MS)
 (insert 'D MS))
```

then the logical value of *MS* is (4 (A B C D NIL)). If we then do (insert 'E *MS*) the logical value is (0 (A B C D E)). Finally, if we do (insert 'F *MS*), the logical value (1 (F B C D E)). However, if we ask ACL2 to print the value of *MS* the result is always the same <ms>.

It is convenient to define a function to display that part of the object in which we are interested. In the case of *MS*, we define (show *MS*) so that it returns the five elements in the ring buffer, starting with the oldest. Thus, for the state of *MS* shown above, (show *MS*) is (B C D E F). So far we have only executed insert. What theorems can we prove about it?

We have proved

```
(defthm show-insert
  (implies (< (ptr MS) 5)
           (equal (show (insert  x MS))
                  (cdr (append (show MS) (list  x))))))
```

Again, note the relatively weak hypothesis, which makes this lemma easier to apply in the future. We do not need to know that *MS* is a well-formed ring buffer, only that its pointer is less than five. [5] This lemma is proved by reasoning about `nth` and `update-nth`.

Now suppose we wish to scan a binary tree and keep track of the last five tips seen. We can write this as follows:

```
(defun scan (x MS)
  (declare (xargs :stobjs (MS)))
  (if (consp x)
      (sequentially
        (scan (car x) MS)
        (scan (cdr x) MS))
    (insert x MS)))
```

Let τ be '(((A . B) . C) . (D . ((E . (F . G)) . (H . I)))), i.e., a binary tree whose fringe consists of the nine symbols A, B, C, ..., I. Then (show (scan τ MS)) is (E F G H I). No new storage is allocated to compute (scan τ MS).

We can prove the following theorem,

```
(defthm show-scan
  (implies (< (ptr MS) 5)
           (equal (show (scan x MS))
                  (lastn 5 (append (show MS) (fringe x))))))
```

where (lastn i x) returns the last n elements of list x and

```
(defun fringe (x)
  (if (consp x)
      (append (fringe (car x))
              (fringe (cdr x)))
    (list x)))
```

Note that this theorem "abuses" our syntactic restrictions on the use of *MS* in a completely unavoidable way. It relates the result of "showing" the object after a `scan` with the result of showing it before the `scan`. Such constructions must be legal if we are to use the language to specify our intentions. The theorem above is proved by reasoning inductively about the tree structure of x. The proof requires knowledge of the properties of `lastn`, `append`, etc., but no new knowledge about the primitives for our single-threaded object *MS*.

Obviously, if the fringe of x contains five or more elements, the initial contents of *MS* is irrelevant. That is, an easy corollary of the above, derived via a lemma about `lastn` and `append`, is

---

[5] The equality by itself is not a theorem. If (ptr MS) exceeds four, then the `insert` on the left-hand side inserts x beyond the end of memory and then `show` on the left-hand side collects the first five elements of the buffer, ignoring the x altogether. Meanwhile, the (show MS) on the right-hand side collects the `nil` beyond the end of memory and then the first four elements of the buffer. The `nil` is `cdr`'d off and the final list of length five contains the first four elements of the buffer, followed by x.

```
(defthm show-scan-corollary
  (implies (and (< (ptr MS) 5)
                (<= 5 (len (fringe  x))))
           (equal (show (scan  x MS))
                  (lastn 5 (fringe  x)))))
```

While these theorems are not fundamentally deep, we offer them to illuminate the claim that we can reason about "destructive" functions such as scan without much trouble thanks to the observation that their syntactic nature allows applicative semantics but von Neumann implementations.

6 Conclusion

Of course, single-threaded objects have not added anything to the expressive power of ACL2; since they are axiomatized entirely in terms of the predefined functions nth and update-nth, we cannot use them to model computing systems previously beyond our grasp. But the new models execute much faster. For example, researchers at Rockwell-Collins, Inc., have used both C and ACL2 to model the same microprocessor. By exploiting single-threaded objects and guards they were able to get the ACL2 model to perform at roughly 90% of the speed of the C model [5,7,6].

It should be noted that the use of single-threaded objects explicitly sequentializes (some of the updates in) any function using them. This reduces the opportunities to introduce parallelism, which is one of the potential payoffs of an applicative language. For this reason, we have sometimes used the name "von Neumann bottlenecks" instead of "single-threaded objects." However, until we realize the potential parallelism in ACL2, we feel that single-threaded objects are very useful.

Our single-threaded objects are similar in spirit to Haskell's "monads." A monad is a type constructor together with two operations that correspond, roughly, to the notions of "update" and "sequentially." Like our single-threaded objects, monads are state-holding objects that are understood applicatively but can be implemented destructively because of syntactic (type) checks analogous to those we implement. It is possible in Haskell for a function to temporarily create a monad for the purpose of some computation. The state-holding object "evaporates" when it is no longer referenced. The ACL2 Version 2.6 supports such a use of single-threaded objects.

The paper [18] relates monads to other popular alternative approaches, including synchronized streams [16], continuations [13], linear logic [4], and side-effects. Our approach shares a lot with linear logic, but we do not regard the provision of single-threaded objects as having produced a new logic. Indeed, the situation is exactly the opposite: if one regards this paper having "added" single-threaded objects to our existing logic, we must stress that we did not alter the logic in any way. Our conventions are merely syntactic restrictions on the executable subset of a conventional first-order, quantifier free logic of recursive functions. We exploit the fact that the syntax of the logic is unchanged so that we can state theorems about the effects of updates.

The presence of single-threaded object encourages the use of let statements binding the state-holding variable name. This insures single-threadedness. In large microprocessor models we typically encounter nests of lets several hundred deep. This has required the invention of special rewriting mechanisms [12] in ACL2.

Our connection of an efficient implementation with a proof engine also exposes the need for an applicative programming language to support not just the execution of such functions on the "live" object but to support execution on "non-live" instances of the object as well. This is necessary since applications of the functions arise in proofs and must be calculated. Indeed, the syntactic restrictions on the use of single-threaded objects must be lifted when one is defining functions or writing formulas for the purpose of expressing specifications. ACL2 supports this.

The main contribution of this work is that we have connected an efficient implementation of state holding objects with an applicative programming language while preserving our ability to reason formally and mechanically about the functions.

Acknowledgments

The introduction of single-threaded objects into ACL2 has a rather complicated history that we recount here for the record.

From 1989 to 1991, we developed the core of ACL2, including its treatment of state, the global state formalizing ACL2's database and file system. We jointly developed the algorithms for checking the syntactic restrictions on the variable state and using destructive modifications on "live state." Boyer then left the ACL2 project and Matt Kaufmann joined it. In 1998, the researchers at Rockwell-Collins, Inc., in particular John Cowles, David Greve, David Hardin and Matt Wilding, lobbied for the behind-the-scenes support for destructive modification of certain structures. Moore recognized their wish-list as describing user-defined state-like objects. Moore then implemented single-threaded objects as described here, by generalizing the pre-existing work of Boyer and Moore for state. Kaufmann later added additional features, such as "local" single-threaded objects that "evaporate" when no longer accessible. Rob Sumners helped us make our arrays extendable.

This work would probably not have been done without the constructive lobbying by the Rockwell researchers who implemented *ad hoc* use of destructive modification to demonstrate the performance gains that could be achieved.

References

1. E. Barendsen and S. Smetsers. Uniqueness typing for functional languages with graph rewriting semantics. In *Mathematical Structures in Computer Science 6*, pages 579–612. 1996. 18

2. R. S. Boyer and J S. Moore. *A Computational Logic*. Academic Press, New York, 1979. 9, 15

3. R. S. Boyer and J S. Moore. *A Computational Logic Handbook, Second Edition*. Academic Press, New York, 1997. 9, 15

4. J.-Y. Girard. Linear logic. In *Theoretical Computer Science*, volume 50, pages 1–102. 1987. 25

5. D. Greve, M. Wilding, and D. Hardin. High-speed, analyzable simulators. In Kaufmann et al. [9], pages 113–136. 25

6. David A. Greve. Symbolic simulation of the JEM1 microprocessor. In G. Gopalakrishnan and P. Windley, editors, *Formal Methods in Computer-Aided Design – FM-CAD*, LNCS 1522. Springer-Verlag, 1998. 25

7. David Hardin, Matthew Wilding, and David Greve. Transforming the theorem prover into a digital design tool: From concept car to off-road vehicle. In Alan J. Hu and Moshe Y. Vardi, editors, *Computer-Aided Verification – CAV '98*, volume 1427 of *Lecture Notes in Computer Science*. Springer-Verlag, 1998. See URL http://pobox.com/users/hokie/docs/concept.ps. 25

8. P. Hudak. Continuation-based mutable abstract data types, or how to have your state and munge it too. Technical Report YaleU/DCS/RR-914, Department of Computer Science, Yale University, July 1992. 9

9. M. Kaufmann, P. Manolios, and J S. Moore, editors. *Computer-Aided Reasoning: ACL2 Case Studies*. Kluwer Academic Press, 2000. 10, 27

10. M. Kaufmann, P. Manolios, and J. S. Moore. *Computer-Aided Reasoning: An Approach*. Kluwer Academic Press, 2000. 12

11. Matt Kaufmann and J. Moore. A precise description of the acl2 logic. In http://www.cs.utexas.edu/users/moore/publications/km97a.ps.Z. Department of Computer Sciences, University of Texas at Austin, 1997. 12

12. J. S. Moore. Rewriting for symbolic execution of state machine models. In *Computer-Aided Verification – CAV'01*, volume 2102 of *Lecture Notes in Computer Science*. Springer-Verlag, 2001. See URL http://www.cs.utexas.edu/users/moore/publications/nu-rewriter. 26

13. G. Plotkin. Call-by-name, call-by-value, and the λ-calculus. In *Theoretical Computer Science*, volume 1, pages 125–159. 1975. 25

14. D. Schmidt. Detecting global variables in denotational specifications. *ACM Trans. Prog. Lang*, 7:299–310, 1985. 9, 10

15. G. L. Steele, Jr. *Common Lisp The Language, Second Edition*. Digital Press, 30 North Avenue, Burlington, MA 01803, 1990. 9, 14

16. W. Stoye. Message-based functional operating systems. 6(3):291–311, 1986. 25

17. P. Wadler. Monads for functional programming. In *Advanced Functional Programming*. Springer Verlag, LNCS 925, 1995. 9, 18

18. P. Wadler. How to declare an imperative. *ACM Computing Surveys*, 29(3):240–263, September 1997. 9, 10, 25

Modeling Engineering Structures with Constrained Objects

Bharat Jayaraman and Pallavi Tambay

Department of Computer Science and Engineering
State University of New York at Buffalo, Buffalo, NY 14260-2000, USA
{bharat,tambay}@cse.buffalo.edu

Abstract. We present a novel programming language based on the concept of *constrained objects* for compositional and declarative modeling of engineering structures. A constrained object is an object whose internal state is governed by a set of (declarative) constraints. When several constrained objects are aggregated to form a complex object, their internal states might further have to satisfy interface constraints. The resultant behavior of the complex object is obtained by logical inference and constraint satisfaction. Our modeling paradigm supports constraints, including quantified and conditional constraints, as well as preferences. We show that, for the domain of engineering modeling, the paradigm of constrained objects is superior to both a pure object-oriented language as well as a pure constraint language. Our current prototype includes tools for authoring constrained-object class diagrams; a compiler that translates class diagrams to CLP(R) code; and domain-specific visual interfaces for building and testing constrained objects.

1 Introduction

In this paper we present a programming language and modeling environment that will facilitate a principled approach to the modeling of complex systems. A domain of particular interest is that of engineering entities such as circuits, trusses, gears, mixers, separators, etc. Modeling such entities involves the specification of both their structure and behavior. In modeling structure, it is natural to adopt a compositional approach since a complex engineering entity is typically an assembly of many components. From a programming language standpoint, we may model each component as an *object*, with internal attributes that capture the relevant features that are of interest to the model. The concepts of classes and hierarchies found in object-oriented (OO) languages, such as C++, Java, and Smalltalk, are appropriate to model the categories of components. However, in modeling the behavior of complex engineering entities, the traditional OO approach of using procedures (or methods) is inappropriate, because it is more natural to think of each component as being governed by certain laws, or invariants. From a programming language standpoint, we may express such behavioral laws as *constraints* over the attributes of an object. When such objects are aggregated to form a complex object, their internal attributes might further have to

S. Krishnamurthi, C. R. Ramakrishnan (Eds.): PADL 2002, LNCS 2257, pp. 28–46, 2002.

satisfy interface constraints. In general, the resultant state of a complex object can be deduced only by satisfying both the internal and the interface constraints of the constituent objects. This paradigm of objects and constraints is referred to as *constrained objects*, and it may be regarded as a declarative approach to object-oriented programming.

To illustrate the notion of constrained objects, consider a resistor in an electrical circuit. (This is a classic example in CLP(R) but there are advantages offered by a constrained object representation, as discussed further below.) Its state may be represented by three variables V, I, and R, which represent respectively its voltage, current, and resistance. However, these state variables may not change independently, but are governed by the constraint V = I * R. Hence a resistor is a *constrained object*. When two or more constrained objects are aggregated to form a complex object, their internal states may be subject to one or more interface constraints. For example, if two resistor objects are connected in series, their respective currents should be made equal. Similarly, in the civil engineering domain, we can model the members and joints in a truss as objects and we can express the laws of equilibrium as constraints over the various forces acting on the truss. In the chemical engineering domain, constrained objects can be used to model mixers and separators, and constraints can be written to express the law of mass balance.

Constraints and Preferences. Sometimes there could be multiple solutions to constraints, and we are interested in the optimal solutions. This in turn necessitates some means of specifying *preferences* that guide the determination of optimal solutions. To take an example from the engineering context, suppose we model a gear train and its constituent gears as objects whose attributes represent the input and output torques, angular speeds, and transmission powers. The efficiency of the gear train can be given in terms of these attributes by a constraint. In addition to these constraints, one may want to specify a preference that the transmission power be as close to 250hp (horse power) as possible and the efficiency be maximized. In our paradigm, such preferences can be specified declaratively using a preference clause.

Domain Specific Visual Interfaces. In the paradigm of constrained objects that we present, a complex object may also have a visual representation, such as a diagram. This visual representation is compositional in nature; that is, each component of the visual form can be traced back to some specific object in the underlying constrained object model. An end-user, i.e., modeler, will be able to access and modify the underlying model using the visual representation. This capability may be contrasted with currently available tools for engineering design such as AutoCAD, Abaqus, etc., where the visual representation contains only geometric information but does not provide access to the underlying logic or constraints. We expect to have different visual interfaces for different domains but a common textual language (described in section 3) for defining the classes of constrained objects.

Modeling Scenario. We expect a modeler to first define the classes of constrained objects, by specifying their attributes and their internal and interface constraints. These classes may be organized into an inheritance hierarchy. Once these definitions have been completed, the modeler can *build* a specific complex object, and execute (*solve*) it to observe its behavior. This execution will involve a process of logical inference and constraint satisfaction [4,5,8,12,20]. A modeler will then need to go through one or more iterations of *modifying* the component objects followed by re-execution. Such modifications could involve updating the internal states of the constituent objects, as well as adding new objects, replacing existing objects, etc. The complex object can be queried to find the values of attributes that will satisfy some given constraints in addition to the ones already present in the constrained objects.

Constrained Objects ≥ Constraints + Objects. Earlier we explained why the paradigm of constrained objects is preferable to the traditional paradigm of imperative objects for engineering modeling. It is also the case that, for the domain of engineering modeling, the paradigm of constrained objects is preferable to a traditional constraint language or constraint logic programming language (such as CLP(R)): (i) It is more natural to model an engineering artifact as a complex object than as a complex constraint. An object has a direct counterpart in the physical world. (ii) The diagrammatic representation can be more easily traced back to an object representation rather than a constraint representation. (iii) Object structure can help in reporting the cause of model inconsistency, and we believe it will also obtain efficiency in constraint solving, especially incremental solving (when a model is revised).

Prototype Implementation. We currently have three tools: (i) A graphical editor for authoring Cob class diagrams using a constraint-based extension of UML [18]. This tool generates textual Cob code from class diagrams. (ii) A translator that takes Cob class definitions as input and generates equivalent CLP(R) predicates as output. We use the underlying CLP(R) engine for constraint handling. (iii) Domain-specific visual interfaces and code generation capabilities. Currently we have visual interfaces (palettes of buttons and drawing primitives) for circuits and trusses, and we generate textual Cob code from these diagrams.

In this paper we describe a programming language called **Cob** and illustrate its use in engineering modeling. While the idea of constrained objects has been discussed to some extent in the literature [3,2,10,13], we extend earlier work by providing a richer set of features for modeling, especially quantified and conditional constraints, preferences, and logic variables. We have developed a formal declarative and operational semantics of Cob, but space precludes their description in this paper. The remainder of this paper is organised as follows: Section 2 briefly surveys related work and provides comparisons. Section 3 outlines the syntax of Cob and presents several motivating examples. Section 4 briefly describes the current Cob programming environment. Finally, section 5 describes our current and future research plans.

2   Related Research

Constrained Objects. An early forerunner in the area of constrained objects is the work of Alan Borning on ThingLab, a constraint-based simulation laboratory [3] intended for interactive graphical simulations. Another language aimed at graphics applications is Bertrand [13] which was extended by Bruce Horn in his constrained object language Siri [11]. This language uses the notion of *event pattern* to declaratively specify state changes: by declaring what constraints must hold after the execution of a method, and also specifying which attributes may and may not change during the method execution. Compared to our language, these approaches provide only a limited capability for expressing constraints, and also provide no support for handling multiple solutions to constraints. (Although ThingLab has a preference construct it orders constraints and not their solutions.) Another constrained object language (also named COB) [17] is intended for analyses integration and automated design. It handles numeric constraints but does not appear to provide logic variables, conditional constraints, aggregate constraints or preferences.

Constraint Imperative Programming. The Kaleidoscope'91 [2] language integrates constraints and object-oriented programming for interactive graphical user interfaces. This 'constraint imperative language' uses constraints to simulate imperative constructs such as updating, assignment, and object identity. For the class of modeling applications that we target, it is not essential for us to consider such imperative concepts. These are important issues in a constraint imperative language [6,14], but not for a declarative object-oriented language such as Cob. In our modeling scenarios, *model execution* and the *model revision* are carried out in mutual exclusion of one another. Changes are made at the level of the modeling environment. Thus we have a clear separation of the declarative and procedural parts of a constrained object.

Constraints, Logic and Objects. Research at the UNH Constraints Computation Center under Prof. Freuder is related to our efforts. From a language standpoint, there are two important differences: (i) we integrate the concepts of object and constraint, and (ii) we adopt the more general CLP paradigm as opposed to a pure constraint language. Our approach to constraints and preferences builds upon our earlier work [7,8], and subsumes the paradigms of CLP as well as HCLP (Hierarchic CLP) [8]. Firstly, CLP does not support conditional constraints or preferences. Also, our provision of conditional constraints allows object creation to take place dynamically and be controlled by constraint satisfaction. Two other related logic-based languages are LIFE [1] and Oz [19]. LIFE combines logic with inheritance, however, it does not deal with full-fledged constraints as we do. Oz is a language combinining constraints and concurrency as well as objects. Both these languages do not support the notion of preference nor do they consider engineering applications.

Constraint-based Specifications. For the sake of completeness, we also mention software specification languages that make use of constraints. The need for a formal representation of constraints in object-oriented programming is illustrated by the development of the Object Constraint Language [21]. For practitioners of object-oriented design and analysis, constraints provide an unambiguous and concise tool for expressing the relations between objects. OCL is a specification language that helps in making explicit these relations that would otherwise be implicit in the code but not apparent to the programmer who reads or modifies it. Eiffel is another language which employs constraints for specifying pre- and post-conditions that must hold on the operations of an object [16]. These languages use constraints as specifications; no constraint solving is done at runtime in order to deduce the values of variables. Contracts [9] provide a formal language for specifying behavioral compositions in object oriented systems. A contract defines a set of communicating participant classes and their contractual obligations as constraints. A class conforming to a contract must implement the methods exactly as specified in the contract. Contracts promote an interaction-oriented design rather than a class-based design.

3   Cob: An Informal Introduction

Syntax. The grammar below defines the structure of a Cob program. A Cob program is a sequence of class definitions, and each constrained object is an instance of some class. The body of a class definition consists of attributes, constraints, predicates, preferences, and constructors. Each of these constituents is optional, and we permit an empty class definition as a degenerate case.

$$
\begin{aligned}
program &::= class\_definition^+ \\
class\_definition &::= [\,\mathtt{abstract}\,]\ \mathtt{class}\ class\_id\ [\,\mathtt{extends}\ class\_id\,]\ \{\ body\ \} \\
body &::= [\,\mathtt{attributes}\ attributes\,]\quad [\,\mathtt{constraints}\ constraints\,] \\
&\quad\ [\,\mathtt{predicates}\ pred\_clauses\,]\quad [\,\mathtt{preferences}\ pref\_clauses\,] \\
&\quad\ [\,\mathtt{constructors}\ constructor\_clause\,]
\end{aligned}
$$

In this paper, we limit attention to single inheritance of classes and at most one constructor for each class. An abstract class is a class without any constructor, and hence cannot be instantiated. Not all of the syntactic details are presented here; a more complete description of the syntax of constraints is given in Appendix A. Below we briefly discuss the more novel aspects of the language.

$$
\begin{aligned}
constraints &::= constraint\ ;\ [\ constraint\ ;]^+ \\
constraint &::= creational\_constraint\ |\ quantified\_constraint \\
&\quad\ |\ simple\_constraint \\
creational\_constraint &::= attribute = \mathtt{new}\ class\_id(terms) \\
quantified\_constraint &::= \mathtt{forall}\ var\ \mathtt{in}\ enum : constraint \\
&\quad\ |\ \mathtt{exists}\ var\ \mathtt{in}\ enum : constraint \\
simple\_constraint &::= conditional\_constraint\ |\ constraint\_atom \\
conditional\_constraint &::= constraint\_atom : -\ literals \\
constraint\_atom &::= term\ \ relop\ \ term\ |\ constraint\_predicate\_id(terms)
\end{aligned}
$$

$$relop ::= = \mid\ != \mid > \mid < \mid >= \mid <=$$
$$term ::= constant \mid var \mid attribute \mid (term) \mid func\_id(terms)$$
$$\mid \textbf{sum } var \textbf{ in } enum : term$$
$$\mid \textbf{prod } var \textbf{ in } enum : term$$
$$\mid \textbf{min } var \textbf{ in } enum : term$$
$$\mid \textbf{max } var \textbf{ in } enum : term$$

A constraint can be either creational, simple or quantified, where the quantification ranges over an enumeration (referred to as *enum*) which may be the indices of an array or the elements of an explicitly specified set. A simple constraint can either be a constraint atom or a conditional constraint. A constraint atom is essentially a relational expression of the form *term relop term*, where *term* is composed of functions/operators from any data domain (e.g. integers, reals, etc.) as well as constants and attributes. A conditional constraint is a constraint atom that is predicated upon a conjunction of literals each of which is a (possibly negated) ordinary atom or a constraint atom.

Often we would like to augment a predicate definition with preference criteria for determining the best solution(s) to goals that make use of this predicate. In Cob, a preference clause is of the form

$p(s1) \le p(s2)$:- *clause_body*,

and it states that the solution *s1* is less preferred than solution *s2* for predicate *p* if the condition specified by *clause_body* is true. We also provide min and max constructs to model optimization problems. The reference [8] provides a more detailed account of this construct.

Date as a Constrained Object. Our first example illustrates the basic features of the language, including the use of conditional constraints.

```
class date {
 attributes
  int Day, Month, Year;
 constraints
  1 ≤ Year;
  1 ≤ Month;    Month ≤ 12;
  1 ≤ Day;      Day ≤ 31;
  Day ≤ 30 :- member(Month, [4,6,9,11]);
  Day ≤ 29 :- Month = 2, leap(Year);
  Day ≤ 28 :- Month = 2, not leap(Year);
 predicates
  member(X, [X|_]).
  member(X, [_|T]) :- member(X,T).
  leap(Y) :- Y mod 4 = 0, Y mod 100 <> 0.
  leap(Y) :- Y mod 400 = 0.
 constructors date(D, M, Y) { Day = D; Month = M; Year = Y; }
}
```

We employ Prolog-like syntax for defining predicates and conditional constraints. For example, the conditional constraint

    Day ≤ 29 :- Month = 2, leap(Year)

requires Day ≤ 29 if the Month is February and the Year is a leap year. Computationally, an important difference between a conditional constraint and a Prolog rule is: If the head of a conditional constraint evaluates to true, then the body need not be evaluated; and, if the head evaluates to false, the body must fail in order for the conditional constraint to be satisfied. In contrast, in Prolog, if the head of a rule unifies with a goal, then the body of the rule must be evaluated; and, if the head does not unify, then the body need not be evaluated.

The above definition can be used to validate a given combination of Day, Month, and Year values, and also be used to generate, for example, a range of Month values for a given a combination of Day and Year. For example, if the Day is set to 31 and the Year to 1999, the set of possible values for Month can be deduced to be any integer between 1 and 12 but not 4, 6, 9, 11, or 2. While 1 ≤ Month ≤ 12 is directly obtained from the unconditional constraints for Month, our computational model can deduce, by a process of *constructive negation* of the goal member(Month, [4,6,9,11]), that Month is not 4, 6, 9, or 11. And, it can deduce that Month is not equal to 2 from the conditional constraint Day ≤ 28 :- Month = 2, not leap(Year).

Conditional constraints can be used to control object creation dynamically. For example, consider the following conditional constraints over attributes X, Y, and Shape of a certain class:

    Shape = rectangle(X, Y) :- Input = 'rectangle'
    Shape = circle(X, Y)   :- Input = 'circle'

Together, they can be used to set a Shape attribute of, for example, a node of a binary tree. In the above example, X and Y stand respectively for the width and height inputs of the **rectangle** constructor; and they stand respectively for the center and radius attributes of the **circle** constructor.

Non-Series/Parallel Circuits. To further illustrate the syntax of Cob and the use of equational and quantified constraints, we present the well-known example of a non-series/parallel electrical circuit. We model the components and connections of such a circuit as objects and their properties and relations as constraints on and amongst these objects. The **component** class models any electrical entity (e.g resistor, battery) that has two ends (referred to as 1 and 2). The attributes of this class represent the currents and voltages at the two ends of the entity. The constraint in class **resistor** represent Ohm's law.

The class **end** represents a particular end of a component. We use the convention that the voltage at end 1 of a component is V1 (similarly for current). A **node** aggregates a collection of ends. When the ends of components are placed together at a node, their voltages must be equal and the sum of the currents through them must be zero (Kirchoff's law). Notice the use of the quantified constraints (**forall**) to specify these laws. Using these classes we can model any non-series/parallel circuit. Given initial values for some attributes, this model can be used to calculate values of the remaining attributes (e.g. the current through a particular component).

```
abstract class component {              class end {
 attributes                              attributes
  real V1, V2, I1, I2;                    component C;
 constraints                             real E, V, I;
  I1 + I2 = 0;                           constraints
}                                         V = C.V1 :- E = 1;
                                          V = C.V2 :- E = 2;
class resistor extends component {        I = C.I1 :- E = 1;
 attributes                               I = C.I2 :- E = 2;
  real R;                                constructors end(C1, E1)
 constraints                              { C = C1; E = E1; }
  V1 - V2 = I1 * R;                      }
 constructors resistor(D) { R = D; }    class node {
}                                         attributes
                                          end [] Ce;
class battery extends component {         real V;
 attributes                              constraints
  real V;                                 sum C in Ce: C.I = 0;
 constraints                              forall C in Ce: C.V = V;
  V2 = 0;                                constructors node(L) {
 constructors battery(X) { V1 = X; }      Ce = L; }
}                                        }
```

Simple Truss. To illustrate the use of constrained objects in engineering design, we define the Cob classes needed to model a simple truss structure, as shown in figure 1. A truss consists of bars placed together at joints. The constraints in the beam class express the standard relations between its modulus of elasticity (E), yield strength (Sy), dimensions (L, W, H), bending, buckling, and tension forces (F_bn, F_bk, F_t), and stress (Sigma). Depending upon the direction of the force in a beam (inward or outward), it acts as either a buckling force or a tension force. This relation is expressed as conditional constraints in the beam class. A bar is a beam placed at an angle (A) and a load is a force applied at an angle (A). The joint class aggregates an array of bars and and an array of loads (that are incident at the joint) and its constraints state that the sum of the forces in the horizontal and vertical directions respectively must be 0. The Cob classes defined here can model a truss with loads and may be used to determine the dimensions of the beams such that they can support the loads. These conditions are taken from the text by Mayne and Margolis [15]. Appendix B shows a sample truss and its Cob model.

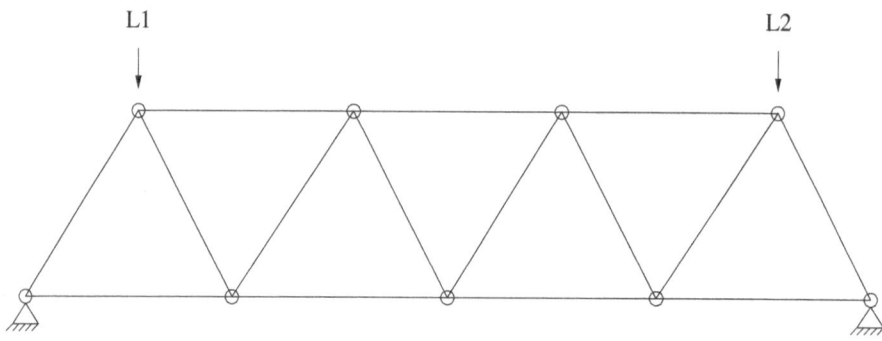

Fig. 1. A Simple Truss

```
class beam {
 attributes
  real E, Sy, L, W, H, F_bn, F_bk, F_t, Sigma, I, F;
 constraints
  Pi = 3.141 ;
  I = F_bk * L *L /Pi * Pi*E;
  I = W * H * H * H / 12;
  F_t = Sy * W * H;
  Sigma = (H * L * F_bn )/ (8 * I);
  F_t = F :- F > 0;
  F_bk = F :- F < 0;
 constructors beam(E1,Sy1,L1,W1,H1,F_bn1,F_bk1,F_t1,Sigma1,I1,F1)
  {  E=E1; Sy=Sy1; L=L1; H=H1; W=W1; F_bn=F_bn1;
    F_bk=F_bk1; F_t=F_t1; Sigma=Sigma1; I=I1; F=F1;  }
}
```

```
class bar {                      class load {
 attributes                       attributes
  beam B; real A;                  real F; real A;
  % beam B placed at angle A      constraints
 constraints                       0 <= A; A <= 360;
  0 <= A; A <= 360;               constructors load(F1, A1)
 constructors bar(B1, A1)          { F = F1; A = A1; }
  { B = B1; A = A1; }            }
}
```

```
class joint {
 attributes
  bar [] Bars; load [] Loads;
 constraints
  sum X in Bars: (X.B.F * sin(X.A)) +
    sum L in Loads: (L.F * sin(L.A)) = 0;
  sum Y in Bars: (Y.B.F * cos(Y.A)) +
    sum M in Loads: (M.F * cos(M.A)) = 0;
 constructors joint(B1, L1) { Bars = B1; Loads = L1; }
}
```

Separators and Mixers. A common problem in chemical engineering, is the use of a combination of mixers and separators to produce a chemical that has specific ingredients in a certain proportion. The arrangement of mixers and separators in figure 2 has two input raw material streams R1 and R2. Each of these streams has certain ingredients in different concentrations. R1 and R2 are split and a part of each (I1 and I2 respectively) is sent to a separator which separates its ingredients. Each separator supplies certain proportion of each ingredient to the mixer which combines them to produce the desired chemical G. W1 and W2 are waste streams from the separators. The problem is to produce G while minimizing I1 and I2 thereby minimizing the cost of processing material in the separators.

Figure 2 describes a typical scenario, and we present below some of the key classes needed for this example. A stream is modeled by the class **stream** with attributes for its rate of flow **FlowRate** and the concentrations of its ingredients (**Concentrations** is an array of reals indexed by the ingredients of the stream). The concentrations of all the ingredients of a stream must sum up to 1. The class **equipment** models any piece of equipment having some input streams and output streams. Every equipment that processes streams is constrained by the law of mass balance. Separators, mixers and splitters are instances of the **equipment** class. The class representing figure 2 (not shown here) will have the preference **min I1 +I2**. This example was worked out with the help of Pratima Gogineni (University at Buffalo).

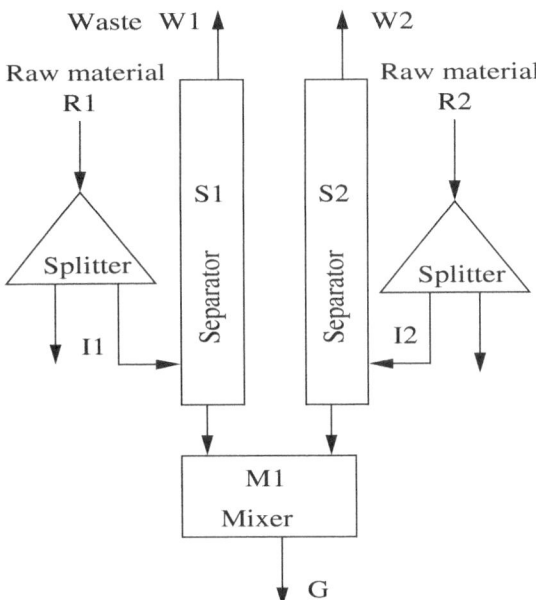

Fig. 2. A Separation Flow Sheet

```
class stream {
 attributes
  real FlowRate;   real [] Concentrations;
 constraints
  sum C in Concentrations : C = 1;
  constructors stream(Q, C) {  FlowRate = Q; Concentrations = C;  }
}
class equipment {
 attributes
  stream [] InStream, OutStream;   int NIngedients;
 constraints
  forall I in 1..NIngredients :
   (sum J in InStream : (J.FlowRate * J.Concentrations[I])) =
   (sum K in OutStream: (K.FlowRate * K.Concentrations[I]));
   % law of mass balance
  constructors equipment(In,Out,NumIng) {
   InStream = In; OutStream = Out; NIngedients = NumIng; }
}
```

Heat Transfer in a Plate. This is another classic program in CLP(R). The problem is to model a plate in which the temperature of any point in the interior of the plate is the average of the temperature of its neighbouring four points. This can be stated mathematically by using 2d Laplace's equations. The Cob representation is shown below in a class called `heatplate`. The constructor initializes the temperature of the border of the 11 x 11 plate. Compared to its CLP(R) representation, the Cob representation of this problem is very concise, owing to the use of quantified constraints. The Cob class below calculates the heat at all the interior points.

```
class heatplate {
 attributes
  real [][] Plate;
 constraints
  forall I in 2..10:
   forall J in 2..10:
    4 * Plate[I,J] =
     (Plate[I-1,J] + Plate[I+1,J] + Plate[I,J-1] + Plate[I,J+1]);
  constructors heatplate(A,B,C,D) {
   forall M in 1..11: Plate[1,M] = A;
   forall N in 1..11: Plate[11,N] = B;
   forall K in 2..10: Plate[K,1] = C;
   forall L in 2..10: Plate[L,11] = D;
  }
}
```

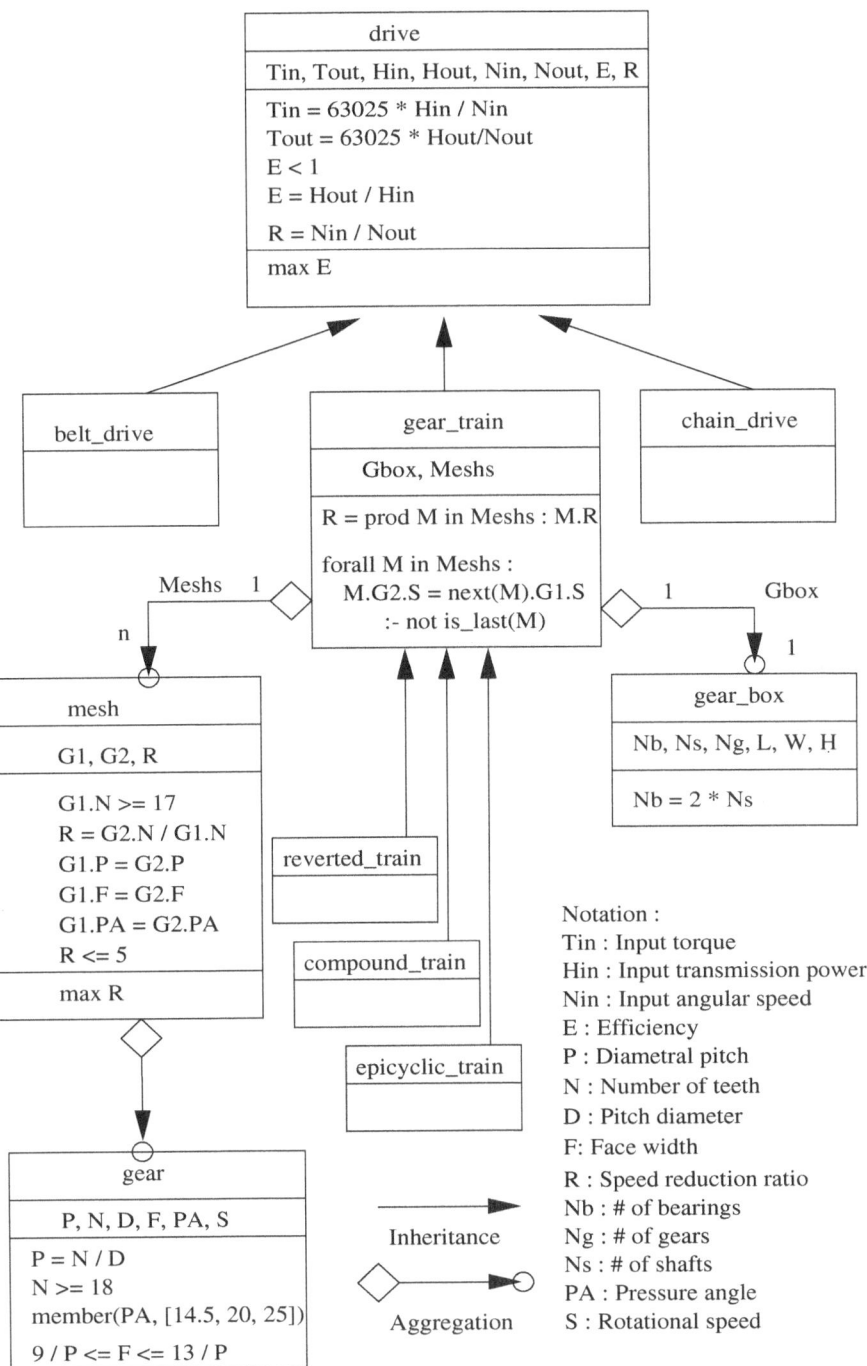

Fig. 3. Gear Train as Constrained Objects

Gear Train. The following problem was proposed by Prof. Li Lin, Dept of Industrial Engineering, University at Buffalo. A gear train is a special kind of drive whose purpose is to transmit rotary power between shafts while reducing angular speed. It consists of an assembly of pairwise engaged gears (meshes) enclosed in a gear box. The efficiency (E) of a drive is given as a relation between its input and output torques, angular speeds and transmission powers. We model this as a constraint in the `drive` class. The attributes and constraints of the remaining Cob classes are described in the class diagram in figure 3. The problem is to design a gear train that meets the designer's constraints and preferences while maximizing its efficiency (stated as a preference in the `drive` class). The Cob model of figure 3 can be used to solve this problem. Given values for `Tin`, `Hin`, and `Nin`, the underlying Cob computational model calculates the numer of meshes and teeth(of a gear) required to maximize the efficiency of the drive. Then using the number of meshes and teeth obtained earlier, the values of `P` (diameteral pitch), `D` (pitch diameter) and `F` (face width) are computed. The details of the above model were clarified by Jason Chen, Dept of Industrial Engineering.

Document Representation The use of constrained objects to model documents brings up the need for constraint optimization and relaxation. In a simplified version of this problem, a book may be thought of as a complex object that aggregates many chapters, each of which aggregates many sections. Each section in turn aggregates many paragraphs, and each paragraph aggregates many words. Thus, the elements of a book, namely, chapter, section, and paragraph become the basic classes of objects in the Cob model. Suppose we are interested in formatting the contents of the book. We may think of a `format` predicate within each class of book-element (chapter, section, etc.), whose purpose is to obtain the optimal (best) layout for the element (The reason for having a *predicate*, instead of a method, will become clear below.) Each formatted element would have a measure of how good or bad its formatting is, viz., its so-called *badness*. We assume that the `format` predicate incorporates some such method for calculating its badness. Also, the `format` predicate of one element would invoke the `format` predicate of its constituent elements in order to construct its optimal layout.

In this example, there are certain important constraints, namely: no section shall begin on the last line of a page, and no section shall end on the first line of a page. Such restrictions are better specified separately from the formatting algorithm, since the algorithm may be modified independently while these still hold. The `constraints` clause is used for specifying these restrictions. Now suppose the formatting algorithm comes up with a format that violates one of these constraints, it would then need to produce another format which will satisfy all constraints. (This is why having a format predicate is more convenient than a method.) Of course, this assumes that such a format exists; otherwise, we need some means of relaxing the constraints. The possibility of multiple solutions necessitates a preference criterion for choosing the best (most preferred) one. This is shown in the class Para, where we state that the format with lesser badness is the preferred one:

```
    format(L1, B1) < format(L2, B2) :- B1 > B2.

class Section {
  attributes
      Para[] paras;
      int begin_ln, end_ln;
  constraints
      begin_ln mod 50 != 49;
      end_ln mod 50 != 1;
      begin_ln = first(paras).begin_ln;
      end_ln = last(paras).end_ln;
      forall p in paras: (p.end_ln + 1 = next(p).begin_ln) :-
          not is_last(p));
  predicates
      format(Sec_lines) :- format(paras, Sec_lines, Badness).
      format([], [], 0).
      format([P|Paras], [L|Lines], Badness) :-
          P.format(L,Badness'),
          format(Paras, Lines, Badness''),
          Badness = Badness' + Badness''.
}
class Para {
  attributes
      int begin_ln, end_ln, Numlines;
      string[] words;
  constraints
      end_ln = begin_ln + Numlines;
      width = 30;
  predicates
      format(Lines, Badness) :- ... details omitted ...
  preference
      format(L1, B1) < format(L2, B2) :- B1 > B2;
}
```

4   Cob Programming Environment

Compiler. We have developed formal declarative and operational semantics of
Cob. In order to validate the language and its semantics, we have developed
a prototype Cob compiler that translates a Cob program into a CLP(R) program. Essentially each class definition translates to one predicate clause. The
constraints and constructor clauses of all classes are translated to appropriate
CLP(R) constraints. Since conditional constraints do not have a direct equivalent in CLP(R), we have implemented them separately. Disequations (!=) and
constructive negation are handled through special predicates. Inheritance and
compound attributes are translated by expanding the attributes of a class to

include the attributes of its superclass. Quantified and aggregation constraints (`forall`, `sum`, etc.) are translated to predicate clauses that iterate over elements of an enumerated type. We use the underlying CLP(R) engine for constraint handling. We are presently extending the tool to handle preferences.

CUML. We have developed a constraint-based extention of the Unified Modeling Language [18]. This extension, called CUML, allows one to define attributes, constraints, and preferences associated with every constrained object class definition. The tool generates textual equivalent of the CUML specification. Figure 3 illustrates the CUML notation for the gear train example. CUML enhances readability of the model and facilitates rapid code development.

Domain Specific Visual Interface. Currently we have a domain-specific visual interface tool for building circuits and trusses that generates textual Cob code that instantiates the appropriate classes. These interfaces include a palette of buttons and drawing primitives for creating instances of electrical components. Each component has a predefined Cob class definition and the value of any of its attributes can be specified through this interface. The components can be placed in any desired configuration and the appropriate classes representing this configuration are automatically instantiated. Once a model/configuration is created, it is translated using the Cob compiler to CLP(R) code. The constraints of the model are then solved, and values of attributes of all the components are displayed. If the model has an inconsistency (some constraint cannot be satisfied), it is detected during this *execution* of the model. Code generation and model execution are important capabilities of this tool not present in drawing tools like AutoCAD.

5 Conclusions, Status, and Further Work

The concept of constrained objects is broadly applicable in the modeling of complex engineering structures. We have illustrated this point in this paper through a variety of examples. We believe the Cob definitions presented are concise and clear. With the aid of domain-specific visual interfaces, the resulting paradigm has considerable potential for both pedagogic purposes as well as for more advanced applications. On a technical level, our language advances previous work by showing the use of a number of new features in modeling, especially conditional and quantified constraints, as well as preferences.

We are working on a number of modeling applications with researchers in the civil, chemical, computer, mechanical, and industrial engineering departments in the University at Buffalo. We are presently investigating a few important issues relating to this paradigm: (i) inconsistency detection, (ii) incrementality, (iii) abstraction. When the state of a model violates its constraints, a response to the effect that an error has occured is often not sufficient. The underlying computational engine should be able to provide a narrow range of possible places where the programmer can look for and correct the error. It is also possible sometimes that there are no solutions to the constraints, and the modeler is interested in understanding the cause of this inconsistency. This is also referred to as an over-constrained system [5] in the literature. A constraint violation could occur due to an incorrectly stated constraint, or an inconsistent value assigned to an attribute and can be corrected with the help of the programer. In conjunction with a visual representation for constrained objects, it is possible to develop techniques showing where the constraint violation occurred.

Another issue of special interest is incrementality. Since a modeler will typically make several changes to an initial model, it is important to support incremental constraint satisfaction, i.e., we should try to compute the new state of the complex object without re-solving all the constraints. When complex object is very large (i.e., consists of many subobjects), it may be very time-consuming to do a detailed simulation. In this case it may be necessary to work with a simplified model, i.e., a "cross-section" of the model so as to get an approximate answer in reasonable time. This problem may be called *model abstraction*.

Acknowledgements

This research was partially supported by grants from the National Science Foundation and the Xerox Foundation.

References

1. H. Ait-Kaci and A. Podelski. Towards a Meaning of LIFE. *Journal of Logic Programming*, 16(3):195–234, 1993. 31
2. A. Borning B. N. Freeman-Benson. Integrating Constraints with an Object Oriented Language. In *Proc. European Conference On Object-Oriented Programming*, pages 268–286, 1992. 30, 31
3. A. Borning. The Programming Language Aspects of Thinglab, A Constraint-Oriented Simulation Laboratory. *ACM TOPLAS*, 3(4):252–287, 1981. 30, 31
4. E. C. Freuder. Partial Constraint Satisfaction. In *Proc. 11th Intl. Jt. Conf. on Artificial Intelligence*, pages 278–283, 1989. 30
5. E. C. Freuder and R. J. Wallace. Heuristic Methods for Over-Constrained Constraint Satisfaction Problems. In *Proc. CP'95 Workshop on Overconstrained Systems*, 1995. 30, 43
6. A. Borning G. Lopez, B. N. Freeman-Benson. Constraints and Object Identity. In *Proc. European Conference On Object-Oriented Programming*, 1994. 31
7. K. Govindarajan. *Optimization and Relaxation in Logic Languages*. PhD thesis, Department of Computer Science, SUNY - Buffalo, 1997. 31
8. K. Govindarajan, B. Jayaraman, and S. Mantha. Optimization and Relaxation in Constraint Logic Languages. In *Proc. 23rd ACM Symp. on Principles of Programming Languages*, pages 91–103, 1996. 30, 31, 33
9. R. Helm, I. Holland, and D. Gangopadhyay. Contracts: Specifying Behavioural Compositions in Object-Oriented Systems. In *Proc. Object-Oriented Programming, Systems, and Applications (OOPSLA)*, 1990. 32
10. B. Horn. Constraint Patterns As a Basis For Object Oriented Programming. In *Proc. Object-Oriented Programming, Systems, and Applications (OOPSLA)*, 1992. 30

11. B. Horn. *Constrained Objects*. PhD thesis, CMU, November 1993. 31
12. J. Jaffar and J. L. Lassez. Constraint Logic Programming. In *Proc. 14th ACM Symp. on Principles of Programming Languages*, pages 111–119, 1987. 30
13. W. J. Leler. *The Specification and Generation of Constraint Satisfaction Systems*. Addison-Wesley, 1987. 30, 31
14. G. Lopez. *The Design and Implementation of Kaleidoscope, A Constraint Imperative Programming Language*. PhD thesis, University of Washington, 1997. 31
15. R. Mayne and S. Margolis. *Introduction to Engineering*. McGraw-Hill, 1982. 35
16. B. Meyer. *Eiffel: The Language*. Prentice-Hall, 1992. 32
17. R. Peak. Automating product data-driven analysis using multifidelity multidirectional constrained objects. Invited Presentation, NASA STEP for Aerospace Workshop, Jet Propulsion Lab, Pasadena CA, Jan 2000. 31
18. James Rumbaugh, Ivar Jacobson, and Grady Booch. *The Unified Modeling Language Reference Manual*. Addison-Wesley, 1998. 30, 42
19. G. Smolka. Constraint Programming in Oz (Abstract). In *Proc. Intl. Conference on Logic Programming*, pages 37–38, 1997. 31
20. P. van Hentenryck. *Constraint Satisfaction in Logic Programming*. MIT Press, 1989. 30
21. Warmer, J., Kleppe, A. *The Object Constraint Language*. Addison-Wesley, 1999. 31

Appendix A: Cob Syntax

The following grammar elaborates on the syntax defined in section 3.

$$
\begin{aligned}
attributes \;&::=\; decl \;;\; [\; decl \;;\;]^{+} \\
decl \;&::=\; type \; id\_list \\
type \;&::=\; primitive\_type\_id \mid class\_id \mid type[\;] \\
primitive\_type\_id \;&::=\; \texttt{real} \mid \texttt{int} \mid \texttt{bool} \mid \texttt{char} \mid \texttt{string} \\
id\_list \;&::=\; attribute\_id \; [\;,\; attribute\_id \;]^{+} \\
attribute \;&::=\; selector[.selector]^{+} \mid attribute[term] \\
selector \;&::=\; attribute\_id \mid selector\_id(terms) \\
selector\_id \;&::=\; \texttt{first} \mid \texttt{next} \mid \texttt{last} \\
terms \;&::=\; term \; [\;,\; term \;]^{+} \\
literals \;&::=\; literal \; [\;,\; literal \;]^{+} \\
literal \;&::=\; [\; \texttt{not} \;]\; atom \\
atom \;&::=\; pred\_id(terms) \mid constraint\_atom \\
pred\_clauses \;&::=\; pred\_clause \;.\; [\; pred\_clause \;.\;]^{+} \\
pred\_clause \;&::=\; clause\_head : - \; clause\_body \\
pred\_clause \;&::=\; clause\_head \\
clause\_head \;&::=\; pred\_id(terms') \\
clause\_body \;&::=\; goal \; [\;,\; goal \;]^{+} \\
goal \;&::=\; [\; \texttt{not} \;]\; pred\_id(terms') \\
terms' \;&::=\; term' \; [\;,\; term' \;]^{+} \\
term' \;&::=\; constant \mid var' \mid attribute \mid function\_id(terms') \\
pref\_clauses \;&::=\; pref\_clause \;.\; [\; pref\_clause \;.\;]^{+} \\
pref\_clause \;&::=\; pred\_id(terms') \;\leq\; pred\_id(terms') : - \; clause\_body \\
&\qquad\quad\mid \texttt{min} \; term \mid \texttt{max} \; term
\end{aligned}
$$

Note that the only variables that may appear in a *term* (defined in section 3) are attributes or those that are introduced in a quantification. These variables are generated by the non-terminal *var*. In the above grammar, the variables that appear in a *pred_clause* are the usual logic variables of Prolog. These are referred to as *var'* in the above syntax.

Appendix B: Sample Truss Code

The truss in figure 4 can be modeled in Cob by the class **sampletruss** given below. The Cob model calculates the cross sectional area of the beams given that they have a square cross section, are made of steel and that the truss must support a load of 15000 lbf.

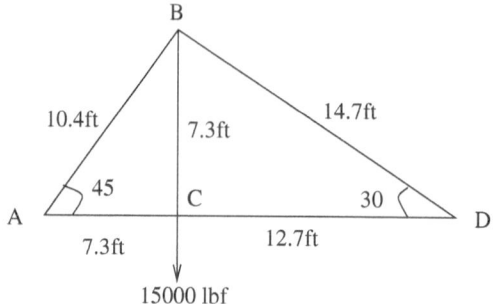

Fig. 4. A Simple Truss

```
class sampletruss {
 attributes
  beam AB, BC, CD, BD, AC; load IAV, IAH, ICV, IDV;
  bar IAB, IAC, IBA, IBC, IBD, ICA, ICB, ICD, IDB, IDC;
  bar [] Ba, Bb, Bc, Bd; load [] La, Lc, Ld;
  real W1, W2, W3, W4, W5, H1, H2, H3, H4, H5, Fab, Fbc, Fcd,
  Fbd, Fac, Fab_bk, Fbc_bk, Fcd_bk, Fbd_bk, Fac_bk, Fab_bn, Fbc_bn,
  Fcd_bn, Fbd_bn, Fac_bn, Fab_t, Fbc_t, Fcd_t, Fbd_t, Fac_t, Fdv,
  Fcv, Fav, Fah, Sigab, Sigbc, Sigcd, Sigac, Sigbd,
  Iab, Ibc, Icd, Ibd, Iac, Es, Sy, Pi;
  joint JA, JB, JC, JD;
 constraints
  Es = 30000000; Sy = 30000; Pi = 3.141;
  W1 = H1; W2 = H2; W3 = H3; W4 = H4; W5 = H5;
 constructors sampletruss() {
  AB=new beam(Es,Sy,10.4,W1,H1,Fab_bn,Fab_bk,Fab_t,Sigab,Iab,Fab);
  BC=new beam(Es,Sy,7.3,W2,H2,Fbc_bn,Fbc_bk,Fbc_t,Sigbc,Ibc,Fbc);
  CD=new beam(Es,Sy,12.7,W3,H3,Fcd_bn,Fcd_bk,Fcd_t,Sigcd,Icd,Fcd);
  BD=new beam(Es,Sy,14.7,W4,H4,Fbd_bn,Fbd_bk,Fbd_t,Sigbd,Ibd,Fbd);
  AC=new beam(Es,Sy,7.3,W5,H5,Fac_bn,Fac_bk,Fac_t,Sigac,Iac,Fac);
  IAB = new bar(AB,Pi/4); IAC = new bar(AC,0);
  IAV = new load(Fav,Pi/2); IAH = new load(Fah,0);
  Ba = [IAB, IAC]; La = [IAV, IAH]; JA = new joint(Ba,La);
  IBA = new bar(AB, 5*Pi/4); IBC = new bar(BC, 3*Pi/2);
  IBD = new bar(BD, 11*Pi/6); Bb = [IBA, IBC, IBD]; Lb = [];
  JB = new joint(Bb, Lb); ICA = new bar(AC, Pi);
  ICB = new bar(BC, Pi/2); ICD = new bar(CD, 0);
  ICV = new load(15000, 3*Pi/2); Bc = [ICA, ICB, ICD];
  Lc = [ICV]; JC = new joint(Bc, Lc); IDB = new bar(BD, 5*Pi/6);
  IDC = new bar(CD, Pi); IDV = new load(Fdv, Pi/2);
  Bd = [IDB, IDC]; Ld = [IDV]; JD = new joint(Bd, Ld);
 }
}
```

Compiler Construction in Higher Order Logic Programming

Chuck C. Liang

Department of Computer Science, Hofstra University
Hempstead, New York 11550, USA
cscccl@hofstra.edu

Abstract. This paper describes a general method of compiler implementation using *higher order abstract syntax* and logic programming. A working compiler written in λProlog is used to demonstrate this method. Various stages of compilation are formulated as higher order logic programming including parsing and the generation of higher order representations, type checking, intermediate representation in continuation-passing style, and machine-dependent code generation. The performance overhead of using higher order representations is also addressed.

1 Introduction

The construction of compilers and translators for programming languages involves much computation that is of a symbolic and deductive nature. Although there has been much study of these aspects of program analysis in the context of declarative languages, logic programming is still not used as a general tool in compiler construction. Implementations of compilers still rely principally on imperative languages, which are less capable of exploiting the inherently declarative aspects of compilation. In particular, *higher order abstract syntax* [27,38], a technique that uses λ-terms in the representation of programs, has been shown to be a valuable tool in the declarative analysis and transformation of programs. This new form of abstract syntax however, is still not applied to practical compiler construction. Studies of higher-order abstract syntax have so far been limited to very small examples.

The aim of the project described here is to develop a method of compiler construction using higher order abstract syntax in general, and a higher order logic programming language in particular. Some of the formulations described here are syntheses and extensions of previous works, while new methods are also introduced when needed. We shall address the various stages of compiler construction, from parsing to machine-dependent code generation, in the context of describing an experimental compiler written in λProlog. Due to space constraints, the discussion here is necessarily limited to outline form, and examples are small to provide clarity. The full implementation, larger examples, and additional notes can be found at www.cs.hofstra.edu/~cscccl/hocompiler/.

It should be stated that we can only present and demonstrate a selected set of compilation techniques. This paper does not seek to be comprehensive in

S. Krishnamurthi, C. R. Ramakrishnan (Eds.): PADL 2002, LNCS 2257, pp. 47–63, 2002.
© Springer-Verlag Berlin Heidelberg 2002

addressing the massive number of approaches developed for compilation, both in general and for particular styles of programming languages. It is inevitable that readers will inquire as to how our body of techniques will be applicable in specific settings, as for instance, in abstract interpretation of logic programs, polymorphism and inheritance in object oriented languages, or register allocation for particular machine architectures. We cannot hope to answer all such questions here. Our purpose is to conduct an experiment on the applicability of higher order abstract syntax in realistic compilation. We hope to *open the door* to the investigation and incorporation of other techniques in this declarative setting.

2   Higher Order Abstract Syntax and λProlog

Conventional abstract syntax representations of source programs cannot capture the *locality* of names that is essential in high level programming languages. As a result, compilers have traditionally relied on external structures, namely symbol tables, to hold this information. Higher order abstract syntax (HOAS) uses λ-terms to represent source programs, thereby capturing the locality of names in a natural and declarative manner. The application of HOAS requires a language in which λ-terms can be used as data-structures, *and* in which enough constructs exists for reasoning with λ-terms. Functional languages may have functions in data structures but they cannot, for example, recognize α-equivalent terms. Thus even languages such as ML cannot fully exploit a higher order representation. The logic programming language λProlog [31] extends standard Prolog by using λ-terms and higher-order unification [18] in place of first order terms and unification. It allows for universal quantification and implication in goals. The following are typical λProlog clauses:[1]

```
kind tm, ty type.              % object-level terms and types
type app tm -> tm -> tm.       % application
type abs (tm -> tm) -> tm.     % abstraction
type --> ty -> ty -> ty.       % type constructor
infixr --> 10.
type typecheck tm -> ty -> o.  % typing judgment
```

```
typecheck (app A B) T :- typecheck A (S --> T), typecheck B S.
typecheck (abs A) (S --> T) :-
    pi v\ (typecheck v S => typecheck (A v) T).
```

The **kind** and **type** clauses declare the signature of an object-level language, which in this case is that of typed λj-terms. Object-level terms and types are categorized by **tm** and **ty** respectively at the meta-level. The infix operator **-->** is the object-level functional type constructor, which should not be confused with

---

[1] These clauses are actually $L\lambda$ clauses. $L\lambda$ [25] is a sublanguage of λProlog that uses a decidable and deterministic form of higher order unification. Most λProlog clauses in practice are in fact in $L\lambda$.

the λProlog type constructor `->`. The predicate `typecheck` represents type judgment. Application is written in Curried form: (`f x`) instead of `f(x)`. The first
`typecheck` clause is an ordinary first order Horn clause. In the second clause, A
is a λ-term variable. λ-abstraction is written with the infix symbol \ (e.g., the
identity is `x\x`). Implication '`=>`' and universal quantification '`pi v\`' can appear
in the bodies of clauses. The operational meaning of these new constructs are
derived from intuitionistic proof theory: $\forall x.A$ holds if A holds under a fresh
eigenvariable x not appearing free elsewhere. $A \Rightarrow B$ holds if B holds with
definite clause A locally visible. When combined with higher-order unification
(or $L\lambda$ unification [25]), these constructs allow recursion over the structure of
λ-terms while preserving the integrity of bound variables. They permit a language to analyze and manipulate the *internal structure* of abstractions, making
it suitable for applying HOAS. The two λProlog clauses above implement type
checking for object-level λ-terms, and are representative of the kind of clauses
used in our compiler.

It should be noted that our use of λProlog is secondary to our use of higher
order abstract syntax. Future developments may permit the application of HOAS
in other systems, possibly including functional-logic hybrid languages. Previous
investigation [28] has determined the critical characteristics of any language
that can truly support HOAS (illustrated by the λProlog extensions described
above). But experimental compiler implementation also requires the practical
features of a realistic programming language. λProlog is currently one of the
only languages that satisfy both criteria. One significant alternative is Elf [37],
which has been used for the theoretical investigation of many topics pertaining to
programming languages, including compiler verification [15]. The justification of
our preference for λProlog lies primarily in the availability of a high-performance
implementation, which is discussed in Sections 3 and 9.

For more information on λProlog and higher order abstract syntax, the reader
is asked to consult [27,31].

3   Obstacles to Application

From the beginning, work in higher order abstract syntax have pointed in the direction of its application in compiler writing. It has been known for some time, for
example, that HOAS can give declarative formulations of type checking. Other
works include using HOAS for the recognition of tail recursion [32], and various program transformations [14]. Interpreters for very small languages (without
parsing) have also been formulated. These experiments are useful in demonstrat-
ing (and even proving) theoretical aspects of programming languages. However,
they are uniformly limited in scale. None has been applied to actual compilation.

We can identify two major factors that have discouraged the application of
HOAS as an actual compilation paradigm:

1. Lack of a high-performance implementation of a suitable programming language, one that can support HOAS.

2. Lack of general tools for *deterministic parsing* (such as Yacc), which are needed to generate HOAS representations from source text.

Recent developments have significantly improved the situation with both of these obstacles. First of all, work in improving the representation and normalization of λ-terms, such those using DeBruijn indices and explicit substitutions [1,30], have lessened the overhead of systems that need to reason with λ-terms. The recent *Teyjus* implementation of λProlog [33] uses such advanced techniques. Teyjus is also *compiler*-based in that it extends Warren's Abstract Machine to accommodate λProlog. In addition, Teyjus has a module system and sufficient I/O capabilities to support compiler construction. We shall further discuss how Teyjus lessens the overhead of HOAS in Section 9. The second obstacle listed above is addressed in the next section.

4   Parsing and the Generation of λ-Syntax Trees

Realistic compilation with HOAS cannot begin unless higher-order representations can be constructed automatically from source text. A parser, coupled with sufficiently expressive "semantic actions" can be used for this purpose. But standard parsing tools (Yacc and derivatives) have been inaccessible to logic programming languages that can support HOAS. Parsing in logic programming has traditionally relied on Definite Clause Grammars (DCG - [35]). Though general in scope, DCGs have no inherent capability to resolve non-determinism. For example, there is nothing that would prevent the user from writing an ambiguous grammar as a DCG. Compilers using DCGs do exist (see [4] for a survey of early work). However, the programmer will have to *manually* provide the mechanisms needed for deterministic parsing (such as lookahead symbols). In contrast, Yacc-style tools generate deterministic parsers from appropriate grammars automatically. Even if DCGs are a viable solution for general compiler writing, they must still be extended to the higher order case, with richer constructs. Attempts to thus extend DCGs exist [8,19], but they have not led to any usable tools.

A deterministic, bottom-up parser generator has recently been developed for λProlog, and is described in [23]. The parser generator requires a different restriction of LR grammars than the LALR grammars used in other Yacc-style tools. It requires the user to write a few more productions: the grammar used in our compiler required eight more productions (out of approximately seventy) compared to traditional Yacc. However, much of the character of Yacc-style parser construction is preserved. The essence of this parser generator is illustrated by the following pair of grammars:

$$
\begin{array}{ll}
\text{LR:} & S \to A \\
& A \to (B) \mid x \\
& B \to (A) \mid x
\end{array}
\qquad\qquad
\begin{array}{ll}
\text{BRC:} & S \to A \\
& A \to (B) \mid x \\
& B \to CA) \mid x \\
& C \to (
\end{array}
$$

Both grammars generate the same language, and both grammars are sensitive to whether the terminal symbol x is surrounded by an even or odd number of pairs of parentheses. For the LR grammar on the left this distinction requires the generation of a finite state machine, which is used to resolve the "reduce-reduce" conflict between $A \rightarrow x$ (even) and $B \rightarrow x$ (odd). The *bounded right context* (BRC) grammar[2] on the right is also an LR grammar. However, the *state information* as to whether an even or odd number of '('s have been read is maintained by the grammar itself, in the form of the extra non-terminal symbol C. In a bottom-up derivation using the second grammar, new '(' symbols will be alternately shifted on to the stack (if it's an odd occurrence) and reduced to C (if it's an even occurrence). x must be reduced to A if it's preceeded by C on the stack, and to B if preceeded by a '('. There is no need to maintain state information externally. Every LR grammar has an equivalent BRC grammar [12,20]. In the context of logic programming, the advantage of this simplification of LR parsing is that it facilitates the formulation of *deterministic bottom-up parsing* as *deterministic proof search*. Instead of implementing general LR parsing algorithms by brute force, a process that destroys much of the character of logic programming, our parser generator constructs inference rules such as the following (which should be read bottom-up):

$$\frac{\ldots(B}{\ldots(x}\ Reduce \qquad \frac{\ldots CA}{\ldots Cx}\ Reduce \qquad \frac{\ldots(C}{\ldots((}\ Reduce \qquad \frac{\ldots C(\sigma}{\ldots C(}\ Shift$$

(σ is the next input symbol.) A pairwise matching of the bottom sides of these rules will confirm that there are no "reduce-reduce" or "shift-reduce" conflicts[3]

The parser generator also contains a customizable lexical analyzer. Since the parser generator is written in λProlog and outputs λProlog code, the semantic actions associated with grammar rules are in fact λProlog goals. These goals can be written so that they generate λ-term syntax trees as source text is parsed bottom-up. The formation of abstractions over text is accomplished by the following *copy* clauses, which first appeared in [26]:

```
copy (app A B) (app C D) :- copy A C, copy B D.
copy (abs A) (abs B) :- pi v\ (copy v v => copy (A v) (B v)).
```

These clauses formulate substitution over object-level λ-terms. The goal

```
pi u\ (copy u S => copy (A u) B)
```

succeeds only if B is β-equivalent to (A S). For example, given source text (in pseudo-ML syntax)

```
"fun f x = (g x);"
```

---

[2] BRC grammars were well-studied in the 1960's and 70's (e.g. see [11,12,16]), but they were eventually overshadowed by general LR parsing. However, they were never considered in the context of logic programming.

[3] The connection between parsing and formal deduction has been studied in the past [36], but *deterministic* parsing in such a framework has received little attention.

the subexpression "(g x)" will be parsed first (since it's bottom-up) into an ordinary syntax tree, namely (app "g" "x"). The abstraction over "x" will be seen next, and at this point the λ-term syntax tree

```
(abs v\ (app "g" v))
```

will be generated by the goal

```
pi u\ (copy u "x" => copy (A u) (app "g" "x")), !
```

The meta-level variable A will be instantiated to the meta-level abstraction v\(app "g" v). Any subsequent "x" encountered in the source text cannot be confused with the bound variable in this abstraction[4]. We use the standard logic programming control feature "!" when necessary. Although "logically perfect" alternatives can be be fashioned with some effort, we are also concerned with efficiency. Our use of λProlog is as a *real programming language*. The declarative paradigm at work here is not merely logic programming, but also the higher-order form of abstract syntax. An alternative method of creating the abstraction A is to use λProlog's built-in higher order unification procedure and provide the programmer means to bias *projections* over *imitations*. The unification goal

```
(A "x") = (app "g" "x")
```

will then accomplish the same purpose.

5   An Experimental Compiler

Once an adequate means of generating higher order representations from source text is available, we can finally begin to apply HOAS in formulating compilers. This and the next few sections describe how HOAS is used in each of the basic compilation stages.

The source language we have chosen for our experimental compiler is an imperative-style language with enough flexibility for experimenting with new features. Many aspects of the language, including its syntax, are based on the "Tiger" language described in [3], which has versions in ML, Java, and C. It is hoped that this choice will facilitate the comparison between our methods of compiler writing with those of other styles of programming. The target language is Sparc assembly language. An existing assembler (gcc in its role as an assembler) is used in the last step to produce Sparc executables. Except for this last step, every aspect of the compiler is written in λProlog.

Although the scale of the source language and compiler is still limited, it is a significant expansion of previous experiments that used HOAS for implementing programming languages (e.g. [14,32]). These early experiments typically used

---

[4] The clauses presented here are stylized for brevity. In reality different copy causes must be defined for each type, i.e, for expressions and for strings. A default clause that copies terms to themselves is also needed so that "g" is preserved before its abstraction is encountered.

source languages with only four or five constructs. None of them involved the building of a complete system that includes efficient parsing, intermediate language, and realistic target language. Clearly a new level of experimentation is required if higher order abstract syntax is to acquire more than theoretical importance.

Our source language admits nested scopes and functions within functions, but it is not higher ordered. To partially compensate for this lack, we implemented Java-style classes and objects (without inheritance, so far)[5]. This means that a function requires an additional parameter that points to heap records with bindings for its free variables (the Sparc registers %o5 and %i5 are reserved for this purpose). Some of the flavor of computing with closures is therefore captured. A higher order, functional language will require a more general treatment of closures. The runtime stack cannot be used easily since local variables may persist in closures, necessitating a garbage collector. These are topics that we wish to explore in the future, but we decided to first demonstrate our methods on a conventional source language.

λ-Syntax Trees

HOAS is applicable to more than one stage of compiler writing (see Section 7). We shall refer to the specific structures generated by the parser as *λ-syntax trees*. We shall continue to use "higher order abstract syntax" to refer to the general technique of using λ-terms in representations.

The λProlog signature for λ-syntax trees of the source language is similar to the abstract syntax structures described in [3], except of course, for its higher-order components. The constructs of the language are defined by type declarations such as the following:[6]

```
kind texp type.    % meta-level type for values
kind ttype type.   % type for object-level types
kind tdec type.    % type for declarations
type intexp int -> texp.     % integer constant
type strexp string -> texp.  % string constant
type opexp string -> texp -> texp -> texp. % binary op.
type ifexp texp -> texp -> texp -> texp.   % if
type whileexp texp -> texp -> texp.        % while
type callexp texp -> (list texp) -> texp.  % function call
type letexp tdec -> texp -> texp.     % let
type dabs (tvar -> tdec) -> tdec. % declaration abstraction
type pabs (tvar -> texp) -> texp. % parameter abstraction
% etc ...
```

---

[5] Classes and instances are represented with bound variables, but (currently) their members are not.

[6] The exact definition of our source language, as well as its abstract syntax structure, is transitory as we explore different strategies for compilation.

The meta-level type for λ-syntax tree expressions is `texp`. The most important higher-order constructors are `dabs` and `pabs`, which abstracts over declarations and formal parameters of functions respectively. `dabs` abstractions are used in `letexp` statements to abstract over the names of a set of (possibly mutually recursive) identifier declarations.

6   Type Checking and Type Inference

A number of compilation strategies, such as static analysis and partial evaluation, can potentially benefit from the ability to reason with a higher order representation directly. Some of these subjects have already been studied in the context of HOAS.

In this section we focus on one essential component of most compilers: type checking. The two type checking clauses presented in Section 2 do not completely suffice in realistic settings. One feature we can expect to find in many languages is mutually-recursive definitions. Higher order logic programming offers interesting solutions for type checking and inference under mutual recursion. Consider an ordinary piece of source code such as

```
let
    var a := 10
    function g(n:int) = if n>0 then f(n-1)
    function f(n) = if n>0 then g(n-1)
in  g(a)   end
```

The type of function `f` is not known while type checking `g`. We also may not have the benefit of any "headers," (as is the case with function `f`). In the λ-syntax tree, this let-structure is represented by two abstractions over a pair consisting of first the declarations followed by the body of the let. In the sample code below, `typeof` is a predicate that associates an expression with a type. `dabs` is a second-order constructor that represents abstraction over a list of declarations followed by an expression in which they appear (its argument will be a λ term). `vardec` and `fixptdec` are constructors for variable and functions declarations respectively. `intexp` and `callexp` are constructors for integer constants and function calls respectively. `namety` is a constructor for (object-level) primitive types, and `-->` is an infix constructor for (object-level) functional types.

```
typeof (let (dabs T)) U :-
  pi v\ (typeof v A => typeof (T v) U).
typeof (vardec Var Exp) :- typeof Var A, typeof Exp A.

typeof (fixptdec F f\(pabs (T f))) (A --> B) :-
    typeof F (A -> B),
    pi f\ (typeof f (A --> B) =>
      pi x\ (typeof x A => typeof (T f x) B)).
```

```
typeof (callexp Fun Arg) B :- typeof Fun (A --> B), typeof Arg A.
typeof (intexp N) (namety "int").
% etc ...
```

The first clause is key: for each abstraction it introduces an eigenvariable for the name of the identifier that will be declared. It also introduces a (meta-level) *free variable* for the initial type of every identifier. Thus for the sample program above the types for f and g are assumed to be distinct free variables initially. These free variables will be instantiated (via unification) into appropriate type expressions when the declarations are processed. For example, for a variable declaration vardec, the type associated with the identifier Var must match the type of its initial value Exp. Subsequent occurrences of Var are therefore constrained to have types consistent with the type of Exp.

Unification is a natural tool for type checking that imperative languages lack. A conventional compiler will also require a symbol table to keep track of types. In the higher order logic programming formulation the symbol table is replaced by the declarative construct of intuitionistic implication (=>), which, together with λ-abstraction, respects scopes in a natural way.

The above formulation of typing suffices for a non-polymorphic language (as is the case with the language used in our experimental compiler). A language with generic type variables such as ML would require the use of a higher order representation of type *schemes* [5]. A quantified type such as $\Pi a.a \rightarrow a$ has a natural higher order representation where the type variable a is bound by an abstraction, i.e., $\Pi\lambda a.a \rightarrow a$ where Π is now a second order constructor. A principal type scheme can now be thought of as an α-equivalence class of terms. Type inference using such representations of type schemes has also been formulated in HOAS [13,22], though they require an indirect way of using meta-level unification than the "mono-typing" described above. In [22] a type inference algorithm is described that targets ML-style let-polymorphism. The expression

```
let val f = (fn x => x) in (f f) end;
```

is typed by associating f with the type scheme $\Pi\lambda a.a \rightarrow a$. α-equivalent instances of this type scheme are then associated for each occurrence of f in the body of the let-expression: $\Pi\lambda a.a \rightarrow a$ and $\Pi\lambda b.b \rightarrow b$. Since the type variables in these instances are bound at the meta-level, they cannot be confused. In a logic programming implementation, each instance can be instantiated with a distinct meta-variable, allowing the correct derivation of the type of the let-expression.

7   A Continuation Passing Style Representation

Modern compilers require intermediate languages. One such language that is based on the λ-calculus already exists, and there is considerable work on translating programs to *continuation passing style* ("CPS" - see for example [2,9,21,39,40]). What can higher order abstract syntax and higher order logic programming add to this well-studied and well-applied subject? In a language that cannot fully support HOAS, including functional languages, a meta-level CPS representation is, ironically, not higher ordered. For example, in [2] a CPS representation is defined in ML, but the ML data structure for CPS expressions is in fact first order. What should be bound variables are represented with ordinary symbols, and not with *abstractions in the meta language*. That is, CPS continuation functions are not represented using ML's native abstractions (`fn =>`). This is due to the inability of ML to *look inside* its abstractions, which is necessary during the analysis and transformation of CPS terms. A HOAS representation of CPS should be able to take advantage of the fact that a CPS term is after all, a λ-term.

We use a higher order CPS-*like* representation as the intermediate language in our experimental compiler. We differ from the traditional CPS representation in the following way. Instead of adding an extra continuation parameter to each function and operator, we modify the application of each function and operator so that they carry a *continuation abstraction*. Essentially, this form of CPS is equivalent to what is referred to as the *direct style* [6] or *A-normal form* [10] representation. It has been shown (see [10]) that this form of CPS is equivalent to the traditional form, with less clutter.

Our CPS intermediate language is essentially a miniaturized version of the source language. Each construct is modified to carry one or more continuations. It has the essential characteristics of CPS in that each operator and function is applied only to primitives. However, it preserves some of the top-down structure of a higher-level abstract syntax representation by duplicating certain essential constructs[7]. In the following signature of our CPS language, recall that `texp` is the type for expressions in the λ-syntax tree:

```
kind kexp type.    % meta-level type for continuation expressions
type cps texp -> kexp -> kexp.      % primitive operation
type kabs (texp -> kexp) -> kexp.  % continuation abstraction
type kreturn  texp -> kexp.        % return value, (stop)
type klet (texp -> kexp) -> kexp. % ''let''
type kformal (texp -> kexp) -> kexp.  % formal parameter
type karg texp -> int -> kexp -> kexp.  % actual parameter
type kcall texp -> int -> kexp -> kexp. % function call
type kvar tvar -> ttype -> texp -> kexp -> kexp. % variable
type kfunc tvar -> ttype -> kexp -> kexp.  % function
type klass tvar -> (list texp) -> kexp -> kexp. % class
type kif kexp -> kexp -> kexp -> kexp -> kexp.  % if-else
type kwhile kexp -> kexp -> kexp -> kexp.       % while loop
```

`kabs` is a second-order constructor for *continuation abstractions*, which are carried by all structures save the terminating `kreturn`. The constructs `kvar`, `kfunc`

---

[7] A strict adherence to the CPS principle can be excessive. For example, if we sequentialize the boolean condition of a while-loop before transforming its body, it will become unclear as to where the while loop actually starts. Some *top-down* structure can be helpful when generating code from the CPS representation.

and `klass` respectively define variables, functions and classes for their continuation. These constructs also carry limited type information due to the presence of classes. Although many constructs carry more than one continuation, only one of these is the "true" continuation surrounding the construct. For example, in `kif`, the condition, "then" and "else" parts of the construct are represented by continuations that terminate in (kabs v\ kreturn v), or essentially $\lambda x.x$. Only the third `kexp` subexpression is the continuation that follows the if-else construct.

An expression such as $a + b * 2$ is represented by the `kexp` term

```
cps (opexp "*" (varexp (simplevar b)) (intexp 2))
   (kabs u\ (cps (opexp "+" (varexp (simplevar a)) u) K))
```

Here K is the continuation that always surrounds any expression. It should be emphasized that the symbols a and b are not strings but *bound variables*, since the higher-level λ-syntax tree is also higher-ordered.

The following are sample clauses that make up the (call-by-value) translation from the λ-syntax tree to the CPS representation. These clauses make use of decidable "higher order pattern" unification:

```
type atomic, primitive  texp -> o.
type formcps kexp -> texp -> kexp -> o.
atomic (intexp A).
atomic (varexp (simplevar S)).
primitive A :- atomic A, !.
primitive (opexp S A B)  :- atomic A, atomic B.

formcps K A (cps A K) :- primitive A.
formcps K (opexp OP A B) AK :- atomic B, !,
  pi v\ (atomic v => (formcps K (opexp OP v B) (L v),
                      formcps (kabs L) A AK)).
formcps K (opexp OP A B) BK :-
  pi v\ (atomic v => (formcps K (opexp OP A v) (L1 v),
                      formcps (kabs L1) B BK)).
% etc ...
```

The `formcps` predicate takes a surrounding continuation (K), an expression, and the resulting continuation as parameters. The use of ! here is for efficiency. It is worthwhile to note that *if* our source language consisted only of application and abstraction, then the CPS transformation would be defined as follows (where `kapply` and `kformal` represent general application and abstraction respectively):

```
type kapply texp -> texp -> kexp -> kexp.
formcps K (app A B) BK :-
  (pi u\ ( formcps (kabs v\ (kapply v u K)) A (L u)) ),
  formcps (kabs L) B BK.
formcps (kabs v\ kreturn v) (abs A) (kformal AK) :-
  (pi u\ (atomic u => formcps (kabs v\ kreturn v) (A u) (AK u))).
```

A similar higher order CPS transformation was given in [7], and was implemented in Elf. However, the purpose of this transformation was to prove a theoretical result with Elf, and was confined to application and abstraction.

It is also possible to use the source language itself to write CPS terms ("direct style"), but we decided to construct a new language to avoid some of the clutter of the source language.

A higher-order representation of CPS expressions can facilitate the formulation of various transformations on the intermediate form. For example, the following optimization clause pushes a purely functional operation inside the "else" case of an kif-statement, if the continuation abstraction (over u) is vacuous over the other components of the construct.

```
optimize (cps A (kabs u\ (kif C THEN (ELSE u) K)))
   (kif C THEN (cps A (kabs ELSE)) K) :- not (side_effect A).
```

The scopes of the variables in upper-case, as per Prolog convention, are over the entire clause, and therefore cannot contain free occurrences of u. ELSE must therefore abstract over u, allowing the continuation abstraction kabs to be pushed inside the else-case. We can similarly formulate dead variable elimination as vacuous abstractions, which are represented by the "higher order pattern" x\A. A first-order meta-level CPS formulation, without the benefit of higher-order pattern matching, would have to manually keep track of and possibly rename bound variables during such transformations.

It may be interesting to consider the formulation of intermediate languages other than CPS in HOAS. However, as argued in [2], there is *nothing wrong* with using CPS. The CPS representation is flexible enough to still allow the application of other techniques, even if they cannot take advantage of the higher order nature of CPS.

8   Code Generation

Higher-order abstract syntax is most useful in the *middle* stages of compilation. At the code generation stage, its benefits become less clear. However, there is nothing to indicate that it is necessarily an impediment if there are enough language features to support it.

Our experimental compiler generates machine-dependent assembly language text for the Sparc architecture [34]. We make use of Sparc's *register windowing* mechanism. Future work will involve an additional intermediate stage that will generate code for a general abstract machine.

The Sparc architecture is first represented in abstract syntax. A meta-level type store is defined to represent Sparc registers, memory locations, immediate constants, and labels. The meta-level type inst represents Sparc instructions. The principal predicate used for generating code for CPS expressions is

```
type gencode int -> int -> kexp -> store -> (list inst) -> o.
```

The first two arguments to this predicate keep track of an integer *label counter,* which is used to generate unique string labels. The "output" of this predicate is first of all a `store` location for the return value of a code fragment, followed by a list of instructions. On processing a CPS term such as a subtraction operation (`cps (opexp "-" A B) (kabs K)`), the appropriate instruction is generated for the subtraction. This involves finding a `store` location to hold the result of the operation. The `store` location, commonly a register, is then *passed* to the continuation abstraction. Each value (`texp`) expression (including A and B above) is therefore always associated with a store location. A predicate `assoc` is used to "remember" the store associated with each expression. A typical `gencode` clause has the form

```
gencode LC0 LC1 (cps A (kabs K)) RETURN [INST | INSTS] :-
    % generate expression A into instruction INST,
    pi v\ (assoc v STORE => gencode LC0 LC1 (K v) RETURN INSTS).
```

where `STORE` is the store location associated with the result of the instruction.

The principal difficulty in defining the `gencode` predicate is register assignment. No matter how declarative a meta-language is, it must deal with the fact that registers in a real machine must be used in special ways. Registers assigned to expressions need to be eventually deallocated, which requires `gencode` to keep track of state information. Our experimental compiler uses intuitionistic implication (`=>`) combined with ! to model mutable information. This method is not entirely satisfactory, not only because it relies heavily on extra-logical features, but also because it is not efficient. An alternative would be to use a table-like data structure, something we have avoided up to this point. That is, `gencode` can carry extra parameters that *lists* expressions and their associated stores.

Perhaps a limited *linear logic programming language* [17] will be able to declaratively formulate register assignment. However, no practical, *higher-order* version of such a language currently exists.

9   Performance Overhead

The use of λ-terms in the representation of programs incurs an extra cost in speed and memory usage during compilation. With a naive implementation of λ-terms and λ-normalization, this extra cost can indeed be overwhelming. However, advanced implementation techniques are being developed [30] to reduce this overhead to a reasonable level.

Reasoning with λ-terms inevitably involves β- and/or α-conversion. For example, consider a CPS term of the form

```
cps A (kabs v\ (cps B (kabs u\ (cps C (kabs w\ ....
```

that involves n nested `cps` terms with `kabs` continuation abstractions. In order to process such a term we would need to look *inside* the λ-abstractions. This is accomplished (as described in the foregoing) by clauses of the representative form

```
process (cps A K) :- process A, process K.
process (kabs K) :- pi v\ (... => process (K v)).
```

The "..." represents clauses containing information associated with the eigenvariable v, such as the register it has been assigned. In a naive implementation of λ-term normalization, The β-reduction of (K v) would involve a complete traversal over the structure of K. All n cps subterms are thus *visited* after reducing just the first redex encountered. The reduced form of (K v) still has $n - 1$ cps subterms, each with a similar continuation abstraction. The process goal will therefore be repeated for the abstraction at the next level, resulting in $n - 1$ additional visitations of cps subterms, and so on. Altogether, the "processing" of the above term will involve $(n^2 + n)/2$ *visitations* of its cps subterms, even though the CPS structure is naturally linear. Since the number of nested continuations n is proportional to the length of the source program, a naive β-reduction strategy can indeed be costly.

The redundant term traversals can be avoided using a more advanced implementation of β-reduction. In particular, an *explicit substitution* calculus [30] can be used to delay the traversal over the term structure until all β-redices have been encountered. The β-reduction of a term $(\lambda x.s)a$ can be *held in suspension* in a structure of the form $\{s; (a, x)\}$.

When a term such as this is encountered in another redex, we can *expand* the suspension environment to capture the substitution of more than one variable: $\{s'; (a, x), (b, y)\}$. The final normalization of the term will involve a single traversal, substituting for all variables simultaneously. This refinement means that the CPS structure above can be "processed" in one pass, which is what one would expect with a conventional, first order representation. Such refinements are used in the Teyjus λProlog implementation [29].

A naive beta-reduction strategy may also need to replicate terms during substitution, resulting in greater memory usage. It was found that, with a modification to Teyjus so that it uses a naive reduction strategy, a heap overflow error occurred while compiling a program just a hundred lines long, while we've successfully compiled programs over a thousand lines long with (standard) Teyjus. Timing comparisons also support our above analysis: using explicit substitutions to delay traversal over terms results in an order-of-magnitude improvement in performance over a naive strategy. In one experiment, a one-page program was compiled (on a 1.1ghz workstation) in approximately 0.3 seconds with (standard) Teyjus and approximately 3.7 seconds with a naive reduction strategy. Future systems that can be used for the practical application of HOAS must implement enhanced strategies for representing and reducing λ-terms[8].

Work is continuing to further reduce the overhead of HOAS. One promising angle of approach is to optimize cases that appear most often in programs, namely the $L\lambda$ subset of λProlog with "β_0-reduction" and second order "pattern" unification [25].

---

[8] A forthcoming paper [24] will further discuss the relative advantages of various λ-term representation and reduction strategies.

10   Conclusion

Although our presentation has been in outline form, we hope to have conveyed a sense of the role that higher order abstract syntax can play during the principal stages of compiler construction. Certainly during portions of this process, namely the initial and final stages, HOAS plays little if any role. But for many of the operations and transformations performed on intermediate forms, HOAS can offer a simpler and cleaner formulation. Our experimental compiler, together with the continuing development of high-performance language support for λ-term representations, shows that HOAS can become useful for general compiler construction. Our compiler also provides a platform for studying new problems previously not considered. For example, with the joining of HOAS and CPS, it is possible to study whether certain optimizations, such as tail-recursion elimination, are better formulated as transformations on λ-syntax trees or on CPS terms.

From a general perspective, with the experimental compiler we have hopefully taken work on higher order abstract syntax to the next logical level. It is a necessary step in the development of higher-order abstract syntax into a practical, declarative programming paradigm. Clearly a great amount of work remain. We have immediate plans, for example, for expanding the compiler by implementing data-flow analyses via abstract interpretation. We now have a platform on which to continue such work.

Acknowledgments

The author wishes to thank Dale Miller and Gopalan Nadathur for their helpful comments.

References

1. M. Abadi, L. Cardelli, P. Curien, and J. Levy. Explicit substitutions. *Journal of Functional Programming*, 1(4):375–416, 1991. 50
2. A. W. Appel. *Compiling with Continuations*. Cambridge University Press, 1992. 55, 56, 58
3. A. W. Appel. *Modern Compiler Implementation in ML*. Cambridge University Press, 1998. 52, 53
4. J. Cohen and T. Hickey. Parsing and compiling using Prolog. *ACM Transactions on Programming Languages and Systems*, 9(2):125–163, 1987. 50
5. L. Damas and R. Milner. Principal type-schemes for functional programs. In *Ninth Annual ACM SIGPLAN-SIGACT Symposium on Principles of Programming Languages*, pages 207–212, January 1982. 55
6. O. Danvy. Back to direct style. *Science of Computer Programming*, 22(3):183–195, 1994. 56
7. O. Danvy, B. Dzafic, and F. Pfenning. On proving syntactic properties of CPS programs. In *Proceedings of the Third International Workshop on Higher Order Operational Techniques in Semantics*, September 1999. 58

8. A. Felty. Defining object-level parsers in λProlog. In *Proceedings of the Work-shop on the λProlog Programming Language*, 1992. Department of Computer and Information Science, University of Pennsylvania, Technical Report MS-CIS-92-86. 50

9. M. Fischer. Lambda calculus schemata. In *ACM Conference on Proving Assertions about Programs, SIGPLAN Notices 7*, number 1, pages 104–109, 1972. 55

10. C. Flanagan, A. Sabry, B. Duba, and M. Felleisen. The essence of compiling with continuations. In *ACM SIGPLAN Conference on Programming Language Design and Implementation*, pages 237–247. ACM Press, 1993. 56

11. R. Floyd. Bounded context syntactic analysis. *Communications of the ACM*, 7(2):62–67, 1964. 51

12. S. L. Graham. On bounded right context languages and grammars. *SIAM Journal on Computing*, 3(3):224–254, 1974. 51

13. J. Hannan. *Investigating a Proof-Theoretic Meta-Language for Functional Programs*. PhD thesis, University of Pennsylvania, August 1990. 55

14. J. Hannan and D. Miller. Uses of higher-order unification for implementing program transformers. In *Fifth International Logic Programming Conference*, pages 942–959, Seattle, Washington, August 1988. MIT Press. 49, 52

15. J. Hannan and F. Pfenning. Compiler verification in LF. In *Seventh Annual IEEE Symposium on Logic in Computer Science*, Santa Cruz, California, June 1992. IEEE Computer Society Press. 49

16. M. Harrison and I. Havel. On the parsing of deterministic languages. *Journal of the ACM*, 21(4):525–548, 1974. 51

17. J. Hodas and D. Miller. Logic programming in a fragment of intuitionistic linear logic. *Information and Computation*, 110(2):327–365, 1994. 59

18. Gérard Huet. A unification algorithm for typed λ-calculus. *Theoretical Computer Science*, 1:27–57, 1975. 48

19. S. Le Huitouze, P. Louvet, and O. Ridoux. Logic grammars and λProlog. In David S. Warren, editor, *Proceedings of the Tenth International Conference on Logic Programming*, pages 64–79. MIT Press, 1993. 50

20. D. E. Knuth. On the translation of languages from left to right. *Information and Control*, 8(6):607–639, 1965. 51

21. D. Kranz, R. Kelsey, J. Rees, P. Hudak, J. Philbin, and N. Adams. ORBIT: An optimizing compiler for Scheme. In *SIGPLAN 1986 Symposium on Compiler Construction, SIGPLAN Notices 21*, number 7, pages 219–233, 1986. 55

22. C. Liang. Let-polymorphism and eager type schemes. In *TAPSOFT '97: Theory and Practice of Software Development*, pages 490–501. Springer Verlag LNCS Vol. 1214, 1997. 55

23. C. Liang. A deterministic shift-reduce parser generator for a logic programming language. In *Computational Logic - CL 2000*, Springer-Verlag LNAI no. 1861, pages 1315–1329, July 2000. 50

24. C. Liang and G. Nadathur. Trade-offs in the intensional representation of lambda terms. Submitted for publication. 60

25. D. Miller. A logic programming language with λ-abstraction, function variables, and simple unification. *Journal of Logic and Computation*, 1(4):497–536, 1991. 48, 49, 60

26. D. Miller. Unification of simply typed lambda-terms as logic programming. In *8th International Logic Programming Conference*, pages 255–269. MIT Press, 1991. 51

27. D. Miller. Abstract syntax for variable binders: An overview. In *Computational Logic - CL 2000*, Springer-Verlag LNAI no. 1861, pages 239–253, July 2000. 47, 49

28. D. Miller, G. Nadathur, F. Pfenning, and A. Scedrov. Uniform proofs as a foundation for logic programming. *Annals of Pure and Applied Logic*, 51:125–157, 1991. 49

29. G. Nadathur. An explicit substitution notation in a λProlog implementation. Technical Report TR-98-01, Department of Computer Science, University of Chicago, January 1998. Also appears in the Proceedings of the First International Workshop on Explicit Substitutions, Tsukuba, Japan, March 1998. 60

30. G. Nadathur. A fine-grained notation for lambda terms and its use in intensional operations. *Journal of Functional and Logic Programming*, 1999(2), March 1999. 50, 59, 60

31. G. Nadathur and D. Miller. An Overview of λProlog. In *Fifth International Logic Programming Conference*, pages 810–827. MIT Press, August 1988. 48, 49

32. G. Nadathur and D. Miller. Higher-order logic programming. In D. Gabbay, C. Hogger, and A. Robinson, editors, *Handbook of Logic in Artificial Intelligence and Logic Programming*, volume 5, pages 499–590. Oxford University Press, 1998. 49, 52

33. G. Nadathur and D. Mitchell. System description: Teyjus—a compiler and abstract machine based implementation of λProlog. In *Automated Deduction–CADE-13*, Springer-Verlag LNAI no. 1632, pages 287–291, July 1999. 50

34. R. Paul. *Sparc architecture, assembly language programming, and C*. Prentice Hall, second edition, 2000. 58

35. F. Pereira and D. Warren. Definite clause grammars for language analysis. *Artificial Intelligence*, 13:231–278, 1980. 50

36. F. Pereira and D. Warren. Parsing as deduction. In *21st Annual Meeting of the Association for Computational Linguistics*, pages 137–144, 1983. 51

37. F. Pfenning. Logic programming in the LF logical framework. In G. Huet and G. D. Plotkin, editors, *Logical Frameworks*. Cambridge University Press, 1991. 49

38. F. Pfenning and C. Elliot. Higher-order abstract syntax. In *ACM-SIGPLAN Conference on Programming Language Design and Implementation*, pages 199–208. ACM Press, 1988. 47

39. A. Sabry and M. Felleisen. Reasoning about programs in continuation-passing style. *Lisp and Symbolic Computation*, 6(3/4):289–360, 1993. 55

40. M. Wand. Correctness of procedure representations in higher-order assembly language. In *Proceedings: Mathematical Foundations of Programming Semantics '91*, pages 294–311. Springer-Verlag LNCS vol. 598, 1992. 55

Declarative Programming and Clinical Medicine
On the Use of Gisela in the MedView Project

Olof Torgersson

Department of Computing Science, Chalmers University of Technology
and Göteborg University, S-412 96 Göteborg, Sweden
`oloft@cs.chalmers.se`

Abstract. In 1995, the MedView project, based on a co-operation between computing science and clinical medicine was initiated. The overall
aim of the project is to develop models, methods, and tools to support
clinicians in their diagnostic work. Today, the system is in daily use at
several clinics and the knowledge base created contains more than 2000
examination records from the involved clinics. Knowledge representation
and reasoning within MedView uses a declarative model based on a theory of definitions. In order to be able to model knowledge declaratively
and integrate reasoning into applications with GUIs a framework for definitional programming has been developed. We give an overview of the
project and of how declarative programming techniques are integrated
with industrial strength object-oriented programming tools to facilitate
the development of real-world applications.

Keywords: Definitional programming, Clinical Medicine, Integration
with GUIs and Objective-C

1 Introduction

Diagnostic work and clinical decision-making are central items in every field of
medical practice, where clinical experience, knowledge and judgement are the
cornerstones of health care management. In order to achieve increased competence, the clinician is confronted with complex information that needs to be
analysed. Accordingly, the clinician needs tools to improve analysis and visualization of data in the diagnostic and learning processes.

The traditional paper record used in medicine does not store information in
a manner that makes it easy to learn from the huge amounts of information
collected over time. Not only does it require that someone manually reads and
organizes the stored information, but even if the records are read the information
stored within them is not sufficiently organized and formalized to form a basis for
a general analysis. Unfortunately most computerized systems developed today
to replace the paper record share the same problem. Systems are designed for
storage and transportation of data, and to simplify administrative tasks.

To remedy these problems systems must be designed which are from the beginning focused on knowledge representation and reasoning, areas where declarative programming tools typically are a natural choice.

S. Krishnamurthi, C. R. Ramakrishnan (Eds.): PADL 2002, LNCS 2257, pp. 64–82, 2002.

In 1995, the Medview project [1], based on a co-operation between computing science and oral medicine, was initiated. The overall goal of the project is to develop models, methods, and tools to support clinicians in their diagnostic work. The project is centered around the question: how can computing technology be used to handle clinical information in everyday work such that clinicians more systematically can learn from their gathered clinical data? That is, how can the chain "formalize-collect-view-analyse-learn" be understood and implemented in the area of clinical medicine.

The basis for formalizing clinical knowledge within MedView is a uniform definitional model suitable for automated reasoning in a computerized system. At the same time, the model is simple enough to have an obvious intuitive reading to the involved clinicians needing no further explanation. To implement the declarative formalized model of clinical knowledge suitable programming tools are needed. Since interacting with users is another very important part of a system for use in a clinical setting we also need programming tools suitable for building graphical user interfaces. The solution taken in the MedView project is to use declarative programming techniques and state-of-the-art object-oriented programming tools in concert using each for the task it performs best. To ensure a smooth integration a framework for definitional programming has been developed that can be seamlessly integrated into applications of various kinds.

The rest of this paper is organized as follows. In Sect. 2 we give some background on definitional programming and the MedView project. Section 3 provides an overview of Gisela, a new framework for definitional programming. In Sect. 4 we describe how Gisela is used in the MedView project. Finally, Sect. 5 gives some notes on related work and possible future directions.

2   Background

2.1   Definitional Programming

Declarative programming comes in many flavors. Common to most declarative paradigms is the concept of a definition. Function definitions are given, predicates are defined etc. However, focus is on what we define, on the functions and predicates respectively. *Definitional programming* is an approach to declarative programming where the definition is the basic notion, that is, focus is on the definitions themselves, not on what we define.

The definitional programming language GCLA[1][3,2,12] was developed as a tool suitable for the design and implementation of knowledge-based systems. In GCLA, programs are regarded as instances of a specific class of definitions, the *partial inductive definitions* (PID) [9]. The definitions of GCLA consist of a number of definitional clauses

$$a = A. \ ,$$

---

[1] To be pronounced Gisela.

where an *atom a* is defined in terms of a *condition A*. The most important operation on definitions is the *definiens* operation, $D(a)$, which gives all the conditions defining the atom a in the definition D.

In GCLA, control information is completely separated from domain information. This is achieved by using two kinds of definitions when constructing programs: The (object) *definition* and the *rule definition*. The intention is that the definition by itself gives a purely declarative description of the problem domain, while the rule definition contains the procedural knowledge needed to perform computations.

From a programming point of view, GCLA is basically a logic programming language, sharing syntax, logical variables, depth-first-search and backtracking with Prolog. The explicit representation of control makes definitional programming a more low-level approach, compared to other declarative programming paradigms, and for most programs, the programmer must be aware of control issues.

Definitional programming in the form of GCLA has been used in a number of applications including construction planning, diagnosis of telecommunication equipment, and music theory. It has also been used to implement a definitional approach to the combination of functional and logic programming [14].

2.2   The MedView Project

Essentially, the MedView project can be divided into two sub-problems: knowledge representation and reasoning, and development of applications for gathering and exploring clinical data. A first strategic decision was to not try to build yet another electronic medical record system, but to focus on knowledge gathering and analysis based on a formal description of the concept "examination". Another to build applied software, for use in the clinical setting, in parallel with the development of theory and implementation of tools for knowledge representation and reasoning. This led to the following things to be done, approximately in the given order:

1. Provide a formal framework and methodology to be used.
2. Formalize the knowledge to be gathered based on this methodology in a close cooperation between odontologists and computer scientists.
3. Develop tools for entering the information gathered at an examination into the knowledge base directly in the examination room.
4. Develop tools for viewing the contents of the knowledge base, both for use in the examination room and later for retrospective studies.
5. Develop tools for analyzing and exploring the knowledge base and for adding concepts built on top of the basic formal method.

Knowledge Representation. In MedView clinical data is seen as definitions of clinical terms. Abstract clinical concepts, like diagnosis, examination, and patient are all given by definitions of collections of specific clinical terms. Knowledge acquisition is modeled as acts of defining a series of descriptive parameters, e.g., anamnesis (disease history), status and diagnosis, in terms of observed

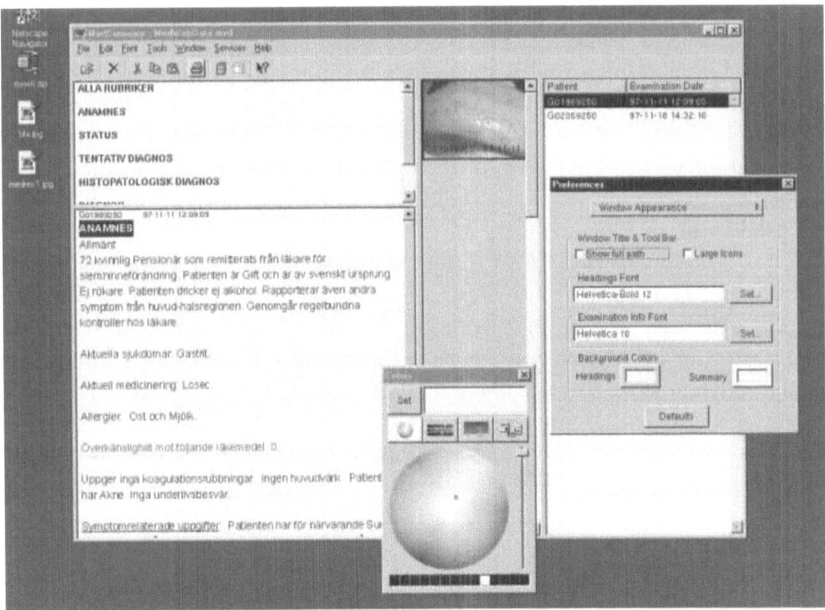

Fig. 1. MedSummary: main and preferences windows. Different texts may be generated by selecting from the headings at the top left. Clicking on a minimized image will show it full-sized in a separate window

values. The basic data thus gathered is collected in the form of definitions which are stored into a large knowledge base. The knowledge base also contains additional definitions describing general medical knowledge.

Status. Today, the system has been in use for a couple of years at several clinics and data from more than 2000 examinations has been collected during patient visits. Apart from applications for use in the clinical setting a number of tools for exploring the database using information visualization techniques have been developed. The most used applications are

- MedRecords, which is used by clinicians to enter detailed formalized examination data during patient visits.
- MedSummary (Fig. 1), which is used to automatically generate textual and pictorial summaries of examination data using natural language generation.
- SimVis and The Cube [8], which are two analysis tools developed to enhance the clinician's ability to intelligibly analyze existing patient material and to allow for pattern recognition and statistical analysis.

Work on a definitional framework for case based reasoning is under way [7].

3   Gisela – A Framework for Definitional Programming

While GCLA is a nice realization of definitional programming it has several drawbacks which became significant when new programming techniques [6] were developed and attempts were made to use GCLA for knowledge representation and reasoning in the MedView project. Most notable were efficiency problems with certain classes of definitions and the problem of interacting well with the tools used to build GUIs.

It was therefore decided that a new definitional programming system should be developed. When we analyzed our needs we realized that what we wanted was not yet another declarative programming language based on a definitional model. Rather, we wanted to create a general framework for definitional programming which would allow us to implement definitional knowledge structures in a flexible way. Equally important was that the framework should allow us to easily build state-of-the-art desktop and web applications with embedded definitional reasoning components.

3.1   Key Properties

The analysis mentioned above led to the development of a framework with the following features important for building real applications:

- The computational model of Gisela treats definitions as abstract objects only, allowing for different kinds of implementation and behaviors.
- Gisela is designed and implemented as an object-oriented framework written in Objective-C.
- Gisela provides a complete object-oriented application programming interface (API) for building definitional components for use in applications.
- Using Gisela in various contexts, e.g,. in desktop or web applications, entails nothing more than allocating some objects, no particular interfacing techniques are needed.
- To allow for "traditional declarative programming" a second API using equational representations is provided.
- Since the computational model is given at a rather abstract level it allows for modification by subclassing the classes defined in the framework allowing for new kinds of definitions and computation methods.

Furthermore, the framework:

- Makes use of the notion of an *observer*, which sets up hooks for interactive computations.
- Gives a description of definitional programming that breaks the links to Prolog present in GCLA.
- Keeps the distinction between declarative and procedural parts of programs used in GCLA, thus separating declarative descriptions and control information.

- Allows any number of distinct definitions in programs. The GCLA system used two: the declarative (object) definition and the procedural (rule) definition.
- Allows for new definitional programming ideas while keeping many techniques developed for GCLA.

Gisela can to some extent be seen as a heir to GCLA. However, the computational model is rather different and the implementation as an extensible object-oriented framework has very little in common with the Prolog-based GCLA system.

3.2   Integration with Objective-C

Gisela was from the start designed to make it simple to build programs directly as objects, from components and classes in the framework instead of using traditional syntactic representations. Indeed, all that is required to use the Gisela framework in an Objective-C program is to create a new instance of the class DFDMachine, some data and method definition objects and start computing.

The general idea behind the Objective-C interface to Gisela is that each kind of entity used to build programs, variables, terms, conditions, definitions, etc., is represented by objects of a corresponding class. Thus, a constant is represented by an object of the class DFConstant, an equation by an object of the class DFEquation and so on. It follows that if we have a conceptually clear definitional model of a system it can be realized directly using object representations.

For example, the equation, a = b. is created by the following code segment:

```
DFConstant *a = [DFConstant constantWithName:@"a"];
DFConstant *b = [DFConstant constantWithName:@"b"];

DFEquation *eq = [DFEquation equationWithLeft:a andRight:b];
```

The basic API for using a DFDMachine performing actual computations is very simple consisting of the methods:

```
// Create a machine that uses the default observer.
- (id)initWithDelegate:(id)anObject;

// Set the query to evaluate.
- (void)setQuery:(DFQuery *)aQuery;

// Returns the next answer if there is one or nil otherwise.
- (DFAnswer *)nextAnswer;

// Returns an  array with all the possible answers.
- (NSArray *)findAllAnswers;
```

The framework provides a number of different definition classes for various purposes. In case these are not sufficient they can be subclassed or simply replaced by custom classes.

3.3 Computing Basics

Giving a full account of Gisela is beyond the scope of this paper. Here we present some basics and a few small examples. For a complete description see [15].

Definitions. A definition D is given by

1. two sets: the *domain* of D, written $dom(D)$, and the *co-domain* of D, written $com(D)$, where $dom(D) \subseteq com(D)$,
2. and a *definiens* operation: $D : com(D) \rightarrow \mathcal{P}(com(D))$.

Objects in $dom(D)$ are referred to as *atoms* and objects in $com(D)$ are referred to as *conditions*.

A natural presentation of a definition is that of a (possibly infinite) system of equations

$$D \begin{cases} a_0 = A_0 \\ a_1 = A_1 \\ \quad \vdots \\ a_n = A_n \\ \quad \vdots \end{cases} n \geq 0,$$

where atoms, $a_0, \ldots, a_n, \ldots \in dom(D)$, are defined in terms of a number of conditions, $A_0, \ldots, A_n, \ldots \in com(D)$, i.e., all pairs (a_i, A_i) such that $A_i \in D(a_i)$, and $a_i \in dom(D)$. Note that an equation $a = A$ is just a notation for A being a member of $D(a)$. Expressed differently, the left-hand sides in an equational presentation of a definition D are the atoms for which $D(a_i)$ is not empty.

Given a definition D the presentation as a system of equations is unique modulo the order of equations. However, given an equational presentation of a definition it is not generally possible to determine which definition the equations represent.

Intuitively, the definiens operation gives further information about its argument. For an atom a, $D(a)$ gives the conditions defining a, that is, $D(a) = \{A \mid (a = A) \in D\}$. For a condition $A \in com(D) \setminus dom(D)$, $D(A)$ gives the constituents of the condition.

Computations. Programs in Gisela consist of an arbitrary number of *data definitions* and *method definitions*. The data definitions describe the declarative content of the program, and the method definitions give the algorithms, or search strategies, used to compute solutions.

Method Definitions. All method definitions presented in this paper will be of the form

$$\text{method } m(D_1, \ldots, D_n). \; n \geq 0$$

$$m = C_1 \# G_1$$

$$\vdots$$

$$m = C_k \# G_k$$

where m is the name of the method definition, $D_1, \ldots, D_n$, are parameters representing the actual data definitions used in computations, each C_i is a computation condition describing a number of operations to perform, and the G_is are guards restricting the applicability of equations in the method definition.

Queries. A computation is a transformation of an initial *state* definition into a final *result* definition. To compute a query, a method definition is applied to an initial state definition. We will write the initial definition as a sequence of equations. The general form of a query is

$$m(D_1, \ldots, D_n)\{e_1, \ldots, e_n\}.$$

where m is a method definition, $D_1, \ldots, D_n$ are the actual data definitions used in the computation, and each e_i is an equation.

If the computation method applied cannot be used to transform the initial state definition into an acceptable result definition the computation fails. If the computation succeeds we take the result definition and any bindings of variables in the initial state definition as the answer to the query. Note that the computation method m provides the particular data definitions describing declarative knowledge to use in the computation. Depending on the context the result of a computation can be interpreted in different ways.

Sample Programs. Programs in Gisela can be built directly from objects programmed in Objective-C based on classes in the framework or using a traditional declarative programming style. We show some simple examples using the later approach to give a flavor of the system.

Example 1. A Toy Expert System. Consider the following toy expert system adopted from [2]. The knowledge base of the system is the data definition:

```
definition diseases.

symptom(high_temp) = disease(pneumonia).
symptom(high_temp) = disease(plague).
symptom(cough) = disease(pneumonia).
symptom(cough) = disease(cold).
```

The data definition, named diseases, contains the connections between symptoms and diseases, but no facts. To ask the system what a possible disease might be, based on observed facts, e.g. symptoms, we form a query using a method definition and an initial state definition. For instance, assume that the patient has the symptom high_temp, from which diseases does this follow?

```
lra(diseases){disease(X) = symptom(high_temp)}.
```

The meaning of the query is "use the method definition lra instantiated with the domain knowledge in the data definition diseases to compute a result definition from the initial state definition {disease(X) = symptom(high_temp)}".

```
G3> lra(diseases){disease(X) = symptom(high_temp)}.
X = pneumonia
? ;
X = plague
```

The answer tells us that `high_temp` could be caused by `pneumonia` or `plague`. Since the result definition is of no particular interest the system has been asked to display only the computed answer substitution.

The method definition `lra` is defined as follows:

```
method lra(D).
    lra = [lra, l:D] # some l:in_dom(D).
    lra = [lra, r:D] # some r:in_dom(D) & all not(l:in_dom(D)).
    lra = [D] # all not(l:in_dom(D); r:in_dom(D)).
```

The first line states that `lra` is a method definition that takes one parameter, a data definition D. The remaining lines are three equations that describe the behavior implemented by `lra`.

The method `lra` attempts to replace left and right-hand sides of equations in the current state definition using the data definition D. If this is not possible, the third equation of `lra` will try to unify the left and right-hand side of some equation in the state definition. If no equation of `lra` can be applied, the answer to the query is `no`.

Example 2. Default Reasoning. Assume we know that an object can fly if it is a bird and if it is not a penguin. We also know that Tweety and Polly are birds as are all penguins, and finally we know that Pengo is a penguin. A data definition expressing this information is the following:

```
definition birds:gcla.

flies(X) =
    bird(X),
    (penguin(X) -> false).

bird(tweety).
bird(polly).
bird(X) = penguin(X).

penguin(pengo).
```

If we want to know which birds can fly, we pose the query

```
G3> gcla(birds){true = flies(X)}.
```

which gives the expected answers. More interesting is that we can also infer negative information, i.e., which birds cannot fly:

```
G3> gcla(birds){flies(X) = false}.
X = pengo
```

The method definition `gcla` is an attempt to emulate general GCLA behavior. More details about how the kind of negation used works can be found in [2].

Example 3. Hamming Distance. The examples above were adopted from GCLA programs. Since GCLA is essentially an extension to logic programming, the interesting part of the answer is the computed answer substitution for variables in the initial state definition. One of the objectives of Gisela is to allow for other ways of computing with definitions, where the computed result definition is the interesting part of the answer. Studying properties of definitions, such as similarity, is an example of this.

Hamming distance is a notion generally used to measure difference with respect to information content. The Hamming distance between two code-words, for example 1101 and 0110, is the number of positions where the words differ. In this example we let each code-word be represented by a data definition. Thus, the word 1101 and the word 0110 are represented by:

definition w1.   definition w2.

w(0) = 1.   w(0) = 0.
w(1) = 1.   w(1) = 1
w(2) = 0.   w(2) = 1.
w(3) = 1.   w(3) = 0.

To compute the Hamming distance between w1 and w2 we ask the query

G3> lr(w1,w2){w(0)=w(0), w(1)=w(1), w(2)=w(2), w(3)=w(3)}

which computes the result definition {1=0, 1=1, 0=1, 1=0}. What we have computed is, so to speak, how *similar* w1 and w2 are. From this similarity measure, it is easy to see that the Hamming distance is 3.

The method `lr` expands the initial state definition as far as possible by replacing atoms according to the actual data definitions used. When a state where no equation can be changed is reached the computation stops.

4   MedView and Gisela

4.1   Application Architecture

The general design approach used in applications is to use the Model-View-Controller (MVC) paradigm. MVC is a commonly used object-oriented software development methodology. When MVC is used, the *model*, that is, data and operations on data, is kept strictly separated from the *view* displayed to the user. The *controller* connects the two together and decides how to handle user actions and how data obtained from the model should be presented in the view.

Applied to the MedView and Gisela setting, the model of what an application should do is implemented using definitional programming in Gisela. The view displayed to the user can be of different kinds, desktop applications, web

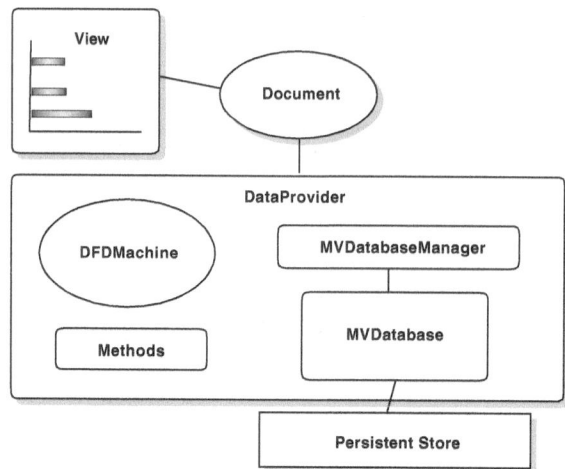

Fig. 2. An example data model

applications etc. In between the view presented to the user and the Gisela machinery there is a controller object which manages communication between the two parts.

One advantage of this approach is, of course, that different views may be used without changing the model. The general architecture is illustrated in Fig. 2. At the center is a `Document` (controller) object, which manages an on-screen window displaying graphs and all resources needed to perform computations. All definitional computations are embedded into a model consisting of an object of the `DataProvider` class. An object of this class creates a `DFDMachine` to perform computations and feeds it with data from an `MVDatabase`. The `MVDatabase` in turn is provided by an `MVDatabaseManager`, which is responsible for things like loading databases and sharing them among objects. Gisela also provides API to load definition objects at run time from text-files. Consequently, any Gisela program developed using equational presentations can smoothly be integrated into an Objective-C application.

4.2   Knowledge Base Structure

The MedView knowledge base consists of a large number of definitions stored in a format that can be read by the Gisela framework. The general structure of the knowledge base is pictured in Fig. 3. It consists of the following:

- A collection of examination records, where each examination is represented by a data definition.
- Additional data definitions describing different kinds of general knowledge.
- Procedural knowledge represented by definitions in terms of method definitions.

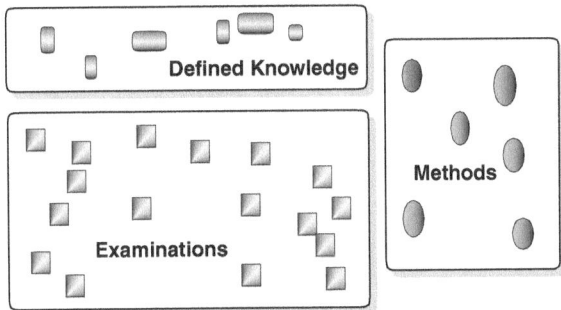

Fig. 3. Schematic view of the MedView knowledge base. The knowledge base consists of a collection of examination records on top of which extra knowledge may be added. To perform computations, methods, shown to the right, are needed

Note the distinction between declarative and procedural knowledge. In addition, the knowledge base contains a large number of digitized images taken at examinations. Each image is associated with a particular examination and can be retrieved by searching the collection of examination records.

Representing Basic Data Assembling information at examinations is modeled as defining a series of descriptive parameters, such as disease history (anamnesis), status, diagnosis, and so on. All examination definitions share a common structure, which so to speak defines the basic concept "examination". A small part of this structure is:

$$
E \begin{cases}
examination = anamnesis \\
examination = status \\
anamnesis = common \\
status = direct \\
common = drug \\
common = smoke \\
direct = mucos \\
direct = palpation \\
mucos = mucos\_site \\
mucos = mucos\_col \\
palpation = palp\_site
\end{cases} \tag{1}
$$

As can be seen from the example, the general structure is hierarchical. An examination consists of *anamnesis*, *status*, etc. Each of these in turn consist of a number of parts, which consist of a number of parts, and so on until we reach the actual *attributes* for which values are collected at an examination. The attributes in (1) are, *drug*, *smoke*, *mucos_site*, *mucos_col*, and *palp_site*. It is important to note that not all attributes must be given values. A missing value simply indicates that we know nothing about it. The structure may be changed as long as it is *extended*, since then old records will remain valid, it is simply that they may have a larger number of attributes without values.

It is natural to view an examination record as being the sum of two definitions. One definition, E, describing the concept examination, and one definition, R, providing data collected at a particular patient visit. Thus, a complete examination is given by $E + R$.

For instance, a set of equations that together with (1) define a particular examination could be

$$R \begin{cases} drug = losec \\ drug = dermovat \\ smoke = no \\ mucos\_site = l122 \\ mucos\_col = white \end{cases}$$

4.3   Additional Knowledge Structures.

On top of the basic collection of examination records additional definitions may be created to represent different kinds of knowledge. We show two examples.

Value Classes. As the number of examinations in the knowledge base grows, it becomes increasingly important to group related values into classes in a hierarchical manner. For example, diseases such as Herpes labialis, Herpetic gingivostomatis, Shingles etc., can be classified into viral diseases. Such classifications facilitate the detection of interesting patterns in the data. Value classes are given as definitions and can be stored in the knowledge base for future use. Examples of existing simple value classes are a division between smokers and non-smokers and between patients with oral lichen planus and patients that do not have oral lichen planus.

A Gisela definition that classifies smoking habits into three groups is:

```
definition smoke_3:constant.
```

```
'1 cigaretter utan filter/dag' = '< 10 cigarettes/day'.
'4 cigaretter utan filter/dag' = '< 10 cigarettes/day'.
'10 filtercigaretter/dag' = '> 10 cigarettes/day'.
'10-15 filtercigaretter/dag' = '> 10 cigarettes/day'.
'40 filtercigaretter/dag' = '> 10 cigarettes/day'.
'Nej' = 'non smoking'.
```

Of course, as the knowledge base grows so will the number of equations in the definition `smoke_3`. To further categorize smoking habits into smokers and non-smokers another definition can be used:

```
definition smoke_2:constant.
```

```
'< 10 cigarettes/day' = smoking.
'> 10 cigarettes/day' = smoking.
```

Note that in the definition `smoke_2` it is assumed that smoking habits have already been grouped using `smoke_3`. A complete value class definition is derived by adding together `smoke_2` and `smoke_3`, that is, conceptually $smoke = smoke\_2 + smoke\_3$.

To examine the use of value classes consider the query

$$m(D_1, \ldots, D_n)\{V = A\}$$

where m is a computation method using the definitions $D_1, \ldots, D_n$, V is the value we are looking for and A some kind of attribute. We will say that a record fulfills the demands of the query if the single equation in the initial state definition can be reduced to identity. For instance a query could be

```
srfi(e1297,smoke_3){'<10 cigarettes/day' = 'Smoke'}.
```

which succeeds if the examination represented by definition `e1297` has a value for the attribute `'Smoke'` indicating that the patient smokes less than 10 cigarettes a day.

A possible method definition encoding the necessary procedural knowledge is:

```
method srfi(Exam,Filter).
    srfi = [] # some identity.
    srfi = [srfi, r:Exam] # some r:in_dom(Exam) &
                            all not(identity).
    srfi = [srfi, r:Filter] # some r:in_dom(Filter) &
                             all not(identity) &
                             all not(r:in_dom(Exam)).
```

The meaning of the equations in `srfi` is: (i) if there is an equation with identical left- and right-hand sides in the current state definition, the computation is finished, (ii) if some attribute can be reduced using `Exam`, reduce it and continue, and (iii) if a value can be grouped using `Filter`, do that and continue.

Computationally, in the query above, `'Smoke'` is first replaced with the value in the definition `e1297`, and then this value is replaced by the appropriate group as given by the definition `smoke_3`.

If we add the definitions `smoke_3` and `smoke` together (an operation supported by the Gisela framework) we could ask the query

```
srfi(e1297,smoke_3+smoke_2){smoking = 'Smoke'}.
```

to check whether a person smokes or not.

Value Corrections. In the MedView project new values for attributes may be freely added by any user. This is necessary since we cannot anticipate all possible values. Also, it is not possible to wait for approval when a new value is encountered, since data is entered during examinations. There are of course at least two major problems with this practice: (i) letting all users add new values might lead to confusion and a less harmonized terminology within the network of users involved, (ii) misspelled words may be introduced into the lists of valid values.

One solution is to monitor the values in the knowledge base regularly and add extra definitions that can be used to find replacements for incorrect values. These definitions can then be used by applications to ensure that a harmonized terminology is used. It is natural to use one definition with corrections for each attribute in the general examination structure that has incorrect values. Which values are correct and which are not is decided by the network of clinicians working with MedView. Solving the problem by making changes in the examination definitions directly is not a viable solution for several reasons, one being the general rule stating that medical record information may not be changed.

As an example, when the values used for the attribute 'Chld-dis' (Child Disease) were inspected, it was found that both "Mässlingen" and "Mässling" were used to denote the same disease (Measles). It was also found that in a number of examinations the disease "Röda Hund" (Rubella) was misspelled "Ruda Hund".

A Gisela definition that describes how to correct values for the attribute 'Chld-dis' is the following:

```
definition 'Chld-dis'.

'Mässling' = 'Mässlingen'.
'Ruda hund' = 'Röda Hund'.
```

It was decided that "Mässlingen" was preferred over "Mässling". Therefore, the value 'Mässling' is defined to be equal to the correct value 'Mässlingen'. Note that only values that are regarded as incorrect are defined in this definition. For simplicity, the name of the definition is the same as the name of the attribute it gives corrections for. From a computational point of view value corrections are essentially identical to value classes.

5   Discussion

The value of Gisela and its use in the MedView project depends on two key issues: (i) To what extent the use of a uniform declarative model facilitates the development of a system such as MedView, and (ii) How well the Gisela system is suited for the task at hand. These issues are discussed briefly here.

5.1   Definitions and MedView

The choice to use definitions as the model underlying knowledge representation and reasoning within MedView was taken in a very early phase of the project based on the expertise of the computer scientists involved. However, the model has proven easy for clinical users to understand and modify. Today, development and maintenance of the general structure of examinations, value lists, value and

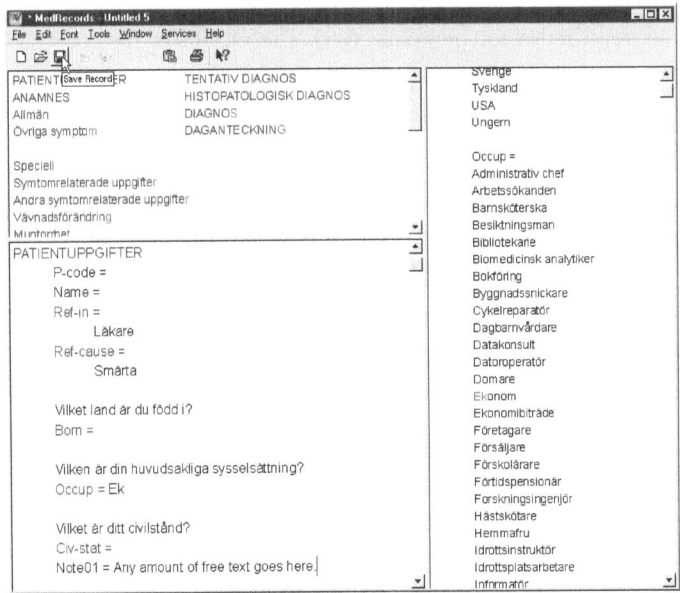

Fig. 4. MedRecords. At the top left is a navigation area which is used to navigate into the appropriate part of the input view (incomplete definition) at the bottom. To the right is a list of values linked to the attributes in the input view

correction definitions etc. is managed by the involved clinicians themselves. An example of this is the MedRecords application shown in Fig.4 used to enter data at examinations. The idea behind this application is to display an incomplete definition (examination record) and provide means to facilitate completing it. The contents of the three views is developed by the users themselves. It is also worth noting that although MedRecords does not make use of Gisela it is definitely colored by the declarative model used.

Clinicians using MedView typically report increased competence resulting from the stringent procedures set-up by using a formalized nomenclature and standardized examination protocols. Furthermore, clinicians rarely have to dictate medical record texts since these can be generated from examination records.

5.2   The Gisela Framework

A major advantage of using declarative programming is that the close gap between the knowledge model and programming model greatly simplifies implementing the reasoning part of the system. While a large number of examinations have been collected in MedView, the work on additional knowledge structures is still in an early phase. In part, this depends on that, prior to the development of the Gisela framework, each kind of new definitional computation to be performed required the development of new specialized procedures for computing with definitions. Accordingly, trying out new ideas in practice was a cumbersome process that required a lot of work. With the Gisela framework different kinds of definitions and computation methods can be expressed easily, something we hope will speed-up the process of trying out new ideas on how to explore the MedView knowledge base.

As the database is approaching a size where it might be meaningful to apply data mining techniques to search for patterns it will become increasingly important to have a tool that is tailored for definitional computing. It will also make it easier to implement, for instance, an intelligent agent in MedRecords helping the user during patient visits.

Of course, most declarative languages have foreign language interfaces. However, there are two things that set Gisela apart most of these: (i) Gisela does not attempt to be a general-purpose programming language, rather it is a system for realizing a certain set of definitional models, (ii) Gisela is a framework with a rather loose definition, specifically aimed at allowing experiments and modifications within the general model set up by the computation model. The aim of declarative systems such as Prolog, Haskell, Mercury [13], and Curry [11], is to provide full-fledged programming languages suitable as alternatives to the commonly used imperative and object-oriented ones. Being general-purpose languages, they also provide libraries to build GUIs [4,10]. An alternative path is taken in [5] which implements Prolog in Java in a manner enabling a tight integration between the two languages.

So far, our experiences from using Gisela are positive: It provides seamless integration with state-of-the-art tools for building desktop and web applications, handles the current database without any problems, and can easily be modified or extended when functionality not present in the framework is needed. If desired the framework can also be used to use declarative programming at different levels. For instance, it is possible to use only data definitions describing a domain and implement the procedural behavior without using Gisela.

5.3 Conclusion

We have described how the declarative programming tool Gisela is used for knowledge representation within the MedView project. The approach taken has been to build a declarative programming tool which can be integrated with ease into a modern object-oriented programming environment. Currently, we have no plans to extend Gisela to handle sophisticated interaction with the user. Instead, we advocate an approach with a definitional model programmed in Gisela and an interface part programmed using other, more suitable, tools. In our experience this is the most practical approach, at least for the time being.

So far, more than 2000 examinations and some 2500 images have been collected into the knowledge base, which in the area of oral medicine is a significant contribution. For the future, both Gisela and MedView are being ported to Java and we are looking into different ways to model and use the knowledge base accumulated during the years.

References

1. Y. Ali, G. Falkman, L. Hallnäs, M. Jontell, N. Nazari, and O. Torgersson. Medview: Design and adoption of an interactive system for oral medicine. In A. Hasman, B. Blobel, J. Dudeck, R. Engelbrecht, G. Gell, and H.-U. Prokosch, editors, *Medical Infobahn for Europe: Proceedings of MIE2000 and GMDS2000*. IOS Press, 2000.

2. M. Aronsson. Methodology and programming techniques in GCLA II. In *Extensions of logic programming, second international workshop, ELP'91*, number 596 in Lecture Notes in Artificial Intelligence. Springer-Verlag, 1992.

3. M. Aronsson, L.-H. Eriksson, A. Gäredal, L. Hallnäs, and P. Olin. The programming language GCLA: A definitional approach to logic programming. *New Generation Computing*, 7(4):381–404, 1990.

4. M. Carlsson and T. Hallgren. Fudgets: A graphical user interface in a lazy functional language. In *FPCA '93 - Conference on Functional Programming Languages and Computer Architecture*, pages 321–330. ACM Press, 1993.

5. E. Denti, A. Omicini, and A. Ricci. tuProlog: a light-weight prolog for internet applications and infrastructures. In *Proc. of the Third International Workshop on Practical Aspects of Declarative Languages (PADL'01)*, volume 1990 of *Lecture Notes in Computer Science*, pages 184–198. Springer-Verlag, 2001.

6. G. Falkman. Program separation and definitional higher order programming. *Computer Languages*, 23(2–4):179–206, 1997.

7. G. Falkman. Similarity measures for structured representations: a definitional approach. In E. Blanzieri and L. Portinale, editors, *EWCBR-2K, Advances in Case-Based Reasoning*, Lecture Notes in Artificial Intelligence, pages 380–392. Springer-Verlag, 2000.

8. G. Falkman. Information visualization in clinical odontology: multidimensional analysis and interactive data exploration. *Artificial Intelligence in Medicine*, 22(2):133–158, 2001.

9. L. Hallnäs. Partial inductive definitions. *Theoretical Computer Science*, 87(1):115–142, 1991.

10. M. Hanus. A functional logic programming approach to graphical user interfaces. In *Proc. of the Second International Workshop on Practical Aspects of Declarative Languages (PADL'00)*, volume 1753 of *Lecture Notes in Computer Science*, pages 47–62. Springer-Verlag, 2000.

11. M. Hanus, H. Kuchen, and J. Moreno-Navarro. Curry: A truly functional logic language. In *Proc. ILPS'95 Workshop on Visions for the Future of Logic Programming*, pages 95–107, 1995.

12. P. Kreuger. GCLA II: A definitional approach to control. In *Extensions of logic programming, second international workshop, ELP91*, number 596 in Lecture Notes in Artificial Intelligence. Springer-Verlag, 1992.

13. Z. Somogyi, F. Henderson, and T. Conway. The execution algorithm of Mercury: an efficient purely declarative logic programming language. *Journal of Logic Programming*, 29(1–3):17–64, 1996.

14. O. Torgersson. A definitional approach to functional logic programming. In R. Dyckhoff, H. Herre, and P. Schroeder-Heister, editors, *Extensions of Logic Programming 5th International Workshop, ELP'96*, number 1050 in Lecture Notes in Artificial Intelligence, pages 273–287. Springer-Verlag, 1996.

15. O. Torgersson. *On GCLA, Gisela, and MedView: Studies in Declarative Programming with Application to Clinical Medicine*. PhD thesis, Department of Computing Science, Chalmers University of Technology and Göteborg University, Göteborg, Sweden, 2000.

Semantics-Based Filtering:
Logic Programming's Killer App?[*]

Gopal Gupta[1], Hai-Feng Guo[2], Arthur I. Karshmer[3], Enrico Pontelli[4],
Juan Raymundo Iglesias[4], Desh Ranjan[4], Brook Milligan[5], Nayana Datta[6],
Omar El Khatib[4], Mohammed Noamany[4], and Xinhong Zhou[7]

[1] Dept. of Computer Science,
UT Dallas, Richardson, TX, USA
gupta@utdallas.edu
[2] Dept. of Computer Science,
SUNY Stony Brook, Stony Brook, NY, USA
[3] National Science Foundation and University of S. Florida,
Tampa, FL, USA
[4] Dept. of Computer Science, New Mexico State University,
Las Cruces, NM, USA
[5] Dept. of Biology, New Mexico State University,
Las Cruces, NM, USA
[6] Synopsis, Inc., Boston, MA, USA
[7] Sabre, Inc.

Abstract. We present a logic programming based framework for rapidly
translating one formal notation $\mathcal{L}_s$ to another formal notation $\mathcal{L}_t$. The
framework is based on Horn logical semantics—a logic programming en-
coding of formal semantics. A Horn logical semantics of the language
$\mathcal{L}_s$ is constructed which employs the parse trees of the language $\mathcal{L}_t$ as
semantic domains for expressing the meaning of sentences in $\mathcal{L}_s$. This
formal semantics, coded in logic programming, immediately yields an
executable (reversible) filter. This (reversible) filter is provably correct,
as it is generated from the semantic specification. Our approach provides a formal basis for interoperability and is illustrated through five
major practical applications: Translating Nemeth Math Braille notation
to LATEX, translating HTML to VoiceXML to make web-pages accessible via an audio-browser or a phone, translating ODBC programs/data
to OQL (Object Query Language) programs/data, automatically generating validating parsers for XML, and interoperating between various
biological software systems developed for phylogenetic inference via the
NEXUS data representation language.

1 Introduction

The need to translate one formal notation to another formal notation arises very
frequently. There are primarily two types of situations where this is needed:

[*] Authors are partially supported by NSF grants CCR 99-00320, CCR 98-20852, CDA-
9729848, HRD 9800209, EIA 98-10732, EIA 9729848, INT 9904063, CCR 9875279
and grant H133G010046 from the US Dept. of Education.

S. Krishnamurthi, C. R. Ramakrishnan (Eds.): PADL 2002, LNCS 2257, pp. 82–100, 2002.

- When a user wants to *migrate* a program from one machine or system to another machine or system. For example, migrating a program written in C from Solaris Unix to Linux or migrating a program developed for Linux to Windows NT. We refer to this migration as *porting*.
- When a user wants to translate a program written in one particular notation to accomplish a particular task to another notation that accomplishes the same task. For example, translating programs written in Fortran to equivalent programs in C, or programs written for Oracle relational database to IBM DB2 relational database, or translating the internal representation of documents written in Word Perfect to that in Microsoft Word. We refer to this translation as *filtering*.

Both porting and filtering are manifestation of the same problem, in which we want to translate the solution to a problem expressed in one formal notation to another. We use the term porting to describe those situations where the changes needed in the notation are minimal (e.g., lexical tools may be enough to accomplish porting). For instance, while porting a C program from Solaris to Windows NT, code involving systems calls may have to be changed as systems calls may have different names/meanings/functions under different operating systems. Additionally, the differences in the two compilers involved may have to be taken into account. We use the term filtering, in contrast, to describe those situations where the notation in which the solution is expressed may have to be completely changed. The new notation may have entirely different syntax and its constructs may have widely differing semantics. Thus, lexical techniques are not enough, and the structure of the notation to be translated has to be inferred via parsing and semantic processing performed. Of course, a filter can be built only if it is possible to map the semantics of the source notation to (a subset of) the target notation. In this paper, we will only concern ourselves with filtering problems, though the framework developed is trivially applicable to porting problems as well.

Suppose we wish to translate a sentence S (a program, a document, etc.) written in a language $\mathcal{L}_s$ to an "equivalent" sentence of $\mathcal{L}_t$. This would first entail building a general translator from $\mathcal{L}_s$ to $\mathcal{L}_t$, and then using this translator to translate S. The translator essentially is a map from semantics of $\mathcal{L}_s$ to the semantics of $\mathcal{L}_t$. In this paper we present an approach based on logic programming and formal semantics for rapidly developing this translator. In our approach the syntax and semantics of $\mathcal{L}_s$ is compositionally specified using Horn logic. The *meaning space* used for specifying the semantics of $\mathcal{L}_s$ consists of parse trees of $\mathcal{L}_t$. This semantic specification is executable and *automatically yields a translator*. This translator can be then used to translate sentences of $\mathcal{L}_s$ to equivalent sentences of $\mathcal{L}_t$. Because the translator is automatically generated from a semantic specification, it is provably correct (w.r.t. the specification).

Traditionally, language filters have been developed using standard compiler technology [1,29]. However, compared to the traditional approach our semantics based filtering framework has a number of advantages:

- If the syntax and semantics are specified with care, then the reverse translator can also be automatically obtained (i.e., a translator for translating sentences of $\mathcal{L}_t$ to equivalent sentences of $\mathcal{L}_s$ is obtained for free). This is, of course, due to relational nature of logic programs.
- Traditionally, porting and to some extent filtering have been done manually. Manual porting and/or filtering can be quite prone to error. However, using our approach, both the forward translator as well as the reverse translator obtained are provably correct as they are automatically obtained from the declarative semantic specifications. Further confidence can be gained by proving the correctness of the semantic specification: the semantic specification consists of (compositionally specified) recursive rules whose correctness can be manually established through inductive proofs.
- Translators for more complex languages, such as those that are context sensitive, can be elegantly specified using our approach. It should be noted that formal notations designed by non-computer scientists tend to be context sensitive [27,24]. Traditional compiling technology is limited to parsing of context free, LR(k) languages [1,3] and is not designed to handle such context sensitive languages. Attempting to handle such languages using traditional compiling technology results in a very complex back-end, that is likely to contain errors, and that is hard to formally prove correct.
- A filter can be obtained in less time using our Horn logic semantics-based approach. Despite the availability of tools such as parser generators, etc., building a language filtering system is still a daunting task. Part of the difficulty comes from the fact that the semantic phase (the back-end) of this compiler is written in an imperative language. In contrast, the syntax and semantic specification in our case is declaratively specified using logic programming.

An approach based on logic programming is ideally suited for translating formal languages, as historically speaking, (natural) language translation was one of the two fields from which logic programming emerged (theorem proving being the other).

Porting and filtering have always been considered important problems in computing, especially in world of business computing, since the underlying software, operating systems, hardware, etc. change very frequently and require the user programs to be modified accordingly as well. It has acquired greater prominence with the advent of XML [8], which gives users the ability to define their own markup languages. Rapidly constructing translators or filters between one DTD/Schema (XML grammar specification) to another will become very important [23], as the number of DTDs/Schemas designed for the same task proliferates. We believe that our logic programming-based technique will prove beneficial for such situations [11,15]. The main advantage gained by using our Horn logic semantics based approach is that *reversible* filters can be built (approaches espoused by W3C for translating DTDs/Schemas, such as XSLT transformation language [10], are good only for one-way translation). Note that building bidirectional translators, in general, is difficult for complex languages; however,

XMLs are notations for tagging documents in a tree-structured manner, thus, building a bidirectional translator between two XMLs is indeed feasible due to their structural simplicity.

We believe that semantic filtering has the potential to become logic programming's killer application. The reversibility of the translation system, the speed with which it can be built and modified, its verifiable and provably correct nature are some of the reasons behind this belief. Our experience in successfully applying this technology to widely varying situations, described in this paper, serves as empirical evidence.

2   Semantics-Based Translation

2.1   Denotational Semantics

Denotational Semantics [31,18,32] is a well-established methodology for the design, description, and analysis of programming languages. In the denotational semantics approach, the semantics of a programming language/notation is specified in terms of mathematical entities, such as sets and functions. The denotational semantics of a language $\mathcal{L}$ has three components:

- *syntax specification:* maps sentences of $\mathcal{L}$ to parse trees; it is commonly specified as a grammar in the BNF format.
- *semantic algebra:* represents the mathematical objects used for expressing the meaning of a program written in the language $\mathcal{L}$; these mathematical objects typically are sets or domains (partially ordered sets, lattices, etc.) along with associated operations to manipulate the elements of the sets.
- *valuation functions:* these are functions mapping parse trees to elements of the semantic algebras.

Given the denotational semantics of a language $\mathcal{L}$, and a program $\mathcal{P}_{\mathcal{L}}$ written in $\mathcal{L}$, the denotation of $\mathcal{P}_{\mathcal{L}}$ w.r.t. the denotational semantics can be obtained by applying the top-level valuation function to the parse tree of $\mathcal{P}_{\mathcal{L}}$. The denotation of $\mathcal{P}_{\mathcal{L}}$ is an entity that is amenable to formal mathematical processing, and thus has a number of applications. For example, it can be used to prove properties of $\mathcal{P}_{\mathcal{L}}$, or it can be transformed to obtain other representations of $\mathcal{P}_{\mathcal{L}}$ (e.g., a compiled representation that can be executed more efficiently [12]). In this paper we assume that the reader is familiar with formal semantics. A detailed exposition can be found in [31,32].

2.2   Horn Logical Semantics

Traditional denotational definitions express syntax as BNF grammars, and the semantic algebras and valuation functions using λ-calculus. The Horn Logical Semantics of a language uses Horn-clause logic (or pure Prolog) to code all three components of the denotational semantics of a language [12]. This simple change in the notation for expressing denotational semantics, while resulting in loss of some declarative purity (the resulting semantics is structural rather than denotational), leads to a number of applications [12]. There are two major advantages:

1. A parser can be obtained from the syntax specification with negligible effort: the BNF specification of a language $\mathcal{L}$ can be trivially translated to a *Definite Clause Grammar* (DCG) [33,28]. This syntax specification, coded as a DCG, can be loaded in a Prolog system, and a parser automatically obtained. This parser can be used to parse programs written in $\mathcal{L}$ and obtain their parse trees. The semantic algebra and valuation functions can also be coded in Horn clause logic. As a result, both the syntax and semantic specifications are executable on any standard logic programming system. What is noteworthy is that different operational models will be obtained both for syntax checking and semantic evaluation by employing different execution strategies during logic program execution. For example, in the syntax phase, if left-to-right, Prolog style, execution is used, then recursive descent parsing is obtained. On the contrary, if a *tabling-based* [4] execution strategy is used then chart parsing is obtained. Likewise, by using different evaluation rules for evaluating the semantic functions, strict evaluation, non-strict evaluation, etc. can be obtained. Thus, interpreters and compilers (via partial evaluation of the interpreter) can also be obtained easily [12]. By using bottom-up [7] or tabled [4] evaluation, the fixpoint of a program's denotation can be computed.

2. Horn logical semantics can be used for automatic verification: the declarative nature of Horn logic can be used to verify interesting properties of programs. The Horn logical semantic of a language $\mathcal{L}_s$ can be viewed as an axiomatization of the language constructs of $\mathcal{L}_s$. The Horn logical meaning (denotation) of a program P written in language $\mathcal{L}_s$ can be thought of as an axiomatization of the logic implicit in the program P or as an axiomatization of the problem that P is supposed to solve. This axiomatization can be used in conjunction with a logic programming engine (extended with negation) or a theorem prover to perform verification [12]. Additionally, as noted earlier, the relational nature of logic programming allows for the state space of a program (i.e., all possible execution paths of the program) written in $\mathcal{L}_s$ to be explored with ease, or to compute the fixpoint of the program's denotation which can be subsequently used for verification and structured debugging. The verification aspect of Horn logical semantics becomes more prominent when Horn logic is generalized to constraints for expressing semantics of languages as it allows for verification of real-time systems & languages [13].

Since both the syntax and semantics of the specification are expressed as logic programs, they are both executable. These syntax and semantic specifications can be loaded in a logic programming system and executed, given a program written in $\mathcal{L}_s$. This provides us with an interpreter that computes the semantics of programs written in the language $\mathcal{L}_s$. If the semantic domain used is that of a memory store, a regular interpreter is obtained, if the semantic domain used is constructs of another language $\mathcal{L}_t$, a translation of the program to the language $\mathcal{L}_t$ is obtained, etc.

2.3   Semantics-Based Language Filtering

Horn logical semantics also provides a formal basis for *porting* or *language filtering*. Specification of a filter can be seen as an exercise in semantics. Essentially, the meaning or semantics of the language $\mathcal{L}_s$ can be given in terms of the constructs of the language $\mathcal{L}_t$. This meaning consists of both syntax and semantic specifications. If these syntax and semantic specifications are executable, then the specification itself acts as a translation system, providing a provably correct filter. The task of specifying the filter from $\mathcal{L}_s$ to $\mathcal{L}_t$ consists of specifying the definite clause grammar (DCG) for $\mathcal{L}_s$ and $\mathcal{L}_t$ and the appropriate valuation predicates which essentially relate (map) parse tree patterns of $\mathcal{L}_s$ to parse tree patterns of $\mathcal{L}_t$. Let $\mathcal{P}_s(S_s, T_s)$ be the top level predicate for the DCG of $\mathcal{L}_s$ that takes a sentence S_s of $\mathcal{L}_s$, parses it and produces the parse tree T_s for it. Let $\mathcal{P}_t(S_t, T_t)$ be the top level predicate for the DCG of $\mathcal{L}_t$ that takes a sentence S_t of $\mathcal{L}_t$, parses it and produces the parse tree T_t for it. Let $\mathcal{M}_{st}(T_s, T_t)$ be the top level valuation predicate that relates parse trees of $\mathcal{L}_s$ and $\mathcal{L}_t$. Then the relation

$$\texttt{translate}(S_s, S_t) \texttt{ :- } \mathcal{P}_s(S_s, T_s),\ \mathcal{M}_{st}(T_s, T_t),\ \mathcal{P}_t(S_t, T_t).$$

declaratively specifies the equivalence of the source and target sentence under the semantic mapping given. The **translate** predicate can be used for obtaining S_t given S_s and *vice versa*. Note, however, that $\mathcal{P}_s, \mathcal{P}_t$ and $\mathcal{M}_{st}$ have to be specified with care for the **translate/2** predicate to be truly reversible under Prolog.

Note that because the semantics is specified denotationally, the syntax and semantics specification of a language are guided by its BNF grammar: there is one syntax rule in the syntax specification per BNF production and one semantics rule in the semantics specification per BNF production. Occasionally, however, some auxiliary predicates may be needed while defining valuation predicates for semantics. Also, extra syntax rules may be introduced if the BNF grammar has left recursive rules which need to be eliminated in the DCG (by converting to right-recursive rules).

3   Applications

We next illustrate our framework with five large applications to which our approach has been successfully applied. Note that the application of our approach to the five cases was motivated by practical needs, where the user of our system was only interested in a one-way translation, and reversibility of the translation process was not an important factor. Thus, the source language parse trees were mapped directly to phrases of the target language (i.e., the parser $\mathcal{P}_t$ was only implicitly specified). In all 5 cases, the translator was specified in a few man months of work, to great surprise of the users whose problem we were solving.

3.1   Translating Nemeth Math Braille Code to LATEX

We first consider the problem of translating Nemeth Math Braille documents to LATEX. This project was done for the MAVIS (Mathematics Accessible to

Visually Impaired Students) group at New Mexico State University and funded by the National Science Foundation. The MAVIS group was set up by NMSU to assist blind students in their study of Mathematics and Science. The goal of the project was to make Mathematics more accessible to visually impaired students and scholars of Mathematics. Nemeth Math Braille is a notation used for encoding Mathematics much in the fashion of LaTeX. It was designed for two main reasons: (i) normal Braille permits only 64 characters (as it is six dots based) and is inadequate for encoding mathematics; and, (ii) to convey the structure of mathematical formulas to blind students. Nemeth Math Braille code was designed in 1951. The rules of grammar are specified in English and are quite complex (the specification runs about 250 pages [27]). Many of the rules are context sensitive in nature, we believe, for three reasons: (i) since the notation is designed for the blind, an attempt is made to keep them aware of the context at all times, resulting in context sensitive features; (ii) the language was designed when very little was understood about grammars and languages; our experience indicates that when non-computer scientists design language, they almost always end up including context-sensitive features in the language; and, (iii) the Nemeth Math Braille Code was primarily designed to transcribe printed mathematics into Braille in a way that the relative spatial placement of symbols is preserved; this also adds to context sensitivity and makes parsing harder (in fact, many features of Nemeth Math Braille code preclude building an LR(k) parser for it.) As a result of all these problems, automatic processing of Nemeth Math Braille code (so as to obtain an equivalent document in LaTeX) was considered an insolvable problem by researchers working on developing assistive technology for the visually impaired [26,30].

The translation to LaTeX is needed to facilitate communication between a sighted course instructor and a blind student: the sighted instructor gives a homework written in LaTeX, which is automatically translated to Nemeth Math Braille code (such a translator has already been built using traditional compiler technology by the MAVIS group, as LaTeX has an easy context free grammar); the blind student "reads" the Nemeth Math Braille coded document, and answers it in Nemeth Math Braille. However, the sighted instructor will not be able to check the answers (since most likely he/she cannot understand Nemeth Math Braille code) unless a translation of the answers to LaTeX is performed.

Nemeth Math Braille code is a complex, context sensitive language, specified informally via examples [27] (first specified in 1951, revised in 1972). An example of context sensitivity found in Nemeth Math Braille code is in the coding of superscripts and subscripts: the mathematical expression $x^a + b$ is represented by the Nemeth Math Braille code as x^a"+b (we use ASCII equivalents instead of writing Braille code for x, ^, a, ", +, and b). However, another mathematical expression y^{x^a+b} is represented by Nemeth Math Braille code as y^x^^a^+b, where ^ is superscript indicator, ^^ means second order superscript indicator, and " is the base line indicator. It is easy to see that the same subexpression $x^a + b$ is represented as x^^a^+b rather than x^a"+b because of the context environment of superscripts. Since the information about the context environment is also encoded in the Nemeth Math Braille code, this context information has to be analyzed during the parsing procedure so that the correct syntax structure will be generated. This makes the grammar of Nemeth Math Braille code very complex, making the syntax hard to specify. Note that several of the context sensitive features (including the example below), can be parsed by first writing a context free grammar that accepts a larger language, and then ruling out the illegal sentences during the semantic phase. However, in case of Nemeth Math Braille code this approach can only be followed in certain cases, as, otherwise, it results in a very complex semantic specification.

Fortunately, Definite Clause Grammars (DCG) of logic Programming can be used for encoding and obtaining a parser for context-sensitive grammars as well. DCG can recover the context information from the source language and then combine it to produce the parse tree. Thus, following our Horn logical semantics framework, we first construct a definite clause grammar for Nemeth Math Braille code, followed by the semantic mappings from Nemeth Math Braille code parse trees to LaTeX. In the semantic specification, the mapped values of some of the terms are dependent on the information in the context environment. That is, the same syntax term (parse tree pattern) will be mapped to different semantics depending on the context information it occurs in. In order to obtain the correct semantics, we have to make the context information visible to the whole or partial sentence being transformed.

We present a (considerably simplified) small fragment of the code below which handles the translation of *polynomials* (these polynomials allow other polynomials to occur as exponents). We first give the syntax of such polynomials (expressed in Nemeth Math Braille code) as a DCG that does the parsing and produces the parse tree (for simplicity we restrict the number of variable names allowed). Then we give the semantics that translates parse trees produced to the corresponding LaTeX mathematics expressions. Since the LaTeX to Nemeth Math Braille code translator already existed at that time, reversibility of the system was not a concern. Thus, the semantics of Nemeth Math Braille code was given directly as LaTeX sentences rather than as LaTeX parse trees.

```
% Definite Clause Grammars            % Semantic Specification
exp(e(X)) --> term(X).                sexp(e(X), INL, L) :-
exp(e(T, O, E)) -->                       sterm(X, INL, ONL, L1),
    term(T), op1(O), exp(E).              getlist(ONL, B1),
term(t(X)) --> vari(X).                   append(L1, B1, L).
term(t(V, H, T)) -->                  sexp(e(T, O, E), NL, L) :-
    vari(V), hats(H), term(T).            sterm(T, NL, OL, L1),
op1(op(H, +)) --> hats(H), [+].           sop(O, OL, NL1),
op1(op('"', +)) --> ['"'], [+].           Close_Braces is OL - NL1,
op1(op(+)) --> [+].                        getlist(Close_Braces, B1),
                                          sexp(E, NL1, L2),
hats([^]) --> [^].                        append(L1, B1, Lp),
hats([^|L]) --> [^], hats(L).             append(Lp, [+|L2], L).
                                      sop(op(H, +), _, Ct) :- shats(H, Ct).
vari(x) --> [x].                      sop(op('"', +), _, 0).
```

```
vari(y) --> [y].                sop(op(+), CL, CL).
vari(a) --> [a].                shats([^], 1).
vari(b) --> [b].                shats([^|L], Ct) :- shats(L, Ct1),
vari(c) --> [c].                          Ct is Ct1 + 1.
                                sterm(t(X), OL, OL, [X]).
                                sterm(t(V, H, T), Ct, OL, [V,^,'{'|R]) :-
                                    Ct1 is Ct + 1, shats(H, Ct1),
                                        sterm(T, Ct1, OL, R).
                                getlist(0, []).
                                getlist(N, ['}'|L]) :- N > 0,
                                          N1 is N - 1, getlist(N1, L).
```

The syntax and semantic specifications are executable, and thus automatically provide us with a translation system. Thus, if we load this program on a logic programming system and ask the following query:

```
?- exp(T, [x, ^, y, ^, ^, a, ^, +, b, '"', +, c], []), sexp(T, 0, L).
```

then the following answer is obtained:

```
T = e(t(x,[^],t(y,[^,^],t(a))),op([^],+),e(t(b),op('"',+),e(t(c))))
L = [x,^,{,y,^,{,a,},+,b,},+,c],
```

which corresponds to the LATEX expression $x^{\hat{}}\{y^{\hat{}}a+b\}+c$, i.e., $x^{y^a+b}+c$.

Thus, the problem of designing a language translator [17,12,22] from Nemeth Math Braille code [27] to LATEX can be easily solved in our formal framework. A translator from Nemeth Math Braille code to LATEX was not available until we built one using our approach. In fact, a complete translator has been developed by our group. It took us only a 3-4 man months of work to produce the translator and to accomplish a task that was considered impossible by researchers in assistive technology [26,30]. Our translator is being α-tested at the Texas School for the Blind and Visually Impaired and other sites. Eventually, it will be made available as an add-on to Scientific Notebook software (a WYSIWYG LATEX based word-processing system) that already has the LATEX to Nemeth Math Braille code translator built in. Our framework is currently being used, with support from the US Dept. of Education, to develop filters between the Marburg notation (a Braille based notation for encoding Mathematics used in Europe) and LATEX and the Nemeth Math notation so that blind and sighted students/scholars/researchers of Mathematics from US and Europe can communicate.

3.2   Interoperability among Bioinformatics Software Systems

Next we look at the application of our translation framework to solving a practical problem in computational biology. The project was done for the National Biotechnology Information Facility (nbif.org), a University-Industry-Government consortium for promoting research in computational biology. The specific problem presented to us was to make various software tools developed for bioinformatics work smoothly with each other. In the bioinformatics field, several

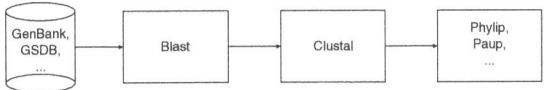

Fig. 1. Ideal pipeline process to analyze a molecular sequence

software tools have been created for very specific tasks in order to make genetic information publicly available and to analyze it. A common bioinformatics analysis usually consists of the following steps:

1. BLAST (Basic Local Alignment Search Tool) [2] is used to query a public database of genetic information like GenBank and GSDB. The result of this process is a molecular sequence.
2. A program like CLUSTAL W [20] is used to align the molecular sequences.
3. The molecular sequences is analyzed to infer phylogenetic information using programs such as PAUP [36], PHYLIP [6], or MACLADE [25].

These steps conform to a straightforward pipeline as shown in Fig. 1. Nevertheless each piece of software intervening in this process was developed independently and as a consequence many different (and complex) file formats are used for each program. For instance, PHYLIP can only accept a PHYLIP format file as input; the input of MACLADE and PAUP has to be specified in NEXUS [24] format; CLUSTAL W produces a specific CLUSTAL W format file as output, and so on.

This diversity of file formats clearly produces a compatibility problem between each of the stages in the pipeline of Fig. 1. To get around this problem, a biologist has to write ad-hoc scripts using tools such as `sed`, `awk` or `Perl` to extract the genetic sequences produced by one program and translate them into the format that can be used for the other programs, or do it manually. Manual translation is error prone and labor intensive. Writing of `Perl/awk/sed` scripts requires the biologist to have a reasonable computing background.

The approach currently taken to solve this problem by some software analysis tools is to make an effort to help by trying to recognize as many types of input formats as possible and trying to generate as many types of output formats as possible. For instance, CLUSTAL W tries to automatically recognize seven different input formats and to generate five different output formats. However, since the main concern of CLUSTAL W is sequence alignment and not sequence translation, the recognition procedure used in CLUSTAL W is not warranted to work all the times, the files generated by CLUSTAL W usually need some editing before they can be used by other programs, and some important file formats are not supported.

Our approach to this problem is to develop a bidirectional translator for inter-program communication using our Horn logical semantics approach [21]. In our design the output of each of the programs depicted in Figure 2 is taken by the translator and transformed into an internal representation. The desired

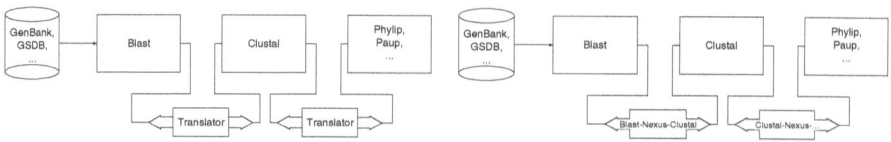

Fig. 2. Proposed approach to achieve the pipeline process to analyze a molecular sequence

Fig. 3. Implemented pipeline

conversion between the stages of the pipeline is achieved transparently through the transformation of the internal representation into the desired output format. The main advantage of using an internal representation is that for every format f we just need a bidirectional translation between f and the internal representation.

As illustrated in Figure 3, the internal representation chosen for the bidirectional translator is NEXUS [24], a modular and expandable format specially designed (by biologists) to comprehensively describe all genetic sequence information ideally needed by a systematic biologist. Even though many other formats exist to represent these sequences, most of them are for a special purpose or contain information that is used by a particular program. On the contrary, NEXUS has gained attention in the last few years because of its interesting features and its goal of providing a uniform input and output format for all types of genetics related softwares. Each different kind of information in NEXUS is enclosed in a block which makes it very readable by a human. Another important concept is that the standard is very flexible allowing to define new kinds of blocks for hosting data for possible future biological applications. NEXUS files are portable since NEXUS is a format independent of any application, while it also allows to define information for a specific program encapsulating it inside a program-specific block. Currently in NEXUS it is possible to define all the structures required for systematic biology applications including, for instance, taxa, states, trees, matrices, unaligned data, distances, codons, and sets.

The tool for format interoperability we have developed has been constructed using the Horn logical semantics approach. Semantics of NEXUS is expressed in terms of the various formats to obtain reversible translators. The core of this approach has been implemented using Prolog (Prolog's built-in DCGs for syntax specification and regular Prolog for semantics specification). Describing the syntax/semantics of the various formats (in particular of NEXUS) has been accomplished following the traditional steps taken by a compiler. First, the program reads the file into a list of character codes. Second, the codes are scanned and converted into a list of tokens. Third, the tokens are parsed using a DCG and a parse tree created. Finally, the parse tree is given an appropriate semantics.

However, the techniques used in each of these phases in this project are nontraditional because the internal format representation, i.e., NEXUS, is in fact a highly context sensitive language (e.g., the interleaved format for matrices [24]).

The flexibility that NEXUS provides is a real implementation challenge and its DCG is very large. In fact NEXUS is in many ways more similar to a human language than to a usual computer language. In the remainder of this section we shall discuss some of the techniques used in the implementation of each of these phases. NEXUS underscores our point regarding language design: formal languages/notations designed by non-computer scientists tend to have context sensitive features.

During scanning a list of character codes is tokenized in a list of syntactic elements with the following format: [Row, Column, Token], representing the token recognized and the row and column coordinates of the token in the file. The coordinates are used in later translation stages to send messages to the user, e.g., warnings and errors. The scanning techniques used in the translator are quite unusual and heavily rely on non-determinism to handle the complexity of token definition in NEXUS. This was due to a number of reasons: (i) tokens in NEXUS are non-case sensitive; (ii) comments can occur inside tokens, (iii) Underscore maybe interpreted as blank space, (iv) comments can be nested and are of multiple types; comments can have impact on the meaning of a file (for example a command-comment [&U] in a tree block means that the tree is unrooted); (v) recognition of tokens and key words is sensitive to the context in which they appear.

The traditional DCG technique consists of creating in advance a list of tokens and using this list as a *difference list* in the DCG to parse the file. It is clear from the previous NEXUS description that it does not make too much sense to create such a list of tokens in advance since the real meaning of the tokens and its real character components are defined by the context. The technique we propose and follow consists in scanning and parsing simultaneously. Every time we reach a rule during parsing that looks for a token we call a predicate match/4, which scans the current input stream *guessing* to check whether the current token corresponds to the token expected. Whenever the input does not correspond to the expected token, match/4 fails leaving the current input intact so that other DCG rule can be applied. This effectively allows multiple symbols look-ahead, which is indispensable for parsing NEXUS. Thus, parsing techniques that use traditional compiling technology will be too cumbersome to use.

The technique is briefly illustrated via a simplified rule fragment shown in Figure 4. The first two arguments of match/4 are the token and the type expected. The third argument tells whether match should either guess or act deterministic. The last argument is the resulting syntactic element matched as described at the beginning of this section.

The creation of a parser in Prolog is relatively simple using DCGs. However many factors had to be taken into account during parsing in this project due to the nature of the translated file formats and using NEXUS as internal file representation [21]. Once parsing is done and the parse tree generated, translation is performed. In the translation stage the parse tree produced is mapped to the required output format using the Horn logical approach described earlier.

```
block_distances( [ N1, N2, N3, N4, N5, N6, N7, N8 ] ) -->
        match( 'distances', _, _, N1 ),
        match( ';', _, y, N2 ),
        dimensions_distances( N3 ),
        format_distances( N4 ),
        taxlabels_optional( N5 ),
        match( 'matrix', _, y, N6 ),
        matrix_data( N7 ), match( ';', _, y, N8 ).
```

Fig. 4. Use of `match/4`

The actual implementation of the translator has been very satisfactory. It was produced in a very short time (less than 6 man months of work). Currently it supports bidirectional translation among NEXUS, Phylip and CLUSTAL W. These translators have been tested on user files provided by biologists; they work for files as big as several hundred kilobytes. More formats are being added (adding support for these formats consists of adding a Prolog module without modifying the entire program).

The Horn logical semantics based approach greatly facilitated the implementation of this project. The complexity of the whole translator is reduced to specifying the BNF grammar; everything else falls through automatically (since only one syntax rule and one semantic rule is needed per BNF production). Coming up with the grammar of each file format and NEXUS was the most time consuming task in this project because of the lack of a formal format definition in the literature. Once we had the grammar for each format, obtaining a DCG and specification of the valuation predicates was simple to achieve. Building these translators took less than few man months of work, most of which was devoted to formalizing the informally specified grammars of the various formats. In fact, the DCG grammar of NEXUS is the first ever complete parser ever built for NEXUS. Most parsers built to date are *ad hoc* parser for smaller subsets of NEXUS; complete parsers will be quite complex to build using traditional technology due to NEXUS' context sensitive and non-LALR(1) nature. In a short time the translation services that use our translator will be available to the bioinformatics user community through the `nbif.org` web server.

3.3 HTML to VoiceXML

The next semantic filtering problem we consider is translation of HTML to VoiceXML. HTML is the mark-up language widely-used to structure documents on the Web. VoiceXML is an XML based languages for marking up voice data. The goal behind VoiceXML is to make the Internet accessible through the phone or an *audio browser*. VoiceXML is being developed by a consortium of IBM, Lucent, Motorola and AT&T and requires a *voice browser* that understands VoiceXML and that reads out the information contained in the VoiceXML marked-up web page. VoiceXML also allows the user to interact (through speech) with the web-page via the audio browser or the phone.

Since HTML has a well-formed context free grammars, it is very natural and easy to write the DCG for it (one DCG rule per BNF grammar rule). The building of the parse tree is also very easily specified, by adding an extra argument in which the parse tree is synthesized. The parse tree of a phrase is constructed in terms of the parse trees of its component sub-phrases. The DCG rules constitute an executable program, as they will be translated into ordinary Prolog clauses automatically when they are loaded into the Prolog system. Thus, one can completely avoid having to deal with the algorithmic or computational aspects of parsing.

Specifying the semantics of HTML in terms of VoiceXML is the next step in the Horn logic semantics-based approach. Predicates that map HTML parse tree patterns to the corresponding sentences of the VoiceXML are specified. These predicates give a meaning to each term in the parse tree a value depending on the values of its subterms.

Note that the semantics is written denotationally, and that there is one semantic rule per grammar rule. Since we have defined the mappings of the valuation functions on all of the options listed in the DCG rules for the subset of HTML, the valuation functions are completely defined. The above syntax and semantics specification can be loaded on a Prolog interpreter and executed to translate sentences from HTML to VoiceXML. Thus, given the input HTML document to the left, an equivalent VoiceXML document shown to the right is obtained.

The main advantage of using Horn logical approach for converting HTML to VoiceXML was the speed with which the task of building the translator was accomplished. Also, for the subset of HTML considered for the project, the translator produced was reversible and could translate VoiceXML documents back to HTML. Note that an approach based on Horn logic can also naturally handle non-well formed HTML (i.e., ending tags may be omitted) through non-determinism in DCGs. Non-well formed HTML does not directly admit an LALR(1) grammar; for this reason, parsers for HTML based on traditional compiler technology are large and quite complex [8]. Work is in progress to build a complete translator from HTML to VoiceXML.

3.4   Database Interoperability

In the final example, we consider the problem of making two databases interoperate with each other—one relational and another object-oriented. We consider the problem of translating programs and data expressed in a relational database format to an object-oriented database format. In particular we consider the translation of ODBC (a standardized SQL) programs and data to OQL (a standardized Object Query Language) programs and data. ODBC (Open Database Connectivity) was developed as a standard to make the development of relational database applications independent from the actual database environment the application was going to run on (Oracle, Sybase, Ingres, etc.). For each vendor's database environment, a driver has to be defined (by that vendor) that maps ODBC programs/data to the vendor's programs/data. The drivers for various relational systems are relatively easy to define, as they map programs/data of ODBC, which can be thought of as a dialect of SQL, to other dialects of SQL. However, if we wish to make ODBC work with object-oriented databases, the driver becomes a lot more complex, as programs and data expressed relationally in ODBC have to be transformed to programs and data expressed in an object-oriented way. A solution to this problem is to build semantic filters that map ODBC programs/data to OQL program/data. OQL (Object Query Language) is a standard devised for query languages for object-oriented databases. The driver can thus be thought as a semantic filter from ODBC to OQL.

We adopt the Horn logical semantics approach once again to perform this translation. In the syntax specification part the syntax of ODBC programs is specified as a DCG. This DCG is extended so as also to generate *parse trees* for the programs. In the semantic specification part, the semantics of ODBC constructs is denotationally given in terms of OQL constructs. Both the syntax and semantic specification are expressed using Horn logic. The Horn logic specification is executable and, thus, automatically yields a system that transforms ODBC programs to OQL programs.

The translation task is facilitated by the fact that the syntax of OQL is very heavily influenced by SQL. The main problem to be handled is mapping relational data representation (relational tables) to object data representation (persistent objects). In our semantic mapping, each table is mapped to a class, the columns are the attributes, and a row of a table is mapped to an instance of an object in that class.

A translator for the full ODBC language was developed, to show the applicability of Horn logic based semantics filtering technology to facilitate database interoperability [5].

Our logic programming based approach to database interoperability can also be used for making heterogeneous databases work together. Essentially, filters can be declaratively described between programs/data of each type of database involved, or the most powerful database (in terms of query expressiveness) identified and programs/data of all other databases semantically mapped to programs/data of this database. Thus, Horn logical semantics arguably provides a theoretical basis to interoperability among heterogeneous databases.

3.5   Generating XML Parsers

Our framework can also be used for automatically generating provably correct validating XML parsers. The grammar of an XML is specified as a DTD. The DTD is a specification of the grammar in the EBNF (extended BNF) format. The W3C consortium has defined a standard language in which this EBNF is specified. One can write the Horn logical semantics of this standard language, giving the meaning of EBNF productions in terms of DCG productions. That is, the semantic specification is a map from EBNF rules in the DTD to the rules of its corresponding DCG. Thus, this semantic specification is a translator of a DTD expressed as an EBNF to one that is expressed as a DCG. The DCG produced, can be used to parse XML documents. Such a validating parser for XML can be built literally in a few of weeks of work. Such a parser has indeed been built [16].

4   A Killer Application for LP

We strongly believe that semantic filtering can be a *killer application* for logic programming. Filtering and porting problems arise very frequently in business and industry. Rapidly solving these problems with the aid of logic programming and Horn logical semantics can lead to considerable productivity gains. These gains are evident from our experience working on building filters for software systems for bioinformatics and building the back-translator for Nemeth Math Braille code to LaTeX.

Also, the advent of XML creates a fertile area for the application of this technology, as the number of DTDs (document type definitions) and schemas proliferates. XML (eXtensible Markup Language) is a notation for specifying mark-up languages for a particular domain. The idea behind XML is to let groups of users define their own task-specific mark-up languages (i.e., their own set of tags with predefined meanings, and syntax rules that govern nesting of these tags, termed DTD/Schemas) for marking up documents so that they can be further processed automatically. With a number of DTDs/Schemas or tagging schemes being defined for the same task, one needs methods to convert documents marked-up using one DTD/Schema to another. One also needs to translate a DTD/Schema to HTML, so that XML documents can be displayed on the web. The WWW consortium has come up with XSL (eXtensible Stylesheet Language) and XSLT (XSL Transformations) for programming these translations. XSL/XSLT are still evolving and are not completely defined yet. We believe that language filtering technology outlined in this paper is more effective in providing solutions to these transformation problem. The major advantage of a Horn logical based technology is that it allows transformations to be expressed in a reversible manner, that is, a translator specified for translating a DTD $D1$ to another DTD $D2$ automatically yields a translator for translating $D2$ to $D1$.

Logic programming based semantic filtering works in situations where other traditional approaches may not, for example, if the language is context sensitive or if it is not LALR(1). In such cases traditional compiler based remedies don't work, or produce a highly complex system. In case of the Nemeth Math Braille code to LaTeX translation problem, the complexity of the problem was such that it was deemed impossible to solve using traditional compiler technology. However, with our Horn logical semantics based approach we were not only able to solve the problem, we were able to build the system in roughly 4 man months of work. The same is true of our work on building translators for bioinformatics software systems.

5   Related Work and Conclusions

Traditionally compiling technology has been used for solving filtering problems. However, as discussed earlier, traditional compiling technology has largely been limited to context free, LR(1) languages. More sophisticated parser generators such as ANTLR [29] have been recently developed that can handle LR(k) grammars. ANTLR also introduces computations into the parser to make parsing decisions (called pred-LL(k) parsing in [29]), allowing it to handle more complex languages. However, we believe that developing parsers for Nemeth Braille Math and NEXUS will still be quite an undertaking in these systems. We believe that the same applies to combinator based parsers that have been recently developed [35]. The work that comes close to ours is that of Stepney [34] who uses a similar approach to declaratively specify compilers: the backend is specified by declaratively mapping parse tree patterns to machine instructions. Stepney's goal is to build compilers in a provably correct way rather than semantic filters.

In this paper we presented an approach based on logic programming and formal semantics for declaratively specifying translators. Our approach was illustrated via practical applications of this technology in five diverse areas: (i) making the web accessible on the phone; (ii) making mathematics accessible to blind students; (iii) making biological software systems developed for phylogenetic inference interoperate with each other; (iv) making relational databases work with object-oriented databases; and, (v) automatically generating provably correct validating parser for an XML. Other applications of this framework are currently being investigated, namely, rapid development of interpreters and compilers of domain specific languages [14].The technology is also being used to develop (i) filters between the Marburg Braille notation, LATEX, and Nemeth Math, (ii) resource (e.g., power, execution time) aware compilers for embedded systems, (iii) a translator from SCR specification language [19] to C code, etc. A general tool for graphically specifying mappings between notations that will automatically generate the Horn logical syntax and semantic specification is also being developed.

References

1. A. Aho, J. D. Ullman, R. Sethi. Compilers: Principles, Techniques, and Tools. Addison Wesley. 1986. 83, 84
2. S. F. Altschul and B. W. Erickson. Significance of nucleotide sequence alignments. *Mol. Biol. Evol.*, 2:526–538, 1985. 91
3. A. Appel. Modern Compiler Construction in ML: Basic Techniques. 1997. Cambridge University Press. 84
4. W. Chen and D. S. Warren. Tabled Evaluation with Delaying for General Logic Programs, *In JACM 43(1):20-74.* 86
5. N. Datta. Semantic basis for Interoperability: An approach based on Horn Logic and Denotational Semantics. MS thesis. NMSU. Aug. 2000. 96
6. J. Felsenstein. PHYLIP: Phylogeny inference package, version 3.5c. Distributed by the author, Deparment of Genetics, Univ. Washington, Seattle, 1993. 91

7. J. W. Lloyd. Foundations of Logic Programming. Springer Verlag. 2nd ed. 1987. 86
8. C. Goldfarb, P. Prescod. The XML Handbook. Prentice Hall. 1998. 84, 95
9. http://www.w3.org/Style/XSL.
10. http://www.w3.org/TR/xslt. 84
11. http://www.w3.org/TR/voicexml/ 84
12. G. Gupta. Horn logic denotations and their applications. In *The Logic Programming Paradigm: The next 25 years*, pages 127–160. Springer Verlag, 1999. 85, 86, 90
13. G. Gupta, E. Pontelli. A Constraint-based Denotational Approach to Specification and Verification of Real-time Systems. In *Proc. IEEE Real-time Systems Symposium*, San Francisco, pp. 230-239. Dec. 1997. 86
14. G. Gupta and E. Pontelli. A Horn logical semantic framework for specification, implementation, and verification of domain specific languages. Essays in honor of Robert Kowalski, Springer Verlag, Lecture Notes in Computer Science, to appear. 98
15. G. Gupta, O. El Khatib, M. Noamany. Building the tower of Babel: Converting XML to VoiceXML for Accessibility. Proc. 7th International Conference on Computers Helping People with Special Needs (ICCHP00). OCG Press (Austria). pp. 267-272. 84
16. G. Gupta, X. Zhou. Auotmatically Generating Validating Parsers for XML. Internal Report. U. T. Dallas. 2001. 97
17. Haifeng Guo. Translating Nemeth Math Braille Code to LaTeX: A Semantics-based Approach. *Master Thesis*. New Mexico State Univ, 1999. 90
18. C. Gunter. Programming Language Semantics. MIT Press. 1992. 85
19. C. Heitmeyer, et al. Automated Consistency Checking of Requirement Specification. In *ACM Trans. on Software Engg. and Methodology*, 1996. 98
20. D. G. Higgins, J. D. Thompson, and T. J. Gibson. Using CLUSTAL for multiple sequence alignments. *Methods in Enzymology*, 266:383–402, 1996. 91
21. J. R. Iglesias, G. Gupta, E. Pontelli, D. Ranjan, B. Milligan. Interoperability between Bioinformatics Tools: A logic programming approach. In *Proc. Practical Aspects of Declarative Langs*, 2001. Springer Verlag LNCS 1990. 91, 93
22. H. Guo, A. Karshmer, G. Gupta, S. Geiger, C. Weaver. A Framework for Translation of Nemeth Braille Code to LaTeX: The MAVIS Project. In *Proc. ACM Conf. on Assistive Technologies*, pp. 136-143, 1998. 90
23. L. Liebmann. Extensible Markup Language, XML's Tower Of Babel. http://www.internetweek.com/indepth01/indepth042401.htm. 84
24. David R. Maddison, David L. Swofford, and Wayne P. Maddison. NEXUS: An extensible file format for systematic information. *Syst. Biol.*, 46(4):590–621, 1997. 84, 91, 92
25. Wayne P. Maddison and David R. Maddison. *MacClade: Analysis of phylogeny and character evolution, version 3.07*. Sinauer, Sunderland, Massachusetts, 1997. 91
26. K. Miesenberger, B. Stöger. Personal Communication. 88, 90
27. A. Nemeth. The Nemeth Braille Code for Mathematics and Science Notation 1972 Revision (Frankfort KY: American Printing House for the Blind, 1972) 84, 88, 90
28. R. A. O'Keefe. The Craft of Prolog. MIT Press. 1990. 86
29. T. Parr. http://www.antlr.org. 83, 98
30. L. Scadden. Making Mathematics and Science Accessible to Blind Students Through Technology. Proceedings of RESNA'96, 1996. 88, 90

31. D. Schmidt. *Denotational Semantics: a Methodology for Language Development.* W. C. Brown Publishers, 1986. 85

32. D. Schmidt. Programming language semantics. In CRC Handbook of Computer Science, Allen Tucker, ed., CRC Press, Boca Raton, FL, 1996. Summary version, ACM Computing Surveys 28-1 (1996) 265-267. 85

33. L. Sterling & S. Shapiro. The Art of Prolog. MIT Press, '94. 86

34. S. Stepney. High Integrity Compilation. Prentice Hall. 1993. 98

35. S. D. Swierstra and L. Duponcheel. Deterministic, Error Correcting Combinator Parsers. In *Advanced Functional Programming: Second international School.* LNCS 1129, pages 184-207, Springer Verlag, Berlin, 1996. 98

36. D. L. Swofford. PAUP: Phylogenetic analysis using parsimony version 3.1.1. Illinois Natural History Survey, Champaign, 1993. 91

Linear Scan Register Allocation in a High-Performance Erlang Compiler

Erik Johansson and Konstantinos Sagonas

Computing Science Department, Uppsala University, Sweden
{happi,kostis}@csd.uu.se

Abstract. In the context of an optimizing native code compiler for the concurrent functional programming language Erlang, we experiment with various register allocation schemes focusing on the recently proposed *linear scan register allocator*. We describe its implementation and extensively report on its behaviour both on register-rich and on register-poor architectures. We also investigate how different options to the basic algorithm and to the compilation process as a whole affect compilation time and quality of the produced code. Overall, the linear scan register allocator is a good choice on register-rich architectures; when compilation time is a concern, it can also be a viable option on register-poor architectures.

1 The Story

During the last years, we have been developing HiPE, a High-Performance native code compiler for the concurrent functional programming language Erlang [2]. Erlang has been designed to address the needs of large-scale soft real-time control applications and is successfully being used in products of the telecommunications industry. The HiPE system significantly improves the performance characteristics of Erlang applications by allowing selective, user-controlled, "just-in-time" compilation of bytecode-compiled Erlang functions to native code. As reported in [7], HiPE currently outperforms all other implementations of Erlang.[1]

Achieving high performance has not come without a price: compilation times are higher than compilation to virtual machine code. Even though HiPE is currently not focusing on dynamic compilation—the compiler is usually used either interactively or through make—compilation times are a significant concern in an interactive development environment which Erlang advocates. Investigating where the HiPE compiler spends time, we have found that HiPE's register allocator, which is based on a variant of graph coloring, is often a bottleneck being responsible for 30–40% of the total compilation time. (This is not atypical; experience reported in the literature is similar.) Worse yet, for functions containing a large number of temporaries, the memory needed to build

---

[1] Since October 2001, HiPE is part of Ericsson's Open Source Erlang release 8 (available from www.erlang.org). See also: www.csd.uu.se/projects/hipe.

S. Krishnamurthi, C. R. Ramakrishnan (Eds.): PADL 2002, LNCS 2257, pp. 101–119, 2002.

the interference graph is often prohibitive. So, we were looking for a more well-behaved register allocator.

In doing so, we found out about the recently proposed *linear scan register allocator* [11]. The method is quite simple and extremely intriguing: with relatively little machinery—and more importantly by avoiding the quadratic cost of heuristic coloring—almost equally efficient code is generated. At first, we were skeptical whether the results of [11] would carry over to HiPE: One reason is because programs written in Erlang—or a functional language in general—may not benefit to the same extent from techniques used for compiling C or 'C [10] programs. More importantly because, even on a register-rich architecture such as the SPARC, HiPE reserves a relatively large set of physical registers which are heavily used by the underlying virtual machine; this increases register pressure and significantly departs from the contexts in which linear scan has previously been used [10,11]. Finally, because we had no idea how the results would look on a register-poor architecture such as IA-32; to our knowledge nobody has ever experimented with linear scan in this setting. Despite our skepticism, we were willing to give it a try. In about two weeks, a straightforward implementation based on the description in [11] was ready, but this was the easy part. The results were encouraging, but we were curious to experiment with various options that [11] also explores, sometimes leaves open, or suggests as future research. We did so and report our findings in this paper.

This paper, besides documenting our implementation (Section 3) and extensively reporting on its performance characteristics (Section 4), describes our experience in using linear scan register allocation in a context which is significantly different from those previously tried. In particular, we are the first ones to investigate the effectiveness of linear scan on the IA-32. Finally, we present results from trying different options to linear scan and report on their effectiveness and on the trade-offs between the speed of register allocation and the quality of the resulting code (Section 5). We thus believe that this paper and our experiences should prove useful not only to other declarative language implementors, but also to all compiler writers considering linear scan register allocation or being involved in a project where compilation time is a concern.

We begin with a description of various schemes for register allocation, focusing on linear scan.

2   Global Register Allocation

2.1   Graph Coloring Register Allocation & Iterated Register Coalescing

The idea behind coloring-based schemes is to formulate register allocation as a graph coloring problem [4], by representing liveness information with an *interference graph*. Nodes in the graph represent variables that are to be allocated to registers. Edges connect variables that are simultaneously live and thus cannot use the same physical register. By using as many colors as physical registers, the register allocation problem can be solved by assigning colors to nodes in the graph such that all directly connected nodes receive different colors.

The classic method by Chaitin *et al.* [4,5] iteratively builds an interference graph and heuristically attempts to color it. If the graph is not colorable, nodes are deleted from the graph, the corresponding temporaries are spilled to memory, and the process is repeated until the graph becomes colorable. Since Chaitin's paper, many variations or improvements to the basic scheme have emerged. In particular, we note the method by Briggs *et al.* [3] which is the one we are using in the HiPE compiler. Compared to [3], iterated register coalescing [6] is a more aggressive coloring-based technique aiming at eliminating many redundant `move` instructions: When the source and destination node of a `move` do not interfere (i.e., are not directly connected in the graph), these nodes can be coalesced into one, and the `move` instruction can be removed.

In practice, coloring-based allocation schemes usually produce good code. However, the cost of register allocation is dominated by the construction of the interference graph, which can take time (and space) quadratic in the number of nodes. When compilation time is a concern, as in just-in-time compilers or interactive development environments, graph coloring may not be the best choice.

2.2 Linear Scan Register Allocation

The linear scan allocation algorithm [11] is simple to understand and implement. It is based on the notion of the *live interval* of a temporary, which is an approximation of its liveness region. The live interval of a temporary is defined so that the temporary is dead at all instructions outside the live interval; the temporary might also be dead at some instructions within the interval.[2] The idea is that the allocator can use this information to easily determine how these intervals overlap and assign temporaries with overlapping intervals to different registers.

The algorithm can be broken down into the following four steps: (1) order all instructions linearly; (2) calculate the set of live intervals; (3) allocate a register to each interval (or spill the corresponding temporary); and finally (4) rewrite the code with the obtained allocation.

Let us look at each step, using Figure 1 as our example.

Ordering Instructions Linearly As long as the calculation of live intervals is correct, an arbitrary linear ordering of the instructions can be chosen. In our example, the control-flow graph of Figure 1(a) can be linearized in many ways; Figures 1(b) and 1(c) show two possible orderings. Different orderings will result in different approximations of live intervals, and the choice of ordering might impact the allocation and the number of spilled temporaries. An optimal ordering is one with as few contemporaneous live intervals as possible, but finding this information at compile-time is time-consuming. It is therefore important to *a priori* choose an ordering that performs best on the average. Poletto and Sarkar

---

[2] Schemes such as [12] for utilizing holes in live ranges will not be considered here.

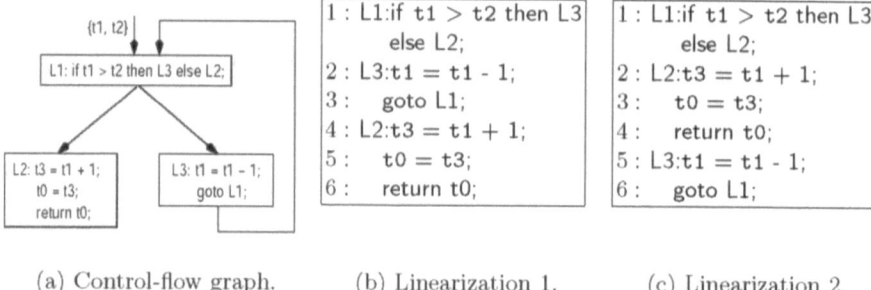

(a) Control-flow graph.   (b) Linearization 1.   (c) Linearization 2.

Fig. 1. Control-flow graph and two of its possible linearizations

in [11] suggest the use of a depth-first ordering of instructions as the most natural ordering and only compare it with the ordering in which the instructions appear in the intermediate code representation. They conclude that these two orderings produce roughly similar code for their benchmarks. We have experimented with other orderings and discuss their impact in Section 5.1.

Calculation of Live Intervals Given a linear ordering of the code, there is a minimal live interval for each temporary. For temporaries not in a loop, this interval starts with the first definition of the temporary and ends with its last use. For temporaries live at the entry of a loop, the interval must be extended to the end of the loop. The optimal interval can be found by first doing a precise liveness analysis and then by traversing the code in linear order extending the intervals of each temporary to include all instructions where the temporary is live. For the first linearization of our example, a valid set of live intervals would be:

$$\texttt{t0} : [5,6], \quad \texttt{t1} : [1,4], \quad \texttt{t2} : [1,3], \quad \texttt{t3} : [4,5]$$

and for the second linearization, a valid set of live intervals would be:

$$\texttt{t0} : [3,4], \quad \texttt{t1} : [1,6], \quad \texttt{t2} : [1,6], \quad \texttt{t3} : [2,3]$$

In the first set of intervals, t2 is only live at the same time as t1, but in the second one, t2 is simultaneously live with all temporaries. There are alternatives to performing the somewhat costly liveness analysis that give correct—but sub-optimal—live intervals. One approach is to use strongly connected components in the control-flow graph; see [11].

Allocation of Registers to Intervals When all intervals are computed, the resulting data structure (Intervals) gets ordered in increasing start-points so as to make the subsequent allocation scan efficient. For our first linearization this would result in:

$$\texttt{t1} : [1,4], \quad \texttt{t2} : [1,3], \quad \texttt{t3} : [4,5], \quad \texttt{t0} : [5,6]$$

Allocation is then done by keeping a set of allocatable free physical registers (FreeRegs), a set of already allocated temporaries (Allocated), and a list containing a mapping of active intervals to registers (Active). The active intervals are ordered on increasing end-points while traversing the start-point-ordered list of intervals. For each interval in Intervals, that is, for each temporary t_i (with interval $[start_i, end_i]$) do:

- For each interval j in Active which ends before or at the current interval (i.e., $end_j \leq start_i$), free the corresponding register and move the mapping to Allocated.

- If there is a free register, r, in FreeRegs, remove r from FreeRegs, add $t_i \mapsto r$ with the interval $t_i : [start_i, end_i]$ to Active (sorted on end).

  If, on the other hand, there are no free registers and the end-point end_k of the first temporary t_k in Active is further away than the current (i.e., $end_k > end_i$), then spill t_k, otherwise spill t_i. By choosing the temporary whose live interval ends last, the number of spilled temporaries is hopefully kept low. (Another way to choose the spilled temporary is discussed in Section 5.4.)

Rewrite of the Code Finally, when the allocation is completed, the code is rewritten so that each use or definition of a temporary involves the physical register where the temporary is allocated to. On RISC architectures, if the temporary is spilled, a `load` or `store` instruction is added to the code and a precolored physical register is used instead of the temporary. On architectures that have fancy addressing modes, such as the IA-32, the location of the spilled temporary can often be used directly in the instruction, in which case no extra instruction for loading or storing the temporary is needed.

3   Implementation of Register Allocators in HiPE

3.1   Graph Coloring and Iterated Register Coalescing Allocators

The graph coloring register allocator was implemented long ago and has been in daily use in the HiPE system ever since. It is a variant of [3], is well-tested, and uses efficient data structures. Despite being *pessimistic* in its spilling strategy (see [9]), it seldom needs to spill on the SPARC.

The iterated register coalescing allocator on the other hand, is *optimistic* in its spilling (similar to the strategy described in [9]), and was implemented having as main goal to obtain a register allocator that follows the algorithm described in [6] so as to establish an approximate lower bound on the number of spills for the benchmarks.

3.2   Linear Scan Register Allocator

As mentioned, the linear scan register allocator was first implemented based on the description in [11]. Afterwards, we experimented with various options and tuned the first implementation considerably. In this section, we only describe the chosen default implementation (i.e., the one using the options that seem to work best in most cases) by looking at how each step of the algorithm is implemented in HiPE. In Section 5 we will improve on [11] by describing and quantifying the impact of the alternatives that we tried.

Ordering Instructions Linearly Since there is no reason to reorder the instructions within a basic block, we just order the basic blocks. The default ordering of blocks is depth-first ordering (also called reverse postorder).

Calculation of Live Intervals Each live interval consists of a start position and an end position: these are instruction numbers corresponding to the first definition and last use of the register in a breadth-first traversal of the basic blocks of the control-flow graph. We use liveness analysis to find out the live-in and live-out sets for each basic block. This information is then used to set up the live intervals for each temporary by traversing the set of basic blocks. All temporaries in the live-in set for a basic block starting at instruction i have a live interval that includes i. All temporaries in the live-out set for a basic block ending at instruction j have a live interval that includes j. Furthermore if a temporary, t, is not included in both the live-in and the live-out set, then the live interval of t needs to be extended to either the first instruction defining t or the last instruction using t within the basic block.

Allocation of Registers to Intervals The allocation is performed by traversing the list of intervals sorted on increasing start-points. During the traversal we use four data structures:

Intervals A list of {`Temporary`,`StartPoint`,`EndPoint`} triples. This is a sorted (on `StartPoint`) representation of the interval structure calculated in the previous step.

FreeRegs Allocatable physical registers (`PhysReg`) which are currently not allocated to a temporary.

Active A list of {`Temporary`,`PhysReg`,`EndPoint`} triples sorted on increasing `EndPoint`, used to keep track of which temporaries are allocated to which physical register for what period, so as to deallocate physical registers when the allocation has passed the `EndPoint`. It is also used to find the temporary with the longest live interval when a temporary needs to be spilled.

Allocation An unsorted list containing the final allocation of temporaries to registers or to spill positions. Tuples have forms {`Temporary`,{`reg`,`PhysReg`}} or {`Temporary`,{`spill`,`Location`}}.

For each interval in the Intervals list, the allocation traversal does the following:

1. Move the information about each interval in the Active list that ends before[3] StartPoint to the Allocation structure. Also add the physical register assigned to the interval to the FreeRegs list.
2. Find an allocation for the current interval:

   - If there is a physical register in the FreeRegs list then tentatively assign this register to the current interval by inserting the interval and the physical register into the Active list, and by removing the physical register from the FreeRegs list.

   - If there is no free register then spill the interval with the furthest EndPoint and move this interval to the Allocation list. If the spilled interval is not the current one, then assign the physical register of the interval that was spilled to the current interval.

Rewrite of the Code When all intervals are processed, the Allocation structure is turned into a tuple that can be used for $O(1)$ mapping from a temporary to its allocated physical register (or spill position). Then all instructions are rewritten using this mapping.

3.3 A Naïve Register Allocator

To establish a base line for our comparisons, we have also implemented an extremely naïve register allocator: it allocates all temporaries to memory positions and rewrites the code in just one pass. For example, on the SPARC, every use of a temporary is preceded by a load of that temporary to a register, and every definition is followed by a store to memory. This means that the number of added load and store instructions is equal to the number of uses and defines in the program. Currently each spill requires three instructions on the SPARC: two to set up the base address to the spill area[4] and one to do the actual load or store. This register allocator is very fast since it only needs one pass over the code, but on the other hand the added loads and stores increase the code size which in turn increases the total compilation time. Obviously, we recommend this "register" allocator to nobody! We simply use it to establish a lower bound on the register allocation time and an upper bound on the number of spills in order to evaluate the performance and effectiveness of the other register allocators.

3.4 The SPARC Back-End

To keep garbage collection times low, all dead objects should look dead to the garbage collector as soon as possible, preferably from the moment that they die.

---

[3] Here one could use "before or at" instead of "before" in order to increase the likelihood that two registers (t1,t2) in a move: t1 = t2 are assigned to the same register. Since HiPE has a multimove instruction (sometimes called parallel move), this is not straightforward since several live intervals might begin at the same program point.
[4] A large constant takes two instructions to create on the SPARC.

In order to achieve this, it is important to not let dead temporaries reside in the root set of a process's memory, for example on the stack. To ensure this, on the SPARC back-end we have chosen to only save live temporaries on the stack during a function call. We also use variable-sized stack frames and place the live temporaries so that there are no holes on the stack. This way, the garbage collector does not need any additional information about the stack other than a pointer to the top and a pointer to the bottom.

This scheme has some drawbacks, one being that all live temporaries have to be written to and read from the stack at function calls. Also, since the frame is trimmed so that only live values reside on the stack, another drawback is that there is no easy way to spill to the stack: the relative offset from the stack pointer to the spill position needs to be calculated *for each use and define* of spilled temporaries. However, since each temporary is saved on the stack at each function call, we know that any spilled values only need to survive till the next function call. This in turn means that we can store all spilled temporaries for a function at a fixed memory area: Even though there might be several processes executing the same code and calling the code recursively, only one of them will use the spill area at a time; all other processes will save their temporaries on their stack.[5]

HiPE is a just-in-time native code compiler extension to a virtual-machine-based runtime system. This has influenced the compiler in several ways: There are for example several special data structures that are part of the virtual machine. Since we know that they are important for the execution of Erlang programs, as they are heavily used, we would like to keep them in registers. On a register-rich architecture such as the SPARC, we have chosen to cache 12 data structures in registers (the stack pointer, stack limit, heap pointer, heap limit, a pointer to the process control block, the reduction counter, the return address, and the first five arguments of Erlang functions), and we have reserved another 4 registers (Zero (%g0), C's SP (%o6) and FP (%i6), and the SPARC API reserved register (%g7)) leaving 16 registers for use by the register allocators. (The allocators can also use the 5 argument registers when they are unused.) As mentioned in the introduction, in this respect, compilation of Erlang programs differs from the contexts to which linear scan has been previously applied [10,12].

3.5   The IA-32 Back-End

The IA-32 back-end was developed after the SPARC one. In its implementation, we decided to try out some new design choices. The most important difference with the SPARC back-end is the use of stack descriptors (*stack maps*), enabling spilling on the stack, while having stack frames of fixed size for each function.

Another difference is in the handling of temporaries that are live across function calls. On the SPARC, a pre-pass ensures that all such temporaries are saved

---

[5] This approach assumes that the runtime system only executes one Erlang process at a time (i.e., that it is single-threaded), which is currently true for the underlying Erlang/OTP system and thus naturally also for HiPE.

on the stack before the call and are restored afterwards. The register allocators can then pretend that all registers are callee-saves. On the IA-32, the allocators assume that the call instruction defines all physical registers, thus preventing any temporaries that are live across a function call from being allocated to any physical register. This means that all these temporaries will be allocated on (spilled to) the stack.[6] The two approaches differ in when a temporary that lives across function calls needs to be read from or written to memory. In the worst case, on the SPARC, a read is needed after each call; on the IA-32, a read is needed at each use. On the SPARC, a write is needed at each call; on the IA-32, a write is needed at each definition. In a pure functional language such as Erlang we suspect that the number of uses plus the number of defines is less than two times the number of calls a temporary is live over. If so, the approach used by the IA-32 back-end is a winner. It remains future work to verify this.

We pre-allocate much fewer, only three, registers on the IA-32: The stack pointer is allocated to %esp and the process pointer to %ebp. At function calls, all arguments are passed on the stack and the return value is passed in %eax. The register allocator will not try to allocate the arguments in registers but keep them in memory (on the stack). The return value on the other hand is always moved to a new temporary directly after the return of the function. Hence, we can use the %eax register as a general purpose register, leaving six registers for the register allocators to play with.

Most instructions of the IA-32 ISA can take a memory location (e.g. register+immediate offset) as one of the operands (or the destination). By using these addressing modes, we can in many cases use spilled temporaries directly, without having to first load them from memory to a register.

Prior to register allocation, the code is in a pseudo-IA-32 intermediate form in which arbitrary operands are allowed in each instruction. After register allocation, a post-pass ensures that each instruction complies with the real IA-32 ISA, e.g. that no binary operation uses more than one memory operand. This is done by rewriting the code to use loads and stores to new temporaries. If any instruction has to be rewritten in this way, then the register allocator is called again with the additional constraint than none of the newly introduced temporaries may be spilled.

The naïve allocator is also using the memory operands of the IA-32. Thus, despite the fact that each temporary is considered spilled by the allocator, an additional load or store instruction is not always needed. (If loads or stores are inserted they use a pre-allocated physical register instead of introducing a new temporary.)

---

[6] For the IA-32 back-end, we had to adjust the linear scan allocator slightly to handle the case when a temporary is defined several times but never used; such is the case of physical registers at function calls. For these temporaries we effectively perform *live-range splitting* and end up with temporaries that have several one-instruction intervals. The alternative would have been that the live intervals of all physical registers would range over most of the function, rendering allocation of other temporaries, and thus use of linear scan, impossible.

4   Performance Results

The register allocator implementations described in the previous section have been evaluated by compiling and running a set of benchmarks. All four register allocators are integrated in the HiPE system (version 0.98) and a compiler option indicates which one to use. We have compiled the code in the same way before and after applying each allocator: The code is compiled to our internal representation of SPARC or pseudo-IA-32 code as a control flow graph. Some simple optimizations are applied to the intermediate stages, such as constant propagation, constant folding, dead code elimination, and removal of unreachable code; see e.g. [8]. The mapping of temporaries to the set of physical registers creates false dependencies, since different temporaries are mapped to the same physical register. This means that register allocation may possibly interfere with optimization passes that come after it; instruction scheduling in particular. In our experimental evaluation we have thus turned off all instruction scheduling. Still, the allocation might affect the scheduling done in hardware.

There is, however, one small difference in the code generated by the different allocators: On the SPARC, the graph coloring and linear scan allocators use a `multimove` instruction, an instruction that performs several `moves` at the same time, while the iterated coalescing allocator does not. For the coalescing allocator each `multimove` is expanded to several ordinary `move` instructions before allocation (many of these `moves` are eliminated by coalescing). For the graph coloring and the linear scan `multimove` instructions are expanded after allocation. This results in slightly different code.

The two platforms we used are: A Linux Pentium-II 333 MHz, 128 MB memory Dell Inspiron 7000 laptop, and a 2-processor Sun Enterprise 3000, 1.2 GB main memory running SunOS 5.7. Each processor is a 248 MHz UltraSPARC-II. (However, the HiPE system uses only one processor.)

4.1   The Benchmarks

Some of the benchmarks (**decode**, **eddie**) have been chosen from the "standard" set of Erlang benchmarks because they incur spilling when compiled with linear scan. We have also included the largest module of the HiPE compiler which is quite troublesome for some register allocators.

spillstress A synthetic benchmark consisting of a recursive function with several continously live variables; its only purpose is to stress the register allocators.
smith The Smith-Waterman DNA sequence matching algorithm.
life Conway's game of life on a 10 by 10 board where each square is implemented as a process.
decode Part of a telecommunications protocol.
huff A Huffman encoder compressing and uncompressing a short string.
estone Measures the number of Estones that an Erlang system can produce. This is an Erlang/OTP benchmark that aims at stressing all parts of an Erlang implementation.

Table 1. Sizes of benchmark programs

Benchmark	Lines	SPARC			IA-32		
		Insts	BasBlks	Temps	Insts	BasBlks	Temps
spillstress	94	1710	338	412	644	188	190
smith	93	2666	764	1004	1637	410	524
life	189	3018	976	1318	1855	516	603
decode	381	3692	1028	1114	2437	612	600
huff	177	4780	1350	1484	2938	768	749
estone	1134	18284	5604	6574	11768	3142	3372
beam2icode	1470	27452	7780	6452	18638	4736	4161
eddie	2233	45324	13155	16210	28625	7250	8242

beam2icode The part of the HiPE compiler that translates BEAM bytecode into intermediate code. The program contains a very big function handling different combinations of instructions. To get measurable execution times, we run this benchmark 10 times.

eddie An Erlang application implementing an HTTP parser which handles http-get requests.

Sizes of benchmark programs (lines of source code, the number of SPARC or IA-32 instructions before register allocation, and the total number of basic blocks and temporaries) are shown in Table 1. We note in passing that, on the SPARC, no allocator spills on many other standard Erlang benchmarks.

4.2   Compilation Times

We have measured both the time to perform register allocation and the time to complete the entire compilation for each program. The results are presented in Table 2 where the Comp columns stand for the total compilation time, and the RA columns stand for the time spent in the register allocator. The table also shows the percentage of compilation time spent in register allocation (RA%).

Note that even though for the naïve implementation the allocation times are usually the shortest, for some benchmarks the total compilation time is the longest (see e.g. **estone** on the SPARC). This is due to the large number of extra instructions which are added to the code due to spilling.

Also, as one can see from Table 2, the complexity of the graph coloring and the coalescing register allocator is not directly dependent on what one could naively consider as the 'size' of the program. Instead the complexity depends on the number of edges in the interference graph, which is for example high for the **spillstress** benchmark on the SPARC. On the other hand, the linear scan allocator is not affected much by the number of simultaneously live temporaries; the allocation time is instead dominated by the time to traverse the code.

The compilation times of **beam2icode** stick out since this program contains one large function with many simultaneously live temporaries. This becomes

Table 2. For each allocator, columns show total compilation time in seconds (Comp), register allocation time (RA), and percentage of total compilation time spent on register allocation (RA%)

	Naïve			Linear Scan			Graph Coloring			Iterated Coalesc.		
	Comp	RA	RA%	Comp	RA	RA%	Comp	RA	RA%	Comp	RA	RA%
SPARC												
spillstress	2.7	0.2	7.1	2.5	0.3	12.4	3.4	1.3	37.2	7.0	4.8	68.5
smith	4.4	0.3	7.0	3.8	0.5	14.0	4.1	0.9	21.0	6.1	3.0	49.8
life	4.8	0.3	6.7	4.3	0.7	15.2	4.7	0.9	20.2	6.0	2.2	37.3
decode	7.7	0.5	6.6	7.0	0.8	11.6	7.8	1.7	21.6	11.8	5.8	49.6
huff	7.3	0.6	8.2	6.2	1.0	16.6	6.8	1.5	22.3	12.6	7.4	58.9
estone	35.5	2.4	6.8	23.8	3.2	13.5	25.2	4.9	19.5	34.3	14.8	43.3
beam2icode	84.1	6.3	7.4	56.7	6.6	11.6	57.8	10.6	18.3	2769.2	2721.5	98.3
eddie	70.0	5.8	8.2	66.3	9.0	13.6	76.4	20.7	27.1	110.6	54.0	48.8
IA-32												
spillstress	1.3	0.03	2.3	1.4	0.24	17.1	1.5	0.35	23.3	1.8	0.73	40.6
smith	1.9	0.04	2.1	2.3	0.62	27.0	2.8	1.14	40.7	3.6	1.86	51.7
life	2.1	0.03	1.4	2.7	0.74	27.4	3.1	1.06	34.2	3.8	1.79	47.1
decode	2.9	0.02	0.7	3.7	1.07	28.9	5.3	2.56	48.3	8.5	5.82	68.5
huff	3.2	0.01	0.3	4.0	1.15	28.7	5.1	2.22	43.5	6.9	3.97	57.5
estone	10.6	0.15	1.4	14.1	4.15	29.4	15.6	5.74	36.8	20.6	10.97	53.3
beam2icode	40.1	0.10	0.2	45.8	21.03	46.0	142.9	117.54	82.3	191.9	167.58	87.3
eddie	34.8	0.21	0.6	44.0	10.20	23.2	51.6	17.92	34.7	73.5	40.25	54.8

troublesome either when many iterations are needed to avoid spilling (which is what happens with iterated register coalescing on the SPARC), or when the number of available registers is low, the produced allocation does not respect the constraints imposed by the ISA, and small corrections to the allocation are needed (such is the case on the IA-32). On the other hand, **estone** and **eddie** consist of a large number of small functions that do not exhibit this behaviour.

Compilation-time-wise, linear scan performs very well: compared to graph coloring, the time for register allocation is significantly reduced, and pathological cases such as **beam2icode** are avoided. In fact, compilation with linear scan is sometimes even faster than the naïve algorithm. This is due to the time needed for rewrite of the code with the allocation. Due to excessive spilling this code is larger for naïve than it is for linear scan; see also Table 4.

4.3   Execution Times

The execution times, in seconds, for each benchmark and allocator are presented in Table 3.

Even though on the SPARC the cost for spilling is higher than necessary (three instructions for each use or define instead of one; see Section 3.4), and linear scan spills more than the other allocators, the effect of spilling on execution times is limited. On a register-rich architecture such as the SPARC, linear scan has in most cases performance comparable to that of the graph coloring and iterated coalescing allocators. Linear scan also performs well on the IA-32; this is partly due to the different calling convention (passing arguments on the stack), and also partly due to the L1 cache being accessed almost as fast as the registers on the Pentium.

Also, note that different register assignments might affect the dynamic instruction scheduling done by the hardware, causing small differences in execution times. These differences might even be large enough to outweigh the cost of a spill. This explains why code produced with linear scan sometimes executes faster than code produced by graph coloring, even though linear scan spills and graph coloring does not (see e.g. **estone** on SPARC).

Table 3. Execution times in seconds

	SPARC				IA-32		
	Naïve	Linear Scan	Graph Color.	Iterated Coalesc.	Naïve	Linear Scan	Graph Color.	Iterated Coalesc.
spillstress	26.1	8.1	8.1	7.7	12.0	9.4	9.4	9.4
smith	31.9	7.1	7.0	6.9	9.0	5.9	6.7	6.0
life	29.1	21.6	21.7	21.6	15.4	14.6	14.4	14.3
decode	21.2	9.3	9.3	9.1	11.8	6.2	6.8	6.3
huff	27.2	9.1	8.9	8.9	11.5	9.5	9.6	10.1
estone	37.2	27.7	27.6	27.8	22.3	19.9	19.6	19.8
beam2icode	13.0	12.2	12.1	12.1	15.4	12.3	13.8	12.1
eddie	22.4	11.2	11.4	11.6	13.6	12.2	13.1	11.8

4.4   Spills on SPARC

Table 4 shows the number of temporaries spilled and the number of instructions after allocation. From these numbers, one can see that even though linear scan spills fewer temporaries than the graph colorer on **decode** and **eddie**, the total number of instructions for graph coloring is lower. This is because the linear scan allocator has a tendency to spill long live intervals with many uses, while the graph colorer spills more temporaries in number but with shorter lives and fewer uses.

As expected, the iterated coalescing allocator always generates fewer spilled temporaries. Also, since the coalescing allocator is usually able to coalesce moves and handles multimoves differently than the graph coloring and linear scan implementations, the resulting number of instructions is smaller for coalescing even when none of the algorithms spills. As mentioned, the naïve allocator spills all non-precolored temporaries, adding load and store instructions at each use or define site. The number of instructions should be compared to the numbers in Table 1 to see the increase in size caused by spills introduced by each algorithm.

4.5   Spills on IA-32

With the IA-32 port of HiPE ready, we were curious to see how our register allocators perform in this back-end by also looking at the number of spills. Besides satisfying our curiosity, this experiment is interesting since to the best of our knowledge the performance of linear scan on a register-poor architecture such as the IA-32 has nowhere been reported.

Table 5 reports, for each benchmark, the number of temporaries that are placed on the stack by the calling convention, and the number of additional spills and instructions after allocation.

Our results are as follows: When the number of available registers is low, the iterated coalescing algorithm is the clear winner as far as its ability to place temporaries in registers is concerned. It manages to minimally spill on this benchmark set. In comparison to graph coloring, this is partly due to the fact that the coalescing allocator is *optimistic* in its spilling strategy. With only few available registers, the linear scan register allocator has trouble keeping temporaries in registers and the number of spills is high compared to coalescing. Compared to the graph colorer, sometimes even though the number of spills is lower, the number of instructions in the resulting code is higher, suggesting that the choice of spilled temporaries is not a good one.

We stress that, due to the different calling conventions used by the SPARC and IA-32 back-ends, the number of spills in Tables 4 and 5 are incomparable.

5   A Deeper Look on Linear Scan: Impact of Some Alternatives

As mentioned, before settling on a default setting, we have experimented with a number of options that one can consider when implementing linear scan. One of these (spilling heuristics) is also considered in [11], another is suggested as possible future work (renaming), and some others (various orderings) are of our own invention. Nevertheless, as experimenting with all these options is time-

Table 4. Number of spilled temporaries and SPARC instructions after allocation

	Naïve		Linear Scan		Graph Color		Iter. Coalesc.	
	Spills	Instrs	Spills	Instrs	Spills	Instrs	Spills	Instrs
spillstress	116	4701	8	2335	4	1981	3	1853
smith	412	6971	0	2666	0	2666	0	2421
life	393	6840	0	3018	0	3018	0	2782
decode	522	9299	27	4360	38	4037	17	3628
huff	633	12061	4	4859	0	4780	0	4334
estone	2393	43430	2	18362	0	18284	0	16650
beam2icode	3936	69140	13	29405	0	27452	0	25198
eddie	6849	113676	31	47688	144	46870	20	43998

Table 5. Number of spilled temporaries and IA-32 instructions after allocation

	on stack	Naïve		Linear Scan		Graph Color		Iter. Coalesc.	
		Spills	Instrs	Spills	Instrs	Spills	Instrs	Spills	Instrs
spillstress	42	60	721	0	701	9	701	0	701
smith	49	299	2056	11	1879	23	1914	0	1868
life	63	265	2322	16	2229	13	2220	3	2205
decode	95	329	3079	8	2949	5	2971	0	2935
huff	125	371	3716	17	3526	25	3521	0	3458
estone	281	1848	14360	72	13493	43	13501	5	13416
beam2icode	801	2612	24534	44	23478	131	23804	0	23345
eddie	821	4638	38387	102	36158	108	36203	0	35871

consuming, we hope that our reporting on them will prove helpful to other implementors. All experiments of this section are conducted on the SPARC.

5.1 Impact of Instruction Ordering

The linear scan algorithm relies on a *linear approximation of the execution order of the code* to determine simultaneously live temporaries. In order to spill as few registers as possible, it is important that this approximation introduces as few false interferences as possible. An interference is false when the linearization places a basic block (B2) where a temporary (T) is not live between two blocks (B1, B3) which define and use T. The live interval for T will then include all instructions in B2, resulting in false interferences between T and any temporaries defined in B2; see Figure 2(a). If, instead, the linearization places B2 and B3 in the opposite order, there will not be a false interference.

Finding the optimal ordering (i.e., the one with the least number of false interferences) is not feasible; this would seriously increase the complexity of the algorithm. It is therefore important to try to find a general ordering that on average gives the best result. To determine such an ordering, we have applied the linear scan algorithm on five different orderings and counted the number of spills and the number of added instructions on our benchmarks.

We will exemplify the following orderings which we have tried (most of them are standard; see e.g. [1,8]) using the control-flow graph shown in Figure 2(b) where edges are annotated with a static prediction (taken/not-taken).

Depth-first ordering The reverse of the order in which nodes are last visited in a preorder traversal. (1,8,2,3,9,4,5,7,6)
Postorder The reverse of the depth-first ordering. (6,7,5,4,9,3,2,8,1)
Prediction The static prediction of branches is used to order the basic blocks in a depth first order. This should correspond to the most executed path being explored first. (1,2,3,4,5,7,8,9,6)
Breadth first ordering The start node is placed first, then its children followed by the grandchildren and so on. (1,2,8,3,4,9,5,6,7)

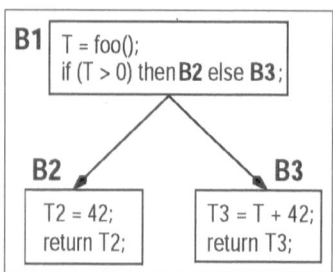

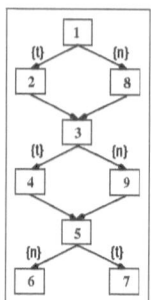

(a) Basic block ordering with false interferences.   (b) A CFG

Fig. 2. Control-flow graphs used to illustrate effects of orderings

Table 6. Impact of using different basic block orderings

Ordering	% Spilled temporaries	Added instructions
Depth-first ordering	0.24	7259
Postorder	0.28	7796
Prediction	6.27	18396
Breadth-first ordering	2.11	21287
'Random'	9.07	26484

'Random' (or rather an approximation of the source code order.) The blocks are ordered by converting the hash-table of basic blocks into a list; this list is approximately ordered on an increasing basic block numbering, which in turn corresponds to the order the basic blocks were created. (1,2,3,4,5,6,7,8,9)

The style in which a program is written has a big impact on which ordering performs best. Factors such as how nested the code is, or the size of each function come into play. The results therefore, as expected, vary from benchmark to benchmark, but provided the range of benchmarks is large and the (weighted) sums of results is taken, a "winner" can be found. As can be seen in Table 6, which shows the total percentage of spilled temporaries and the total number of added **loads** and **stores**, the depth-first ordering performs best. In HiPE, we are currently using it as the default.

5.2 Impact of Performing Liveness Analysis

In [11], a fast live interval analysis is described that does not use an iterative liveness analysis. Instead, it extends the intervals of all live temporaries in a strongly connected component (SCC) to include the whole SCC. After presenting the method, the authors conclude that although compilation using linear

Table 7. Execution times in secs with (w) and without (w/o) variable renaming (VR)

	Linear Scan		Graph Coloring			Iter. Coalesing		
	w VR	w/o VR	w VR	w/o VR		w VR	w/o VR	
spillstress	8.1	8.0	8.1	7.9	(-2)	7.7	8.0	
smith	7.1	7.0	7.0	7.0		6.9	6.9	
life	21.6	21.6	21.7	21.7		21.6	21.8	
decode	9.3	10.5	(-4)	9.3	9.3	(-16)	9.1	9.8	(+1)
huff	9.1	8.9	(-3)	8.9	8.4		8.9	8.9	
estone	27.7	27.8	(+1)	27.6	27.8		27.8	28.0	
beam2icode	12.2	12.2	(+8)	12.1	12.3		12.1	12.3	
eddie	11.2	11.4	(+16)	11.4	11.6	(-18)	11.6	11.8	

scan based on this method is sometimes faster than normal linear scan, the resulting allocation is usually much worse. We have independently confirmed their findings. In fact, the allocation is sometimes so bad that excessive spilling increases the time it takes to rewrite the code so much that the SCC-based linear scan allocator becomes slower than linear scan with a full liveness analysis. In our benchmark set, even compilation-time-wise linear scan with liveness analysis is faster on more than half of the benchmarks. Execution-time-wise, performing liveness analysis pays off.

5.3   Impact of Renaming

The HiPE compiler translates bytecode for a register-based virtual machine into an intermediate language with unlimited temporaries. This translation process introduces false dependencies since some registers of the virtual machine will be reused at different points in the program for different values. These false dependencies have a negative impact on the performance of some optimizations in the compiler. This can be remedied either by SSA conversion or by a renaming pass which gives a unique variable name to each value; see e.g. [8]. The effects of the renaming on execution times can be seen in Table 7; the difference in the number of spills w.r.t. the spills reported in Table 4 is shown within parentheses. Since all optimizations after the renaming become faster and more accurate, we recommend the use of this pass.

5.4   Impact of Spilling Heuristics

We have also experimented with the use of a spilling heuristic based on usage counts instead of interval length. Since information about the length of intervals is needed by the linear scan algorithm anyway (in order to free registers when an interval ends) this information can be used "for free" to guide spilling. The usage count heuristic is slightly more complicated to implement since it needs some extra information: the usage count of each temporary. There is also a cost in finding the temporary with the least use. As Table 8 shows, the usage count heuristic spills more (as expected) but spills temporaries which are not used much, so the size of the resulting code is sometimes smaller; see e.g. **decode** or **estone**. However, looking at the performance of the generated code, a clear winner between the two heuristics cannot be found. We thus do not recommend the use of usage counts.

Table 8. Impact of spilling heuristics

	Spills (Instructions)		Execution Time	
	Interval length	*Usage count*	*Interval length*	*Usage count*
spillstress	8 (2335)	27 (2298)	8.1	8.5
smith	0 (2666)	0 (2666)	7.1	7.1
life	0 (3018)	0 (3018)	21.6	21.0
decode	27 (4360)	78 (4336)	9.3	10.8
huff	4 (4859)	52 (5077)	9.1	9.7
estone	2 (18362)	9 (18333)	27.7	27.2
beam2icode	13 (29405)	490 (31642)	12.2	12.5
eddie	31 (47688)	256 (47698)	11.2	11.9

6   Concluding Remarks

We have experimented with register allocation, focusing on linear scan, and reported on its performance in the context of a just-in-time native code compiler for a virtual-machine-based implementation of a concurrent functional language. Besides describing our experiences in using linear scan in a significantly different context than those in which it has so far been employed, and reporting on its performance on the IA-32, we thoroughly investigated how various options to the basic algorithm affect compilation time and the quality of the resulting code. In many cases, we have independently confirmed results of [11]; in many others, we provide a deeper look or improve on those results in the hope that this will prove useful to other declarative programming language implementors.

Stated briefly, our experience is that in a register-rich environment, such as the SPARC (or the upcoming IA-64), linear scan is a very respectable register allocator: It is significantly faster than algorithms based on graph coloring, resulting in code that is almost as efficient. When compilation time is a concern, or at low optimization levels, it should be used.[7] Disregarding compilation-time concerns, on register-poor architectures, an optimistic iterated coalescing register allocator (which can eliminate most register-register moves) is a better approach to obtaining high-performance.

---

[7] On the SPARC, HiPE currently uses linear scan as default register allocator in optimization levels up to -O2; graph coloring is used in -O3.

References

1. A. V. Aho, R. Sethi, and J. D. Ullman. *Compilers: Principles, Techniques and Tools.* Addison-Wesley, Reading, MA, 1986. 115
2. J. Armstrong, R. Virding, C. Wikström, and M. Williams. *Concurrent Programming in Erlang.* Prentice-Hall, second edition, 1996. 101
3. P. Briggs, K. D. Cooper, and L. Torczon. Improvements to graph coloring register allocation. *ACM Trans. Prog. Lang. Syst.*, 16(3):428–455, May 1994. 103, 105
4. G. J. Chaitin. Register allocation & spilling via graph coloring. In *Proceedings of the SIGPLAN Symposium on Compiler Construction*, pages 98–105. ACM Press, June 1982. 102, 103
5. G. J. Chaitin, M. A. Auslander, A. K. Chandra, J. Cocke, M. E. Hopkins, and P. W. Markstein. Register allocation via coloring. *Computer Languages*, 6(1):47–57, Jan. 1981. 103
6. L. George and A. W. Appel. Iterated register coalescing. *ACM Trans. Prog. Lang. Syst.*, 18(3):300–324, May 1996. 103, 105
7. E. Johansson, M. Pettersson, and K. Sagonas. HiPE: A High Performance Erlang system. In *Proceedings of the ACM SIGPLAN International Conference on Principles and Practice of Declarative Programming*, pages 32–43. ACM Press, Sept. 2000. 101
8. S. S. Muchnick. *Advanced Compiler Design & Implementation.* Morgan Kaufman Publishers, San Fransisco, CA, 1997. 110, 115, 117
9. J. Park and S.-M. Moon. Optimistic register coalescing. In *Proceedings of the 1998 International Conference on Parallel Architecture and Compilation Techniques*, pages 196–204. IEEE Press, Oct. 1998. 105
10. M. Poletto, W. C. Hsieh, D. R. Engler, and M. F. Kaashoek. 'C and tcc: A language and compiler for dynamic code generation. *ACM Trans. Prog. Lang. Syst.*, 21(2):324–369, Mar. 1999. 102, 108
11. M. Poletto and V. Sarkar. Linear scan register allocation. *ACM Trans. Prog. Lang. Syst.*, 21(5):895–913, Sept. 1999. 102, 103, 104, 105, 106, 114, 116, 118
12. O. Traub, G. Holloway, and M. D. Smith. Quality and speed in linear-scan register allocation. In *Proceedings of SIGPLAN Conference on Programming Language Design and Implementation*, pages 142–151. ACM Press, June 1998. 103, 108

Compiling Embedded Programs to Byte Code

Morten Rhiger

[1] BRICS – Basic Research in Computer Science*
www.brics.dk
[2] Department of Computer Science, University of Aarhus
Ny Munkegade, Building 540, DK-8000 Aarhus C, Denmark
mrhiger@brics.dk
http://www.brics.dk/~mrhiger

Abstract. Functional languages have proven substantially useful for hosting embedded domain-specific languages. They provide an infrastructure rich enough to define both a convenient syntax for the embedded language, a type system for embedded programs, and an evaluation mechanism for embedded programs. However, all existing host languages either interpret embedded programs instead of compiling them or require an expensive pre-compilation phase. In this article we close this gap in an implementation of the functional language OCaml: We provide a library of OCaml byte-code combinators that is reminiscent of quasi-quotation in Lisp and of 'C and that enables just-in-time compilation of embedded programs. We illustrate these byte-code combinators on a prototypical domain-specific language.

Keywords. Just-in-time compilation, OCaml, domain-specific language, embedded language.

1   Introduction

Embedded languages have been devised as an alternative to implementing compilers for domain-specific languages [2,31]. An embedded language adds domain-specific functionality (such as domain-specific values, their types, and operations on them) to an existing general-purpose language. The general-purpose language provides the domain-independent linguistic features (such as a type system and an evaluation strategy) and the means to execute programs (such as a compiler or an interpreter). This style of programming was already envisioned in the 1960's by Landin who observed that the design of programming languages splits into "the choice of written appearances of programs" and "the choice of abstract entities that can be referred to in the language" [23,29].

Embedded languages provide practically useful compromises in both language development and application development. The language designer need not define and implement new domain-specific languages from scratch and the

---

* Funded by the Danish National Research Foundation.

S. Krishnamurthi, C. R. Ramakrishnan (Eds.): PADL 2002, LNCS 2257, pp. 120–136, 2002.

application programmer need not use general-purpose languages to solve domain-specific problems. Furthermore, embedded languages that share the same host language can easily be combined without the need for foreign-language interfaces.

Declarative languages provide powerful domain-independent linguistic features that make them well suited as host languages. Typed functional languages, such as Haskell [14] and ML [28], are particularly useful as host languages because they provide a rich infrastructure of higher-order functions, polymorphic types, and modules [20]. Like all other languages, an embedded language consists of

- a syntax of valid programs,
- a static semantics (such as, e.g., a type system), and
- a dynamic semantics (such as, e.g., a definitional interpreter or compiler).

Functional languages often enable convenient syntactic representations of embedded programs using either macro systems or a mixture of prefix and infix operators. Recent work have also shown how embedded programs can be type-checked in a statically typed host language using "phantom types" [12,15,22,24,32]. Currently, however, embedded programs must either be translated into the host languages by a pre-processor [12] or they must be executed by an interpreter implemented in the host language. (If the domain-specific operations cannot be expressed in the host language then the evaluation mechanism for embedded programs is provided by a stand-alone processor. We do not consider this third alternative.) Neither of these approaches is satisfactory. The first because integrating a pre-processor is difficult and inflexible in the presence of the interactive sessions of most functional languages. The second because it introduces an overhead of interpreting embedding programs. It would be desirable to enable direct execution of embedded programs without the burden of pre-processing and without the penalty of interpretation.

In this article we extend OCaml [27], a dialect of ML, with support for generating embedded programs directly as executable code. We provide a collection of combinators for constructing higher-order programs as OCaml byte-code instructions instead of as text and we provide the means to execute such byte-code instructions. The combinators can be used to translate an interpreter for embedded programs into a compiler that directly generates executable byte-code instructions. Existing compilers for embedded languages generate target code as program text which must be then be compiled into executable code [12]. These compilers can essentially be seen as source-to-source optimizing macro transformers. In comparison, we take one step further and generate byte-code executables directly. In addition, our approach also enables source-to-source optimizing macros.

This article uses a prototypical domain-specific language, namely regular expressions, as a running example. However, the technique presented here is directly applicable to other examples. The hitherto largest application is in specializing the term rewriter of MetaPRL, a theorem prover implemented in OCaml [32].

In Section 2 we embed regular expressions into OCaml using an interpreter. This example highlights the limitations of interpreting embedded programs. In Section 3 we present our main contribution, an implementation of byte-code combinators for OCaml. We return to embedding regular expressions into OCaml using the byte-code combinators in Section 4. In Section 5 we briefly discuss the experiments with the MetaPRL theorem prover. We outline related work in Section 6 and conclude in Section 7.

2   Interpreting Embedded Programs

Lex and Yacc-like pre-processing tools are prototypical examples of embedded domain-specific applications. They provide a practically useful alternative to implementing parsers for regular or context-free languages directly as general-purpose programs. To this end, they extend an existing general-purpose language with high-level declarations for grammars. The pre-processor compiles an embedded grammar into a parser implemented in the host language while the remaining program parts supply the code that constructs tokens or parse trees.

To illustrate embedded languages in OCaml, we consider a particularly simple variant of parsing, namely regular-expression matching. The concrete syntax of regular expressions is as follows.

$$r ::= \mathbf{0} \mid \mathbf{1} \mid c \mid r_1 + r_2 \mid r_1 r_2 \mid r^*$$

where c denotes a character symbol. The language accepted by a regular expression is defined inductively as follows. (Here, ϵ denotes the empty string.)

$$\mathcal{L}(\mathbf{0}) = \emptyset$$
$$\mathcal{L}(\mathbf{1}) = \{\epsilon\}$$
$$\mathcal{L}(c) = \{c\}$$
$$\mathcal{L}(r_1 + r_2) = \mathcal{L}(r_1) \cup \mathcal{L}(r_2)$$
$$\mathcal{L}(r_1 r_2) = \mathcal{L}(r_1)\mathcal{L}(r_2)$$
$$\mathcal{L}(r^*) = \bigcup_{i \geq 0}(\mathcal{L}(r))^i$$

For the purpose of simplification, we use a regular-expression matcher that backtracks. (An alternative is to translate a regular expression into a deterministic automaton which can be either interpreted or compiled.) Figure 1 presents the abstract syntax of regular expressions and a matching function `accept`. The matcher is applied to a regular expression, a list of characters, and a continuation. If the regular expression matches a portion of the characters then the continuation is applied to the remaining characters. Otherwise, the matcher directly returns false. The clause for r^* (`STAR`) is recursive and uses an explicit fixed-point operator. In this clause, the continuation immediately fails if matching does not progress. This extra check ensures that matching pathological regular expressions such as $\mathbf{1}^*$ terminates [7,17].

Embedding regular expressions into OCaml using an interpreter is more flexible than the Lex and Yacc-like approach where grammars are compiled into

```
type re = ZERO | ONE | CHAR of char
         | CAT of re * re | SUM of re * re | STAR of re

let rec fix f x = f (fix f) x

let rec accept re s k =
  match re with
    ZERO              -> false
  | ONE               -> k s
  | CHAR c            ->
      (match s with c'::s' -> c = c' && k s'
                  | []      -> false)
  | CAT (re1, re2) -> accept re1 s (fun s' -> accept re2 s' k)
  | SUM (re1, re2) -> accept re1 s k || accept re2 s k
  | STAR re1          ->
      fix (fun star s ->
              k s || accept re1 s
                      (fun s' -> if s==s' then false else star s'))
        s

let matches re s = accept re s (fun s' -> s' = [])
```

Fig. 1. Interpreted regular expression matching in OCaml

parsers in a pre-processing phase. The reason is that regular expressions, our notion of grammars, are first-class objects, and hence can be manipulated within OCaml. For example, instead of the cumbersome prefix data type constructors we can use infix operators such as the following.

```
let (++) re1 re2 = SUM(re1, re2)
let (@@) re1 re2 = CAT(re1, re2)
```

A regular expression such as $a(b + c)$ can then be transliterated in OCaml as

```
CHAR 'a' @@ (CHAR 'b' ++ CHAR 'c')
```

which matches the strings $\{ab, ac\}$. We can also exploit algebraic identities such as $\mathcal{L}(0 + r) = \mathcal{L}(r + 0) = \mathcal{L}(r)$ and $\mathcal{L}(1r) = \mathcal{L}(r1) = \mathcal{L}(r)$ to generate improved regular expressions. For example, alternative definitions of ++ and @@ read as follows.

```
let (++) re1 re2 =
  match re1, re2 with
    ZERO, _    -> re2
  | _,   ZERO -> re1
  | _,   _    -> SUM(re1, re2)

let (@@) re1 re2 =
```

```
match re1, re2 with
   ONE,  _     -> re2
 | _,    ONE  -> re1
 | _,    _    -> CAT(re1, re2)
```

Finally, the following two functions produce regular expressions for sums $c_1 + c_2 + \cdots + c_n$ and concatenations $c_1 c_2 \cdots c_n$ from a given string of characters "$c_1 c_2 \cdots c_n$". They serve as macros defining regular expressions for classes of characters and for sequences of characters, respectively. (Here, explode maps a string into the list of its characters.)

```
let cclass s =
  List.fold_right (++)
    (List.map (fun c -> CHAR c) (explode s))
    ZERO

let string s =
  List.fold_right (@@)
    (List.map (fun c -> CHAR c) (explode s))
    ONE
```

The regular-expression matcher may be used in a parser to recognize tokens of characters. A fragment of such a parser reads as follows. (Here we assume, for simplicity, that the input is already separated into chunks of characters).

```
let digit = cclass "0123456789"
let alpha = cclass "abcdefghijklmnopqrstuvwxyz"
let alnum = alpha ++ digit

let lex s =
  if matches ( string "if" ++ string "then" ++ string "else" ) s then
       (* Code for generating keywords *)
  else if matches ( STAR digit ) s then
       (* Code for generating numerals *)
  else if matches ( alpha @@ STAR alnum ) s then
       (* Code for generating identifiers *)
  ...
  else error "Unexpected token"
```

However, such a function inherits an interpretive overhead from matching regular expressions against a string. In the following section we develop the machinery that enables us to compile regular expressions (and other embedded programs) into efficient OCaml code.

3   Run-Time Byte-Code Generation in OCaml

The implementation of OCaml consists of a byte-code compiler and a runtime system with a virtual machine for running byte-code executables. The compiler is implemented in OCaml and the run-time system is implemented in C. The run-time system consists of a byte-code interpreter, a garbage collector, and a set of pre-defined library procedures.

The byte-code compiler consists of modules each implementing a phase. The initial input is a stream of characters, either read from a file (in batch mode) or from standard input (in interactive mode). Each phase produces a refined representation of the source program.

- Lexical analysis and parsing: Together, lexical analysis and parsing read a sequence of characters and produce an abstract-syntax tree.
- Type analysis: This phase type-checks the source program. It produces a type-annotated abstract-syntax tree.
- Semantics-preserving translation: This phase translates OCaml expressions into an extended λ-calculus. The major difference between an OCaml expression and a λ-term is that modules and functors are represented as tuples and higher-order functions in the λ-terms.
- Code generation: This phase produces a list of symbolic byte-code instructions from a λ-term.
- Byte-code emission: This phase writes a list of symbolic byte-code instructions to a file (in batch mode) or into memory (in interactive mode).

Since OCaml is an interactive system, the compiler is present during all stages of execution. It is our intention to use parts of the OCaml compiler to generate byte-code instructions directly for embedded programs. The first step is therefore to translate embedded programs into a suitable representation of OCaml programs. There are several viable representations of OCaml programs corresponding to the input to each of the phases described above. (We describe the translation technique itself in Section 4.) At the extremes, we can represent programs as their text and pass them though all phases, from lexical analysis and parsing to byte-code emission, or we can represent programs as symbolic byte-code instructions and pass them through only the byte-code emission phase. Neither of these approaches are satisfactory, however: Passing programs through the entire compiler is typically too costly and generating byte-code instructions directly is typically too cumbersome.

As a convenient intermediate representation of OCaml programs, we shall instead choose the λ-terms that are input to the code generation phase. These terms are defined by the following data type in the compiler.

```
type lambda =
      Lvar         of Ident.t
    | Lconst       of structured_constant
    | Lapply       of lambda * lambda list
    | Lfunction    of function_kind * Ident.t list * lambda
    | Llet         of let_kind * Ident.t * lambda * lambda
    | Lprim        of primitive * lambda list
    | Lifthenelse  of lambda * lambda * lambda
    | Lsequence    of lambda * lambda
    | ...
```

The compiler provides a function

```
val comp_expr :
    env -> lambda -> int
      -> instruction list -> instruction list
```

for compiling λ-terms. Here, `env` is the type of compilation environments and `instruction` is the type of symbolic byte-code instructions. The call

comp_expr env exp sz cont

compiles an expression *exp* in compilation environment *env*, in a stack frame of size *sz*, and where *cont* is the list of instructions to execute afterwards (i.e., a byte-code representation of the continuation of the expression). The result is a list of instructions that evaluate *exp* and then perform *cont*.

The data type `lambda` defines an abstract-syntax tree of λ-terms. It provides a representation of programs which is more flexible than a representation of symbolic byte-code instructions. For example, identifiers are represented by their name (`Ident.t`) instead of by their position on the run-time stack and functions are represented as λ-abstractions (`Lfunction`) instead of as closures. However, λ-terms are constructed as abstract-syntax trees only to be mapped into byte-code instructions by the function `comp_expr` immediately afterwards. We eliminate the syntax dispatch of `comp_expr` by using a non-standard *Church-encoded* representation of λ-terms. To this end, λ-term are constructed by *byte-code combinators* instead of by data-type constructors.

A byte-code combinator is a triple that encapsulates enough information that it can be reassembled into a sequence of byte-code instructions.

1. A byte-code combinator carries a list of the variables that occur free in the expression it represents. Such a list is used to construct the byte-code instructions for creating closures.
2. If a byte-code combinator represents a variable, then it carries the name of that variable. This information is used in generating byte-code combinators for let-expressions that preserve tail calls. Instead of generating byte-code instructions corresponding to an expression let x = E in x they generate simply the byte-code instructions corresponding to E.
3. A byte-code combinator carries a function that generates the actual byte-code instructions. It takes two arguments, an environment mapping variable names to stack or environment positions and a byte-code representation of the continuation. It adds code for the current byte-code combinator to the front of the continuation.

Byte-code combinators efficiently support two key operations, namely concatenation of byte-code instructions and instantiation of free variables. When the code-generating function of a complete byte-code combinator is applied to an environment and a continuation, byte-code instructions are generated in a backwards manner using the continuation and the positions of variables are resolved using the environment. There is no copying of the generated byte-code

```
let mkint i =
  ([],
   None,
   fun(rho, k) ->
     Kconst(Lambda.Const_base(Asttypes.Const_int i)) :: k)

let mkapp (vsa, _, fa) ((vsb, _, fb) as arg) =
  (union(vsa, vsb),
   None,
   function
       (rho, Kreturn n :: k)          ->
         fb(rho, Kpush :: fa(installTmp rho, Kappterm(1, n+1) :: k))
     | (rho, Kappterm(i, j) :: k) ->
         fb(rho, Kpush :: fa(installTmp rho, Kappterm(i+1, j+1) :: k))
     | (rho, k)                        ->
         fb(rho, Kpush :: fa(installTmp rho, Kapply 1 :: k)))
```

Fig. 2. Example byte-code combinators for integers and applications

instructions and they are not traversed once they are created. The type of byte-code combinators, `exp`, is as follows.

```
type code = instruction list
type exp  = ide list * ide option * (env * code -> code)
```

For byte-code combinators involving variables and bindings (such as variables, λ-abstractions, and let-expressions) we provide both a low-level first-order interface and a higher-order interface similar to a higher-order abstract syntax [30]. The low-level interface allows direct generation and manipulation of variables, λ-abstractions, and let-expressions. The higher-order interface groups common patterns involving bindings into convenient functions. In addition to the following byte-code combinators, we have implemented byte-code combinators for operations on tuples, lists, integers, booleans, strings, mutable data structures, and global variables.

```
mkint  : int -> exp
mkapp  : exp -> exp -> exp
mklam  : (exp -> exp) -> exp
mklet  : exp -> (exp -> exp) -> exp
mkif   : exp -> exp -> exp -> exp
...
```

Figure 2 show the byte-code combinators for generating integers and applications. The byte-code combinator for applications generates optimized tail calls and it groups together several curried calls into one instruction. These byte-code combinators generate the following instructions.

Kconst p:	Loads the accumulator with the operand p.
Kpush:	Pushes the contents of the accumulator onto the stack.
Kappterm(i, j):	Performs a tail call with i arguments and where the current stack frame contains j elements.
Kapply i:	Performs an ordinary non-tail call with i arguments.
Kreturn n:	Removes n arguments from the stack and then pops a saved return address and a saved environment off the stack.

On the average, the definition of a byte-code combinator requires less than 8 lines of OCaml code and it typically generates between 3 and 6 instructions. Experiments show that the byte-code combinators typically generate up to 170000 byte-code instructions per second [32].

To run a byte-code combinator, its code-generating function is first applied to an empty environment and a continuation consisting only of a return instruction. The result is a list of symbolic instructions. Using functions provided by OCaml's interactive run-time system, the list of symbolic instructions is then written to the memory in the form of executable byte-code instructions. We use the following two auxiliary functions as a front-end to the internals of the run-time system.

```
run_code : instruction list -> 'a
run_exp  : exp  -> 'a
```

The function run_code writes a list of symbolic byte-code instructions to the memory, relocates global pointers in the allocated block, and passes it to the virtual machine for execution. The function run_exp instantiates a byte-code combinator and executes the resulting list of instructions. It is defined in terms of run_code as follows.

```
let run_exp (_, _, f) = run_code (f ([], [Kreturn 1]))
```

Together, byte-code combinators and run_exp support run-time code generation in the same way as Lisp-like S-expressions and eval [3].

4   Compiling Embedded Programs

We return to the regular-expression matcher from Section 2 but now using the byte-code combinators to compile regular expressions instead of interpreting them. To this end, we derive a compiler for regular expressions from the interpreter presented in Figure 1 using standard partial-evaluation techniques [21]. Such a compiler is the "generating extension" of the regular-expression matcher and can be obtained by self-applying a partial evaluator [16]. However, when the operations executed at translation time and those executed at run time are cleanly separated, which is indeed the case with the regular-expression matcher, then a generating extension can simply be obtained from the interpreter by replacing run-time operations with code-generating operations. We use byte-code combinators as code-generating primitives.

```
let rec mkaccept re s k =
  match re with
    ZERO          -> mkfalse
  | ONE           -> k s
  | CHAR c        ->
      mkif (mknull s)
        mkfalse
        (mkand (mkeqint (mkint (int_of_char c)) (mkhd s))
               (mklet (mktl s) (fun s' -> k s')))
  | CAT (re1, re2) -> mkaccept re1 s (fun s' -> mkaccept re2 s' k)
  | SUM (re1, re2) ->
      generalize k
        (fun k' -> mkor (mkaccept re1 s k') (mkaccept re2 s k'))
  | STAR re1      ->
      mkapp (mkfix (mklam2 (fun star s ->
                      mkor (k s)
                           (mkaccept re1 s (fun s' ->
                             mkif (mkeqint s s')
                               mkfalse
                               (mkapp star s'))))))
            s

let mkmatches re : char list -> bool =
  run_exp (mklam (fun s -> mkaccept re s (fun s' -> mknull s')))
```

Fig. 3. Embedded compiler for regular expressions

The compiler for regular expressions is shown in Figure 3. In partial-evaluation terminology, the regular expression is "static", the list of characters "dynamic", and continuations are static functions on dynamic arguments (lists of characters) producing dynamic results (booleans). Hence, we have systematically replaced operations on lists of characters by the equivalent byte-code combinators. Apart from the byte-code combinators already mentioned in Section 3, we also use byte-code combinators for generating booleans (mkfalse and mktrue), short-circuit boolean conjunction and disjunction (mkand and mkor, defined in terms of mkif), integer comparison (mkeqint), and fixed-point operators (mkfix, defined in terms of the global variable fix).

Generating extensions for continuation-passing style programs often face the problem of code duplication: When a static continuation is applied twice its corresponding code may be inlined twice in the generated program. In the regular expression compiler, continuations are passed to both recursive calls in the clause for SUM. Therefore, to avoid code duplication, this continuation is bound and inlined in the generated program using the following generalization directive which produces a standard two-level η-redex.

```
let generalize k f = mklet (mklam k) (fun k' -> f (mkapp k'))
```

```
        closure L1, 0        ; fun s ->
        return 1             ;
L1:     acc 0                ;    if null s
        push                 ;
        const 0a             ;
        eqint                ;
        branchifnot L4       ;
        const 0a             ;    then false
        branch L2            ;
L4:     acc 0                ;    else if 97 = hd s
        getfield 0           ;
        push                 ;
        const 97             ;
        eqint                ;
        branchifnot L3       ;
        acc 0                ;       then let s' = tl s
        getfield 1           ;
        push                 ;
        acc 0                ;          in
        push                 ;
        const 0a             ;
        eqint                ;             null s'
        pop 1                ;
        branch L2            ;
L3:     const 0a             ;       else false
L2:     return 1             ;
```

Fig. 4. Byte-code instructions for the regular expression a.

The main function of the regular-expression compiler generates and evaluates the byte-code combinator corresponding to a given regular expression. It has the type

```
mkmatches : re -> char list -> bool
```

which agrees with the type of the interpreter for regular expressions.

As an example, Figure 4 shows the byte-code instructions corresponding to the regular expression a. (The ASCII code for the character a is 97.) Matching compiled regular expressions using Figure 3 is more efficient than matching interpreted regular expressions using Figure 1. For example, matching the regular expression language against the first 600 words in this article takes 3.09 ms (milliseconds) using the interpreted version and 1.33 ms using the compiled version. (The measures were performed on an IBM ThinkPad 600 equipped with a 266MHz Pentium II processor and 96 Mb of RAM and which runs RedHat Linux 2.2.1. We have not measured the space usage. The running times are averaged over 1000 runs.) Matching the regular expression $\{a, b, c, d, e, k, l, m, n\}^*$ against the same 600 words takes 23.08 ms using the interpreted version and 13.73 ms using the compiled version.

The generated byte codes are executed by the OCaml virtual machine that itself runs "at native speed." Thus, in the example presented here, a regular expression is matched by interpreting its byte-code counterpart (using the OCaml virtual machine). In comparison, we can compile the original regular-expression matcher using OCaml's native-code compiler. A regular expression is then matched by interpreting its abstract syntax (using the original matcher). Both cases have "one level" of interpretive overhead. The latter approach yields running times 0.40 ms and 2.61 ms for the regular expressions language and $\{a, b, c, d, e, k, l, m, n\}^*$, respectively. Thus, in these cases, directly interpreting regular expressions (at native speed) is faster that interpreting their compiled byte-code counterparts (at native speed).

5   Application: The MetaPRL Term Rewriter

One application area for run-time code generation is in the proof-search engines of automated theorem provers. Higher-order logical frameworks provide an expressive foundation for reasoning about formal systems. They permit concise problem descriptions and re-use of logical models. MetaPRL is a logical programming environment that combines OCaml with a higher-order logical framework [18]. The MetaPRL tactic prover consists of a proof editor, logic definitions, and a refiner. The logic definitions describes the language of a logic. It also contains *primitive inference rules* that define axioms and theorems of the logic, *rewrites* that define computational equivalences, and *theorems* which provide proofs for derived inference rules and axioms. Inference rules are compiled to a byte-code language. The refiner interprets the byte-code instructions during rule application and term rewriting.

Since reasoning about programs is expensive, it is crucial that proof searching is efficient. To this end, MetaPRL provides specialized implementations for the parts of a logic, such as term representations and proof-search strategies [19]. Furthermore, the set of inference rules is fixed for a particular proof search so the term rewriter can be specialized to the set of inference rules at the time a proof search is initiated.

We have applied the byte-code combinators presented in this article to specialize MetaPRL's term rewriter. Similar to the above, we have implemented the generating extension of the term rewriter in a straightforward manner. MetaPRL applies the term rewriter rather extensively. For example, reducing a factorial function with an argument of 100 requires several hundred thousands of rewrites of a total of around 1500 rewrites. Thus, it is eminently reasonable to specialize the term rewriter to the rewrites. We are currently working on benchmarks for these experiments.

6 Related Work

Elliot, Finne, and de Moor present an embedded compiler for a first-order language [12]. They base their compiler on macros that exploit algebraic identities to generate efficient source programs and on a separate back-end for code generation. In comparison, we have presented a general approach to evaluating embedded programs that enables programs to be interpreted or compiled directly into byte-code executables at run time.

Sperber and Thiemann present a run-time specializer for Scheme that generates byte code [33]. They have composed an existing partial evaluator for Scheme with an existing Scheme compiler producing byte code [35]. Their run-time specializer does not construct intermediate residual programs as text. Instead, they have obtained a set of byte-code combinators directly from the Scheme compiler by deforesting the data type of abstract-syntax trees. The result is a set of byte-code combinators similar to those presented in this article. Sperber and Thiemann use byte-code combinators to built residual programs in a partial evaluator whereas we suggest to use them directly to built generating extensions (i.e. compilers) from interpreters. Conceptually, both Sperber and Thiemann's combinators and the combinators presented in this article can be obtained from the (recursively descending) compilers for Scheme and OCaml, respectively. For practical purposes, however, both sets of combinators have been written by hand. (In fact, Sperber and Thiemann start out with a handwritten compiler for a subset of Scheme.)

Balat and Danvy have designed a run-time specializer for OCaml using type-directed partial evaluation [1]. They have composed standard type-directed partial evaluation with a compiler from normal forms into OCaml byte code. They have exploited the fact that normal forms form a subset of full OCaml to implement a fast dedicated compiler. In contrast, we do not use a compiler but integrate the generation of byte-code instructions into the byte-code combinators.

In dialects of Lisp, quasi-quotation and `eval` provide an interface to generating programs as S-expressions and executing them at run time [3]. S-expressions may be "taken apart" and they may contain nested applications of `eval` and nested quasiquatations. Together, S-expressions, quasiquatations, and `eval` therefore allows for "peep-hole optimizing" code at run-time before executing it and they support multi-stage code generation. In comparison, the byte-code combinators presented in this article do not support multi-level code generation and they may not be taken apart. In order to provide an `eval` procedure, the Lisp compiler or interpreter must coexist with the run-time system. In comparison, executing a byte-code combinator only require a simple translation of symbolic instructions into (integer) byte codes. Hence, the OCaml compiler need not coexist at run-time and our solution can be used with compiled OCaml programs.

Traditional macro preprocessors, such as CamlP4 for OCaml and the macro systems of most dialects Lisp, sometimes support program specialization at compile time. However, since macros are expanded at compile time, these macro systems do not provide run-time specialization or run-time code generation. For example, it is not possible for a standard macro preprocessor alone to generate specialized regular-expression matchers based on regular expressions input by the user. This is exactly achieved by some form of run-time code generation such as `eval` or the byte-code combinators presented in this article.

'C is an extension of the C language with Lisp-like quasi-quotation for specifying dynamically generated code [13]. The main concerns of 'C is generating efficient code at run time with as little overhead as possible. 'C generates machine code instead of byte code as in this work.

Tempo is a run-time specialization systems for C [4]. Based on an initial binding-time signature, Tempo splits the source program into static and dynamic parts. While the dynamic parts do contain unknowns, they can be compiled into binary code by an almost standard C compiler. From the binding-time annotations the static compiler also generates a *template* that specifies how the pre-compiled blocks should be re-assembled at run time. When the source program is split into few large blocks, they may provide enough flow information that an optimizing C compiler can generate efficient code for them. In contrast, byte-code programs, such as those generated by the byte-code combinators that we present, are difficult to optimize since the set of instructions is highly specialized. Instead, byte-code run-time systems often provide a fast virtual machine.

The Fabius system by Leone and Lee is a run-time code generator of machine code for a first-order subset of ML [25,26]. Fabius specializes curried functions to their first argument using standard partial evaluation techniques: Given an application $f\ a$ in the source program, Fabius constructs the generating extension of f at compile time. The generating extension is then applied to the argument a at run time to produce the executable code corresponding the specialized version of f with respect to a. In comparison, our system generates byte code and is not restricted to specializing curried functions.

There is a strong similarity between an interpreter and its generating extension [6,29]. Both can be expressed as a fold function over the data type for the input language. The only structural difference is that the interpreter uses evaluating primitives while the compiler uses code-generating primitives for operations on run-time values. We can emphasize this binding-time separation by parameterizing an interpreter over a collection of primitives. Type-directed partial evaluation precisely expect such binding-time separated programs as input [5]. By instantiating the parameterized interpreter with either evaluating or code-generating primitives we obtain an interpreter or a compiler that generates executable code directly. Furthermore, by instantiating the interpreter with primitives that generate a textual representation of programs (such as a data type of OCaml terms) we obtain a translator that generates OCaml programs. Hence, this parameterized approach is able to express both pre-processing, interpretation, and just-in-time compilation. Using OCaml's module system we can conveniently represent parameterized interpreters as functors and primitives as modules.

We have also used the byte-code combinators presented in this article as a code-generating back-end for a type-directed partial evaluator [32]. The result is a run-time specializer for typed higher-order programs. Using this system, we have successfully specialized the term rewriter in the back-end of a large theorem prover [18].

In typed languages that support program manipulation it is desirable that only well-typed programs are generated. Static typing in the context of run-time code generation, however, is still somewhat of an open problem. Davies's $\lambda^{\bigcirc}$-calculus [8], motivated by linear-time temporal logic, provides a type system able to describe standard partial evaluation. However, in $\lambda^{\bigcirc}$, there is no way to express immediate evaluation of sub-terms because generated programs may contain free variables. Davies and Pfenning's $\lambda^{\square}$-calculus [9], motivated by modal logic, provides a type system for manipulating closed program. In $\lambda^{\square}$, direct evaluation of generated programs can be expressed but these often contain administrative redexes [10]. At any rate, neither $\lambda^{\bigcirc}$ nor $\lambda^{\square}$ have been designed for a strict language with mutable state such as OCaml.

7   Conclusions

The ability to generate code at run time can increase the efficiency of embedded programs while retaining their flexibility. We have designed a set of byte-code combinators for directly generating OCaml byte-code instructions. The implementation is integrated in the latest version of the OCaml compiler. It consists of less than 500 lines of OCaml code.

The byte-code combinators can be used as code-generating primitives for deriving a compiler, or generating extension, from an interpreter. This style of programming amounts to implementing generating extensions by hand and occurs in macro-systems and partial evaluation. We have illustrated this programming style using a regular-expression matcher but it also applies to other embedded languages.

Acknowledgements

The author would like to thank the anonymous referees for constructive suggestions and Olivier Danvy for extensive comments.

References

1. Vincent Balat and Olivier Danvy. Strong normalization by type-directed partial evaluation and run-time code generation. In Xavier Leroy and Atsushi Ohori, editors, *Proceedings of the Second International Workshop on Types in Compilation*, number 1473 in Lecture Notes in Computer Science, pages 240–252, Kyoto, Japan, March 1998. 132
2. Thomas Ball, editor. *Proceedings of the Second USENIX Conference on Domain-Specific Languages*, Austin, Texas, October 1999. 120
3. Alan Bawden. Quasiquotation in Lisp. In Olivier Danvy, editor, *Proceedings of the ACM SIGPLAN Workshop on Partial Evaluation and Semantics-Based Program Manipulation*, number NS–99–1 in BRICS Note Series, pages 4–12, San Antonio, Texas, January 1999. 128, 132

4. Charles Consel and François Noël. A general approach for run-time specialization and its application to C. In Steele [34], pages 145–156. 133

5. Olivier Danvy. Type-directed partial evaluation. In John Hatcliff, Torben Æ. Mogensen, and Peter Thiemann, editors, *Partial Evaluation – Practice and Theory; Proceedings of the 1998 DIKU Summer School*, number 1706 in Lecture Notes in Computer Science, pages 367–411, Copenhagen, Denmark, July 1998. Springer-Verlag. 133

6. Olivier Danvy. Programming techniques for partial evaluation. In Friedrich L. Bauer and Ralf Steinbrüggen, editors, *Foundations of Secure Computation*, NATO Science series, pages 287–318. IOS Press Ohmsha, 2000. 133

7. Olivier Danvy and Lasse R. Nielsen. Defunctionalization at work. In Harald Søndergaard, editor, *Proceedings of the Third International Conference on Principles and Practice of Declarative Programming*, Firenze, Italy, September 2001. ACM Press. To appear. 122

8. Rowan Davies. A temporal-logic approach to binding-time analysis. In Edmund M. Clarke, editor, *Proceedings of the Eleventh Annual IEEE Symposium on Logic in Computer Science*, pages 184–195, New Brunswick, New Jersey, July 1996. IEEE Computer Society Press. 134

9. Rowan Davies and Frank Pfenning. A modal analysis of staged computation. In Steele [34], pages 258–283. 134

10. Rowan Davies and Frank Pfenning. A modal analysis of staged computation. Technical report CMU–CS–99–153, School of Computer Science, Carnegie Mellon University, Pittsburgh, Pennsylvania, 1999. To appear in JACM. 134

11. Premkumar Devanbu and Jeff Poulin, editors. *Proceedings of the Fifth International Conference on Software Reuse*, Victoria, British Columbia, June 1998. IEEE Computer Society Press. 136

12. Conal Elliott, Sigbjorn Finne, and Oege de Moor. Compiling embedded languages. In Walid Taha, editor, *Proceedings of the International Workshop on Semantics, Applications, and Implementation of Program Generation*, number 1924 in Lecture Notes in Computer Science, pages 9–27, Montréal, Canada, September 2000. 121, 132

13. Dawson R. Engler, Wilson C. Hsieh, and M. Frans Kaashoek. 'C: A language for high-level, efficient, and machine-independent dynamic code generation. In Steele [34], pages 131–144. 133

14. Joseph H. Fasel, Paul Hudak, Simon Peyton Jones, and Philip Wadler. Haskell special issue. *SIGPLAN Notices*, 27(5), May 1992. 121

15. Sigbjorn Finne, Daan Leijen, Erik Meijer, and Simon Peyton Jones. Calling hell from heaven and heaven from hell. In Peter Lee, editor, *Proceedings of the 1999 ACM SIGPLAN International Conference on Functional Programming*, pages 114–125, Paris, France, September 1999. ACM Press. 121

16. Yoshihiko Futamura. Partial evaluation of computation process – an approach to a compiler-compiler. *Higher-Order and Symbolic Computation*, 12(4):381–391, 1999. Reprinted from Systems, Computers, Controls 2(5), 1971. 128

17. Robert Harper. Proof-directed debugging. *Journal of Functional Programming*, 9(4):463–469, July 1999. 122

18. Jason Hickey. Nuprl-light: An implementation framework for higher-order logics. In William McCune, editor, *14th International Conference on Automated Deduction*, number 1249 in Lecture Notes in Artificial Intelligence, pages 395–399. Springer-Verlag, 1997. 131, 134

19. Jason J. Hickey and Aleksey Nogin. Fast tactic-based theorem proving. In J. Harrison and M. Aagaard, editors, *Theorem Proving in Higher Order Logics: 13th International Conference, TPHOLs 2000*, volume 1869 of *Lecture Notes in Computer Science*, pages 252–266. Springer-Verlag, 2000. 131

20. Paul Hudak. Modular domain specific languages and tools. In Devanbu and Poulin [11], pages 134–142. 121

21. Neil D. Jones, Carsten K. Gomard, and Peter Sestoft. *Partial Evaluation and Automatic Program Generation*. Prentice Hall International Series in Computer Science. Prentice-Hall, 1993. Available online at
http://www.dina.kvl.dk/~sestoft/pebook/pebook.html. 128

22. Simon Peyton Jones, Erik Meijer, and Daan Leijen. Scripting COM components in Haskell. In Devanbu and Poulin [11], pages 224–233. 121

23. Peter J. Landin. The next 700 programming languages. *Communications of the ACM*, 9(3):157–166, 1966. 120

24. Daan Leijen and Erik Meijer. Domain specific embedded compilers. In Thomas Ball, editor, *Proceedings of the 2nd USENIX Conference on Domain-Specific Languages*, pages 109–122, 1999. 121

25. Mark Leone and Peter Lee. Lightweight run-time code generation. In Peter Sestoft and Harald Søndergaard, editors, *Proceedings of the ACM SIGPLAN Workshop on Partial Evaluation and Semantics-Based Program Manipulation*, Technical Report 94/9, University of Melbourne, Australia, pages 97–106, Orlando, Florida, June 1994. 133

26. Mark Leone and Peter Lee. Optimizing ML with run-time code generation. In *Proceedings of the ACM SIGPLAN'96 Conference on Programming Languages Design and Implementation*, SIGPLAN Notices, Vol. 31, No 5, pages 137–148. ACM Press, May 1996. 133

27. Xavier Leroy. *The Objective Caml system, release 3.01*. INRIA, Rocquencourt, France, March 2001. 121

28. Robin Milner, Mads Tofte, Robert Harper, and David MacQueen. *The Definition of Standard ML (Revised)*. The MIT Press, 1997. 121

29. Lockwood Morris. The next 700 formal language descriptions. *Lisp and Symbolic Computation*, 6(3/4):249–258, 1993. 120, 133

30. Frank Pfenning and Conal Elliott. Higher-order abstract syntax. In Mayer D. Schwartz, editor, *Proceedings of the ACM SIGPLAN'88 Conference on Programming Languages Design and Implementation*, SIGPLAN Notices, Vol. 23, No 7, pages 199–208, Atlanta, Georgia, June 1988. ACM Press. 127

31. Chris Ramming, editor. *Proceedings of the First USENIX Conference on Domain-Specific Languages*, Santa Barbara, California, October 1997. 120

32. Morten Rhiger. *Higher-Order Program Generation*. PhD thesis, BRICS PhD School, University of Aarhus, Aarhus, Denmark, July 2001. 121, 128, 133

33. Michael Sperber and Peter Thiemann. Two for the price of one: composing partial evaluation and compilation. In Ron K. Cytron, editor, *Proceedings of the ACM SIGPLAN'97 Conference on Programming Languages Design and Implementation*, SIGPLAN Notices, Vol. 32, No 5, pages 215–225, Las Vegas, Nevada, June 1997. ACM Press. 132

34. Guy L. Steele, editor. *Proceedings of the Twenty-Third Annual ACM Symposium on Principles of Programming Languages*, St. Petersburg Beach, Florida, January 1996. ACM Press. 135

35. Peter Thiemann. Combinators for program generation. *Journal of Functional Programming*, 9(5):483–525, 1999. 132

Typed Combinators for Generic Traversal

Ralf Lämmel[1,2] and Joost Visser[1]

[1] CWI
Kruislaan 413, NL-1098 SJ Amsterdam
Phone: +31 20 592 {4090|4266}, Fax: +31 20 592 4199
{Ralf.Laemmel,Joost.Visser}@cwi.nl
http://www.cwi.nl/~{ralf,jvisser}
[2] Vrije Universiteit
De Boelelaan 1081a, NL-1081 HV Amsterdam

Abstract. Lacking support for generic traversal, functional programming languages suffer from a scalability problem when applied to large-scale program transformation problems. As a solution, we introduce *functional strategies*: typeful generic functions that not only can be applied to terms of any type, but which also allow generic traversal into subterms. We show how strategies are modelled inside a functional language, and we present a combinator library including generic traversal combinators. We illustrate our technique of programming with functional strategies by an implementation of the *extract method* refactoring for Java.

Keywords: Genericity, traversal, combinators, program transformation

1 Introduction

Our domain of interest is program transformation in the context of software re-engineering [4,2,3]. Particular problems include automated refactoring (e.g., removal of duplicated code, or goto elimination) and conversion (e.g., Cobol 74 to 85, or Euro conversion). In this context, the bulk of the functionality consists of traversal over the syntax of the involved languages. Most problems call for various different traversal schemes. The involved syntaxes are typically complex (50-2000 grammar productions), and often one has to cope with evolving languages, diverging dialects, and embedded languages. In such a setting, genericity regarding traversal is indispensable [3,15].

By lack of support for generic term traversal, functional programming suffers from a serious and notoriously ignored scalability problem when applied to program transformation problems. To remedy this situation, we introduce functional *strategies*: generic functions that cannot only (i) be applied to terms of any type, but which also (ii) allow generic traversal into subterms, and (iii) may exhibit non-generic (ad-hoc) behaviour for particular types.[1] We show how

---

[1] We use the term *generic* in the general sense of type- or syntax-independent, not in the stricter senses of parametric polymorphism or polytypism. In fact, the genericity of functional strategies goes beyond these stricter senses.

S. Krishnamurthi, C. R. Ramakrishnan (Eds.): PADL 2002, LNCS 2257, pp. 137–154, 2002.
© Springer-Verlag Berlin Heidelberg 2002

these strategies can be modelled inside the functional language Haskell[2], and we present a strategy combinator library that includes traversal combinators.

A generic traversal problem Let us consider a simple traversal problem and its solution. Assume we want to accumulate all the variables on use sites in a given abstract syntax tree of a Java program. We envision a traversal which is independent of the Java syntax except that it must be able to identify Java variables on use sites. Here is a little Java fragment:

```
//print details
System.out.println("name:" + _name);
System.out.println("amount" + amount);
```

For this fragment, the traversal should return the list ["_name","amount"] of variables on use sites.

Using the techniques to be presented in this paper, the desired traversal can be modelled with a function of the following type:

$$collectUseVars \quad :: \quad TU \; Maybe \; [String]$$

Here, *TU Maybe* [*String*] is the type of *type-unifying* generic functions which map terms of any type to a list of *String*s. The *Maybe* monad is used to model partiality. In general, a function f of type *TU m a* can be applied to a term of *any* type to yield a result of type a (of a monadic type $m \; a$ to be precise). Besides type-unifying strategies, we will later encounter so-called *type-preserving* strategies where input and output type coincide.

The definition of *collectUseVars* can be based on a simple and completely generic traversal scheme of the following name and type:

$$collect \quad :: \quad MonadPlus \; m \Rightarrow TU \; m \; [a] \to TU \; m \; [a]$$

The strategy combinator *collect* maps a type-unifying strategy intended for identification of collectable entities in a node to a type-unifying strategy performing the actual collection over the entire syntax tree. This traversal combinator is included in our library. We can use the combinator in the following manner to collect Java variables on use sites:

$$
\begin{array}{lll}
collectUseVars & :: & TU \; Maybe \; [String] \\
collectUseVars & = & collect \; (monoTU \; useVar) \\[4pt]
useVar & :: & Expression \to Maybe \; [String] \\
useVar \; (Identifier \; i) & = & Just \; [i] \\
useVar \; \_ & = & Nothing
\end{array}
$$

The non-generic, monomorphic function *useVar* identifies variable names in Java expressions. To make it suitable as an argument to *collect*, it is turned into a type-unifying generic function by feeding it to the combinator *monoTU*. The resulting traversal *collectUseVars* can be applied to any kind of Java program fragment, and it will return the variables identified by *useVar*. Note that the constructor functions *Just* and *Nothing* are used to construct a value of the *Maybe* datatype to represent the list of identified variables.

---

[2] Throughout the paper we use Haskell 98 [10], unless stated otherwise.

Generic functional programming Note that the code above does not mention any of Java's syntactical constructs except the syntax of identifiers relevant to the problem. Traversal over the other constructs is accomplished with the fully generic traversal scheme *collect*. As a consequence of this genericity, the solution to our example program is extremely concise and declarative. In general, functional strategies can be employed in a scalable way to construct programs that operate on large syntaxes. In the sequel, we will demonstrate how generic combinators like *collect* are defined and how they are used to construct generic functional programs that solve non-trivial program transformation problems.

Structure of the paper In Section 2 we model strategies with abstract data types (ADTs) to be implemented later, and we explain the primitive and defined strategy combinators offered by our strategy library. In Section 3, we illustrate the utility of generic traversal combinators for actual programming by an implementation of an automated program refactoring. In Section 4, we study two implementations for the strategy ADTs, namely an implementation based on a universal term representation, and an implementation that relies on rank-2 polymorphism and type case. The paper is concluded in Section 5.

Acknowledgements We are grateful to Johan Jeuring for discussions on the subject.

2   A Strategy Library

We present a library for generic programming with strategies. To this end, we introduce ADTs with primitive combinators for strategies (i.e., generic functions). For the moment, we consider the representation of strategies as opaque since different models are possible as we will see in Section 4. The primitive combinators cover concepts we are used to for ordinary functions, namely application and sequential composition. There are further important facets of strategies, namely partiality or non-determinism, and access to the immediate subterms of a given term. Especially the latter facet makes clear that strategies go beyond parametric polymorphism. A complete overview of all primitive strategy combinators is shown in Figure 1. In the running text we will provide definitions of a number of defined strategies, including some traversal schemes.

2.1   Strategy Types and Application

There are two kinds of strategies. Firstly, the ADT *TP* m models type-preserving strategies where the result of a strategy application to a term of type t is of type $m\ t$. Secondly, the ADT *TU* m a models type-unifying strategies where the result of strategy application is always of type $m\ a$ regardless of the type of the input term. These contracts are expressed by the types of the corresponding combinators *applyTP* and *applyTU* for strategy application (*cf.* Figure 1). In both cases, m is a monad parameter [22] to deal with effects in strategies such as state passing or non-determinism. Also note that we do not apply strategies

Strategy types (opaque)

data *Monad m*	$\Rightarrow$	*TP m* = ... *abstract*
data *Monad m*	$\Rightarrow$	*TU m a* = ... *abstract*

Strategy application

applyTP :: (*Monad m*, *Term t*)	$\Rightarrow$	*TP m* → *t* → *m t*
applyTU :: (*Monad m*, *Term t*)	$\Rightarrow$	*TU m a* → *t* → *m a*

Strategy construction

polyTP :: *Monad m*	$\Rightarrow$	(∀x. *x* → *m x*) → *TP m*
polyTU :: *Monad m*	$\Rightarrow$	(∀x. *x* → *m a*) → *TU m a*
adhocTP :: (*Monad m*, *Term t*)	$\Rightarrow$	*TP m* → (*t* → *m t*) → *TP m*
adhocTU :: (*Monad m*, *Term t*)	$\Rightarrow$	*TU m a* → (*t* → *m a*) → *TU m a*

Sequential composition

seqTP :: *Monad m*	$\Rightarrow$	*TP m* → *TP m* → *TP m*
letTP :: *Monad m*	$\Rightarrow$	*TU m a* → (*a* → *TP m*) → *TP m*
seqTU :: *Monad m*	$\Rightarrow$	*TP m* → *TU m a* → *TU m a*
letTU :: *Monad m*	$\Rightarrow$	*TU m a* → (*a* → *TU m b*) → *TU m b*

Choice

choiceTP :: *MonadPlus m*	$\Rightarrow$	*TP m* → *TP m* → *TP m*
choiceTU :: *MonadPlus m*	$\Rightarrow$	*TU m a* → *TU m a* → *TU m a*

Traversal combinators

allTP :: *Monad m*	$\Rightarrow$	*TP m* → *TP m*
oneTP :: *MonadPlus m*	$\Rightarrow$	*TP m* → *TP m*
allTU :: (*Monad m*, *Monoid a*)	$\Rightarrow$	*TU m a* → *TU m a*
oneTU :: *MonadPlus m*	$\Rightarrow$	*TU m a* → *TU m a*

Fig. 1. Primitive strategy combinators

to arbitrary types but only to instances of the class *Term* for term types. This is sensible since we ultimately want to traverse into subterms.

The strategy application combinators serve to turn a generic functional strategy into a non-generic function which can be applied to a term of a specific type. Recall that the introductory example is a type-unifying traversal with the result type [*String*]. It can be applied to a given Java class declaration *myClassDecl* of type *ClassDeclaration* as follows:

applyTU collectUseVars myClassDecl :: *Maybe* [*String*]

Prerequisite for this code to work is that an instance of the class *Term* is available for *ClassDeclaration*. This issue will be taken up in Section 4.

2.2   Strategy Construction

There are two ways to construct strategies from ordinary functions. Firstly, one can turn a parametric polymorphic function into a strategy (*cf. polyTP* and *polyTU* in Figure 1). Secondly, one can *update* a strategy to apply a monomorphic function for a given type to achieve type-dependent behaviour (*cf. adhocTP* and *adhocTU*). In other words, one can dynamically provide ad-hoc cases for a strategy. Let us first illustrate the construction of strategies from parametric polymorphic functions:

$$
\begin{array}{lll}
identity & :: & Monad\ m \Rightarrow TP\ m \\
identity & = & polyTP\ return
\end{array}
\qquad
\begin{array}{lll}
build & :: & Monad\ m \Rightarrow a \rightarrow TU\ m\ a \\
build\ a & = & polyTU\ (const\ (return\ a))
\end{array}
$$

The type-preserving strategy *identity* denotes the generic (and monadic) identity function. The type-unifying strategy *build a* denotes the generic function which returns *a* regardless of the input term. As a consequence of parametricity [21], there are no further ways to inhabit the argument types of *polyTP* and *polyTU*, unless we rely on a specific instance of *m* (see *failTU* below).

The second way of strategy construction, i.e., with the *adhoc* combinators, allows us to go beyond parametric polymorphism. Given a strategy, we can provide an ad-hoc case for a specific type. Here is a simple example:

$$
\begin{array}{lll}
gnot & :: & Monad\ m \Rightarrow TP\ m \\
gnot & = & adhocTP\ identity\ (return \circ not)
\end{array}
$$

The strategy *gnot* is applicable to terms of any type. It will behave like *identity* most of the time, but it will perform Boolean negation when faced with a Boolean. Such type cases are crucial to assemble traversal strategies that exhibit specific behaviour for certain types of the traversed syntax.

2.3   Sequential Composition

Since the strategy types are opaque, sequential composition has to be defined as a primitive concept. This is in contrast to ordinary functions where one can define function composition in terms of λ-abstraction and function application. Consider the following parametric polymorphic forms of sequential composition:

$$
\begin{array}{lll}
g \circ f & = & \lambda x \rightarrow g\ (f\ x) \\
f\ `mseq`\ g & = & \lambda x \rightarrow f\ x \ggg g \\
f\ `mlet`\ g & = & \lambda x \rightarrow f\ x \ggg \lambda y \rightarrow g\ y\ x
\end{array}
$$

The first form describes ordinary function composition. The second form describes the monadic variation. The third form can be regarded as a let-expression with a free variable x. An input for x is passed to both f and g, and the result of the first application is fed to the second function. The latter two polymorphic forms of sequential composition serve as prototypes of the strategic combinators for sequential composition. The strategy combinators *seqTP* and *seqTU* of Figure 1 correspond to *mseq* lifted to the strategy level. Note that the first strategy is always a type-preserving strategy. The strategy combinators *letTP* and *letTU* are obtained by lifting *mlet*. Note that the first strategy is always a type-unifying strategy.

Recall that the *poly* combinators could be used to lift an ordinary parametric polymorphic function to a strategy. We can not just use *poly* to lift the prototypes for sequential composition because they are function *combinators*. For this reason, we supply the combinators for sequential composition as primitives of the ADTs, and we postpone their definition to Section 4.

Let us illustrate the utility of *letTU*. We want to lift a binary operator o to the level of type-unifying strategies by applying two argument strategies to the same input term and combining their intermediate results by o. Here is the corresponding strategy combinator:

$$comb \qquad :: \quad Monad\ m \Rightarrow (a \to b \to c) \to TU\ m\ a \to TU\ m\ b \to TU\ m\ c$$
$$comb\ o\ s\ s' \quad = \quad s\ `letTU`\ \lambda a \to s'\ `letTU`\ \lambda b \to build\ (o\ a\ b)$$

Thus, the result of the first strategy argument s is bound to the variable a. Then, the result of the second strategy argument s' is bound to b. Finally, a and b are combined with the operator o, and the result is returned by the *build* combinator which was defined Section 2.2.

2.4   Partiality and Non-determinism

Instead of the simple class *Monad* we can also consider strategies w.r.t. the extended class *MonadPlus* with the members *mplus* and *mzero*. This provides us with means to express partiality and non-determinism. It is often useful to consider strategies which might potentially fail. The following ordinary function combinator is the prototype for the *choice* combinators in Figure 1.

$$f\ `mchoice`\ g \qquad = \quad \lambda x \to (f\ x)\ `mplus`\ (g\ x)$$

As an illustration let us define three simple strategy combinators which contribute to the construction of the introductory example.

$$failTU \qquad\quad :: \quad MonadPlus\ m \Rightarrow TU\ m\ x$$
$$failTU \qquad\quad = \quad polyTU\ (const\ mzero)$$
$$monoTU \qquad :: \quad (Term\ a, MonadPlus\ m) \Rightarrow (t \to m\ a) \to TU\ m\ a$$
$$monoTU\ f \quad\ = \quad adhocTU\ failTU\ f$$
$$tryTU \qquad\quad :: \quad (MonadPlus\ m, Monoid\ a) \Rightarrow TU\ m\ a \to TU\ m\ a$$
$$tryTU\ s \qquad\ = \quad s\ `choiceTU`\ (build\ mempty)$$

The strategy *failTU* denotes unconditional failure. The combinator *monoTU* updates failure by a monomorphic function f, using the combinator *adhocTU*. That is, the resulting strategy fails for all types other than f's argument type. If f is applicable, then the strategy indeed resorts to f. The combinator *tryTU* allows us to recover from failure in case we can employ a neutral element *mempty* of a monoid.

Recall that the *monoTU* combinator was used in the introductory example to turn the non-generic, monomorphic function *useVar* into a type-unifying strategy. This strategy will fail when applied to any type other than *Expression*.

2.5   Traversal Combinators

A challenging facet of strategies is that they might descend into terms. In fact, any program transformation or program analysis involves traversal. If we want to employ genericity for traversal, corresponding basic combinators are indispensable. The *all* and *one* combinators in Figure 1 process all or just one of the *immediate* subterms of a given term, respectively. The combinators do not just vary with respect to quantification but also for the type-preserving and the type-unifying case. The type-preserving combinators *allTP* and *oneTP* preserve the outermost constructor for the sake of type-preservation. Dually, the type-unifying combinators *allTU* and *oneTU* unwrap the outermost constructor in order to migrate to the unified type. More precisely, *allTU* reduces all pre-processed children by the binary operation *mappend* of a monoid whereas *oneTU* returns the result of processing one child. The *all* and *one* combinators have been adopted from the untyped language Stratego [20] for strategic term rewriting.

We are now in the position to define the traversal scheme *collect* from the introduction. We first define a more parametric strategy *crush* which performs a deep reduction by employing the operators of a monoid parameter. Then, the strategy *collect* is nothing more than a type-specialized version of *crush* where we opt for the list monoid.

$$
\begin{aligned}
&crush && :: && (MonadPlus\ m, Monoid\ a) \Rightarrow TU\ m\ a \rightarrow TU\ m\ a \\
&crush\ s && = && comb\ mappend\ (tryTU\ s)\ (allTU\ (crush\ s)) \\
\\
&collect && :: && MonadPlus\ m \Rightarrow TU\ m\ [a] \rightarrow TU\ m\ [a] \\
&collect\ s && = && crush\ s
\end{aligned}
$$

Note that the *comb* combinator is used to combine the result of *s* on the current node with the result of crushing the subterms. The *tryTU* combinator is used to recover from possible failure of *s*. In the introductory example, this comes down to recovery from failure of *monoTU useVar* at non-*Expression* nodes, and at nodes of type *Expression* for which *useVar* returns *Nothing*.

2.6   Some Defined Combinators

We can subdivide defined combinators into two categories, one for the control of strategies, and another for traversal schemes. Let us discuss a few examples of defined combinators. Here are some representatives of the category for the control of strategies:

$$
\begin{aligned}
&repeatTP && :: && MonadPlus\ m \Rightarrow TP\ m \rightarrow TP\ m \\
&repeatTP\ s && = && tryTP\ (seqTP\ s\ (repeatTP\ s)) \\
\\
&ifthenTP && :: && Monad\ m \Rightarrow TP\ m \rightarrow TP\ m \rightarrow TP\ m \\
&ifthenTP\ f\ g && = && (f\ `seqTU`\ (build\ ()))\ `letTP`\ (const\ g) \\
\\
&notTP && :: && MonadPlus\ m \Rightarrow TP\ m \rightarrow TP\ mentity \\
&notTP\ s && = && ((s\ `ifthenTU`\ (build\ True))\ `choiceTU`\ (build\ False)) \\
& && && `letTP`\lambda b \rightarrow \textbf{if}\ b\ \textbf{then}\ failTP\ \textbf{else}\ identity \\
\\
&afterTU && :: && Monad\ m \Rightarrow (a \rightarrow b) \rightarrow TU\ m\ a \rightarrow TU\ m\ b \\
&afterTU\ f\ s && = && s\ `letTU`\ \lambda a \rightarrow build\ (f\ a)
\end{aligned}
$$

The combinator *repeatTP* applies its argument strategy as often as possible. As an aside, a type-unifying counter-part of this combinator would justly not be typeable. The combinator *ifthenTP* precedes the application of a strategy by a guarding strategy. The guard determines whether the guarded strategy is applied at all. However, the guarded strategy is applied to the original term (as opposed to the result of the guarding strategy). The combinator *notTP* models negation by failure. The combinator *afterTU* adapts the result of a type-unifying traversal by an ordinary function.

Let us also define a few traversal schemes (in addition to *crush* and *collect*):

$$
\begin{array}{lll}
bu & :: & Monad\ m \Rightarrow TP\ m \rightarrow TP\ m \\
bu\ s & = & (allTP\ (bu\ s))\ `seqTP`\ s \\
oncetd & :: & MonadPlus\ m \Rightarrow TP\ m \rightarrow TP\ m \\
oncetd\ s & = & s\ `choiceTP`\ (oneTP\ (oncetd\ s)) \\
select & :: & MonadPlus\ m \Rightarrow TU\ m\ a \rightarrow TU\ m\ a \\
select\ s & = & s\ `choiceTU`\ (oneTU\ (select\ s))
\end{array}
$$

$$
selectenv :: MonadPlus\ m \Rightarrow e \rightarrow (e \rightarrow TU\ m\ e) \rightarrow (e \rightarrow TU\ m\ a) \rightarrow TU\ m\ a
$$
$$
selectenv\ e\ s'\ s = s'\ e\ `letTU`\ \lambda e' \rightarrow (s\ e)\ `choiceTU`\ (oneTU\ (selectenv\ e'\ s'\ s))
$$

All these schemes deal with recursive traversal. The combinator *bu* serves for unconstrained type-preserving bottom-up traversal. The argument strategy has to succeed for every node if the traversal is to succeed. The combinator *oncetd* serves for type-preserving top-down traversal where the argument strategy is tried until it succeeds once. The traversal fails if the argument strategy fails for all nodes. The type-unifying combinator *select* searches in top-down manner for a node which can be processed by the argument strategy. Finally, the combinator *selectenv* is an elaboration of *select* to accomplish explicit environment passing. The first argument strategy serves for updating the environment before descending into the subterms. As will be demonstrated in the upcoming section, traversal schemes like these can serve as building blocks for program transformations.

3   Application: Refactoring

Refactoring [9] is the process of step-wise improving the internal structure of a software system without altering its external behaviour. The *extract method refactoring* [9, p. 110] is a well-known example of a basic refactoring step. To demonstrate the technique of programming with strategy combinators, we will implement the extract method refactoring for Java.

3.1   The *Extract Method* Refactoring

In brief, the extract method refactoring is described as follows:

> *Turn a code fragment that can be grouped together into a reusable method whose name explains the purpose of the method.*

For instance, the last two statements in the following method can be grouped into a method called `printDetails`.

```
void printOwning(double amount) {
  printBanner ();
  //print details
  System.out.println("name:" + _name);
  System.out.println("ammount" + amount);
}
```

$$\Downarrow$$

```
void printOwning(double amount) {
  printBanner ();
  printDetails(amount);
}
void printDetails(double amount) {
  System.out.println("name:" + _name);
  System.out.println("amount" + amount);
}
```

Note that the local variable `amount` is turned into a parameter of the new method, while the instance variable `_name` is not. Note also, that the *extract method* refactoring is valid only for a code fragment that does not contain any return statements or assignments to local variables.

3.2   Design

To implement the *extract method* refactoring, we need to solve a number of subtasks.

Legality check The focused fragment must be analysed to ascertain that it does not contain any return statements or assignments to local variables. The latter involves detection of variables in the fragment that are defined (assigned into), but not declared (i.e., free *defined* variables).

Generation The new method declaration and invocation need to be generated. To construct their formal and actual parameter lists, we need to collect those variables that are used, but not declared (i.e., free *used* variables) from the focused fragments, with their types.

Transformation The focused fragment must be replaced with the generated method invocation, and the generated method declaration must be inserted in the class body.

These subtasks need to be performed at specific moments during a traversal of the abstract syntax tree. Roughly, our traversal will be structured as follows:

1. Descend to the class declaration in which the method with the focused fragment occurs.

$typed\_free\_vars :: (MonadPlus\ m, Eq\ v)$
$\Rightarrow [(v, t)] \rightarrow TU\ m\ [v] \rightarrow TU\ m\ [(v, t)] \rightarrow TU\ m\ [(v, t)]$
$typed\_free\_vars\ env\ getvars\ declvars$
$= afterTU\ (flip\ appendMap\ env)\ (tryTU\ declvars)\ `letTU`\ \lambda env' \rightarrow$
  $choiceTU\ (afterTU\ (flip\ selectMap\ env')\ getvars)$
    $(comb\ diffMap\ (allTU\ (typed\_free\_vars\ env'\ getvars\ declvars))$
      $(tryTU\ declvars))$

Fig. 2. A generic algorithm for extraction of free variables with their declared types

2. Descend into the method with the focused fragment to (i) check the legality of the focused fragment, and (ii) return both the focused fragment and a list of typed free variables that occur in the focus.
3. Descend again to the focus to replace it with the method invocation that can now be constructed from the list of typed free variables.

3.3   Implementation with Strategies

Our solution is shown in Figures 2 through 4.

Free variable analysis As noted above, we need to perform two kinds of free variable collection: variables used but not declared, and variables defined but not declared. Furthermore, we need to find the types of these free variables. Using strategies, we can implement free variable collection in an extremely generic fashion. Figure 2 shows a generic free variable collection algorithm. This algorithm was adapted from an untyped rewriting strategy in [19]. It is parameterized with (i) an initial type environment *env*, (ii) a strategy *getvars* which selects any variables that are used in a certain node of the AST, and (iii) a strategy *declvars* which selects declared variables with their types. Note that no assumptions are made with respect to variables or types, except that equality is defined on variables so they can appear as keys in a map.

The algorithm basically performs a top-down traversal. It is not constructed by reusing one of the defined traversal combinators from our library, but directly in terms of the primitive combinator *allTU*. At a given node, first the incoming type environment is extended with any variables declared at this node. Second, either the variables used at the node are looked-up in the type environment and returned with their types, or, if the node is not a use site, any declared variables are subtracted from the collection of free variables found in the children (cf. *allTU*). Note that the algorithm is typeful, and fully generic. It makes ample use of library combinators, such as *afterTU*, *letTU* and *comb*.

As shown in Figure 3, this generic algorithm can be instantiated to the two kinds of free variable analyses needed for our case. The functions *useVar*, *defVar*, and *declVars* are the Java-specific ingredients that are needed. They determine

$$
\begin{array}{lll}
use\,Var\ (Identifier\ i) & = & return\ [i] \\
use\,Var\ \_ & = & mzero \\
defVar\ (Assignment\ i\ \_) & = & return\ [i] \\
declVars & :: & MonadPlus\ m \Rightarrow TU\ m\ [(Identifier,\ Type)] \\
declVars & = & adhocTU\ (monoTU\ declVarsBlock)\ declVarsMeth \\
\end{array}
$$

$$\quad\quad \textbf{where}\ declVarsBlock\ (BlockStatements\ vds\ \_) = return\ vds$$
$$\quad\quad\quad\quad declVarsMeth\ (MethodDecl\ \_\ \_\ (FormalParams\ fps)\ \_) = return\ fps$$

$$freeUseVars\ env = afterTU\ nubMap\ (typed\_free\_vars\ env\ (monoTU\ useVar)\ declVars)$$
$$freeDefVars\ env = afterTU\ nubMap\ (typed\_free\_vars\ env\ (monoTU\ defVar)\ declVars)$$

Fig. 3. Instantiations of the generic free variable algorithm for Java

the used, defined, and declared variables of a given node, respectively. We use them to instantiate the generic free variable collector to construct *freeUseVars*, and *freeDefVars*.

Method extraction The remainder of the extract method implementation is shown in Figure 4. The main strategy *extractMethod* performs a top-down traversal to the class level, where it calls *extrMethFromCls*. This latter function first obtains parameters and body with *ifLegalGetParsAndBody*, and then replaces the focus with *replaceFocus*. Code generation is performed by two functions *constructMethod* and *constructMethodCall*. Their definitions are trivial and not shown here. The extraction of the candidate body and parameters for the new method is performed in the same traversal as the legality check. This is a top-down traversal with environment propagation. During descent, the environment is extended with declared variables. When the focus is reached, the legality check is performed. If it succeeds, the free used variables of the focused fragment are determined. These variables are paired with the focused fragment itself, and returned. The legality check itself is defined in the strategy *isLegal*. It fails when the collection of variables that are defined but not declared is non-empty, or when a return statement is recognized in the focus. The replacement of the focus by a new method invocation is defined by the strategy *replaceFocus*. It performs a top-down traversal. When the focus is found, the new method invocation is generated and the focus is replaced with it.

4   Models of Strategies

We have explained what strategy combinators are, and we have shown their utility. Let us now change the point of view, and explain some options for the implementation of the strategy ADTs including the primitives. Recall that functional strategies have to meet the following requirements. Firstly, they need to be applicable to values of any term type. Secondly, they have to allow for updating in the sense that type-specific behaviour can be enforced. Thirdly, they have to

$extractMethod$ :: $(Term\ t, MonadPlus\ m) \Rightarrow t \rightarrow m\ t$
$extractMethod\ prog$
$\quad\quad\quad = \quad applyTP\ (oncetd\ (monoTP\ extrMethFromCls))\ prog$
$extrMethFromCls$ $MonadPlus\ m \Rightarrow ClassDeclaration \rightarrow m\ ClassDeclaration$
$extrMethFromCls\ (ClassDecl\ fin\ nm\ sup\ fs\ cs\ ds)$
$\quad\quad\quad = \quad \textbf{do}\ (pars, body) \leftarrow ifLegalGetParsAndBody\ ds$
$\quad\quad\quad\quad\quad\quad\quad ds' \leftarrow replaceFocus\ pars\ (ds +\!\!+ [constructMethod\ pars\ body])$
$\quad\quad\quad\quad\quad\quad\quad return\ (ClassDecl\ fin\ nm\ sup\ fs\ cs\ ds')$
$ifLegalGetParsAndBody$
$\quad\quad\quad$ :: $(Term\ t, MonadPlus\ m) \Rightarrow t \rightarrow m\ ([([Char], Type)], Statement)$
$ifLegalGetParsAndBody\ ds$
$\quad\quad\quad = \quad applyTU\ (selectenv\ []\ appendLocals\ ifLegalGetParsAndBody1)\ ds$
$\quad\quad\quad\quad\quad \textbf{where}\ ifLegalGetParsAndBody1\ env$
$\quad\quad\quad\quad\quad\quad\quad\quad = getFocus\ `letTU`\ \lambda s \rightarrow$
$\quad\quad\quad\quad\quad\quad\quad\quad\quad ifthenTU\ (isLegal\ env)$
$\quad\quad\quad\quad\quad\quad\quad\quad\quad (freeUseVars\ env\ `letTU`\ \lambda pars \rightarrow$
$\quad\quad\quad\quad\quad\quad\quad\quad\quad build\ (pars, s))$
$\quad\quad\quad\quad\quad\quad\quad appendLocals\ env$
$\quad\quad\quad\quad\quad\quad\quad\quad = comb\ appendMap\ (tryTU\ declVars)\ (build\ env)$
$replaceFocus$ :: $(Term\ t, MonadPlus\ m) \Rightarrow [(Identifier, Type)] \rightarrow t \rightarrow m\ t$
$replaceFocus\ pars\ ds$
$\quad\quad\quad = \quad applyTP\ (oncetd\ (replaceFocus1\ pars))\ ds$
$\quad\quad\quad\quad\quad \textbf{where}\ replaceFocus1\ pars$
$\quad\quad\quad\quad\quad\quad\quad = getFocus\ `letTP`\ \lambda\_ \rightarrow$
$\quad\quad\quad\quad\quad\quad\quad\quad monoTP\ (const\ (return\ (constructMethodCall\ pars)))$
$isLegal$ :: $MonadPlus\ m \Rightarrow [([Char], Type)] \rightarrow TP\ m$
$isLegal\ env$ = $freeDefVars\ env\ `letTP`\ \lambda env' \rightarrow$
$\quad\quad\quad\quad \textbf{if}\ null\ env'\ \textbf{then}\ notTU\ (select\ getReturn)\ \textbf{else}\ failTP$
$getFocus$ :: $MonadPlus\ m \Rightarrow TU\ m\ Statement$
$getFocus$ = $monoTU\ (\lambda s \rightarrow \textbf{case}\ s\ \textbf{of}\ (StatFocus\ s') \rightarrow return\ s'$
$\quad\quad\quad\quad\quad\quad\quad\quad\quad\quad\quad\quad\quad \_ \rightarrow mzero)$
$getReturn$ :: $MonadPlus\ m \Rightarrow TU\ m\ (Maybe\ Expression)$
$getReturn$ = $monoTU\ (\lambda s \rightarrow \textbf{case}\ s\ \textbf{of}\ (ReturnStat\ x) \rightarrow return\ x$
$\quad\quad\quad\quad\quad\quad\quad\quad\quad\quad\quad\quad\quad \_ \rightarrow mzero)$

Fig. 4. Implementation of the *extract method* refactoring

be able to descend into terms. The first model we discuss uses a universal term representation. The second model employs rank-2 polymorphism with type case.

4.1   Strategies as Functions on a Universal Term Representation

One way to meet the requirements on functional strategies is to rely on a universal representation of terms of algebraic datatypes. Such a representation can easily be constructed in any functional language in a straightforward manner. The challenge is to hide the employment of the universal representation to rule out inconsistent representations, and to relieve the programmer of the burden to deal explicitly with representations rather than ordinary values and functions.

The following declarations set up a representation type *TermRep*, and the ADTs for strategies are defined as functions on *TermRep* wrapped by datatype constructors *MkTP* and *MkTU*:

type *TypeId*	$=$	*String*
type *ConstrId*	$=$	*String*
data *TermRep*	$=$	*TermRep TypeRep ConstrId* [*TermRep*]
data *TypeRep*	$=$	*TypeRep TypeId* [*TypeRep*]
newtype *TP m*	$=$	*MkTP* (*TermRep* $\to$ *m TermRep*)
newtype *TU m a*	$=$	*MkTU* (*TermRep* $\to$ *m a*)

Thus, a universal value consists of a type representation (for a potentially parameterized data type), a constructor identifier, and the list of universal values corresponding to the immediate subterms of the encoded term (if any). The strategy ADTs are made opaque by simply not exporting the constructors *MkTP* and *MkTU*. To mediate between *TermRep* and specific term types, we place members for implosion and explosion in a class *Term*.

class *Term t* **where**
  explode   :: $t \to TermRep$
  implode   :: $TermRep \to t$

  explode (*Identifier i*) = *TermRep* (*TypeRep* "Expr" []) "Identifier" [*explode i*]
  implode (*TermRep* _ "Identifier" [*i*]) = *Identifier* (*implode i*)

The instances for a given term type follow a trivial scheme, as illustrated by the two sample equations for Java *Identifier*s. In fact, we extended the DrIFT tool [25] to generate such instances for us (see Section 5). For a faithful universal representation it should hold that explosion can be reversed by implosion. Implosion is potentially a partial operation. One could use the *Maybe* monad for the result to enable recovery from an implosion problem. By contrast, we rule out failure of implosion in the first place by hiding the representation of strategies behind the primitive combinators defined below. It would be easy to prove that all functions on *TermRep* which can be defined in terms of the primitive combinators are implosion-safe.

The combinators *polyTP* and *polyTU* specialize their polymorphic argument to a function on *TermRep*. Essentially, the combinators for sequential composition and choice are also defined by specialisation of the corresponding prototypes *mseq*, *mlet*, and *mchoice*. In addition, we need to unwrap the constructors *MkTP* and *MkTU* from each argument and to re-wrap the result.

	seqTP f g = MkTP ((*unTP f*) '*mseq*' (*unTP g*))
polyTP f = MkTP f	*seqTU f g = MkTU* ((*unTP f*) '*mseq*' (*unTU g*))
polyTU f = MkTU f	*letTP f g = MkTP* ((*unTU f*) '*mlet*' ($\lambda a \to unTP$ (*g a*)))
unTP (*MkTP f*) = *f*	*letTU f g = MkTU* ((*unTU f*) '*mlet*' ($\lambda a \to unTU$ (*g a*)))
unTU (*MkTU f*) = *f*	*choiceTP f g = MkTP* ((*unTP f*) '*mchoice*' (*unTP g*))
	choiceTU f g = MkTU ((*unTU f*) '*mchoice*' (*unTU g*))

The combinators for strategy application and updating are defined as follows:

$$
\begin{aligned}
applyTP\ s\ t\ &=\ unTP\ s\ (explode\ t) \ggg \lambda t' \to return\ (implode\ t') \\
applyTU\ s\ t\ &=\ unTU\ s\ (explode\ t) \\
adhocTP\ s\ f\ &=\ MkTP\ (\lambda u \to \textbf{if}\ applicable\ f\ u \\
&\qquad\qquad\qquad \textbf{then}\ f\ (implode\ u) \ggg \lambda t \to return\ (explode\ t) \\
&\qquad\qquad\qquad \textbf{else}\ unTP\ s\ u) \\
adhocTU\ s\ f\ &=\ MkTU\ (\lambda u \to \textbf{if}\ applicable\ f\ u \\
&\qquad\qquad\qquad \textbf{then}\ f\ (implode\ u) \\
&\qquad\qquad\qquad \textbf{else}\ unTU\ s\ u)
\end{aligned}
$$

As for application, terms are always first exploded to *TermRep* before the function underlying a strategy can be applied. This is because strategies are functions on *TermRep*. In the case of a type-preserving strategy, the result of the application also needs to be imploded afterwards. As for update, we use a type test (*cf. applicable*) to check if the given universal value is of the specific type handled by the update. For brevity, we omit the definition of *applicable* but it simply compares type representations. If the type test succeeds, the corresponding implosion is performed so that the specific function can be applied. If the type test fails, the generic default strategy is applied.

The primitive traversal combinators are particularly easy to define for this model. Recall that these combinators process in some sense the immediate subterms of a given term. Thus, we can essentially perform list processing. The following code fragment defines a helper to apply a list-processing function on the immediate subterms. We also show the implementation of the primitive *allTP* which directly employs the standard monadic map function *mapM*.

$$
\begin{aligned}
applyOnKidsTP\ &::\ Monad\ m \Rightarrow ([\,TermRep\,] \to m\,[\,TermRep\,]) \to TP\ m \\
applyOnKidsTP\ s\ &=\ MkTP\ (\lambda(\,TermRep\ sort\ con\ ks) \to \\
&\qquad\qquad\qquad\qquad s\ ks \ggg \lambda ks' \to return\ (\,TermRep\ sort\ con\ ks')) \\
allTP\ s\ &=\ applyOnKidsTP\ (mapM\ (unTP\ s))
\end{aligned}
$$

4.2   Strategies as Rank-2 Polymorphic Functions with Type Case

Instead of defining strategies as functions on a universal representation type, we can also define them as a kind of polymorphic functions being directly applicable to terms of the algebraic datatypes. But, since strategies can be passed as arguments to strategy combinators, we need to make use of *rank-2 polymorphism*[3]. The following declarations define *TP m* and *TU m a* in terms of universally quantified components of datatype constructors. This form of wrapping is the Haskell approach to deal with rank-2 polymorphism while retaining decidability of type inference [14].

$$
\begin{aligned}
\textbf{newtype}\ Monad\ m \Rightarrow TP\ m\ &=\ MkTP\ (\forall t.\ Term\ t \Rightarrow t \to m\ t) \\
\textbf{newtype}\ Monad\ m \Rightarrow TU\ m\ a\ &=\ MkTU\ (\forall t.\ Term\ t \Rightarrow t \to m\ a)
\end{aligned}
$$

---

[3] Rank-2 polymorphism is not part of Haskell 98, but available in the required form as an extension of the Hugs implementation.

Note that the functions which model strategies are not simply universally quanti-fied, but the domain is also constrained to be an instance of the class *Term*. The following model-specific term interface provides traversal and ad-hoc primitives to meet the other requirements on strategies.

$$
\begin{array}{ll}
\textbf{class } \textit{Update } t \Rightarrow \textit{Term } t \textbf{ where} & \\
\quad allTP' :: \textit{Monad } m & \Rightarrow \textit{TP } m \to t \to m \; t \\
\quad oneTP' :: \textit{MonadPlus } m & \Rightarrow \textit{TP } m \to t \to m \; t \\
\quad allTU' :: (\textit{Monad } m, \textit{Monoid } a) & \Rightarrow \textit{TU } m \; a \to t \to m \; a \\
\quad oneTU' :: \textit{MonadPlus } m & \Rightarrow \textit{TU } m \; a \to t \to m \; a \\
\quad adhocTP' :: (\textit{Monad } m, \textit{Update } t') & \Rightarrow (t' \to m \; t') \to (t \to m \; t) \to (t' \to m \; t') \\
\quad adhocTU' :: (\textit{Monad } m, \textit{Update } t') & \Rightarrow (t' \to m \; a) \to (t \to m \; a) \to (t' \to m \; a)
\end{array}
$$

We use primed names because the members are only rank-1 prototypes which still need to be lifted by wrapping and unwrapping. The term interface is instantiated by defining the primitives for all possible term types.

The definitions of the traversal primitives are as simple as the definitions of the *implode* and *explode* functions for the previous model. They are not shown for brevity. To define *adhocTP'* and *adhocTU'* for each datatype, an additional technique is needed: we model strategy update as a type case [7,5]. The instances of the *Update* class, mentioned in the context of class *Term*, implement this type case via an encoding technique for Haskell inspired by [24]. In essence, this technique involves two members *dUpdTP* and *dUpdTU* in the *Update* class for each datatype *d*. These members for *d* select their second argument in the instance for *d*, and default to their first argument in all other instances.

Given the rank-1 prototypes, the derivation of the actual rank-2 primitive combinators is straightforward:

$$
\begin{array}{ll}
applyTP \; s \; t = (unTP \; s) \; t & allTP \; s = MkTP \; (allTP' \; s) \\
applyTU \; s \; t = (unTU \; s) \; t & oneTP \; s = MkTP \; (oneTP' \; s) \\
adhocTP \; s \; f = MkTP \; (adhocTP' \; (unTP \; s) \; f) & allTU \; s = MkTU \; (allTU' \; s) \\
adhocTU \; s \; f = MkTU \; (adhocTU' \; (unTU \; s) \; f) & oneTU \; s = MkTU \; (oneTU' \; s)
\end{array}
$$

Note that application does not involve conversion with *implode* and *explode*, as in the previous model, but only unwrapping of the rank-2 polymorphic function. As for sequential composition, choice, and the *poly* combinators, the definitions from the previous model carry over.

4.3   Trade-Offs and Alternatives

The model relying on a universal term representation is simple and does not rely on more than parametric polymorphism and class overloading. It satisfies extensibility in the sense that for each new datatype, one can provide a new instance of *Term* without invalidating previous instances. The second model is slightly more involved. But it is more appealing in that no conversion is needed, because strategies are simply functions on the datatypes themselves, instead of on a representation of them. However, extensibility is compromised, as the em-ployed coding scheme for type cases involves a closed world assumption. That is, the encoding technique for type case requires a class *Update* which has members for each datatype. Note that these trade-offs are Haskell-specific. In a different language, e.g., a language with built-in type case, strategies would be supported via different models. In fact, a simple language extension could support strategies directly.

Regardless of the model, it is intuitively clear that a full traversal visiting all nodes should use time linear in the size of the term, assuming a constant node-processing complexity. Both models expose this behaviour. However, if a traversal stops somewhere, no overhead for non-traversed nodes should occur. The described universal representation is problematic is this respect since the non-traversed part below the stop node will have to be imploded before the node can be processed. Thus, we suffer a penalty linear in the number of non-traversed nodes. Similarly, implosion is needed when a strategy is applied which involves an ad-hoc update. This is because a universal representation has to be imploded before a non-generic function can be applied on a node of a specific datatype. Short of switching to the second model, one can remedy these performance problems by adopting a more involved universal representation. The overall idea is to use dynamic typing [1] and to do stepwise explosion by need, that is, only if the application of a traversal primitive requires it.

5   Conclusion

Functional software re-engineering Without appropriate technology large-scale software maintenance projects cannot be done cost-effectively within a reasonable time-span, or not at all [4,6,3]. Currently, declarative *re*-technologies are usually based on term rewriting frameworks and attribute grammars. There are hardly (published) attempts to employ functional programming for the development of large-scale program transformation systems. One exception is AnnoDomini [8] where SML is used for the implementation of a Y2K tool. The traversal part of AnnoDomini is kept to a reasonable size by a specific normalisation that gets rid of all syntax not relevant for this Y2K approach. In general, re-engineering requires generic traversal technology that is applicable to the full syntax of the language at hand [3]. In [15], we describe an architecture for functional transformation systems and a corresponding case study concerned with a data expansion problem. The architecture addresses the important issues of scalable parsing and pretty-printing, and employs an approach to generic traversal based on combinators for updatable generalized folds [17]. The functional strategies described in the present paper provide a more lightweight and more generic solution than folds, and can be used instead.

Of course, our techniques are not only applicable to software re-engineering problems, but generally to all areas of language and document processing where type-safe generic traversal is desirable. For example, our strategy combinators can be used for XML processing where, in contrast to the approaches presented in [23], document processors can at once be typed and generic.

Generic functional programming Related forms of genericity have been proposed elsewhere. These approaches are not just more complex than ours, but they are even insufficient for a faithful encoding of the combinators we propose. With intensional and extensional polymorphism [7,5] one can also encode type-parametric functions where the behaviour is defined via a run-time type case. However, as-is the corresponding systems do not cover algebraic data types, but only products, function space, and basic data types. With polytypic programming (*cf.* PolyP and Generic Haskell [12,11]), one can define functions by induction on types. However, polytypic functions are not first class citizens: due to the restriction that polytypic parameters are quantified at the top level, polytypic *combinators* cannot be defined. Also, in a polytypic definition, though one can provide fixed ad-hoc cases for specific data types, an *adhoc* combinator is absent. It may be conceivable that polytypic programming is generalized to cover the functionality of our strategies, but the current paper shows that strategies can be modelled within a language like Haskell without type-system extensions.

The origins of functional strategies The term 'strategy' and our conception of generic programming were largely influenced by strategic term rewriting [18,20,16]. In particular, the overall idea to define traversal schemes in terms of basic generic combinators like *all* and *one* has been adopted from the untyped language Stratego [20] for strategic term rewriting. Our contribution is that we integrate this idea with typed and higher-order functional programming. In fact, Stratego was not defined with typing in mind.

Availability The strategy library *StrategyLib* is available as part of a generic functional programming bundle called *Strafunski* at http://www.cs.vu.nl/Strafunski. Complete source of *StrategyLib* are included in the report version of this paper which can also be downloaded from the Strafunski web page. The bundle also contains an extended version of DrIFT (formerly called Derive [25]) which can be used (pending native support for strategies) to generate the instances of class *Term* according to the model in Section 4.1 for any given algebraic data type.

References

1. M. Abadi, L. Cardelli, B. Pierce, and G. Plotkin. Dynamic Typing in a Statically Typed Language. *ACM Transactions on Programming Languages and Systems*, 13(2):237–268, Apr. 1991. 152
2. G. Arango, I. Baxter, P. Freeman, and C. Pidgeon. TMM: Software maintenance by transformation. *IEEE Software*, 3(3):27–39, May 1986. 137
3. M. Brand, M. Sellink, and C. Verhoef. Generation of Components for Software Renovation Factories from Context-free Grammars. *Science of Computer Programming*, 36(2–3):209–266, 2000. 137, 152
4. E. Chikofsky and J. C. II. Reverse Engineering and Design Recovery: A Taxonomy. *IEEE Software*, 7(1):13–17, Jan. 1990. 137, 152
5. K. Crary, S. Weirich, and G. Morrisett. Intensional polymorphism in type-erasure semantics. *ACM SIGPLAN Notices*, 34(1):301–312, Jan. 1999. 151, 153

6. A. Deursen, P. Klint, and C. Verhoef. Research Issues in the Renovation of Legacy Systems. In J. Finance, editor, *Proc. of FASE'99*, volume 1577 of *LNCS*, pages 1–21. Springer-Verlag, 1999. 152

7. C. Dubois, F. Rouaix, and P. Weis. Extensional polymorphism. In *Conference record of POPL'95*, pages 118–129. ACM Press, 1995. 151, 153

8. P. H. Eidorff, F. Henglein, C. Mossin, H. Niss, M. H. B. Sørensen, and M. Tofte. AnnoDomini: From type theory to year 2000 conversion tool. In *Conference Record of POPL'99*, pages 1–14. ACM press, 1999. Invited paper. 152

9. M. Fowler. *Refactoring: Improving the Design of Existing Code*. Addison Wesley, 1999. 144

10. *Haskell 98: A Non-strict, Purely Functional Language*, Feb. 1999. http://www.haskell.org/onlinereport/. 138

11. R. Hinze. A generic programming extension for Haskell. In E. Meijer, editor, *Proceedings of the 3rd Haskell Workshop, Paris, France*, Sept. 1999. Technical report, Universiteit Utrecht, UU-CS-1999-28. 153

12. P. Jansson and J. Jeuring. PolyP - a polytypic programming language extension. In *Conference record of POPL'97*, pages 470–482. ACM Press, 1997. 153

13. J. Jeuring, editor. *Proc. of WGP'2000, Technical Report, Universiteit Utrecht*, July 2000. 154

14. M. Jones. First-class polymorphism with type inference. In *Conference record of POPL'97*, pages 483–496, Paris, France, 15–17 Jan. 1997. 150

15. J. Kort, R. Lämmel, and J. Visser. Functional Transformation Systems. In *9th International Workshop on Functional and Logic Programming*, Benicassim, Spain, July 2000. 137, 152

16. R. Lämmel. Typed Generic Traversals in S'_γ. Technical Report SEN-R0122, CWI, Aug. 2001. 153

17. R. Lämmel, J. Visser, and J. Kort. Dealing with Large Bananas. In Jeuring [13], pages 46–59. 152

18. L. Paulson. A Higher-Order Implementation of Rewriting. *Science of Computer Programming*, 3(2):119–149, Aug. 1983. 153

19. E. Visser. Language Independent Traversals for Program Transformation. In Jeuring [13], pages 86–104. 146

20. E. Visser, Z. Benaissa, and A. Tolmach. Building Program Optimizers with Rewriting Strategies. In *Proc. of ICFP'98*, pages 13–26, Sept. 1998. 143, 153

21. P. Wadler. Theorems for Free! In *Proc. of FPCA'89, London*, pages 347–359. ACM Press, New York, Sept. 1989. 141

22. P. Wadler. The essence of functional programming. In *Conference record of POPL'92*, pages 1–14. ACM Press, 1992. 139

23. M. Wallace and C. Runciman. Haskell and XML: Generic combinators or type-based translation? *ACM SIGPLAN Notices*, 34(9):148–159, Sept. 1999. Proceedings of ICFP'99. 152

24. S. Weirich. Type-safe cast: (functional pearl). *ACM SIGPLAN Notices*, 35(9):58–67, Sept. 2000. 151

25. N. Winstanley. Derive User Guide, version 1.0. Available at http://www.dcs.gla.ac.uk/~nww/Derive/, June 1997. 149, 153

Event-Driven FRP*

Zhanyong Wan, Walid Taha, and Paul Hudak

Department of Computer Science, Yale University
New Haven, CT, USA
{wan-zhanyong,taha,hudak-paul}@cs.yale.edu

Abstract. Functional Reactive Programming (FRP) is a high-level declarative language for programming reactive systems. Previous work on FRP has demonstrated its utility in a wide range of application domains, including animation, graphical user interfaces, and robotics. FRP has an elegant continuous-time denotational semantics. However, it guarantees no bounds on execution time or space, thus making it unsuitable for many embedded real-time applications. To alleviate this problem, we recently developed *Real-Time FRP* (RT-FRP), whose operational semantics permits us to formally guarantee bounds on both execution time and space.

In this paper we present a formally verifiable compilation strategy from a new language based on RT-FRP into imperative code. The new language, called *Event-Driven FRP* (E-FRP), is more tuned to the paradigm of having multiple external events. While it is smaller than RT-FRP, it features a key construct that allows us to compile the language into efficient code. We have used this language and its compiler to generate code for a small robot controller that runs on a PIC16C66 micro-controller. Because the formal specification of compilation was crafted more for clarity and for technical convenience, we describe an implementation that produces more efficient code.

1 Introduction

Functional Reactive Programming (FRP) [12,19] is a high-level declarative language for programming reactive systems. A *reactive system* is one that continually responds to external stimuli. FRP has been used successfully in domains such as interactive computer animation [6], graphical user interface design [5], computer vision [15], robotics [14], and control systems. FRP is sufficiently high-level that, for many domains, FRP programs closely resemble equations naturally written by domain experts to specify the problems. For example, in the domain of control systems, our experience has been that we can go from a traditional mathematical specification of a controller to running FRP code in a matter of minutes.

FRP is implemented as an embedded language in Haskell [7], and so provides no guarantees on execution time or space: programs can diverge, consume large

---

* Funded by NSF CCR9900957, NSF ITR-0113569, and DARPA F33615-99-C-3013 and DABT63-00-1-0002

amounts of space, and introduce unpredictable delays in responding to external stimuli. In many applications FRP programs have been "fast enough," but for real-time applications, careful FRP programming and informal reasoning is the best that one can do.

In trying to expand the scope of FRP to these more demanding settings, we recently identified a subset of FRP (called RT-FRP) where it can be statically guaranteed that programs require only limited resources [20]. In RT-FRP there is one global clock, and the state of the whole program is updated when this clock ticks. Hence every part of the program is executed at the same frequency.

One key application domain that we are interested in is micro-controllers. In addition to being resource bounded, these hardware devices have a natural programming paradigm that is not typical in functional programming languages. In particular, they are event-driven. In such systems, an event affects only a statically decidable part of the system state, and hence there is no need to propagate the event throughout the whole system. Unfortunately, RT-FRP was not designed with this concern in mind.

This paper addresses the issue of compiling a variant of RT-FRP, called *Event-driven FRP (E-FRP)*. In this variant, the RT-FRP global clock is generalized to a set of events. This framework makes it clear that there is no need for RT-FRP's built-in notion of time, since we can now implement it as a special case of an event stream that is treated as a clock. Indeed, now we can have many different time bases, not necessarily linearly related, and in general can deal with complex event-driven (and periodic) reactive systems in a natural and effective manner. We have found that E-FRP is well-suited for programming interrupt-driven micro-controllers, which are normally programmed either in assembly language or some dialect of C.

In what follows, we present the basic ideas of E-FRP with an example from our work on the RoboCup challenge [16].

1.1   A Simple Robot Controller in E-FRP

The Yale RoboCup team consists of five radio-controlled robots, an overhead vision system for tracking the two teams and a soccer ball, and a central FRP controller for guiding the team. Everything is in one closed control loop. Even in this relatively small system, certain components must be developed in low level languages. Of particular interest to us is the controller running on-board the robots. Based on the speed sensor feedback and increase/decrease speed instructions coming from the central FRP controller, the on-board controller must determine the exact signals to be sent to the motors. In each robot, a PIC16C66 micro-controller [13] is used to execute the code that controls the robot. Initially, this low-level controller was programmed in a specialized subset of C, for which a commercial compiler targeting PIC16C66 exists. Written at this level, however, these controllers can be quite fragile, and some important features of the design of the controller can easily become obscured. Reasoning about the combination of the main FRP controller and these separate controllers is also non-trivial. This problem would not exist if the controllers are written in FRP, or a subset thereof.

The Physical Model Each robot has two wheels mounted on a common axis and each wheel is driven by an independent motor. For simplicity we focus on one wheel, and do not discuss the interaction between the two.

The amount of power sent to the motor is controlled using a standard electrical engineering technique called *Pulse-Width Modulation* (PWM): instead of varying the voltage, the power is rapidly switched off and on. The percentage of time when the power is on (called the *duty cycle*) determines the overall power transmission.

Each wheel is monitored through a simple stripe detection mechanism: The more frequently the stripes are observed by an infrared sensor, the faster the wheel is deemed to be moving. For simplicity, we assume the wheel can only go in one direction.

The Computational Model The main goal of the controller is to regulate the power being sent to the motor, so as to maintain a desired speed ds for the wheel. The control system is driven by five independent interrupt sources:

- *IncSpd* and *DecSpd* increment and decrement the desired speed;
- *Stripe* occurs 32 times for every full revolution of the wheel;
- *Timer0* and *Timer1* are two timers that occur at regular, but different, intervals. The frequency of *Timer0* is much higher than that of *Timer1*.

A register output determines the ON/OFF state of the motor.

The E-FRP Execution Model Before presenting the code for the controller, some basic features of the E-FRP execution model need to be explained.

As with FRP, the two most important concepts in E-FRP are *events* and *behaviors*. Events are time-ordered sequences of discrete event occurrences. Behaviors are values that react to events, and can be viewed as time-indexed signals. Unlike FRP behaviors that can change over continuous time, E-FRP behaviors can change value only when an event occurs.

E-FRP events are mutually exclusive, meaning that no two events ever occur simultaneously. This decision avoids potentially complex interactions between event handlers, and thus greatly simplifies the semantics and the compiler.

Finally, on the occurrence of an event, execution of an E-FRP program proceeds in *two distinct phases*: The first phase involves carrying out computations that depend on the previous state of the computation, and the second phase involves updating the state of the computation. To allow maximum expressiveness, E-FRP allows the programmer to insert annotations to indicate in which of these two phases a particular change in behavior should take place.

Source Code

$ds = \mathsf{init}\ x = 0\ \mathsf{in}$
$\quad \{\ IncSpd \Rightarrow x + 1,$
$\quad\quad DecSpd \Rightarrow x - 1\},$
$s = \mathsf{init}\ x = 0\ \mathsf{in}$
$\quad \{\ Timer1 \Rightarrow 0\ \mathsf{later},$
$\quad\quad Stripe \Rightarrow x + 1\},$
$dc = \mathsf{init}\ x = 0\ \mathsf{in}$
$\quad \{\ Timer1 \Rightarrow$
$\quad\quad\quad \mathsf{if}\ x < 100\ \mathsf{and}\ s < ds$
$\quad\quad\quad\quad \mathsf{then}\ x + 1$
$\quad\quad\quad \mathsf{else\ if}\ x > 0\ \mathsf{and}\ s > ds$
$\quad\quad\quad\quad \mathsf{then}\ x - 1$
$\quad\quad\quad \mathsf{else}\ x\},$
$count = \mathsf{init}\ x = 0\ \mathsf{in}$
$\quad \{\ Timer0 \Rightarrow$
$\quad\quad\quad \mathsf{if}\ x \geq 100\ \mathsf{then}\ 0$
$\quad\quad\quad \mathsf{else}\ x + 1\},$
$output = \mathsf{if}\ count < dc\ \mathsf{then}\ 1\ \mathsf{else}\ 0$

Target Code

$(IncSpd,$
$\quad \langle ds := ds^+ + 1;$
$\quad\quad output := \mathsf{if}\ count < dc\ \mathsf{then}\ 1\ \mathsf{else}\ 0\rangle,$
$\quad \langle ds^+ := ds;$
$\quad\quad output := \mathsf{if}\ count < dc\ \mathsf{then}\ 1\ \mathsf{else}\ 0\rangle),$
$(DecSpd,$
$\quad \langle ds := ds^+ - 1;$
$\quad\quad output := \mathsf{if}\ count < dc\ \mathsf{then}\ 1\ \mathsf{else}\ 0\rangle,$
$\quad \langle ds^+ := ds;$
$\quad\quad output := \mathsf{if}\ count < dc\ \mathsf{then}\ 1\ \mathsf{else}\ 0\rangle),$
$(Timer1,$
$\quad \langle s^+ := 0;$
$\quad\quad dc := \mathsf{if}\ dc^+ < 100\ \mathsf{and}\ s < ds$
$\quad\quad\quad\quad \mathsf{then}\ dc^+ + 1$
$\quad\quad\quad \mathsf{else\ if}\ dc^+ > 0\ \mathsf{and}\ s > ds$
$\quad\quad\quad\quad \mathsf{then}\ dc^+ - 1$
$\quad\quad\quad \mathsf{else}\ dc^+;$
$\quad\quad output := \mathsf{if}\ count < dc\ \mathsf{then}\ 1\ \mathsf{else}\ 0\rangle,$
$\quad \langle s := s^+;\ dc^+ := dc;$
$\quad\quad output := \mathsf{if}\ count < dc\ \mathsf{then}\ 1\ \mathsf{else}\ 0\rangle),$
$(Stripe,$
$\quad \langle s := s^+ + 1;$
$\quad\quad output := \mathsf{if}\ count < dc\ \mathsf{then}\ 1\ \mathsf{else}\ 0\rangle,$
$\quad \langle s^+ := s;$
$\quad\quad output := \mathsf{if}\ count < dc\ \mathsf{then}\ 1\ \mathsf{else}\ 0\rangle),$
$(Timer0,$
$\quad \langle count := \mathsf{if}\ count^+ >= 100\ \mathsf{then}\ 0$
$\quad\quad\quad\quad\quad\quad\quad \mathsf{else}\ count^+ + 1;$
$\quad\quad output := \mathsf{if}\ count < dc\ \mathsf{then}\ 1\ \mathsf{else}\ 0\rangle,$
$\quad \langle count^+ := count;$
$\quad\quad output := \mathsf{if}\ count < dc\ \mathsf{then}\ 1\ \mathsf{else}\ 0\rangle)$

Fig. 1. The Simple RoboCup Controller (SRC)

An E-FRP Controller Figure 1 presents an E-FRP controller, together with the target code produced by our compiler. In what follows we explain the definition of each of ds, s, dc, $count$, and $output$ in detail.

The desired speed ds is defined as an "init … in …" construct, which can be viewed as a state machine that changes state whenever an event occurs. The value of ds is initially 0, then it is incremented (or decremented) when $IncSpd$ (or $DecSpd$) occurs. The local variable x is used to capture the value of ds just before the event occurs.

The current speed measurement s is initially 0, and is incremented whenever a stripe is detected (the *Stripe* interrupt). This value, however, is only "inspected" when $Timer1$ occurs, at which point it is reset to zero. The later annotation means that this resetting is not carried out until all other first-phase activities triggered by $Timer1$ have been carried out (that is, it is done in the second phase of execution).

The duty cycle dc directly determines the amount of power that will be sent to the motor. On $Timer1$, the current speed s is compared with the desired speed ds (Recall that s is reset by $Timer1$ in the second phase, after all the first-phase computations that depend on the penultimate value of s have been completed). If the wheel is too slow (or too fast) then the duty cycle is incremented (or decremented). Additional conditions ensure that this value remains between 0 and 99.

The current position in the duty cycle is maintained by the value *count*. This value is incremented every time $Timer0$ occurs, and is reset every 100 $Timer0$ interrupts. Hence it counts from 0 to 99 repeatedly. The actual 0/1 signal going to the motor is determined by the value *output*. Since *output* is 1 only when $count < dc$, the larger dc is, the more power is sent to the motor, and hence the more speed. Note that *output* is updated whenever *count* or dc changes value.

Our compiler produces SimpleC, a restricted form of C. The target code is a group of event handlers. Each event handler is responsible for one particular event source, and consists of two sequences of assignments, one for each of the two phases. When the event occurs, the two assignment sequences are executed in turn to update the values of the behaviors.

Highlights The source program is easy to read and concise. It is also a minor extension on a subset of FRP, and hence inherits its denotational semantics. As we will show in this paper, it also has a simple operational semantics from which it is immediate that the program is resource bounded. The compiler generates resource bounded, but bloated, target code. However, we are able to substantially enhance the target code by a four-stage optimization process.

1.2   Contribution and Organization of This Paper

The key contribution of this paper is identifying a subset of FRP that can be compiled into clearly efficient and resource bounded code, and that is suitable for programming event-driven applications. The compilation strategy and the optimization techniques we present are also interesting.

Section 2 presents the syntax and semantics of E-FRP. Section 3 introduces the target language. Section 4 defines a compilation strategy from E-FRP into imperative code. Section 5 explains the optimization techniques.

2   Syntax and Semantics of E-FRP

Notation 1 We write $\langle f_j \rangle^{j \in \{1..n\}}$ for the sequence $\langle f_1, f_2, \ldots, f_n \rangle$. We omit the superscript $j \in \{1..n\}$ when obvious from the context. We write $\{f_j\}^{j \in \{1..n\}}$ or

---

$$\boxed{d, r, H, \varphi, b, P}$$

Non-reactive behaviors	d	$::= x \mid c \mid f \langle d_i \rangle$	Phases	$\varphi \in \Phi ::= \varepsilon \mid \text{later}$
Reactive behaviors	r	$::= \text{init } x = c \text{ in } H$	Behaviors b	$::= d \mid r$
Event handlers	H	$::= \{I_i \Rightarrow d_i \; \varphi_i\}$	Programs P	$::= \{x_i = b_i\}$

$$\boxed{FV(b)}$$

$$FV(x) \equiv \{x\}, \quad FV(c) \equiv \emptyset, \quad FV(f \langle d_i \rangle) \equiv \bigcup_i FV(d_i)$$

$$FV(\text{init } x = c \text{ in } \{I_i \Rightarrow d_i \; \varphi_i\}) \equiv \bigcup_i FV(d_i) - \{x\}$$

Fig. 2. Raw Syntax of E-FRP and definition of free variables

$\{f_j\}$ for the set $\{f_1, f_2, \cdots, f_n\}$. We write $x_1 :: \langle x_2, \ldots, x_n \rangle$ for the sequence $\langle x_1, x_2, \ldots, x_n \rangle$. We write $A +\!\!\!+ A'$ for the concatenation of the sequences A and A'. We write $A \uplus B$ for $A \cup B$ assuming that $A \cap B = \emptyset$. Finally, we write $\text{prim}(f, \langle c_i \rangle) \equiv c$ for that applying primitive function f on arguments $\langle c_i \rangle$ results in c.

2.1   Syntax of E-FRP

Figure 2 defines the syntax of E-FRP and the notion of free variables. The categories x, c and f are for variables, constants and primitive functions respectively. When a function symbol f is an infix operator, we write $d_1 \; f \; d_2$ instead of $f \; d_1 \; d_2$. The category I is for event names drawn from a finite set $\mathcal{I}$. On different target platforms, events may have different incarnations, like OS messages, or interrupts (as in the case of micro-controllers). For simplicity, an E-FRP event does not carry a value with its occurrence. The category ε stands for the empty string. An event I cannot occur more than once in an event handler H, and a variable x cannot be defined more than once in a program P.

A non-reactive behavior d is not directly updated by any event. Such a behavior could be a variable x, a constant c, or a function application on other non-reactive behaviors.

A reactive behavior $r \equiv \text{init } x = c \text{ in } \{I_i \Rightarrow d_i \; \varphi_i\}$ initially has value c, and changes to the *current* value of d_i when event I_i occurs. Note that x is bound to the old value of r and can occur free in d_i. As mentioned earlier, the execution of an E-FRP program happens in two phases. Depending on whether φ_i is ε or later, the change of value takes place in either the first or the second phase.

A program P is just a set of mutually recursive behavior definitions.

2.2   Operational Semantics

A store S maps variables to values:

$$S ::= \{x_i \mapsto c_i\}$$

$$\boxed{P \vdash b \xrightarrow{I} c}$$

$$\frac{P \vdash b \xrightarrow{I} c}{P \uplus \{x = b\} \vdash x \xrightarrow{I} c} \qquad \frac{}{P \vdash c \xrightarrow{I} c}$$

$$\frac{\left\{ P \vdash d_i \xrightarrow{I} c_i \right\} \quad \mathrm{prim}(f, \langle c_i \rangle) \equiv c}{P \vdash f \langle d_i \rangle \xrightarrow{I} c}$$

$$\frac{P \vdash d[x := c] \xrightarrow{I} c'}{P \vdash \mathsf{init}\ x = c\ \mathsf{in}\ \{I \Rightarrow d\} \uplus H \xrightarrow{I} c'}$$

$$\frac{H \not\equiv \{I \Rightarrow d\} \uplus H'}{P \vdash \mathsf{init}\ x = c\ \mathsf{in}\ H \xrightarrow{I} c}$$

$$\boxed{P \vdash b \xrightarrow{I} b'}$$

$$\frac{}{P \vdash d \xrightarrow{I} d}$$

$$\frac{H \equiv \{I \Rightarrow d\ \varphi\} \uplus H' \quad P \vdash d[x := c] \xrightarrow{I} c'}{P \vdash \mathsf{init}\ x = c\ \mathsf{in}\ H \xrightarrow{I} \mathsf{init}\ x = c'\ \mathsf{in}\ H}$$

$$\frac{H \not\equiv \{I \Rightarrow d\ \varphi\} \uplus H'}{P \vdash \mathsf{init}\ x = c\ \mathsf{in}\ H \xrightarrow{I} \mathsf{init}\ x = c\ \mathsf{in}\ H}$$

$$\boxed{P \vdash b \xrightarrow{I} c; b'}$$

$$\frac{P \vdash b \xrightarrow{I} c \quad P \vdash b \xrightarrow{I} b'}{P \vdash b \xrightarrow{I} c; b'}$$

$$\boxed{P \xrightarrow{I} S; P'}$$

$$\frac{\left\{ \{x_i = b_i\}^{i \in K} \vdash b_j \xrightarrow{I} c_j; b'_j \right\}^{j \in K}}{\{x_i = b_i\}^{i \in K} \xrightarrow{I} \{x_i \mapsto c_i\}^{i \in K}; \{x_i = b'_i\}^{i \in K}}$$

Fig. 3. Operational Semantics of E-FRP

Figure 3 defines the operational semantics of an E-FRP program by means of four judgments. The judgments can be read as follows:

- $P \vdash b \xrightarrow{I} c$: "on event I, behavior b yields c."
- $P \vdash b \xrightarrow{I} b'$: "on event I, behavior b is updated to b'."
- $P \vdash b \xrightarrow{I} c; b'$: "on event I, behavior b yields c, and is updated to b'." This is shorthand for $P \vdash b \xrightarrow{I} c$ and $P \vdash b \xrightarrow{I} b'$.
- $P \xrightarrow{I} S; P'$: "on event I, program P yields store S and is updated to P'."

Note the difference between phase 1 stepping ($\varphi \equiv \varepsilon$) and phase 2 stepping ($\varphi \equiv \mathsf{later}$): The first returns the updated state, while the second returns the old state.

$$\boxed{S \vdash d \hookrightarrow c}$$

$$\frac{}{S \uplus \{x \mapsto c\} \vdash x \hookrightarrow c} \quad \frac{}{S \vdash c \hookrightarrow c} \quad \frac{\{S \vdash d_i \hookrightarrow c_i\} \\ \mathrm{prim}(f, \langle c_i \rangle) \equiv c}{S \vdash f \langle d_i \rangle \hookrightarrow c}$$

$$\boxed{S \vdash A \hookrightarrow S'}$$

$$\frac{}{S \vdash \{\} \hookrightarrow S} \quad \frac{\{x \mapsto c\} \uplus S \vdash d \hookrightarrow c' \\ \{x \mapsto c'\} \uplus S \vdash A \hookrightarrow S'}{\{x \mapsto c\} \uplus S \vdash x := d :: A \hookrightarrow S'}$$

$$\boxed{S \vdash Q \overset{I}{\hookrightarrow} S'; S''}$$

$$\frac{I \notin \{I_i\}}{S \vdash \{(I_i, A_i, A_i')\} \overset{I}{\hookrightarrow} S; S} \quad \frac{S \vdash A \hookrightarrow S' \quad S' \vdash A' \hookrightarrow S''}{S \vdash \{(I, A, A')\} \uplus Q \overset{I}{\hookrightarrow} S'; S''}$$

Fig. 4. Operational Semantics of SimpleC

3   SimpleC: An Imperative Language

The PIC16C66 does not need to be programmed in assembly language, as there is a commercial compiler that takes as input a restricted C. We compile E-FRP to a simple imperative language we call SimpleC, from which C or almost any other imperative language code can be trivially generated.

3.1   The Syntax of SimpleC

The syntax of SimpleC is defined as follows:

Assignment Sequences $A ::= \langle x_i := d_i \rangle$ Programs $Q ::= \{(I_i, A_i, A_i')\}$

A program Q is just a collection of event handler function definitions, where I_i is the name of the function. The function body is split into two consecutive parts A_i and A_i', which are called *the first phase* and *the second phase* respectively. The idea is that when an interrupt I_i occurs, first the associated A_i is executed to generate a store matching the store yielded by the source program, then the associated A_i' is executed to prepare the store for the next event.

3.2   Operational Semantics of SimpleC

Figure 4 gives an operational semantics to SimpleC, where the judgments are read as follows:

- $S \vdash d \hookrightarrow c$: "under store S, d evaluates to c."
- $S \vdash A \hookrightarrow S'$: "executing assignment sets A updates store S to S'."
- $S \vdash Q \overset{I}{\hookrightarrow} S'; S''$: "when event I occurs, program Q updates store S to S' in the first phase, then to S'' in the second phase."

It is obvious that the operational semantics of SimpleC is deterministic.

4   Compilation

A compilation strategy is described by a set of judgments presented in Figure 5. The judgments are read as follows:

- $(x := d) < A$: "d does not depend on x or any variable updated in A. "
- $\vdash_I^1 A : P$: "A is the first phase of P's event handler for I."
- $\vdash_I^2 A : P$: "A is the second phase of P's event handler for I."
- $P \rightsquigarrow Q$: "P compiles to Q."

In the object program, besides allocating one variable for each behavior defined in the source program, we allocate a *temporary variable* x^+ for each reactive behavior named x. Temporary variables are needed for compiling certain recursive definitions.

The compilation relation is clearly decidable. But note that given a program P, $P \rightsquigarrow Q$ does not uniquely determine Q. Hence, this is not a just specification of our compiler (which is deterministic), but rather, it allows many more compilers than the one we have implemented. However, we can prove that *any* Q satisfying $P \rightsquigarrow Q$ will behave in the same way.

Note also that if there is cyclic data dependency in an E-FRP program P, we will not be able to find a Q such that $P \rightsquigarrow Q$. The restriction that the set of possible events is known at compile time and the events are mutually exclusive (i.e. no two events can be active at the same time) allows us to perform this check.

Since the target code only uses fixed number of variables, has finite number of assignments, has no loops, and does not dynamically allocate space, it is obvious that the target code can be executed in bounded space and time.

4.1   Compilation Examples

The workings of the compilation relation are best illustrated by some examples. Consider the following source program:

$$x_1 = \text{init } x = 0 \text{ in } \{I_1 \Rightarrow x + x_2\},$$
$$x_2 = \text{init } y = 1 \text{ in } \{I_2 \Rightarrow y + x_1\}$$

Here x_1 depends on x_2, and x_2 depends on x_1, but they only depend on each other in different events. Within each event, there is no cyclic dependency. Hence this program can be compiled to the following SimpleC program:

$$(I_1, \langle x_1 := x_1^+ + x_2 \rangle, \langle x_1^+ := x_1 \rangle),$$
$$(I_2, \langle x_2 := x_2^+ + x_1 \rangle, \langle x_2^+ := x_2 \rangle)$$

Consider the following source program:

$$x_1 = \text{init } x = 0 \text{ in } \{I \Rightarrow x + x_2\},$$
$$x_2 = \text{init } y = 1 \text{ in } \{I \Rightarrow x_1 \text{ later}\}$$

$\boxed{(x := d) < A}$

$$\frac{FV(d) \cap (\{x\} \uplus \{x_i\}) \equiv \emptyset}{(x := d) < \langle x_i := d_i \rangle}$$

$\boxed{\vdash^1_I A : P}$

$$\vdash^1_I \langle\rangle : \{\} \qquad \frac{\vdash^1_I A : P \quad (x := d) < A}{\vdash^1_I x := d :: A : \{x = d\} \uplus P} \;\cdot$$

$$\frac{\vdash^1_I A : P \quad (x := d[y := x^+]) < A}{\vdash^1_I x := d[y := x^+] :: A : \{x = \text{init } y = c \text{ in } \{I \Rightarrow d\} \uplus H\} \uplus P}$$

$$\frac{\vdash^1_I A : P \quad (x^+ := d[y := x]) < A}{\vdash^1_I x^+ := d[y := x] :: A : \{x = \text{init } y = c \text{ in } \{I \Rightarrow d \text{ later}\} \uplus H\} \uplus P}$$

$$\frac{\vdash^1_I A : P \quad H \not\equiv \{I \Rightarrow d\,\varphi\} \uplus H'}{\vdash^1_I A : \{x = \text{init } y = c \text{ in } H\} \uplus P}$$

$\boxed{\vdash^2_I A : P}$

$$\vdash^2_I \langle\rangle : \{\} \qquad \frac{\vdash^2_I A : P \quad (x := d) < A}{\vdash^2_I x := d :: A : \{x = d\} \uplus P}$$

$$\frac{\vdash^2_I A : P}{\vdash^2_I x^+ := x :: A : \{x = \text{init } y = c \text{ in } \{I \Rightarrow d\} \uplus H\} \uplus P}$$

$$\frac{\vdash^2_I A : P}{\vdash^2_I x := x^+ :: A : \{x = \text{init } y = c \text{ in } \{I \Rightarrow d \text{ later}\} \uplus H\} \uplus P}$$

$$\frac{\vdash^2_I A : P \quad H \not\equiv \{I \Rightarrow d\,\varphi\} \uplus H'}{\vdash^2_I A : \{x = \text{init } y = c \text{ in } H\} \uplus P}$$

$\boxed{P \rightsquigarrow Q}$

$$\frac{P \equiv \{x_i = b_i\} \quad \{\vdash^1_I A_I : P \quad \vdash^2_I A'_I : P\}^{I \in \mathcal{I}} \quad \bigcup_i FV(b_i) \subseteq \{x_i\}}{P \rightsquigarrow \{(I, A_I, A'_I)\}^{I \in \mathcal{I}}}$$

Fig. 5. Compilation of E-FRP

Here x_1 and x_2 are mutually dependent in I, but their values are updated in different phases. In each phase, the dependency graph is acyclic. Hence this program compiles too, and one acceptable compilation for it is:

$$(I, \langle x_1 := x_1^+ + x_2; \; x_2^+ := x_1 \rangle, \langle x_1^+ := x_1; \; x_2 := x_2^+ \rangle)$$

However, if the definition for x_2 were

$$x_2 = \text{init } y = 1 \text{ in } \{I \Rightarrow x_1\}$$

then the code would have been rejected.

If we let both x_1 and x_2 be updated in the later phase, i.e. let the program P be

$$x_1 = \text{init } x = 0 \text{ in } \{I \Rightarrow x + x_2 \text{ later}\},$$
$$x_2 = \text{init } y = 1 \text{ in } \{I \Rightarrow x_1 \text{ later}\}$$

then one possible translation of P in SimpleC is

$$(I, \langle x_1^+ := x_1 + x_2; \ x_2^+ := x1 \rangle, \langle x_1 := x_1^+; \ x_2 := x_2^+ \rangle$$

In concrete C syntax, the code would look like

```
void on_I( void ) {
        x1_ = x1 + x2;   x2_ = x1;
later:  x1  = x1_;       x2  = x2_;
}
```

4.2 Correctness

When an event I occurs, a behavior x in an E-FRP program can be updated to have a new value c. To prove that our compiler is correct, we need to show that after executing the event handler for I, the corresponding variable(s) of x in the target program will have the same value c. The following concept is useful for formalizing this intuition:

Definition 1 The **state** of a program P, written as state(P), is a store defined by:

$$\text{state}(P) \equiv \{x_i \mapsto \text{state}_P(d_i)\} \uplus \{x_j \mapsto \text{state}_P(r_j), x_j^+ \mapsto \text{state}_P(r_j)\}$$

where $P \equiv \{x_i = d_i\} \uplus \{x_j = r_j\}$ and

$$
\begin{array}{ll}
\text{state}_{P \uplus \{x=b\}}(x) & \equiv \text{state}_P(b) \\
\text{state}_P(c) & \equiv c \\
\text{state}_P(f \ \langle d_i \rangle) & \equiv \text{prim}(f, \langle \text{state}_P(d_i) \rangle) \\
\text{state}_P(\text{init } x = c \text{ in } H) & \equiv c
\end{array}
$$

Finally, we show that the compilation is correct in the sense that updating an E-FRP program does not change its translation in SimpleC, and that the source program generates the same result as the target program:

Theorem 1 (*Compilation Correctness*)

1. $P \rightsquigarrow Q \wedge P \xrightarrow{I} S; P' \implies P' \rightsquigarrow Q$;
2. $P \rightsquigarrow Q \wedge P \xrightarrow{I} S; P' \wedge \text{state}(P) \vdash Q \xrightarrow{I} S_1; S_2 \implies \exists S'. \ S_1 \equiv S \uplus S' \wedge S_2 \equiv \text{state}(P')$.

The proof of Theorem 1 is omitted as this paper focuses on practical rather than theoretical results.

$$\boxed{P \vdash Q \Rightarrow_1 Q'} \quad \frac{(x = d) \in P \quad FV(d) \cap LV(A) = \emptyset}{P \vdash Q \uplus \{(I, A + x := d + A', A'')\} \Rightarrow_1 Q \uplus \{(I, A + A', A'')\}}$$

$$\frac{(x = d) \in P \quad FV(d) \cap LV(A') = \emptyset}{P \vdash Q \uplus \{(I, A, A' + x := d + A'')\} \Rightarrow_1 Q \uplus \{(I, A, A' + A'')\}}$$

$$\boxed{P \vdash Q \Rightarrow_2 Q'} \quad \frac{x^+ \in FV(d)}{\begin{array}{c} P \vdash Q \uplus \{(I, A + x := d + A', A'')\} \Rightarrow_2 \\ Q \uplus \{(I, A + x := d[x^+ := x] + A', A'')\} \end{array}}$$

$$\boxed{P \vdash Q \Rightarrow_3 Q'} \quad \frac{FV(d) \cap LV(A_2) = \emptyset}{\begin{array}{c} P \vdash Q \uplus \{(I, A_1 + x^+ := d + A_2, A_3 + x := x^+ + A_4)\} \Rightarrow_3 \\ Q \uplus \{(I, A_1 + A_2 + x := d, x^+ := x + A_3 + A_4)\} \end{array}}$$

$$\boxed{P \vdash Q \Rightarrow_4 Q'} \quad \frac{Q \equiv Q' \uplus \{(I, A + x^+ := d + A', A'')\} \quad x^+ \notin RV(Q)}{P \vdash Q \Rightarrow_4 Q' \uplus \{(I, A + A', A'')\}}$$

$$\frac{Q \equiv Q' \uplus \{(I, A, A' + x^+ := d + A'')\} \quad x^+ \notin RV(Q)}{P \vdash Q \Rightarrow_4 Q' \uplus \{(I, A, A' + A'')\}}$$

$$\boxed{P \vdash Q \Rightarrow_i^* Q'} \quad \frac{}{P \vdash Q \Rightarrow_i^* Q} \qquad \frac{P \vdash Q \Rightarrow_i^* Q' \quad P \vdash Q' \Rightarrow_i Q''}{P \vdash Q \Rightarrow_i^* Q''}$$

$$\boxed{P \vdash Q \Rightarrow_{|i} Q'} \quad \frac{P \vdash Q \Rightarrow_i^* Q' \quad \nexists Q''. P \vdash Q' \Rightarrow_i Q''}{P \vdash Q \Rightarrow_{|i} Q'}$$

$$\boxed{P \vdash Q \Rightarrow_| Q'} \quad \frac{P \rightsquigarrow Q \quad P \vdash Q \Rightarrow_{|1} Q_1 \quad P \vdash Q_1 \Rightarrow_{|2} Q_2 \quad P \vdash Q_2 \Rightarrow_{|3} Q_3 \quad P \vdash Q_3 \Rightarrow_{|4} Q'}{P \vdash Q \Rightarrow_| Q'}$$

Fig. 6. Optimization of the Target Code

5 Optimization

The compiler that we have described, although provably correct, generates only naïve code that leaves a lot of room for optimization. Besides applying known techniques for optimizing sequential imperative programs, we can improve the target code by taking advantage of our knowledge on the compiler. In particular, we implemented a compiler that does:

1. Ineffective code elimination: Given a definition $x = b$ in the source program, x is affected by a particular event I only when one of the following is true:
   (a) b is a reactive behavior that reacts to I; or
   (b) b is a non-reactive behavior, and one of the variables in $FV(b)$ is affected by I.

It is obvious that whether x is affected by I can be determined statically. If x is not affected by I, the code for updating x in the event handler for I can be eliminated. This optimization helps reduce the code size as well as the response time.

2. Temporary variable elimination: The value of a temporary variable x^+ cannot be observed by the user of the system. Hence there is no need to keep x^+ around if it can be eliminated by some program transformations. This technique reduces memory usage and the response time.

We define the *right-hand-side variables* (written RV) of a collection of assignments, and the *left-hand-side variables* (written LV) of a collection of assignments, as

$$\boxed{RV(A)} \qquad RV(\langle x_i := d_i \rangle) \equiv \bigcup_i FV(d_i)$$

$$\boxed{RV(Q)} \qquad RV(\{(I_i, A_i, A'_i)\}) \equiv \bigcup_i (RV(A_i) \cup RV(A'_i))$$

$$\boxed{LV(A)} \qquad LV(\langle x_i := d_i \rangle) \equiv \{x_i\}$$

The optimizations are carried out in four stages, where each stage consists of a sequence of one particular kind of transformations. In each stage, we keep applying the same transformation to the target code till it cannot be applied any further.

The purpose of stage 1 is to eliminate unnecessary updates to variables. One such update is eliminated in each step.

The code produced by the unoptimizing compiler has the property that at the beginning of phase 1 of any event handler, x and x^+ always hold the same value. Stage 1 optimization preserves this property. Hence in stage 2, we can safely replace the occurrences of x^+ on the right hand side of an assignment in phase 1 with x. This reduces the usage of x^+ and thus helps stage 4.

Since stage 1 and stage 2 are simple, we can easily write a compiler that directly generates code for stage 3. However the proof of the correctness of this partially-optimizing compiler then becomes complicated. Therefore we choose to present stage 1 and stage 2 as separate optimization processes.

We call the transformation in stage 3 "castling" for its resemblance to the castling special move in chess: if an event handler updates x^+ in phase 1 and assigns x^+ to x in phase 2, under certain conditions we can instead update x at the end of phase 1 and assign x to x^+ at the beginning of phase 2. This transformation reduces right-hand-side occurrences of x^+, thus making it easier to be eliminated in stage 4. Note that the correctness of this transformation is non-trivial.

If the value of a temporary variable x^+ is never used, then there is no need to keep x^+ around. This is what we do in stage 4.

Figure 6 formally defines the optimization. Given a source program P, we write $P \vdash Q \Rightarrow_i Q'$ for that Q is transformed to Q' in *one step* in stage i, where $1 \leq i \leq 4$; we write $P \vdash Q \Rightarrow_i^* Q'$ for that Q is transformed to Q' in *zero or more steps* in stage i; and we write $P \vdash Q \Rightarrow|_i Q'$ for that Q' is the *furthest* you can

$$Q_1 \equiv (IncSpd, \langle ds := ds^+ + 1 \rangle, \langle ds^+ := ds \rangle),$$
$$(DecSpd, \langle ds := ds^+ - 1 \rangle, \langle ds^+ := ds \rangle),$$
$$(Timer1, \langle s^+ := 0; dc := \text{if } dc^+ < 100 \text{ and } s < ds \text{ then } dc^+ + 1$$
$$\text{else if } dc^+ > 0 \text{ and } s > ds \text{ then } dc^+ - 1 \text{ else } dc^+;$$
$$output := \text{if } count < dc \text{ then } 1 \text{ else } 0 \rangle,$$
$$\langle s := s^+; \ dc^+ := dc \rangle),$$
$$(Stripe, \ \langle s := s^+ + 1; \rangle, \langle s^+ := s; \rangle),$$
$$(Timer0, \langle count := \text{if } count^+ >= 100 \text{ then } 0 \text{ else } count^+ + 1;$$
$$output := \text{if } count < dc \text{ then } 1 \text{ else } 0 \rangle,$$
$$\langle count^+ := count \rangle)$$

$$Q_2 \equiv (IncSpd, \langle ds := ds + 1 \rangle, \langle ds^+ := ds \rangle),$$
$$(DecSpd, \langle ds := ds - 1 \rangle, \langle ds^+ := ds \rangle),$$
$$(Timer1, \langle s^+ := 0; dc := \text{if } dc < 100 \text{ and } s < ds \text{ then } dc + 1$$
$$\text{else if } dc > 0 \text{ and } s > ds \text{ then } dc - 1 \text{ else } dc;$$
$$output := \text{if } count < dc \text{ then } 1 \text{ else } 0 \rangle,$$
$$\langle s := s^+; \ dc^+ := dc \rangle),$$
$$(Stripe, \ \langle s := s + 1; \rangle, \langle s^+ := s; \rangle),$$
$$(Timer0, \langle count := \text{if } count >= 100 \text{ then } 0 \text{ else } count + 1;$$
$$output := \text{if } count < dc \text{ then } 1 \text{ else } 0 \rangle,$$
$$\langle count^+ := count \rangle)$$

$$Q_3 \equiv (IncSpd, \langle ds := ds + 1 \rangle, \langle ds^+ := ds \rangle),$$
$$(DecSpd, \langle ds := ds - 1 \rangle, \langle ds^+ := ds \rangle),$$
$$(Timer1, \langle dc := \text{if } dc < 100 \text{ and } s < ds \text{ then } dc + 1$$
$$\text{else if } dc > 0 \text{ and } s > ds \text{ then } dc - 1 \text{ else } dc;$$
$$output := \text{if } count < dc \text{ then } 1 \text{ else } 0; s := 0 \rangle,$$
$$\langle s^+ := s; \ dc^+ := dc \rangle),$$
$$(Stripe, \ \langle s := s + 1; \rangle, \langle s^+ := s; \rangle),$$
$$(Timer0, \langle count := \text{if } count >= 100 \text{ then } 0 \text{ else } count + 1;$$
$$output := \text{if } count < dc \text{ then } 1 \text{ else } 0 \rangle,$$
$$\langle count^+ := count \rangle)$$

$$Q_4 \equiv (IncSpd, \langle ds := ds + 1 \rangle, \langle \rangle),$$
$$(DecSpd, \langle ds := ds - 1 \rangle, \langle \rangle),$$
$$(Timer1, \langle dc := \text{if } dc < 100 \text{ and } s < ds \text{ then } dc + 1$$
$$\text{else if } dc > 0 \text{ and } s > ds \text{ then } dc - 1 \text{ else } dc;$$
$$output := \text{if } count < dc \text{ then } 1 \text{ else } 0; s := 0 \rangle, \langle \rangle),$$
$$(Stripe, \ \langle s := s + 1; \rangle, \langle \rangle),$$
$$(Timer0, \langle count := \text{if } count >= 100 \text{ then } 0 \text{ else } count + 1;$$
$$output := \text{if } count < dc \text{ then } 1 \text{ else } 0 \rangle, \langle \rangle)$$

Fig. 7. Optimization of the Simple RoboCup Controller

get from Q by applying stage i transformations. Finally, we write $P \vdash Q \Rightarrow\!\mid Q'$ for that P compiles to Q, which is then optimized to Q'.

As an example, Figure 7 presents the intermediate and final results of optimizing the SRC program. Stage 1 optimization generates Q_1, where all unnecessary updates to *output* have been eliminated. Then stage 2 gets rid of all right-hand-side temporary variables in phase 1, as in the change from $ds := ds^+ + 1$ to $ds := ds + 1$, and the result is Q_2. In stage 3 we rearrange the updating to s and s^+ and get Q_3. Finally, we are able to remove all temporary variables in stage 4, resulting in Q_4, the optimized final code.

6   Discussion and Related Work

We refer the reader to [17] for a general introduction on the use of functional programming for reactive (especially real-time) applications.

E-FRP is a slightly extended subset of FRP. To make the relation precise, we present a partial function $[\![\_]\!]$ that translates E-FRP to FRP:

$$
\begin{aligned}
&[\![x]\!] &&\equiv x\\
&[\![c]\!] &&\equiv \mathsf{lift0}\ c\\
&[\![f\ \langle d_i\rangle^{i\in\{1..n\}}]\!] &&\equiv \mathsf{liftn}\ f\ \langle[\![d_i]\!]\rangle^{i\in\{1..n\}}\\
&[\![\mathsf{init}\ x = c\ \mathsf{in}\ \{I_i \Rightarrow d_i\}]\!] &&\equiv \mathsf{iStepAccum}\ c\ [\![\{I_i \Rightarrow d_i\}]\!]_x\\
&[\![\mathsf{init}\ x = c\ \mathsf{in}\ \{I_i \Rightarrow d_i\ \mathsf{later}\}]\!] &&\equiv \mathsf{stepAccum}\ c\ [\![\{I_i \Rightarrow d_i\}]\!]_x\\
&[\![\{x_i = b_i\}]\!] &&\equiv \{x_i = [\![b_i]\!]\}\\
&\quad\text{where}\quad [\![\{I_i \Rightarrow d_i\}^{i\in K}]\!]_x \equiv \mathsf{foldr}\ (.|.)\ \mathsf{neverE}\ [\![d_i]\!]_{x,I_i}{}^{i\in K}\\
&\qquad\qquad [\![d]\!]_{x,I} \equiv (\mathsf{snapshot}n\ I\ \langle x_i\rangle^{i\in\{1..n\}}) \Rightarrow \lambda\langle x_i\rangle^{i\in\{1..n\}}.\lambda x.d\\
&\qquad\qquad\quad \text{where}\ \{x_i\}^{i\in\{1..n\}} \equiv FV(d) - \{x\}
\end{aligned}
$$

The key facility missing from FRP is the ability to mix now and later operations, which is exactly the reason why $[\![\_]\!]$ is not total. Our experience with E-FRP shows that this is a very useful feature, and extending FRP with such functionality would be interesting future work.

Several languages have been proposed around the *synchronous data-flow* notion of computation, including SIGNAL, LUSTRE, and ESTEREL, which were specifically designed for control of real-time systems. SIGNAL [8] is a block-diagram oriented language, where the central concept is a *signal*, a time-ordered sequence of values. This is analogous to the sequence of values generated in the execution of an E-FRP program. LUSTRE [3] is a functional synchronous data flow language, rooted again in the notion of a sequence. ESTEREL is a synchronous imperative language devoted to programming control-dominated software or hardware reactive systems [1]. Compilers exist to translate ESTEREL programs into automata or electronic circuits [2]. Although these languages are similar to E-FRP, there are subtle differences whose significance deserves further investigation.

To guarantee bounded space and time, the languages above do not consider recursion. The language of synchronous Kahn networks [4] was developed as an extension to LUSTRE that adds recursion and higher-order programming. Such an extension yields a large increase in expressive power, but sacrifices resource-boundedness. In RT-FRP we have shown that, using some syntactic restrictions and a type system, it is possible to have recursion and guarantee resource bound. We expect to be able to extend E-FRP with the RT-FRP style recursion.

The SCR (Software Cost Reduction) requirements method [10] is a formal method based on tables for specifying the requirements of safety-critical software systems. SCR is supported by an integrated suite of tools called SCR* [11], which includes among others a *consistency checker* for detecting well-formedness errors, a *simulator* for validating the specification, and a *model checker* for checking application properties. SCR has been successfully applied in some large projects to expose errors in the requirements specification. We have noticed that the tabular notation used in SCR for specifying system behaviors has a similar flavor as that of E-FRP, and it would be interesting future work to translate E-FRP into SCR and hence leverage the SCR* toolset to find errors in the program.

Throughout our work on E-FRP, more systematic approaches for semantics-based program generation, for example MetaML, have been continually considered for the implementation of the final program generation phase of the compiler [18]. So far, we have used an elementary technique for the generation of programs instead. There are a number of practical reasons for this:

- The code we generate does not involve the generation of new variable names, and thus there is no apparent need for MetaML hygiene (fresh name generation mechanism).
- MetaML does not currently support generating code in languages other than MetaML.
- The target language, has only a very simple type system, and essentially all the instructions we generated have the same type. In other words, assuring type safety of the generated code, a key feature of MetaML, is not a significant issue.
- The standard way for using MetaML is to stage a denotational semantics. While such a denotational semantics exists for FRP, it is not yet clear how we can use staging to introduce the imperative implementation of behaviors in a natural way. We plan to pursue this direction in future work.

An alternative approach to semantics-based program generation is the use of an appropriate monad, as in the work of Harrison and Kamin [9]. However, we have not identified such a monad at this point, and this is also interesting future work.

7   Conclusions

We have presented a core, first-order subset of FRP and showed how it can be compiled in a natural and sound manner into a simple imperative language. We have implemented this compilation strategy in Haskell. The prototype produces C code that is readily accepted by the PIC16C66 C compiler. Compared to previous work on RT-FRP, our focus here has shifted from the integration with the lambda language to the scrutiny of the feasibility of implementing this language and using it to program real event-driven systems. In the immediate future, we intend to extend the language with more constructs (especially behavior switching), to investigate the correctness of some basic optimizations on the generated programs, and to continue the development of the compiler.

References

1. Gerard Berry and Laurent Cosserat. The Esterel synchronous programming language and its mathematical semantics. In A. W. Roscoe S. D. Brookes and editors G. Winskel, editors, *Seminar on Concurrency*, volume 197 of *Lect. Notes in Computer Science*, pages 389–448. Springer Verlag, 1985. 169

2. Gerard Berry and the Esterel Team. *The Esterel v5.21 System Manual*. Centre de Mathématiques Appliquées, Ecole des Mines de Paris and INRIA, March 1999. Available at `http://www.inria.fr/meije/esterel`. 169

3. Paul Caspi, Halbwachs Halbwachs, Nicolas Pilaud, and John A. Plaice. Lustre: A declarative language for programming synchronous systems. In *the Symposium on Principles of Programming Languages (POPL '87)*, January 1987. 169

4. Paul Caspi and M. Pouzet. Synchronous Kahn networks. In *International Conference on Functional Programming*. ACM SIGPLAN, May 1996. 169

5. Antony Courtney and Conal Elliott. Genuinely functional user interfaces. In *Haskell Workshop*, 2001. 155

6. Conal Elliott and Paul Hudak. Functional reactive animation. In *International Conference on Functional Programming*, pages 163–173, June 1997. 155

7. John Peterson et al. Haskell 1.4: A non-strict, purely functional language. Technical Report YALEU/DCS/RR-1106, Department of Computer Science, Yale University, Mar 1997. World Wide Web version at `http://haskell.cs.yale.edu/haskell-report`. 155

8. Thierry Gautier, Paul Le Guernic, and Loic Besnard. Signal: A declarative language for synchronous programming of real-time systems. In Gilles Kahn, editor, *Functional Programming Languages and Computer Architecture*, volume 274 of *Lect Notes in Computer Science, edited by G. Goos and J. Hartmanis*, pages 257–277. Springer-Verlag, 1987. 169

9. William L. Harrison and Samuel N. Kamin. Modular compilers based on monad transformers. In *Proceedings of the IEEE International Conference on Computer Languages*, 1998. 170

10. Constance Heitmeyer. Applying *Practical* formal methods to the specification and analysis of security properties. In *Proc. Information Assurance in Computer Networks, LNCS 2052*, St. Petersburg, Russia, May 2001. Springer-Verlag. 170

11. Constance Heitmeyer, James Kirby, Bruce Labaw, and Ramesh Bharadwaj. SCR*: A toolset for specifying and analyzing software requirements. In *Proc. Computer-Aided Verification*, Vancouver, Canada, 1998. 170

12. Paul Hudak. *The Haskell School of Expression – Learning Functional Programming through Multimedia*. Cambridge University Press, New York, 2000. 155

13. Microchip Technology Inc. *PIC16C66 Datasheet*. Available on-line at `http://www.microchip.com/`. 156

14. John Peterson, Gregory Hager, and Paul Hudak. A language for declarative robotic programming. In *International Conference on Robotics and Automation*, 1999. 155

15. Alastair Reid, John Peterson, Greg Hager, and Paul Hudak. Prototyping real-time vision systems: An experiment in DSL design. In *Proceedings of International Conference on Software Engineering*, May 1999. 155

16. RoboCup official site. `http://www.robocup.org/`. 156

17. Walid Taha, Paul Hudak, and Zhanyong Wan. Directions in functional programming for real(-time) applications. In Thomas A. Henzinger and Christoph M. Kirsch, editors, *Proc. First International Workshop, EMSOFT, LNCS 2211*, pages 185–203, Tahoe City, CA, USA, October 2001. Springer-Verlag. 169

18. Walid Taha and Tim Sheard. Multi-stage programming with explicit annotations. In *Proceedings of Symposium on Partial Evaluation and Semantics Based Program manipulation*, pages 203–217. ACM SIGPLAN, 1997. 170
19. Zhanyong Wan and Paul Hudak. Functional reactive programming from first principles. In *Proceedings of Symposium on Programming Language Design and Implementation*. ACM, 2000. 155
20. Zhanyong Wan, Walid Taha, and Paul Hudak. Real-time FRP. In *Proceedings of Sixth ACM SIGPLAN International Conference on Functional Programming*, Florence, Italy, September 2001. ACM. 156

Adding Apples and Oranges

Martin Erwig and Margaret Burnett ·

Oregon State University, Department of Computer Science
Corvallis, OR 97331, USA
{erwig,burnett}@cs.orst.edu

Abstract. We define a unit system for end-user spreadsheets that is based on the concrete notion of units instead of the abstract concept of types. Units are derived from header information given by spreadsheets. The unit system contains concepts, such as dependent units, multiple units, and unit generalization, that allow the classification of spreadsheet contents on a more fine-grained level than types do. Also, because communication with the end user happens only in terms of objects that are contained in the spreadsheet, our system does not require end users to learn new abstract concepts of type systems.

Keywords: First-Order Functional Language, Spreadsheet, Type Checking, Unit, End-User Programming

1 Introduction

The early detection of type errors is a well-known benefit of static typing, but static typing has not been used in programming languages intended for end users not formally schooled in programming. A possible reason for this omission is that the introduction of static types incurs learning cost: either the cost of learning about type declarations, or the cost of understanding a type inference system well enough to understand the error messages it generates. End users are not usually interested in paying these costs, because their use of programming is simply a means to an end, namely helping them get their "real" jobs done faster.

The number of end-user programmers in the United States alone are expected to reach 55 million by 2005, as compared to only 2.75 million professional programmers [4]. This estimate was originally made in 1994 based on Bureau of Labor Statistics and Bureau of Census figures, and a 1999 assessment of the model shows that its predictions are so far reasonably on track. The "programming" systems most widely used by end users are members of the spreadsheet paradigm. Henceforth, we use the term spreadsheet languages[1] to refer to all systems following the spreadsheet paradigm, in which computations are defined by cells and their formulas. Although spreadsheet languages have not been taken

---

[1] We have chosen this terminology to emphasize the fact that even commercial spreadsheet systems are indeed languages for programming, although they differ in audience, application, and environment from traditional programming languages.

S. Krishnamurthi, C. R. Ramakrishnan (Eds.): PADL 2002, LNCS 2257, pp. 173–191, 2002.
© Springer-Verlag Berlin Heidelberg 2002

seriously by the programming language community, two recent NSF workshops' results included the conclusion that serious consideration of languages such as these is indeed needed [2].

There is extensive evidence that many spreadsheets contain errors. For example, field audits of real-world spreadsheets have found that 20% to 40% of all spreadsheets contain errors, and several controlled spreadsheet experiments have reported even higher error rates [3,16,14]. These errors can have serious consequences. For example, a Dallas oil and gas company lost millions of dollars in an acquisition deal because of spreadsheet errors [13].

To help prevent some of these spreadsheet errors, we are developing an approach to reasoning about units. Like other research into units and dimensions [17,9], the goal of our approach is to detect errors related to illegal combinations of units. Unlike other works, we aim to detect any such error as soon as it is typed in, to make use of information such as column headers the end user has entered for reasons other than unit inference, and to support a kind of polymorphism of units through generalization. Note that our notion of "unit" is completely application dependent and is generally not related to the idea that units represent scales of measurement for certain dimensions [10].

Consider the following scenario. Suppose a user has created the example spreadsheet in Figure 1. From the labels the user has placed, the system can guess that, for example, the entries of column B are apples. The system confirms its guesses by interacting with the user, and the user can correct the guesses and add additional information about the units structure as well. This mechanism for getting explicit information about units is a "gentle slope" language feature [12,11]: the user does not have to "declare" any unit information at all, but the more such information the user enters through column headers or later clarifications in correcting the system's guesses, the more the system can use this information to reason about errors.

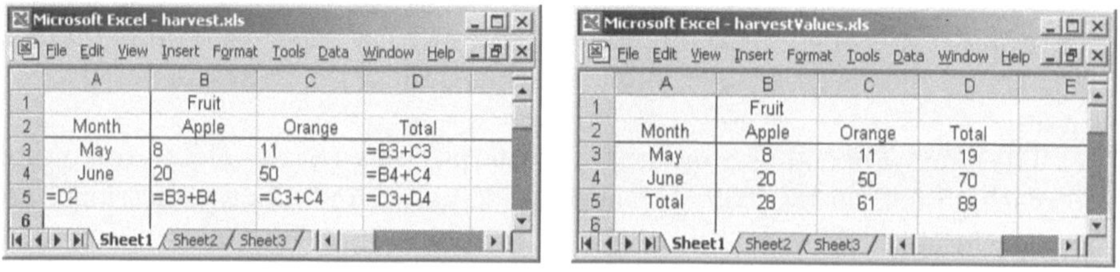

(a) Formulas   (b) Resulting values

Fig. 1. A fruit production spreadsheet

From the information gleaned, the system can deduce that the total at the bottom of column B is also in apples, which is a legal combination of units. The entry in D3 adds apples and oranges, which at first glance may seem an illegal combination of units; however, it represents the total of all of row 3, which is in units of May as well as in units of all the fruits. Thus, the total is in units of May apples or May oranges, which reduces to May fruits, and is legal as well. As this demonstrates, in cells such as B3 there is a collaborative relationship between two kinds of units: apples and May. By similar reasoning, the total in D5 is legal; it turns out to be the sum of all fruits in all months, and its units reflect a collaborative relationship between fruits and months.

Now suppose the user attempts to add May apples to June oranges (B3+C4). The system immediately detects a unit error in this formula, because there is no match on specific units (apples versus oranges), and not enough is being combined to cover all fruits in a way that also matches either one month or generalizes to all months. Adding May apples to June oranges is the kind of error that arises when a user accidentally refers to the wrong cell in a formula, through typographical error or selecting the wrong cell with the mouse.

The rest of this paper is structured as follows. In Section 2 we discuss specific aspects of spreadsheets that influence the design of our unit system. In Section 3 we define a small language that serves as a model of spreadsheets. In Section 4 we develop a notion of units and unit expressions that can be used to describe units for expressions and cells. In particular, we have to describe what well-formed units are. Then in Section 5 we describe the process of checking the units of (cells in) a spreadsheet. We draw some conclusions and give remarks on future work in Section 6. Formal definitions appear in the Appendices A to C.

2 Features of Spreadsheet Languages that Impact Reasoning about Units

Like other members of the applicative family, spreadsheet languages are declarative languages, and hence computations are specified by providing arguments to operations. It is not impossible for a spreadsheet language to support higher-order functions (for example, see [8]), but since higher-order functions are not commonly associated with spreadsheets, for the purposes of this paper we will consider only first-order functions. The restriction to first-order functions makes rich type systems feasible, such as by including use of dependent types. Taking advantage of this opportunity, the unit system presented here includes a similar notion: dependent units.

In spreadsheets, the distinction between "static" and "dynamic" is subtly different than in other languages, because spreadsheets automatically execute after every edit through the "automatic recalculation" feature. Thus, each static edit is immediately followed by dynamic computations. We choose to ignore this advantage to some extent, because by staying only with static (but incremental) devices, the reasoning mechanism can function the same under both eager and lazy evaluation mechanisms, since it will not depend on which cells have been evaluated. Note that the only "input" device for spreadsheets is the entry of constant formulas into cells, and we will consider the evaluation of constant formulas to be a static operation, at least for constant formulas that identify new units. Because "input values" are thus available to the static reasoning system, dependent units are feasible.

The question may arise as to why we have chosen to make the reasoning system static if the intertwining of static-time operations with runtime operations means that complete runtime information is available. The answer is that we would like the reasoning system to work regardless of a spreadsheet's evaluation mechanism. It should work even with lazy evaluation, in which off-screen cells are not computed until they are scrolled on-screen or needed for on-screen calculations. Also, we would like the reasoning system to work even if the user turns off the "automatic recalculation" feature, such as to load a legacy spreadsheet primarily to check it for unit errors.

Still, to be consistent with spreadsheets' default behavior of automatically updating after every edit, a design constraint of the reasoning system is that it must support immediate feedback. Thus, we require the following design constraint to be met:

Constraint 1 (*Incremental*): The reasoning mechanism should give immediate visual feedback as to the unit safety of the most recently entered spreadsheet formula as soon as it is entered.

Recent studies in the realm of one type of problem-solving, namely web searching, indicate that users performed consistently better if they had a basic understanding of the system's selection mechanism [1]. Further, there needs to be a meaningful way to communicate with users about the errors the reasoning system detects. What both of these points suggest is that the reasoning system itself should be in terms of concrete elements explicitly put in the spreadsheet by the user, because the user is familiar with these elements. We have decided to adopt this approach, and we state it as design constraint 2:

Constraint 2 (*Directness*): The reasoning mechanisms should directly be in terms of elements with which the user is working, such as labels and operation names.

Most static type inference systems introduce new vocabularies that relate only abstractly and indirectly to the objects and formulas on the screen. Design constraint 3 follows directly from design constraint 2:

Constraint 3 (*Not type based*): The reasoning mechanism should require no formal notion of types per se other than what is expressed by units.

Another important difference between other applicative languages and spreadsheet languages is that in spreadsheets, if something goes wrong, such as a (dynamic) type error or a divide-by-zero, computations still continue. This is different from other declarative languages featuring static type checking, which do not allow execution until all type errors are removed. This implies that a reasoning system for spreadsheets must allow reasoning to happen even when a type error (or unit error, in our case) is present somewhere in the spreadsheet.

Further, since end users do not have the training professional programmers have, many of their spreadsheets have characteristics of which computer scientists would not approve. We have a collection of real spreadsheets gathered from office workers, professors, and a variety of web pages. These spreadsheets show inconsistent labeling, odd layouts, formulas with repeated constants rather then references, cells whose formulas return error values resulting from exceptions [5], and many other oddities. It would not be practical to design an approach purportedly intended for end users that did not work for those kinds of programs, because those are the kinds of programs end users write. We express this point in our fourth design constraint:

> **Constraint 4** (*Practical*): The reasoning mechanism must support the kind of spreadsheets end users really build. In particular, the approach cannot rest upon assumptions that end users will create "the right kind" of formulas, be complete in their labeling practices, or that their spreadsheets will be free of statically detectable errors.

3   A Spreadsheet Calculus

In this section we will define a simple model of spreadsheets, the σ-calculus, to have a notation for spreadsheet cells and expressions that can be related to units. The model should be simple enough to facilitate the definition of a unit system and expressive enough to support the end-user requirements discussed in Section 2.

The syntax of the σ-calculus is defined in Figure 2. A spreadsheet (s) consists of a set of named cells. Names, or addresses, (a) are taken from a set N and are distinct from all other values and expressions. Each cell contains an expression (e), which evaluates to a value. A value can be of any suitable type, in particular, values need not be restricted to be numbers or strings. Two distinguished values are the error value ϵ and the blank value $\sqcup$, which are introduced for practical reasons to take into account design constraint 4: spreadsheets often include blank cells and errors. Expressions that are not constants are given by applications of operations to other expressions or by references to other cells. Since we are modeling a first-order language, we do not allow partial applications of operations.

We consider operations (ω) to be indexed by the number of required arguments. Hence, ω^0 ranges over all constants that are different from $\sqcup$ and ϵ. We use v as a synonym for ω^0 whereas $v^{\sqcup}$ ranges over all constants, including $\sqcup$, and v^{ϵ} ranges over all constants, including $\sqcup$ and ϵ. When we use ω^n we implicitly assume $n > 0$ if not explicitly stated otherwise. A spreadsheet is given by a collection of cells whose names are distinct. We can thus regard a spreadsheet as a mapping from names to expressions. We use $dom(s)$ and $rng(s)$ to denote a spreadsheet's domain and range, respectively. More generally, we call a mapping $N \rightarrow \alpha$ a *named α-collection*, or just *α-collection* for short. Hence, a spreadsheet is an e-collection.

$$
\begin{array}{lll}
a & & \text{Names} \\
e & ::= & \sqcup \mid \epsilon \mid \omega^n(e_1, \ldots, e_n) \mid a \qquad \text{Expressions } (n \geq 0) \\
s & ::= & (a_1, e_1) ; \ldots ; (a_m, e_m) \qquad \text{Spreadsheets } (m \geq 1) \\
& & i \neq j \Rightarrow a_i \neq a_j
\end{array}
$$

Fig. 2. The σ-calculus—abstract syntax of spreadsheets

We deliberately do not require a rectangular structure among the cells since such a restriction is not needed for the investigation performed in this paper and would rule out unnecessarily certain spreadsheet languages, such as Forms/3 [6].

Spreadsheets (that is, e-collections) like the one shown in Figure 1 (a) are evaluated to v-collections where all expressions have been evaluated to values; see Figure 1 (b). This evaluation is formally defined through a reduction relation given in Appendix A.

In the following we refer to the expression or value contained in a spreadsheet s in the cell a by $s(a)$. Hence, if we name our example spreadsheet *Harvest* and the evaluated sheet *Result*, we have, for example, *Harvest*(D3) = +(B3, C3) and *Result*(D3) = 19. In discussing examples we sometimes identify cells by their content, for example, if we speak of cell Total, we mean the cell named D2.

4   The Nature of Units

The unit information for the cells in a spreadsheet are completely contained in the spreadsheet itself because units are defined by values. More precisely, each value in a spreadsheet (except $\sqcup$) defines a unit. We can imagine that all the values in a spreadsheet define a unit universe from which the units for cells are drawn. Although all values are units, not all values are generally used as units. For example, in the spreadsheet *Harvest* the text Total is by definition a unit, but it is not used as a unit for cells in the spreadsheet. In the following three subsections we define how basic unit information is provided by headers, how complex units are obtained by unit expressions, and what well-formed units are.

4.1   Headers

Intuitively, a header is a label that gives a unit for a group of cells. For example, in Figure 1 Month is a header for the cells May and June. In this simple form, headers may seem similar to data types in Haskell or ML, but there are some important differences: first, "constructors" like May might be used as headers for other cells, thus leading to something like "dependent data types". Moreover, a cell might have more than one header, which would correspond to overloaded constructors. For example, the cell B3 has *two* headers, namely Apple and May Another difference is that numbers can be used as constructors. Consider, for

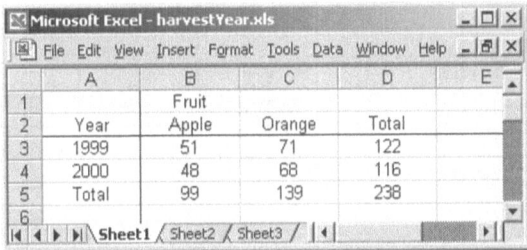

Fig. 3. Yearly production

example, a variation of the harvest spreadsheet that gives data for different years; see Figure 3. Here, the number 1999 is used as unit for the cells B3, C3, and D3. The formal definition of headers is given in Appendix B.

A header definition represents explicit unit information and is used in the unit checking process. This information has to be provided in some way by the user; it corresponds to type declarations in programming languages. Since we cannot expect end users to spend much of their time on declaring units for cells, we have to infer as much unit information as possible automatically or from other user actions that are not directly concerned with units. A header definition can be obtained by exploiting, for instance, the following sources of information:

1. *Predefined unit information.* For instance, the fact that May is a month is known in advance.
2. *Formatting.* For example, if a user devises a specific table format for part of a spreadsheet, unit information can be obtained automatically from the borders of the table.
3. *Spatial & content analysis.* By analyzing a spreadsheet with respect to different kinds of cell contents (for example, text, constant numbers, formulas) and their spatial arrangements, regions can be identified that contain header information (typically the left and top part of tables), footer information (sum formulas at the end of rows and columns), and table data (the constant numbers in between).

In this paper we are not concerned with the process of "header inference"; we assume that the header information is given through the mentioned mechanisms.

4.2   Unit Expressions

We distinguish between simple and complex units. In particular, values like Month or Fruit that do not themselves have a unit are *simple units*. In contrast, *complex units* can be constructed from other units in three different ways to be explained in more detail below.

1. Since units are values, they can themselves have units; hence, we can get chains of units called *dependent units.*

	A	B	C	D
1				
2		B1	B1	
3	A2	A3, B2	A3, C2	
4	A2	A4, B2	A4 ,C2	
5				

Fig. 4. Header information for the *Harvest* spreadsheet

2. Since values in a spreadsheet can be classified according to different categories at the same time, values can principally have more than one unit, which leads to *and units.*
3. Operations in a spreadsheet combine values that possibly have different units. In some cases, these different units indicate a unit error, but in other cases the unit information can be generalized to a common "superunit". Such generalizations are expressed by *or units.*

In the next three subsections we will discuss each of the described unit forms.

Dependent Units Consider the header information for the spreadsheet from Figure 1, shown as a table in Figure 4:

We observe in the table that B3 has B2 as a header which in turn has B1 as a header. This hierarchical structure is reflected in our definition of units. In this example, the unit of the cell B3 is not just Apple, but Fruit[Apple]. In general, if a cell c has a value v as a unit which itself has unit u, then c's unit is a *dependent unit* $u[v]$.

Dependent units are not limited to two levels. For example, if we distinguished red and green apples, a cell containing Green would have unit Fruit[Apple], and a cell whose header is Green would have the dependent unit Fruit[Apple][Green], which is the same as Fruit[Apple[Green]] (see also Appendix B).

Dependent units express a hierarchy of units that results from the possibility of values being and having units at the same time. The topmost level of this hierarchy is given by the unit **1**, which is not a value and does not have a unit itself. **1** is assigned to all cells for which no more specific unit can be inferred. In a dependent unit, **1** can appear only at the outermost position since it is the unit of all nondependent units. (In other words, unit expressions like $u[\mathbf{1}]$ do not make sense since **1** is not a value and cannot have a unit u.)

The dependencies given by a header definition h define a directed graph whose nodes are cell names and whose edges are given by the set $\{(a, a') \mid a' \in h(a)\}$, that is, edges are directed toward headers. We require this dependency graph to be acyclic. More specifically, we require that all nodes except the roots (sources) have at most one outgoing edge. (This constraint ensures that the unit for each value is given by a simple path.)

And Units Cells might have more than one unit. For example, the number 11 in cell C3 gives a number of oranges, but at the same time describes a number that is associated with the month May. Cases like this are modeled with *and* units, which are similar to intersection types [15]. In our example, C3 has the unit Fruit[Orange]&Month[May]. It should be clear that the order of units does not matter in an *and* unit. Likewise, the &-unit operator is associative.

An *and* unit of dependent units that have a prefix in common is meaningless and represents an error because subunits define different alternatives for their superunit that exclude each other. For example, it makes no sense for a cell to have the unit Fruit[Apple]&Fruit[Orange] because a number cannot represent numbers of oranges and apples at the same time; such a unit is a contradiction in itself. The same is true for units like Fruit[Apple[Green]]&Fruit[Apple[Red]] and Fruit[Apple[Green]]&Fruit[Orange]. In contrast, a unit like Month[May]&Fruit[Orange] is reasonable because a number can be classified according to different unit hierarchies.

Or Units The dual to *and* units are *or* units that correspond to union types. *Or* units are inferred for cells that contain operations combining cells of different, but related units. For example, cell D3's formula corresponds to the σ-calculus expression $+(B3, C3)$. Although the units of B3 and C3 are not identical, they differ only in one part of their *and* unit, Fruit[Apple] and Fruit[Orange]. Moreover, these units differ only in the innermost part of their dependent units. In other words, they share a common prefix that includes the complete path of the dependency graph except the first node. This fact makes the $+$ operation applicable. The unit of D3 is then given as an *or* unit of the units of B3 and C3, that is, Fruit[Apple]&Month[May]|Fruit[Orange]&Month[May]. This unit expression can be transformed by commutativity of &, by distributivity of & over |, and prefix factoring for | to Month[May]&Fruit[Apple|Orange]; see Section 5.3. In general, an *or* unit is valid only if it can be transformed into a unit expression in which *or* is applied only to values (that is, not unit expressions) that all have the same unit.

4.3   Well-Formed Units

The preceding discussion leads to the following definition of unit expressions:

$$u \quad ::= \quad v \quad | \quad u_1[u_2] \quad | \quad u_1 \& u_2 \quad | \quad u_1 | u_2 \quad | \quad 1 \quad | \quad \epsilon$$

In addition to the context-free syntax of units, the previously described constraints can be formalized through the concept of *well-formed units* that is defined with respect to a spreadsheet s and a header definition h. Five rules are needed to define when a unit is well-formed:

1. **1** is always a well-formed unit.
2. Every value that does not have a header is a well-formed unit. For example, in Figure 1, Fruit is a well-formed unit.

3. If a cell has value v and header u, then $u[v]$ is a well-formed unit. For example, in Figure 1, Fruit[Apple] is a well-formed unit, and in Figure 3, Year[1999] is a well-formed unit.

4. Where there is no common header ancestor, it is legal to *and* units. For example, in Figure 1, Fruit[Apple]&Month[May] is a well-formed unit because Apples and May have no common ancestor.

5. Where there is a common header ancestor, it is legal to *or* units. For example, in Figure 1, Fruit[Apple|Orange] is well-formed. More precisely, we require that all the values except the most nested ones agree. This is the reason why the unit Fruit[Apple[Green]]|Fruit[Orange] is not well-formed.

These rules are formalized in Appendix B.

The described constraints are also a reason for *not* employing a subset model for units: if units were interpreted as sets and dependent units as subsets, we would expect *or* and *and* units to behave like set union and set intersection, respectively. In such a model we certainly require, for example, Apple ∩ Apple = Apple, however, we have just seen that the corresponding *and* unit is meaningless, which demonstrates that a simple (sub)set/lattice model for units is not adequate.

Not all of a spreadsheet's legal units are actually used as units. For example, in Figure 1, Total is a value and thus also a unit, but it is not used as a unit for another value. Likewise, the well-formed unit Fruit[Apple[8]] is not used in the spreadsheet.

5   A Spreadsheet Unit System

We have defined what spreadsheets and units are; next we have to describe how units are inferred for cells in a spreadsheet.

We need to consider three kinds of judgments: first, we have judgments of the form $(a, e) :: u$ that associate units to cells and that can exploit header information. Second, for the unit inference for operations we also need judgments $e : u$ that give units for expressions regardless of their position (context). Third, for expressing the units of a spreadsheet we need a further kind of judgment $(a_1, e_1); \ldots; (a_m, e_m) ::: (a_1, u_1); \ldots; (a_m, u_m)$, which expresses the fact that the unit information for a spreadsheet is given by a u-collection, also called a *unitsheet*.

We have not yet integrated type checking into unit checking. Recall that by design constraints 2 and 3, we deliberately avoid including a notion of abstract types in the reasoning system for units. We are currently investigating ways of treating types as units, so that type checking and unit checking are communicated in the same way to the end user. However, this approach complicates the structure of dependent units (they are no longer paths but DAGs) and seems to make the unit inference more difficult.

5.1   Unit Inference Rules

The main rules for inferring units for cells are given below. The rule names are given to help reference the formal rules in Appendix C and the examples discussed in Section 5.3.

VAL$_{::}$ All cells that do not have a header, have the unit 1. For example, cell Total has unit 1.

DEP$_{::}$ If cell a has a header cell b that contains a value v and has a well-formed unit u, then a's unit is $u[v]$. More generally, if a cell has multiple headers with values v_i and units u_i, then its unit is given by the *and* unit of all the $u_i[v_i]$. An example is the cell containing 8 whose unit is Fruit[Apple]&Month[May].

REF$_{::}$ If cell a's formula is a reference to cell b, then b's unit, say u_b is propagated to a. For example, cell A5 contains a reference to D2 which has unit 1. Hence, A5's unit is also 1. If a has itself a header definition, say u_a, then u_a must conform with u_b, which is achieved by defining a's unit to be $u_a\&u_b$.

APP$_{::}$ Each operator has its own definition of how the units of its parameters combine.

Regarding the latter point, we define a function μ_ω for each operator ω^n, which defines how the operation transforms the units of its parameters. Note that the definition of μ_ω takes also into account the unit that can be derived from a possible header definition for that cell. Both sources of unit information have to be unified. This unification is particularly helpful to retain unit information in the case of multiplication and division because these two operations have in our current model only a weak unit support.

A proper treatment of multiplication and division requires the concept of dimensions [17,9]. Extending our unit system by dimensions would complicate it considerably; in particular, end users would probably be confused if required to cope with both unit and dimension error messages. Therefore, we equip operations like $*$ and $/$ with a rather weak unit transformation: basically, the unit of a product is given by the unit of one factor if all other factors have unit 1, otherwise the unit is weakened to 1. In contrast, the unit of a division is always given by the unit of its dividend.[2] If a header definition is present for the cell containing an operation ω, the corresponding unit u is taken into account by creating an *and* unit of u and the computed unit u'. This *and* unit implements a further level of unit consistency checking.

The definition of μ_ω is shown for some operations in Figure 5 (we also abbreviate $u_1, \ldots, u_n$ by $\bar{u}$). u is the cell's header unit; $\bar{u}$ are all the units of the parameters.

The unit transformations show how operations are defined for different, but related, units and expose a kind of polymorphism, which we call *unit polymorphism*. Unit polymorphism is similar to parametric polymorphism in the sense

---

[2] Division is not commutative, hence choosing one particular operand is justified. Moreover, the dividend is dominant in specifying the unit, for example, if we had to decide on the unit of "salary per month", we would probably choose "salary".

$$
\begin{aligned}
\mu_+(u, \bar{u}) &= (u_1 | \ldots | u_n) \& u \\
\mu_{\mathsf{count}}(u, \bar{u}) &= (u_1 | \ldots | u_n) \& u \\
\mu_*(u, \bar{u}) &= \downarrow(\bar{u}) \& u \\
\mu_/(u, \bar{u}) &= u_1 \& u \\
\ldots
\end{aligned}
\qquad
\downarrow(\bar{u}) = \begin{cases} u_i & \text{if } u_i \neq \mathbf{1} \wedge \forall j \neq i : u_j = \mathbf{1} \\ \mathbf{1} & \text{otherwise} \end{cases}
$$

Fig. 5. Unit transformations

that the operations use the same implementation regardless of the units of their arguments. The hierarchy of units also reminds of inclusion polymorphism [7].

5.2   Unit Simplification

We can observe that by applying operations we can obtain arbitrarily complex unit expressions that do not always meet the conditions for well-formed units. We need equations on unit expressions that allow us to simplify complex unit expressions. Whenever simplification to a well-formed unit is possible, it can be concluded that the operation is applied in a "unit-correct" way. Otherwise, a unit error is detected. The complete set of equations is given in Appendix C. Some important cases are:

- *Commutativity.* The order of arguments in *or* and *and* units does not matter. For example, the expressions Fruit[Apple]&Month[May] and Month[May]& Fruit[Apple] denote the same unit.
- *Generalization.* A dependent unit $u[u_1 | \ldots | u_k]$ whose innermost unit expression is given by an *or* unit that contains *all* the units $u_1, \ldots, u_k$ that have u as a header denotes the same unit as u. For example, the unit expression Fruit[Apple|Orange] expresses the same unit information as just Fruit since the two cells Apple and Orange are the only cells that have Fruit as a header.
- *Factorization.* An *or* unit whose arguments share a common prefix is identical to the unit in which the *or* unit is moved inside. For example, the unit expression Fruit[Apple]|Fruit[Orange] expresses the same unit information as Fruit[Apple|Orange] (which in turn is equal to Fruit).
- *Distributivity* (of *and* over *or*). If one argument of an *and* unit is an *or* unit, then the *and* can be moved into the *or* expression. Likewise, *and* units with a common unit can be moved out of an *or* unit. For example, if a number represents May apples or May oranges (that is, has the unit Month[May]&Fruit[Apple]|Month[May]&Fruit[Orange]), then we can as well say that it represents apples or oranges and at the same time a number for May, which is expressed by the unit Month[May]&(Fruit[Apple]|Fruit[Orange]). Note, however, that *or* units do not distribute over *and*.

5.3 Unit Checking in Action

Next we demonstrate the unit inference rules and the unit simplifications with the example spreadsheet from Figure 1 and the corresponding header information from Figure 4. We have combined both tables and show the spreadsheet with some of its headers represented as arrows in Figure 6.

Since B1 has no header definition, Fruit has unit 1 by rule VAL$_{::}$; as a judgment this is written $(B1, Fruit) :: 1$. Then by rule DEP$_{::}$ we know that Orange has the unit $1[Fruit]$ (or: $(C2, Orange) :: 1[Fruit]$) because

- the header of C2 is B1,
- the value of the cell B1 is Fruit (that is, $Harvest(B1) = Fruit$), and
- cell Fruit has unit 1.

Since all units except 1 are of the form $1[\ldots]$ we omit the leading 1 for brevity in the following. Hence we also say: $(C2, Orange) :: Fruit$. Similarly, we can reason that $(A3, May) :: Month$. Finally, using the last two results and the fact that the header of C3 is defined to be the two cells A3 and C2 we can conclude by rule DEP$_{::}$ that $(C3, 11) :: Month[May]\&Fruit[Orange]$.

Next we infer the unit for the cell D3. First, we have to infer the unit $(B3, 8) :: Month[May]\&Fruit[Apple]$, which can be obtained in the same way as the unit for the cell C3. To infer the unit of D3 we apply rule APP$_{::}$. We already have the units for both arguments; since we have no header information for D3, u is 1 in this case. So we can apply μ_+ and obtain as a result an *or* unit for D3, namely:

$$Month[May]\&Fruit[Apple]|Month[May]\&Fruit[Orange]$$

We can now perform rule simplification several times, first exploiting distributivity, which yields the unit:

$$Month[May]\&(Fruit[Apple]|Fruit[Orange]).$$

then we apply factorization, which yields the unit:

$$Month[May]\&Fruit[Apple|Orange].$$

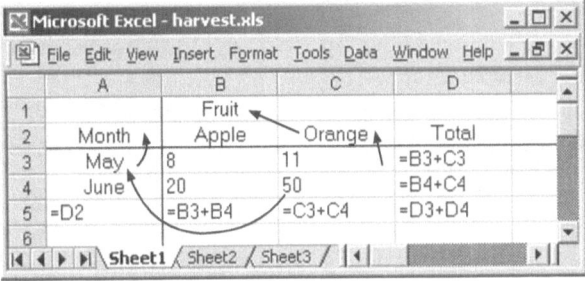

Fig. 6. Some headers for the *Harvest* spreadsheet

Finally, using generalization, we obtain the unit:

$$\text{Month}[\text{May}]\&\text{Fruit}.$$

On the other hand, a cell with an expression $+(\text{B3}, \text{C4})$ would lead to a unit error because we get two different months and two different fruits, which prevents the application of the distributivity rule and thus prevents the unit expression from being reduced to a well-formed unit. Therefore, we cannot infer a unit for such a cell, so the system reports a unit error for that cell.

5.4   Unit Safety

The traditional approach of showing soundness for type systems works for our unit system, too, but it does not yield a very powerful result. (See Appendix C for a formal treatment.) The problem is that soundness does not capture the essential contribution of the unit system, namely preventing unit errors. The reason is that the operational semantics is defined on values that are not differentiated by units. In other words, computations that are unit incorrect still yield reasonable values since the unit information is ignored by the semantics.

Hence, we need a semantics of values and functions that operate on a finer granularity than types. We can achieve this by tagging values with unit information and defining the semantics in such a way that error values are returned for applications of operations that yield non-well-formed units with their results. The semantics definition for operations must incorporate the unit transformation and the simplification rules (like generalization and factorization). The details will be investigated in a future paper.

6   Conclusions and Future Research

In this paper, we have presented an approach to reasoning about units in spreadsheets. The approach is a "gentle slope" approach in the sense that the user does not have to learn anything new to start using it, but the more information he or she chooses to provide to the system, the more helpful the system can be in reasoning about whether the spreadsheet's different units are being combined correctly. Significant features of the approach are:

- With units, reasoning about application of operations happens on a more fine-grained level than types.
- The reasoning system includes dependent units.
- The reasoning system, while not supporting parametric polymorphism (for *types*), supports a kind of polymorphism of units.
- The reasoning system is intended for end-user programming of spreadsheets.

In our approach, unit information is given explicitly, which is one reason for the expressiveness of the unit system and for the existence of a simple unit checking procedure. Nevertheless, the often-cited problem of inherent verbosity of explicit type disciplines is not a problem in our approach since the unit information is already present (for example, for documentation) and can be reused. In a sense, our approach can be described as having "implicitly explicit units".

In future work, we will investigate the unit-aware semantics and corresponding unit safety results for the unit system. Moreover, we will investigate the possibilities for header inference. A particular problem is how we can minimize the interaction with the user while trying to get as much unit information as possible. Furthermore, we will try to find a stronger unit treatment of operations requiring dimensions.

References

1. N. Belkin. Helping People Find What They Don't Know. *Communications of the ACM*, 41(8):58–61, 2000. 176
2. B. Boehm and V. Basili. Gaining Intellectual Control of Software Development. *Computer*, 33(5):27–33, 2000. 174
3. B. Boehm and V. Basili. Software Defect Reduction Top 10 List. *Computer*, 34(1):135–137, 2001. 174
4. B. W. Boehm, C. Abts, A. W. Brown, S. Chulani, K. C. Bradford, E. Horowitz, R. Madachy, D. J. Reifer, and B. Steece, editors. *Software Cost Estimation with COCOMO II*. Prentice-Hall International, Upper Saddle River, NJ, 2000. 173
5. M. M. Burnett, A. Agrawal, and P. van Zee. Exception Handling in the Spreadsheet Paradigm. *IEEE Transactions on Software Engineering*, 26(10):923–942, 2000. 177
6. M. M. Burnett, J. Atwood, R. Djang, H. Gottfried, J. Reichwein, and S. Yang. Forms/3: A First-Order Visual Language to Explore the Boundaries of the Spreadsheet Paradigm. *Journal of Functional Programming*, 11(2):155–206, 2001. 178
7. L. Cardelli and P. Wegner. On Understanding Types, Data Abstraction, and Polymorphism. *Computing Surveys*, 17(4):471–522, 1985. 184
8. W. de Hoon, Rutten L., and M. van Eekelen. Implementing a Functional Spreadsheet in CLEAN. *Journal of Functional Programming*, 5(3):383–414, 1995. 175
9. A. Kennedy. Dimension Types. In *5th European Symp. on Programming*, LNCS 788, pages 348–362, 1994. 174, 183
10. A. Kennedy. Relational Parametricity and Units of Measure. In *24th ACM Symp. on Principles of Programming Languages*, pages 442–455, 1997. 174
11. B. Myers, S. Hudson, and R. Pausch. Past, Present, and Future of User Interface Software Tools. *ACM Transactions on Computer-Human Interaction*, 7(1):3–28, 2000. 174
12. B. Myers, D. Smith, and B. Horn. Report of the 'End-User Programming' Working Group. In B. Myers, editor, *Languages for Developing User Interfaces*, pages 343–366. A. K. Peters, Ltd., Wellesley, MA, 1992. 174
13. R. Panko. Finding Spreadsheet Errors: Most Spreadsheet Models Have Design Flaws that May Lead to Long-Term Miscalculation. *Information Week*, (May 29):100, 1995. 174
14. R. Panko. What We Know about Spreadsheet Errors. *Journal of End User Computing*, (Spring), 1998. 174
15. B. C. Pierce. Intersection Types and Bounded Polymorphism. *Mathematical Structures in Computer Science*, 7(2):129–193, 1997. 181
16. T. Teo and M. Tan. Quantitative and Qualitative Errors in Spreadsheet Development. In *30th Hawaii Int. Conf. on System Sciences*, pages 25–38, 1997. 174

17. M. Wand and P. O'Keefe. Automatic Dimensional Inference. In J.-L. Lassez and G. Plotkin, editors, *Computational Logic: Essays in Honor of Alan Robinson*, pages 479–483. MIT Press, Cambridge, MA, 1991. 174, 183

Appendix

A   Operational Semantics of Spreadsheets

The operational semantics of spreadsheets is defined through a reduction relation ($\twoheadrightarrow$) on cell expressions that depends on the definition of the evaluation of operations ($\to$), which, in particular, has to include a specification of the behavior of operations with respect to the value $\sqcup$; see Figure 7.

$$
\begin{aligned}
+^n(v_1^\sqcup, \ldots, v_n^\sqcup) &\to x_1 + \ldots + x_n &&\text{where } x_i = \text{ if } v_i^\sqcup = \sqcup \text{ then } 0 \text{ else } v_i^\sqcup \\
\text{count}^n(v_1^\sqcup, \ldots, v_n^\sqcup) &\to x_1 + \ldots + x_n &&\text{where } x_i = \text{ if } v_i^\sqcup = \sqcup \text{ then } 0 \text{ else } 1 \\
{}^n(v_1^\sqcup, \ldots, v_n^\sqcup) &\to x_1 * \ldots * x_n &&\text{where } x_i = \text{ if } v_i^\sqcup = \sqcup \text{ then } 1 \text{ else } v_i^\sqcup \\
&\cdots \\
\omega^n(\ldots, \epsilon, \ldots) &\to \epsilon
\end{aligned}
$$

Fig. 7. Reduction of basic operations

The reduction relation is defined relatively to a spreadsheet s, which does not change during evaluation and can thus be treated as a global variable. All cell expressions that cannot be reduced to a value according to the reduction relation are defined to reduce to ϵ. This applies, for example, to definitions containing cycles.

The reduction relation $\twoheadrightarrow$ extends naturally to a spreadsheet by application to all of its cells; see Figure 8. A reduced spreadsheet is a v^ϵ-collection, which we also call a *valuesheet*, an example of which was shown in Figure 1 (b).

$$
\begin{array}{lll}
\text{VAL}_{\twoheadrightarrow} \dfrac{}{v^\epsilon \twoheadrightarrow v^\epsilon} &
\text{REF}_{\twoheadrightarrow} \dfrac{s(a) \twoheadrightarrow v^\epsilon}{a \twoheadrightarrow v^\epsilon} &
\text{REF}^\epsilon_{\twoheadrightarrow} \dfrac{a \notin dom(s)}{a \twoheadrightarrow \epsilon} \\[2em]
\text{APP}_{\twoheadrightarrow} \dfrac{e_i \twoheadrightarrow v_i^\epsilon \quad \omega^n(v_1^\epsilon, \ldots, v_n^\epsilon) \to v^\epsilon}{\omega^n(e_1, \ldots, e_n) \twoheadrightarrow v^\epsilon} &&
\text{APP}^\epsilon_{\twoheadrightarrow} \dfrac{k \neq n}{\omega^n(e_1, \ldots, e_k) \twoheadrightarrow \epsilon} \\[2em]
\text{SHEET}_{\twoheadrightarrow} \dfrac{e_1 \twoheadrightarrow v_1^\epsilon \quad \ldots \quad e_m \twoheadrightarrow v_m^\epsilon}{(a_1, e_1); \ldots; (a_m, e_m) \twoheadrightarrow (a_1, v_1^\epsilon); \ldots; (a_m, v_m^\epsilon)}
\end{array}
$$

Fig. 8. Operational semantics of spreadsheets

A spreadsheet is said to be ϵ-*free* if its reduction does not contain an error value, that is, $s = (a_1, e_1) ; \ldots ; (a_m, e_m)$ is ϵ-free $\Longleftrightarrow \twoheadrightarrow s(a_1, v_1^{\sqcup}) ; \ldots ; (a_m, v_m^{\sqcup})$.

B   Definition of Headers and Units

We formalize the notion of header through a $\{a\}$-collection, called *header defini-tion*: $h(a) = \{a_1, \ldots, a_k\}$ means that cell a has the cells $a_1, \ldots, a_k$ as headers.[3]

Unit expressions are defined by the grammar given in Section 4.3. The syntax allows unit expressions for dependent units to be arbitrary binary leaf trees, but we consider all trees that have the same order of leaves to be equal; see also Figure 11. We select the right-spine tree, which corresponds to the unit expression $u_1[u_2[\ldots u_{n-1}[u_n]\ldots]]$, as the canonical representative for the class of all equivalent dependent units.

Well-formed units are expressed by judgments $\vdash u$ defined in Figure 9. For notational brevity we omit the spreadsheet s and the header definition h and consider them as global constants since they are changed within the rules.

$$
\text{ONE} \vdash \frac{}{\vdash \mathbf{1}} \qquad\qquad \text{VAL} \vdash \frac{a \notin dom(h) \qquad s(a) = v}{\vdash \mathbf{1}[v]}
$$

$$
\text{DEP} \vdash \frac{a' \in h(a) \qquad s(a) = v \qquad \vdash u \qquad \vdash u[s(a')]}{\vdash u[s(a')[v]]}
$$

$$
\text{AND} \vdash \frac{\vdash \mathbf{1}[u_1[\ldots u_{n-1}[u_n]\ldots]] \qquad \vdash \mathbf{1}[u_1'[\ldots u_{m-1}'[u_m']\ldots]] \qquad u_i \neq_u u_i'}{\vdash u_1[\ldots u_{n-1}[u_n]\ldots]\& u_1'[\ldots u_{m-1}'[u_m']\ldots]}
$$

$$
\text{OR} \vdash \frac{\vdash \mathbf{1}[u_1[\ldots u_n[v_1]\ldots]] \quad \ldots \quad \vdash \mathbf{1}[u_1[\ldots u_n[v_k]\ldots]] \quad n > 1 \quad k > 1 \quad v_i \text{ distinct}}{\vdash \mathbf{1}[u_1[\ldots u_n[v_1|\ldots|v_k]\ldots]]}
$$

Fig. 9. Well-formed units

C   Unit Inference

We can give the set of inference rules for determining units for (all cells of) a spreadsheet, formalizing the examples given in the previous section. See Figure 10. As in the definition for well-formed units, we regard s and h as global constants.

The rules EQ. and EQ.. exploit the equations shown in Figure 11, which define equality of units. (Note that $\&$ distributes over $|$, but not vice versa, and that although $\mathbf{1}$ is the unit for $\&$, it leads to a non-valid unit when combined with $|$.)

---

[3] We require $k > 0$ since $h(a) = \emptyset$ would be interpreted in the same way as the case $a \notin dom(h)$.

$$\text{VAL:} \quad \frac{}{v^{\sqcup} : \mathbf{1}} \qquad \text{REF:} \quad \frac{(a, s(a)) :: u \qquad \vdash u}{a : u} \qquad \text{EQ:} \quad \frac{e : u \qquad u =_u u'}{e : u'}$$

$$\text{APP:} \quad \frac{e_i : u_i \qquad \vdash u_i}{\omega^n(e_1, \ldots, e_n) : \mu_\omega(\mathbf{1}, u_1, \ldots, u_n)}$$

$$\text{VAL::} \quad \frac{a \notin dom(h)}{(a, v^{\sqcup}) :: \mathbf{1}} \qquad \text{REF::} \quad \frac{(a, s(a)) :: u \quad (a', s(a')) :: u' \quad \vdash u \quad \vdash u'}{(a, a') :: u \& u'}$$

$$\text{APP::} \quad \frac{e_i : u_i \qquad \vdash u_i \qquad (a, \sqcup) :: u \qquad \vdash u}{(a, \omega^n(e_1, \ldots, e_n)) :: \mu_\omega(u, u_1, \ldots, u_n)} \qquad \text{EQ::} \quad \frac{(a, e) :: u \quad u =_u u'}{(a, e) :: u'}$$

$$\text{DEP::} \quad \frac{h(a) = \{a_1, \ldots, a_k\} \qquad s(a_i) = v_i^{\sqcup} \qquad (a_i, v_i^{\sqcup}) :: u_i \qquad \vdash u_i}{(a, v^{\sqcup}) :: u_1[v_1^{\sqcup}] \& \ldots \& u_k[v_k^{\sqcup}]}$$

$$\text{SHEET:::} \quad \frac{i \in J_m \qquad (a_i, e_i) :: u_i \qquad \vdash u_i \qquad j \in \bar{J}_m \qquad u_j = \epsilon}{(a_1, e_1); \ldots; (a_m, e_m) :::: (a_1, u_1); \ldots; (a_m, u_m)}$$

Fig. 10. A unit system for the σ-calculus

The condition (*) for generalization is that the *or* unit expression consists exactly of all units $u_1, \ldots, u_n$ that have u as a header. Moreover, this condition must hold for all definitions (copies) of u (that is, for all cells containing u):

$$\forall a \in s^{-1}(u) : h^{-1}(\{a\}) = \{a_1, \ldots, a_k\} \wedge s(a_1) = u_1 \wedge \ldots \wedge s(a_k) = u_k$$

In the rule SHEET::: we use the notation J_m for a subset of $\{1, \ldots, m\}$ and $\bar{J}_m$ to denote $\{1, \ldots, m\} - J_m$. The rule SHEET::: can be used to derive different u-collections for one spreadsheet. We can define an ordering on the u-collections based on the number of ϵ-values contained in them, so that we can select the u-collection containing the least number of ϵ-values as *the* u-collection for a spreadsheet (which we could call the spreadsheet's *principal u-collection*.)

The fact that the principal u-collection is always uniquely defined follows from the structure of the unit system: the unit for each cell can be computed in a syntax-directed way without having to make any choices, so that it is not possible, for example, to remove a unit error in one cell by "allowing" an error in another cell.

For completeness, we mention as a straightforward result that the defined unit system is sound. First, we have the following lemma for individual cells:

Lemma 1 (Unit Soundness for Cells). $(a, e) :: u \wedge \vdash u \Longrightarrow e \twoheadrightarrow v^{\sqcup}$

Since reduction and the units for a spreadsheet are directly derived from the corresponding relations on cells, the unit soundness for spreadsheets follows directly from Lemma 1:

$$
\begin{aligned}
u_1 \& u_2 &=_u u_2 \& u_1 & \text{(commutativity)} \\
u_1 | u_2 &=_u u_2 | u_1 \\
(u_1 \& u_2) \& u_3 &=_u u_1 \& (u_2 \& u_3) & \text{(associativity)} \\
(u_1 | u_2) | u_3 &=_u u_1 | (u_2 | u_3) \\
u \& (u_1 | u_2) &=_u (u \& u_1) | (u \& u_2) & \text{(distributivity)} \\
u \& u &=_u u & \text{(idempotency)} \\
u | u &=_u u \\
\mathbf{1} \& u &=_u u & \text{(unit)} \\
u[u_1] | u[u_2] &=_u u[u_1 | u_2] & \text{(factorization)} \\
u[u_1 | \dots | u_k] &=_u u \quad \Leftarrow (*) & \text{(generalization)} \\
(u_1[u_2])[u_3] &=_u u_1[u_2[u_3]] & \text{(linearization)}
\end{aligned}
$$

Fig. 11. Unit equality

Corollary 1 (Unit Soundness for Spreadsheets).

$(a_1, e_1) ; \dots ; (a_m, e_m) ::: (a_1, u_1) ; \dots ; (a_m, u_m) \wedge \vdash u_i \Longrightarrow$
$(a_1, e_1) ; \dots ; (a_m, e_m) \twoheadrightarrow (a_1, v_1^{\sqcup}) ; \dots ; (a_m, v_m^{\sqcup})$

In other words, a spreadsheet that does not contain unit errors is guaranteed to be ϵ-free.

WASH/CGI: Server-Side Web Scripting with Sessions and Typed, Compositional Forms

Peter Thiemann

Universität Freiburg
Georges-Köhler-Allee 079, D-79085 Freiburg, Germany
Phone: +49 761 203 8051, Fax: +49 761 203 8052
thiemann@informatik.uni-freiburg.de

Abstract. The common gateway interface (CGI) is one of the prevalent methods to provide dynamic contents on the Web. Since it is cumbersome to use in its raw form, there are many libraries that make CGI programming easier.

WASH/CGI is a Haskell library for server-side Web scripting. Its implementation relies on CGI, but its use avoids most of CGI's drawbacks. It incorporates the concept of a session, provides a typed, compositional approach to constructing interaction elements (forms), and relies on callbacks to specify control flow. From a programmer's perspective, programming WASH/CGI is like programming a graphical user interface (GUI), where the layout is specified using HTML via a novel monadic interface.

Keywords: Haskell, Monads, CGI Programming

1   Introduction

The common gateway interface (CGI) is one of the oldest methods for deploying dynamic Web pages based on server-side computations. As such, CGI has a number of advantages. Virtually every Web server supports CGI. CGI requires no special functionality from the browser, apart from the standard support for HTML forms. And, on the programming side, CGI communicates via standard input/output streams and environment variables so that CGI is not tied to a particular architecture or implementation language. Hence, CGI is the most portable approach to providing dynamic contents on the Web.

The basic idea of CGI is straightforward. Whenever the Web server receives a request for a CGI-enabled URL, it treats the local file determined by the URL as an executable program, a *CGI script*, and starts it in a new process. Such a script receives its input through the standard input stream and through environment variables and delivers the response to its standard output stream as defined by the CGI standard [1].

CGI programming in raw form is fairly error-prone. A common source of errors lies in the parameter passing scheme between forms and CGI scripts. A form is an HTML element that contains named input elements. Each input element implements one particular input widget. When a special submit button

S. Krishnamurthi, C. R. Ramakrishnan (Eds.): PADL 2002, LNCS 2257, pp. 192–208, 2002.

is pressed, the browser sends a list of pairs of input element names and their string values to the server. This message in its raw form is passed to a CGI script, which must extract the values by name. Unfortunately, there is no guarantee that the form uses the names expected by the script and vice versa.

In particular, since parameter passing between forms and CGI scripts is string-based, it is completely untyped. It is not possible to specify the expected type of an input field. Of course, it is possible to check the input value upon receipt but this requires extra programming.

Another painful limitation of CGI is due to the statelessness of the underlying protocol, HTTP. Every single request starts a new CGI process, which produces a response page and terminates. There is no concept of a *session*, *i.e.*, a sequence of interactions between browser and server, and more importantly of *session persistence*. Session persistence means that the value of a variable is available throughout a session. Some applications even require global persistence where the lifetime of a variable is not tied to any session. Usually, CGI programmers build support for sessions and persistence from scratch. They distribute the units of a session over a number of CGI scripts and link them manually. To provide a notion of session persistence, they put extra information in their response pages (hidden input fields or cookies) or they maintain a session identification using URL rewriting. Clearly, all those solutions are tedious and error-prone.

The present work provides a solution to all the issues mentioned above. Our WASH/CGI library makes CGI programming simple and intuitive. It is implemented in Haskell [2] and includes the following features:

- a callback style of programming user interaction;
- input fields which are first-class entities; they can be typed and grouped to compound input fields (compositionality);
- the specification of an input widget and the collection of the input data are tied together so that mismatches are impossible;
- support for sessions and persistence.

The library is available through the WASH web page[1]. The web page also contains some live examples with sources. Beyond the topics discussed in this paper, WASH/CGI provides first-class clickable images where each pixel can be bound to a different action, as well as a simple implementation of global persistence.

Familiarity with the Haskell language [2] as well as with the essential HTML elements is assumed throughout.

Overview We follow the structure of the library in a bottom-up manner to give the reader a feel for the awkwardness of raw CGI programming, which is discussed in Sec. 2. The worst edges are already smoothed by using functional wrappers for input and output. In Section 3, we consider a structured way of specifying HTML documents, so that we can describe more complex output. Section 4 explains the concept of a session in WASH/CGI and discusses its implementation. Section 5 explains the construction of HTML documents with

---

[1] http://www.informatik.uni-freiburg.de/~thiemann/WASH

active elements, forms and input fields. The issue of persistent store is considered in Sec. 6. Finally, Section 7 explains an extended example of using the library, followed by a section on related work (Sec. 8), and a conclusion with some pointers for further work.

2   Raw CGI Programming

A CGI script receives its input through the standard input stream and through environment variables. The input can be divided into meta-information and the actual data. Meta-information includes the URL of the script, the protocol, the name and address of the requesting host, and so on. The data arrives (conceptually) as a list of name-value pairs. The actual encoding is not important for our purposes and many approaches to Web programming contain facilities to access these inputs conveniently. For example, Meijer's CGI library [3] provides functionality similar to that explained in this section.

Our raw library RawCGI implements parameter passing through the function

```
start :: (CGIInfo -> CGIParameters -> IO a) -> IO a
```

where CGIInfo is a record containing the meta-information and CGIParameters is a list of (name-value) pairs of strings. Now, a CGI programmer just has to write a function of type CGIInfo -> CGIParameters -> IO a that processes the input and creates an output document and returns an IO action. The intention is that this action writes a CGI response to the standard output, but it can also do other things, e.g., access a data base or communicate with other hosts.

The output of a CGI script also has to adhere to a special format, which is parsed by the web server. Since that format depends on the type of the output data, it is natural to implement this output format generically using a type class.

```
class CGIOutput a where
  cgiPut :: a -> IO ()
```

This declaration introduces an overloaded function cgiPut which can be instantiated differently for each type a. Currently, the library includes instances for HTML, strings, files, return status (to indicate errors), and relocation requests.

Here is a very simple CGI script written with this library.

```
main =
  start cgi
cgi info parms =
  case assocParm "test" parms of
    Nothing -> cgiPut "Parameter 'test' not provided"
    Just x  -> cgiPut ("Value of test = "++x)
```

It checks whether the parameter test was supplied on invocation of the script and generates an according message. The value of assocParm "test" parms is Nothing if there is no binding for the name test, and Just x if the value of test is the string x.

```
type Element    -- abstract
type Attribute -- abstract

element_  :: String -> [Attribute] -> [Element] -> Element
doctype_  :: [String] -> [Element] -> Element

attr_     :: String -> String -> Attribute

add_      :: Element -> Element    -> Element
add_attr_ :: Element -> Attribute -> Element
```

Fig. 1. Signature of HTMLBase (excerpt)

3   Generation of HTML

The next ingredient for CGI programming is a disciplined means to generate HTML. This task is split into a low-level ADT HTMLBase (Fig. 1), which provides the rudimentary functionality for constructing an internal representation of HTML pages and printing it, and a high-level module HTMLMonad.

In the low-level ADT, the function element_ constructs a HTML element from a tag, a list of attributes, and a list of children. The function doctype_ constructs the top-level element of a document. Given an attribute name and a value, attr_ constructs an attribute. The expression add_ e e' adopts the element e' as a child of e, and add_attr_ attaches an attribute to an element.

The interface in Fig. 1 is not intended for direct use but rather as a stepping stone to provide representation independence for the high-level interface. A key point of the high-level interface is its parameterization. Later on, it will be necessary to thread certain information through the construction of an HTML document. Since the particulars of this threading may vary, we parameterize the construction by a monad that manages the threading. Later, we will instantiate the parameter to the IO monad and to the CGI monad, a new monad which is discussed below.

Given that the parameter is a monad, we formulate HTML generation as a monad transformer WithHTML [4]. Hence, if m is a monad, then WithHTML m is a monad, too. In particular, it composes m with a state transformer that transforms HTML elements:

```
data WithHTML m a = WithHTML (Element -> m (a, Element))
```

For each HTML tag, the library provides a function of the same name, that constructs the corresponding element. This function maps one WithHTML action into another and has a generic definition.

```
makeELEM :: Monad m => String -> WithHTML m a -> WithHTML m a
makeELEM tag (WithHTML g) =
  WithHTML (\elem ->
    g (element_ tag" [] []) >>= \(a, tableElem) ->
    return (a, add_ elem tableElem))
```

The argument action WithHTML g is applied to the newly created, empty table element. The intention is that this action adds children and attributes to the new element. Afterwards, it includes the new element in the list of children of the current element, elem, which is threaded through by the state transformer. The resulting value, a, is the value returned by g after constructing the children.

From this it is easy to define special instances like the table function.

```
table :: Monad m => WithHTML m a -> WithHTML m a
table = makeELEM "table"
```

Attributes are also attached to the current element. The corresponding function attr is straightforward.

```
attr :: Monad m => String -> String -> WithHTML m ()
attr a v =
  WithHTML (\elem -> return ((), add_attr_ elem (attr_ a v)))
```

Due to the underlying language Haskell, parameterized documents and (higher-order) document templates can be implemented by functions. As an example for the elegant coding style supported by the library, we show the definition of a standard document template, which is parameterized over the title of the page, ttl, and over the actual contents, elems.

```
standardPage :: String -> WithHTML m a -> WithHTML m a
standardPage ttl elems =
  html (head (title (text ttl))
     ## body (h1    (text ttl)  ## elems))
```

Only two combinators must be explained. The function text constructs a textual node from a string. The operator ## composes state transformations. Intuitively, ## concatenes (lists of) nodes.

Using a monad for HTML generation has further advantages. For example, standard monadic operations and in particular the do notation can be used to construct HTML. The ## operator behaves very much like the >> operator, but its typing is different. While ## returns the result of its first parameter action, the >> operator returns the result of the second parameter:

```
(>>) :: Monad m => m a -> m b -> m b
(##) :: Monad m => m a -> m b -> m a
```

4   Sessions

A session is a sequence of interactions between the server and a browser that logically belong together. In raw CGI programming, sessions must be implemented by the programmer. For example, Figure 2 shows a typical session which guides a user through a couple of forms (ask), performs some I/O (io), and finally yields some document as an answer (tell). Usually, each of the blocks A, B, C, and D must be implemented as a separate program. In contrast, our library provides combinators ask, tell, and io in such a way that the entire interaction can be described in one program.

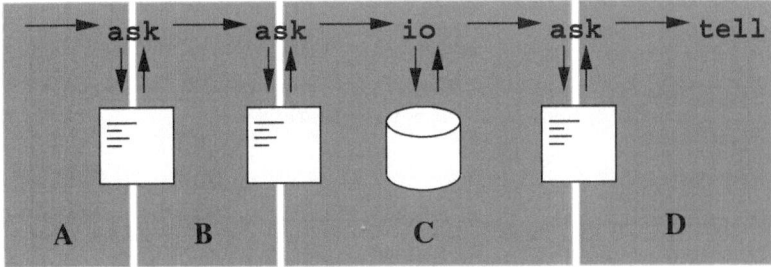

Fig. 2. A CGI session

Since we cannot change the CGI protocol, our program also has to terminate each time a user interaction is required: at each **ask**. However, **ask** saves the current state and arranges matters so that receipt of the user's response reloads the state and makes the program continue exactly where it left off.

CGI programmers have a number of alternatives for saving the state, and these are exactly the alternatives for implementing **ask**. The simplest approach is to include a so-called hidden input field in the form sent to the user and store the state in that field. Hidden input fields are not displayed by the browser, but are always transmitted on submittal of the form. Clearly, this approach is only feasible when the state is small. Once the state gets bigger, it should be stored in a local file on the server and only a pointer to it is put into a hidden field, a cookie, or in an extension of the script's URL. The present version of our library puts the whole state in a hidden field.

The next question is which part of the state we save: for efficiency reasons, it is not feasible to save the entire program state. In our approach, we save a log of the responses from the user and from I/O operations. These responses are the only factors that affect the flow of control in the program. Since we are in a pure language, all other values can be recomputed with equal outcomes. This approach proved sufficiently efficient for the applications that we considered.

Our implementation encapsulates this machinery in the monad CGI.

```
data CGI a = CGI { unCGI :: CGIState -> IO (Maybe a, CGIState) }
```

This definition declares the selector **unCGI** along with the data constructor **CGI**. It defines, again, a state monad composed with the **IO** monad. The **CGIState** contains two copies of the log mentioned. The first copy is used to provide responses to questions that have been answered in previous parts of the session. The second copy retains the whole log so that it can be sent to the browser. Both copies are used like queues: each input operation tries to get its result from the front of the first queue. Only if the queue is empty it performs the actual input. The second queue is only used to register new results, which are put at the end of the queue. Whenever the CGI program (re-) starts, both queues are initialized to the same restored state.

The **CGI** monad has the following actions.

```
tell :: CGIOutput a => a -> CGI ()
tell a = CGI (\cgistate -> cgiPut a >> exitWith ExitSuccess)
```

The action `tell` takes any value whose type is an instance of `CGIOutput`, prints it as a CGI response, and terminates the program.

```
io :: (Read a, Show a) => IO a -> CGI a
```

The combinator `io` implements the embedding of IO into CGI. If `ioa :: IO a` is an IO action returning values of type `a`, then `io ioa` is the corresponding CGI action. Its implementation is slightly complicated because IO actions can return different results each time they are run. Hence, an IO action must be executed at most once in a session and its value must be saved for later invocations of the script.

First, `io ioa` must check if the result of action `ioa` is already present in the first queue. In that case, it simply returns the logged answer and removes the front element. If the first queue is empty, `io ioa` executes the action `ioa`, logs the result (enqueues it in the second queue), and returns it. The result type of the operation must be an instance of the classes `Show` and `Read`, so that each result can be stored as a string (`Show`) and reconstructed from a string (`Read`)[2].

To understand the `ask` operation that sends a form to the browser and waits for the user's response, we first need to examine `cgistate` more closely. Beyond the queues explained above, there is a `pageInfo` field that contains information pertinent to the currently created HTML page. From this information and a document to display, the function in the `nextaction` field determines the CGI action that is executed by `ask`. The type of this function is `Element -> CGI ()`. There is also a function, `nextCGIState`, that removes the front element from the first queue and resets a few internal data structures (e.g., `pageInfo`) that are required to implement forms and input fields.

```
ask :: WithHTML CGI a -> CGI ()
ask ma =
  do doc <- build_document ma
     CGI (\cgistate ->
       unCGI (nextaction (pageInfo cgistate) doc) (nextCGIState cgistate))
```

First, the element `ma` is wrapped into a document, `doc`, using `build_document`. Then, `ask` grabs the current `cgistate` and performs the CGI action `next-action (pageInfo cgistate) doc` on the advanced CGI state `nextCGIState cgistate`.

The computation of `nextaction` is necessary because the action depends on a number of things which cannot be determined in advance.

– If there is no response in the log, then the constructed page must be sent to the user and the program must terminate.

---

[2] More efficient means for storing and restoring are possible, but currently not implemented.

– If there is a logged response, then the response is analyzed during the construction of the request page (which is not sent anymore). This analysis also registers the required action in the **pageInfo** field.

Now we see why the construction of HTML is parameterized over a monad, in this case over **CGI**. During the construction, the input parameters are analyzed and saved in the **pageInfo** field. The next logical step is to examine the construction of forms.

5 Forms

The constructors for active HTML components, like input fields and forms, have a more specific type than constructors for passive HTML elements.

```
type HTMLField a = WithHTML CGI () -> WithHTML CGI a
```

The constructor for forms takes a collection of attributes and child elements and returns a `<form>` element. Each input field must have exactly one enclosing form element.

```
makeForm :: HTMLField ()
```

It is not necessary to set the standard attributes of the form element. The `action` attribute, which contains the URL for processing the content of the form, the `enctype` attribute, which determines the encoding of the content of the form, and the `method` attribute are all determined automatically by WASH/CGI.

Input elements specify the input widgets that appear in a form. The function

```
textInputField :: HTMLField (InputField String)
```

generates a simple textual input field whereas

```
inputField :: Read a => HTMLField (InputField a)
```

generates a text input field, which is restricted to values of type **a**. The resulting value of type **InputField a** is the *handle* for the input field. The handle contains the actual input value, which is accessible through the functions

```
value  :: InputField a -> Maybe a
string :: InputField a -> Maybe String
```

The **value** function extracts the parsed value (if there was a parsable input), whereas the **string** function is meant for error analysis and provides access to the raw input (if the input element was filled in at all).

Further input widgets are specified in the same manner (see Fig. 3). A **fileInputField** returns the contents of the chosen file as a string. A **resetField** just clears all input fields, it has no I/O functionality. Radio buttons and selection boxes have a slightly more complicated interface. They are omitted for brevity.

It remains to discuss the **submitField**. It takes a **CGI** action and generates a button in the HTML page. Clicking such a button executes its action. The action is similar to a continuation. Since a form may contain more than one

```
passwordInputField :: HTMLField (InputField String)
checkboxInputField :: HTMLField (InputField Bool)
fileInputField     :: HTMLField (InputField String)
resetField         :: HTMLField (InputField ())
submitField        :: CGI () -> HTMLField ()
```

Fig. 3. Input fields (excerpt)

submit button, multiple continuations are possible. In particular, a large form may be composed from small interaction groups that consist of input fields and one or more submit buttons.

For example, consider programming a simple login screen:

```
login = ask $ standardPage "LOGIN" $ makeForm $ table $
  do nameF <- tr (td (text "Enter your name ") >>
                  td (textInputField (attr "size" "10")))
     passF <- tr (td (text "Enter your password ") >>
                  td (textInputField (attr "size" "10")))
     submitField (check nameF passF) (attr "value" "LOGIN")

check nameF passF =
  htell $ standardPage "LOGIN" $
    (text "You said " ## fromJust (value nameF) ##
     text " and " ## fromJust (value passF))
```

This program is self-explanatory with a small amount of knowledge on HTML. Clicking the submit field triggers the callback action `check name pass` and the variables `name` and `pass` are bound to the handles for the two `textInputField`s. This is due to our convention that HTML constructors always return the value constructed by their children.

Executing the `login` function generates the HTML page in Fig. 4 (see also Fig. 5, left part). In this page, the widgets are automatically named (`f0`, `f1`, `f3`, and `s2`). The numbers are assigned during construction of the page in a depth-first traversal. The `pageInfo` field administers this information.

This functionality is largely implemented in the constructors for the input fields like `textInputField`. They have the following responsibilities, beyond constructing the HTML element and creating the field's handle:

- Assign a unique name `f i` to the input field.
- Check the log for an input pair with name `f i`.
- If such a pair is present, the corresponding value is put into the handle. In the case of a typed field, the value is parsed from the input string.
- If no suitable pair is present (either because there is no logged response, yet, or because the browser did not send it), then `string` and `value` of the handle are set to `Nothing`.

```
<html><head><title>LOGIN</title></head>
<body><h1>LOGIN</h1>
<form enctype="application/x-www-form-urlencoded" name="f3" method="POST"
     action="http://localhost:80">
<table><tr><td>Enter your name </td>
<td><input size="10" name="f0" type="text"></td>
</tr>
<tr><td>Enter your password </td>
<td><input size="10" name="f1" type="text"></td>
</tr>
<input value="LOGIN" name="s2" type="submit">
</table>
<input value="%5B%5D" name="=CGI=parm=" type="hidden">
</form></body></html>
```

Fig. 4. Generated HTML form

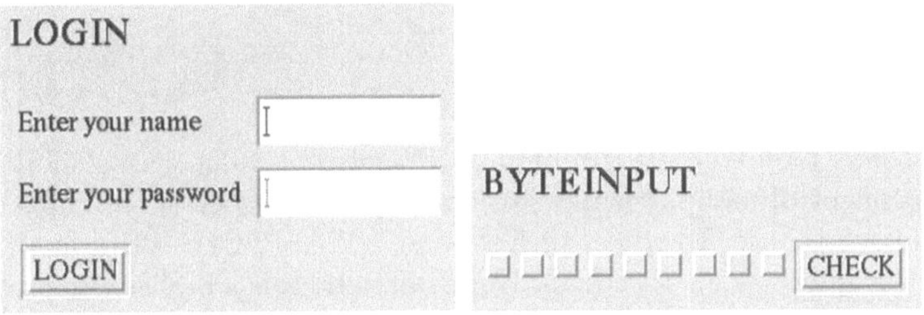

Fig. 5. Generated Web forms

Fields of type "submit" are counted separately because there may be several such fields for each form and each submit field may be bound to a different action. The constructor submitField for a submit field works as follows:

- Assign a unique name si to the submit field.
- Check the log for an input with name si.
- If such an input is present, it registers the callback action in the action component of the pageInfo.
- Otherwise, nothing happens.

The constructor makeForm of the form element is only responsible to set up the attributes and to include the hidden field that contains the log (=CGI=parm= in Fig. 4) in the document. The value attribute contains the log information (in this case, the empty list []), which is URL encoded.

It is easy to define custom input elements from the given primitives. For example, a byte-input widget might be programmed from checkboxes as shown in Fig. 6. The code generates a sequence of eight checkboxes, extracts their boolean values, multiplies them by the place value, and adds them all together.

```
byteInput = byteInput' 256 InputField{string=Just "", value=Just 0}
byteInput' i acc attr =
  if i > 0 then return acc else
  do bi    <- checkboxInputField attr
     acc' <- byteInput' (i 'div' 2) acc attr
     return acc'{value= value acc' >>= \v ->
                        value bi >>= \b ->
                        return (v + i * b2i b)}
  where b2i False = 0
        b2i True = 1
```

Fig. 6. A Byte-Input Widget

The first checkbox determines the most significant bit. Like any other HTML element constructor, `byteInput` accepts a parameter `attr` which is distributed to all the checkboxes. Fig. 5 (right part) displays the result.

6   Persistency

In the context of Web Programming, a persistent value has a lifetime which is independent of any particular session. Typically, a persistent value would be stored in a database. To access such a value, a WASH/CGI-script might perform a database query as an IO action. Unfortunately, this simplistic approach has a number of drawbacks.

- The (potentially big) result of the query would appear in the log.
- It is virtually impossible to guarantee that a value read earlier in a session is still consistent with the value stored in the database at a later point in a session. Hence, it is impossible to implement an update operation.

For these reasons, we designed an interface for accessing persistent data which overcomes these problems.

The basic idea of the library is to manage all accesses to persistent data via time-stamped handles. The type of a handle is

```
data T a      -- abstract
```

where the type parameter `a` indicates the type of the persistent value. To obtain a handle, it must be initialized:

```
init    :: (Read a, Show a, Types a) => String -> a -> CGI (Maybe (T a))
```

The operation `init` takes the name of a persistent value and an initial value (of type `a`) and returns a `CGI` action, which may return a handle for the value. If the persistent value does not exist, yet, then the system creates it, fills it with the initial value and returns a handle to it. Otherwise, the handle contains the most recently stored value. The contexts `Read a` and Show a indicate that a textfile is used to store the actual data. The context **Types a** indicates that it must be possible to generate a type stamp from type **a**. This type stamp is used to guarantee type consistency across module boundaries. When trying to **init** an existing persistent value at the wrong type then the **CGI** action returns **Nothing**.

The **get** operation retrieves the value from a handle:

```
get     :: Read a => T a -> CGI a
```

The implementation guarantees that **get h**, for a fixed handle **h**, always returns the same value.

The **set** operation stores a value in the persistent store.

```
set     :: (Read a, Show a) => T a -> a -> CGI (Maybe (T a))
```

Interestingly, the action **set h v** may fail (*i.e.*, return **Nothing**). Failure occurs if the handle **h** is not *current*. A handle is current if the value accessible via the handle has not been set otherwise since the handle was created. In other words, a **get** operation on a non-current handle does not return the last value **set** through the handle.

Hence, the last operation

```
current :: Read a => T a -> CGI (T a)
```

takes a handle and returns its most recent version.

As said above, the implementation stores the persistent value in a textfile. Since many scripts accessing the persistent value may run concurrently on the server, we need some kind of concurrency control. Hence, the module **Persistent** locks each file before it starts using it and unlocks it once it is done with the file. Locks are implemented in a portable way by creating a lock directory for each persistent value.

7   Extended Example

As an extended example, we consider a time tabling service[3]. It implements a collaborative interface to construct time tables and publish them on the Web. Time tables can be entered from scratch, saved on the server, and later reviewed. Changing a time table requires a password, whereas viewing is possible for anybody who knows the URL. The whole application is implemented in just 136 lines of Haskell.

Clearly, this task requires global persistence, which is implemented in a module **Persistent**. As an example, here is the code implementing the anonymous view function.

```
cgigen owner =
  do Some hdl <- Persistent.init ('T':'T':owner) Nothing
     alltt <- get hdl
     case alltt of
```

---

[3] http://nakalele.informatik.uni-freiburg.de:80/cgi/WASH/TimeTable.cgi

```
Nothing ->
  htell (standardPage "Time Table Service"
         (text "No time table available for " ## text owner))
Just (passwd, headers, tt) ->
  timetable owner passwd headers tt True
```

The code accesses the timetable for `owner` by first creating a *persistence handle*, hdl, using the function `Persistent.init` applied to the name of the persistent value and its initial value. If the persistent value already exists, the handle points to its current value. Otherwise, `init` creates a new persistent value initialized to `Nothing`, in this case. We access the persistent value through function `get`. It returns the current contents of the handle.

The function `timetable`, which is invoked if the time table is available, performs the main formatting work. It is heavily parameterized and we only show an excerpt from this function.

```
timetable owner passwd headers tt final =
  ask $ standardPage (Prelude.head hdrs) $ makeForm $
  do xys <- table $
  do attr "border" "3"
     thead $ tr $ mapM_ (\d -> th (text d ## attr "width" "150")) hdrs
     mapM (\hour -> tr (td (text (show hour) ## attr "align" "right") >>
                    mapM (\d -> ttentry final tt d hour)
                        [1 .. 5]))
              [8 .. 19]
  unless final
   (submitField
         (updateAction owner passwd hdrs (concat xys) Nothing True)
         (fieldVALUE "SUBMIT"))
```

The code either generates a form with 60 input fields or the final output formatted as a table, depending on the value of `final`. The second `do` specifies the contents of the table. First, its `border` attribute is set to 3. Next, it creates the header line of the table `thead`. It creates the header entries by applying the monadic map operator `mapM_` to the list of headers. The second `mapM` is responsible for the contents of the table. It uses the monadic map operator `mapM` for constructing a rectangular arrangement of 5×12 input fields, where each single field is generated by `ttentry`. The submit button (last three lines) only appears if we are generating an input form (`final == False`).

It is interesting to consider how the return value `xys` from the `table` combinator is computed. The innermost `mapM` generates a list of handles to input elements. This list is also returned as the value of the `\hour` lambda expression. The outer `mapM` wraps each of the items into a list.

8   Related Work

Meijer's CGI library [3] implements a low-level facility for accessing the input to a CGI script and for creating its output. It is nicely engineered and its functionality is at about the level of our own `RawCGI` library. Meijer's library offers additional features like cookies and its own HTML representation, which we felt should be separated from the functionality of `RawCGI`.

Hughes [5] has devised the powerful concept of arrows, a generalization of monads. His motivating application is the design of a CGI library that implements sessions. Indeed, the functionality of his library was the major source of inspiration for our work. Our work indicates that monads are sufficient to implement sessions (Hughes also realized that [6]). Furthermore, it extends the functionality offered by the arrow CGI-library with a novel representation of HTML and typed compositional forms. Also, the callback-style of programming advocated here is not encouraged by the arrow library.

Hanus's library [7] for server-side scripting in the functional-logic language Curry comes close to the functionality that we offer. In particular, its design inspired our investigation of a callback-style programming model. While his library uses logical variables to identify input fields in HTML forms, we are able to make do with a purely functional approach. Our approach only relies on the concept of a monad, which is fundamental for a real-world functional programmer.

Further approaches to Web programming using functional languages are using the Scheme language [8,9]. The main idea is to use a continuation to take a snapshot of the state of the script after sending the form to the browser. This continuation is then stored on the server and the form contains a key for later retrieval of the continuation. Conceptually, this is similar to the log that we are using. Technically, there are two important differences. First, we have to reconstruct the current state from the log when the next user request arrives. Using a continuation, this reconstruction is immediate. Second, our approach relies only on CGI whereas the continuation approach implies that the script runs inside the Web server and hence that the Web server is implemented in Scheme, too.

A recent revision of the continuation-based approach overcomes the tight coupling of scripts to the server. Graunke et al [10] present an approach to transform arbitray interactive programs into CGI scripts. The transformation consists of three steps, a transformation to continuation-passing style, lambda lifting, and defunctionalization. The resulting program consists of a number of dispatch functions (arising from defunctionalization) and code pieces implementing interaction fragments. Compared to our approach, they reconstruct the state from a marshalled closure whereas we replay the interaction. Furthermore, they implement mutable state using cookies stored on the client side. It is not clear whether such functionality is needed for Haskell scripts since the language discourages the use of mutable state.

Bigwig [11] is a system for writing Web applications. It provides a number of domain specific customizable languages for composing dynamic documents, specifying interactions, accessing databases, etc. It compiles these languages into a combination of standard Web technologies, like HTML, CGI, applets, JavaScript. Like our library, it implements a session facility, which is more restrictive in that sessions may neither be backtracked nor forked. Each Bigwig session has a notion of a current state, which cannot be subverted. However, the implementation of sessions is different and relies on a special runtime system that improves the efficiency of CGI scripts [12]. In addition, Bigwig provides a sophisticated facility for generating documents and typed document templates. Moreover, there is a type system for forms. WASH/CGI provides typed document templates in the weak sense of Bigwig by keeping strings and values of type Element apart. A special type system for forms is not required since (typed) field values are directly passed to (typed) callback-actions. Hence, all necessary type checking is done by the Haskell compiler.

MAWL [13,14] is a domain specific language for specifying form-based interactions. It was the first language to offer a typing of forms against the code that received its input from the form. It provides a subset of Bigwig's functionality, for example, the facilities for document templates are much more limited.

Guide [15] is a rule-based language for CGI programming. It supports a simple notion of document templates, similar in style to that offered by MAWL. It provides only rudimentary control structure: it sequentially processes a list of predicates and takes the action (that is, it displays a HTML page) associated to the first succeeding predicate. It supports the concept of a session, a limited form of concurrency control, as well as session-wide and global variables. However, it neither supports typed input, nor composition of input fields, nor facilities to ensure that the variables used in a script match the variables defined in a form.

In comparison to a GUI library [16,17,18,19] a CGI library does not have to deal with concurrency. All interaction is limited to exchanging messages between Web browser and Web server, so that nested interactions are not possible. This greatly simplifies the implementation. However, HTML is an expressive language to specify layout and Web-based user interfaces are ubiquitous, so there is a market for the kind of library that we are proposing.

In previous work[20,21], we have investigated the use of Haskell for generating valid HTML and XML documents, where the type system enforces adherence to the DTD. That work is completementary to the present one. While the user interface is identical, the present work constructs HTML elements in a different way and it only guarantees well-formed output. It would be possible to join both works, but we have not done this, yet.

Java Server Pages [22] and Servlets are recent approaches to the convenient specification of dynamic contents. They also provide a notion of session Persistence and encapsulate its implementation. Unfortunately, they do not guarantee type safety and they do not provide the advanced support for generating HTML and forms as we do.

9   Conclusions and Future Work

The WASH/CGI library brings new power to CGI programmers. It offers a simple and declarative way to implement complicated interactive Web-based user interfaces. In particular, it treats the display of the Web browser like a graphical user interface with restricted facilities. This approach results in a natural use of

HTML for the layout. Further, we can attach callback-actions to active input elements to specify the flow of control.

The WASH/CGI approach is not only suitable for CGI programming, but also for other kinds of server-side Web scripting. For example, it would be interesting to investigate a combination with Haskell server pages [23], with Bigwig's runtime system [12], or with proprietary APIs (NSAPI, ISAPI).

Ongoing work addresses the integration with WASH/HTML, a generic typed representation of HTML, which representation ensures that only valid documents are generated [20]. Further, we investigate the integration with a Web server written in Haskell. Using Concurrent Haskell [24], there will be one thread in the server for each session. This approach reduces the management of session state via logs to thread management, as in the continuation approach discussed above. It also greatly simplifies issues like persistency and concurrency control. Last but not least, we are including support for style sheets and JavaScript.

References

1. Cgi: Common gateway interface. (http://www.w3.org/CGI/) 192
2. Haskell 98, a non-strict, purely functional language.
   http://www.haskell.org/definition (1998) 193
3. Meijer, E.: Server-side web scripting with Haskell. Journal of Functional Programming **10** (2000) 1–18 194, 204
4. Jones, M. P.: Functional programming with overloading and higher-order polymorphism. In: Advanced Functional Programming. Volume 925 of Lecture Notes in Computer Science. Springer-Verlag (1995) 97–136 195
5. Hughes, J.: Generalising monads to arrows. Science of Computer Programming **37** (2000) 67–111 205
6. Hughes, J. Private communication (2000) 205
7. Hanus, M.: High-level server side Web scripting in Curry. In: Practical Aspects of Declarative Languages, Proceedings of the Third International Workshop, PADL'01. Lecture Notes in Computer Science, Las Vegas, NV, USA, Springer-Verlag (2001) 205
8. Graunke, P., Krishnamurthi, S., Hoeven, S. V. D., Felleisen, M.: Programming the Web with high-level programming languages. In Sands, D., ed.: Proc. 10th European Symposium on Programming. Lecture Notes in Computer Science, Genova, Italy, Springer-Verlag (2001) 122–136 205
9. Queinnec, C.: The influence of browsers on evaluators or, continuations to program Web servers. [25] 23–33 205
10. Graunke, P., Findler, R. B., Krishnamurthi, S., Felleisen, M.: Automatically restructuring programs for the Web. In: Proceedings of ASE-2001: The 16th IEEE International Conference on Automated Software Engineering, San Diego, USA, IEEE CS Press (2001) 205
11. Sandholm, A., Schwartzbach, M. I.: A type system for dynamic web documents. In Reps, T., ed.: Proc. 27th Annual ACM Symposium on Principles of Programming Languages, Boston, MA, USA, ACM Press (2000) 290–301 205
12. Brabrand, C., Møller, A., Sandholm, A., Schwartzbach, M. I.: A runtime system for interactive web services. Journal of Computer Networks (1999) 206, 207

13. Ladd, D. A., Ramming, J. C.: Programming the Web: An application-oriented language for hypermedia service programming, World Wide Web Consortium (1995) 567–586   206
14. Atkinson, D., Ball, T., Benedikt, M., Bruns, G., Cox, K., Mataga, P., Rehor, K.: Experience with a domain specific language for form-based services. In: Conference on Domain-Specific Languages, Santa Barbara, CA, USENIX (1997)   206
15. Levy, M. R.: Web programming in Guide. Software—Practice & Experience **28** (1998) 1581–1603   206
16. Carlsson, M., Hallgren, T.: FUDGETS: A graphical interface in a lazy functional language. In Arvind, ed.: Proc. Functional Programming Languages and Computer Architecture 1993, Copenhagen, Denmark, ACM Press, New York (1993) 321–330   206
17. Vullinghs, T., Tuijnman, D., Schulte, W.: Lightweight GUIs for functional programming. In Swierstra, D., Hermenegildo, M., eds.: International Symposium on Programming Languages, Implementations, Logics and Programs (PLILP '95). Number 982 in Lecture Notes in Computer Science, Utrecht, The Netherlands, Springer-Verlag (1995) 341–356   206
18. Finne, S., Peyton Jones, S.: Composing Haggis. In: Proc. 5th Eurographics Workshop on Programming Paradigms in Graphics, Maastricht, NL (1995)   206
19. Sage, M.: FranTk — a declarative GUI language for Haskell. [25] 106–117   206
20. Thiemann, P.: Modeling HTML in Haskell. In: Practical Aspects of Declarative Languages, Proceedings of the Second International Workshop, PADL'00. Number 1753 in Lecture Notes in Computer Science, Boston, Massachusetts, USA (2000) 263–277   206, 207
21. Thiemann, P.: A typed representation for HTML and XML in Haskell. Journal of Functional Programming (2001) To appear.   206
22. Peligrí-Llopart, E., Cable, L.: Java Server Pages Specification. http://java.sun.com/products/jsp/index.html (1999)   206
23. Meijer, E., van Velzen, D.: Haskell Server Pages, functional programming and the battle for the middle tier. In: Draft proceedings of the 2000 ACM SIGPLAN Haskell Workshop, Montreal, Canada (2000) 23–33   207
24. Peyton Jones, S., Gordon, A., Finne, S.: Concurrent Haskell. In: Conference Record of POPL '96: The 23$^{\rm rd}$ ACM SIGPLAN-SIGACT Symposium on Principles of Programming Languages, St. Petersburg Beach, Florida, USA (1996) 295–308 207
25. Wadler, P., ed.: International Conference on Functional Programming. In Wadler, P., ed.: Proc. International Conference on Functional Programming 2000, Montreal, Canada, ACM Press, New York (2000)   207, 208

A Better XML Parser
through Functional Programming

Oleg Kiselyov

Software Engineering, Naval Postgraduate School
Monterey, CA 93943
oleg@pobox.com
oleg@acm.org

Abstract. This paper demonstrates how a higher-level, declarative view of XML parsing as folding over XML documents has helped to design and implement a better XML parser. By better we mean a full-featured, algorithmically optimal, pure-functional parser, which can act as a stream processor. By better we mean an efficient SAX parser that is *easy to use*, a parser that does not burden an application with the maintenance of a global state across several callbacks, a parser that eliminates classes of possible application errors.

This paper describes such better XML parser, SSAX. We demonstrate that SSAX is a better parser by comparing it with several XML parsers written in various (functional) languages, as well as with the reference XML parser Expat. In the experience of the author the declarative approach has greatly helped in the development of SSAX. We argue that the more expressive, reliable and easier to use application interface is the outcome of implementing the parsing engine as an enhanced tree fold combinator, which fully captures the control pattern of the depth-first tree traversal.

Keywords: XML parsing, traversal, tree fold, Scheme, Haskell

1   Introduction

On the surface of it, parsing of XML presents no problems. We merely need to apply yacc/lex or a similar tool to the Extended BNF grammar in the XML Recommendation. XML parsing ought to be even easier in functional languages, thanks to the development of intuitive parsing combinator libraries.

It comes as a surprise then that all but two functional-style XML parsers barely comply even with a half of the XML Recommendation [13]. None of the pure or mostly functional-style XML parsers support XML Namespaces. With the exception of FXP [10], the existing functional-style parsers cannot process XML documents in a stream-wise fashion. These parsers thus exhibit significant processing latency and are limited to documents that can fit within the available memory. The application interface of the only one functional, full-featured,

S. Krishnamurthi, C. R. Ramakrishnan (Eds.): PADL 2002, LNCS 2257, pp. 209–224, 2002.
© Springer-Verlag Berlin Heidelberg 2002

stream-oriented parser FXP mirrors the API of the reference XML parser Expat [4]. The latter is notorious for its difficult and error-prone application interface.

XML is markedly more difficult to parse than it is commonly thought. It is by no means sufficient for a parser merely to follow the Extended BNF grammar of XML. Besides the grammar, the XML Recommendation [13] specifies a great number of rules (e.g., whitespace handling, attribute value normalization, entity references expansion) as well as well-formedness and validity constraint checks, which a parser must implement. Whitespace handling rules in particular require an unusually tight coupling between tokenizing and parsing.

The second peculiar aspect of XML parsing is its strong emphasis on efficiency and the convenience of the application interface. The traditional view of parsing as a transformation of a source document into an abstract syntax tree is deficient for several classes of XML applications. We should note first that the traditional approach does apply to XML, where it is called a Document Object Model (DOM) parsing. The DOM approach is a necessity for applications that repeatedly traverse and search the abstract syntax tree of a document. Other applications however scan through the document tree entirely, and only once. Such applications can potentially process an XML document as it is being read. Loading the whole document into memory as an abstract syntax tree is then inefficient both in terms of time and memory. Such applications can benefit from a lower-level, event-based model of XML parsing called a Simple Application Programming Interface for XML (SAX). A SAX parser applies user-defined actions to elements, attributes and other XML entities as they are identified. The actions can transform received elements and character data on the fly, or can incorporate them into custom data structures, including the DOM tree. Therefore, a SAX parser can always act as a DOM parser. The converse is not true.

Although the SAX XML parsing model is more general, more memory efficient and faster, SAX parsers are regarded as difficult to use: "It feels like you are trapped inside an eternal loop when writing code. You find yourself using many global variables and conditional statements" [3].

Is it possible to implement an efficient, compliant, stream-oriented XML parser with a convenient user interface that minimizes the amount of user-application state? Furthermore, can functional programming help to design and to implement such a parser?

This paper proves by construction that the answer to both questions is yes. The contribution of this paper is a SSAX parser [7], a compliant SAX XML parser that is being used in several industrial applications. SSAX is not a toy parser: it fully supports XML Namespaces, character, internal and external parsed entities, `xml:space`, attribute value normalization, processing instructions and CDATA sections. At the same time, SSAX minimizes the amount of application-specific state that has to be shared among user-supplied event handlers. SSAX makes the maintenance of an application-specific element stack unnecessary, which eliminates several classes of common bugs. SSAX is written in a pure-functional subset of Scheme. Therefore, the event handlers are referentially transparent, which makes them easier for a programmer to write and to reason about. The superior user application interface for the event-driven XML parsing is in itself a contribution of the paper. The paper demonstrates that this interface is not an accident but the outcome of a correctly chosen control abstraction, which captures the pattern on depth-first traversal of trees.

The key design principle of SSAX was a view of an XML document as an n-ary tree laid out in a depth-first order. XML parsing is then a tree traversal. We review the topic of functional-style tree traversals in Section 2. We will concentrate on efficiency and on capturing the pattern of such traversals in a higher-order combinator, `foldts`. In Section 3 we describe the SSAX parser, which is an implementation of `foldts` with the tree in question being an XML document. Section 4 demonstrates on several concrete examples that the SSAX parser is indeed efficient, easier to use and less error-prone, compared to other SAX parsers, in particular the reference XML parser Expat and its pure functional analogue FXP. We conclude in Section 5 that functional programming is intuitive and helpful not only for processing XML but for parsing it as well.

2   Depth-First Traversals of Trees

We start with a very simple example of a functional-style depth-first tree traversal and gradually extend it to improve efficiency and to abstract the pattern of the traversal. Although the SSAX parser has been implemented in Scheme, this section will use Haskell notation. The latter is more succinct; furthermore, it is more convenient for direct comparison with important papers on tree folding [5][6], which use Haskell notation.

Our trees are represented by the datatype

```
data Tree = Leaf String | Nd [Tree]
```

Given such a tree, we turn to our first problem of concatenating strings attached to all leaves, in their depth-first traversal order. If we view our trees as realizations of an XML information set [14], our first problem becomes that of computing a *string-value* for the root node of the information set .

The obvious solution to the problem

```
str_value1:: Tree -> String
str_value1 (Leaf str) = str
str_value1 (Nd kids) = foldr (++) "" (map str_value1 kids)
```

where

```
foldr:: (a->b->b) -> b -> [a] -> b
foldr f z [] = z
foldr f z (x:xs) = f x (foldr f z xs)
```

although elegant, is deficient. Indeed, let us apply `str_value1` to a full binary tree of depth k whose leaves are one-character strings (2^k leaves total). Executing `str_value1` then requires $k2^k$ character-moving operations and produces $(k-1)2^k$ garbage characters. The algorithm can be improved by noting that we do not have to concatenate the strings eagerly. Instead, we can accumulate strings in a list and join them after the traversal.

```
str_value2:: Tree -> String
str_value2 = concat . str_value2'

str_value2' (Leaf str) = [str]
str_value2' (Nd kids) = concat (map str_value2' kids)
```

This halves the amount of garbage and the number of character movements. However, appending two lists of size 2^i takes 2^i operations. The algorithm still has the time complexity of $O(k2^k)$; it still produces $k2^{k-1} + 2^{k+1}$ list cells of garbage. The best solution is to build a list of strings in the reverse order – with the reversal and concatenation at the very end:

```
str_value3:: Tree -> String
str_value3 = concat . reverse . (str_value3' [])

str_value3' seed (Leaf str) = str : seed
str_value3' seed (Nd kids) = foldl str_value3' seed kids
```

where

```
foldl:: (a->b->a) -> a -> [b] -> a
foldl f z [] = z
foldl f z (x:xs) = foldl f (f z x) xs
```

Some language systems offer a string-concatenate-reverse function, which halves the amount of the produced garbage. The running time of `str_value3` is linear in the size of the tree. The amount of garbage – while unavoidable – grows only linearly with the size of the tree. The function `str_value3` differs from `str_value1` and `str_value2` in another aspect. The actions at children nodes of the same node are no longer independent. The actions are threaded through the seed argument and must be performed in order. The independence of actions in `str_value1` and `str_value2` manifested itself in the presence of `map`, which is absent in `str_value3`.

We now turn to the next example – computing a digest of a tree. We want to traverse a tree depth-first and to compute an MD5 hash of all encountered nodes and leaf values. A hash function is generally non-associative. Therefore, we have no choice but to use a stateful traversal similar to that of `str_value3`.

```
md5Init:: MD5Context
md5Update:: String -> MD5Context -> MD5Context
md5Final:: MD5Context -> String
```

```
tree_digest:: Tree -> String

tree_digest = md5Final . (tree_digest' md5Init)
tree_digest' ctx (Leaf str) =
  md5Update "/leaf" $ md5Update str $ md5Update "leaf" ctx
tree_digest' ctx (Nd kids) =
  md5Update "/node" $ foldl tree_digest' (md5Update "node" ctx)
                                                              kids
```

Can we separate the task of tree traversal and recursion from the task of transformation of a node and a state? The benefits of encapsulating common patterns of computation as higher-order operators instead of using recursion directly are well-known [11][5]. For lists, the common pattern of traversal is captured by the familiar `foldl` and `foldr` operators, which can be generalized to trees [11][6]:

```
foldt:: (String -> a) -> ([a] -> a) -> Tree -> a
foldt f g (Leaf str) = f str
foldt f g (Nd kids) = g (map (foldt f g) kids)
```

Unlike the functions `str_value1` and `str_value2`, the efficient `str_value3'` cannot be expressed via `foldt` in a simple way because the actions at branches are dependent on the history of the traversal and cannot be simply mapped to children nodes. Such functions are often distinguished [11] by an extra parameter, which acts as a an accumulator or a continuation: (cf. `str_value2'` with `str_value3'` above). Such functions can be written as second-order folds [11], which return procedures as results. In our example:

```
str_value31 tree = concat $ reverse $ (str_value31' tree [])
    where
        str_value31' = foldt (\str seed -> str : seed)
               (\new_kids seed -> foldl (flip ($)) seed new_kids)
```

This representation requires higher-order features of the language and often not as efficient because (`str_value31' tree`) creates as many closures as there are nodes in the `tree`. The closures are then applied to `[]`, which generates the final result. In strict languages such as ML or Scheme (used in the following sections), closure creation is relatively expensive.

   To make "mapping" of an accumulating function to a tree efficient, we introduce a more general control operator:

```
foldts :: (a->a) -> (a->a->a) -> (a->[Char]->a) -> a-> Tree-> a
foldts fdown fup fhere seed (Leaf str) = fhere seed str
foldts fdown fup fhere seed (Nd kids) =
       fup seed $ foldl (foldts fdown fup fhere) (fdown seed) kids
```

A user instantiates `foldts` with *three* actions; for comparison, `foldr` requires only one action and `foldt` needs two. The three `foldts` actions are threaded via a `seed` parameter, which maintains the local state. An action accepts a seed as one of its arguments and returns a new seed as the result. The action `fhere` is applied to a leaf of the tree. The action `fdown` is invoked when a non-leaf node is entered and before any of the node's children are visited. The `fdown` action has to generate a seed to be passed to the first visited child of the node. The action `fup` is invoked after all children of a node have been seen. The action is a function of two seeds: the first seed is the local state at the moment the traversal process enters the branch rooted at the current node. The second seed is the result of visiting all child branches. The action `fup` is to produce a seed that is taken to be the state of the traversal after the process leaves the current branch.

The two previously considered examples – computation of a string value and of a digest for a tree – can easily be written with `foldts`:

```
str_value32 = concat . reverse . (str_value32' [])
   where
          str_value32' = foldts id (\_->id) (flip (:))
```

In this example, the seed is the list of leaf values accumulated in the reverse order. The `fhere` action prepends the value of the visited leaf to the list. The actions `fdown` and `fup` are trivial: they merely propagate the seed.

```
tree_digest2 = md5Final . (foldts fd fu fh md5Init)
    where fh ctx str = md5Update "/leaf" $  md5Update str $
                                            md5Update "leaf" ctx
          fd ctx = md5Update "node" ctx
          fu _ ctx = md5Update "/node" ctx
```

The computation of the tree digest is no more complex. The seed is the MD5 context. The `fdown` and `fup` actions mark the fact of entering and exiting a non-leaf node. This example clearly demonstrates that consuming node values and updating the local state are separated from the task of traversing the tree and recurring into its branches. This separation makes operations on tree nodes simpler to write and to comprehend.

3   XML Parsing as Tree Traversal

The enhanced tree fold, `foldts`, has more than theoretical interest. The `foldts` combinator is literally at the core of the pure functional XML parser SSAX. To see how `foldts` applies to XML parsing, we note that an XML document with familiar angular brackets is a concrete representation of a tree laid out in a depth-first order. Elements, processing instructions, CDATA sections and character data are the nodes of such a tree. The latter three are always the leaf nodes. Attributes are collections of named values attached to element nodes. Since element nodes can be non-terminal nodes, the moments the traversal enters and leaves an element node must be specifically marked, respectively as the start and the end tags. XML parsing then is a depth-first traversal of an XML document regarded as a tree. XML parsing is a pre-post-order, down-and-up traversal as it invokes user actions when the traversal process enters a node and again when the process has visited all child branches and is about to leave the node.

Just like the `foldts`, the SSAX framework captures the pattern of the XML document traversal (i.e., parsing). To be more precise, the framework carries out such parsing chores as tokenizing, XML namespace resolution and the namespace context propagation, the whitespace mode propagation, the expansion of character and parsed entity references, attribute value normalization, maintaining the traversal order. The user can therefore concentrate on the meaningful work – what to do at encountered nodes.

At the heart of SSAX is a function `SSAX:make-parser`, which takes user-supplied node action procedures (also called content handlers) and instantiates the corresponding XML parser. Similarly to `foldts`, `SSAX:make-parser` requires three mandatory handlers: `new-level-seed`, `finish-element`, and `char-data-handler`. These handlers closely correspond to the procedural parameters `fdown`, `fup` and `fhere` passed to `foldts`. The output of `SSAX:make-parser` is a procedure `Port -> Seed -> Seed`. The first argument is a port from which to read the input XML document. The port is treated throughout the SSAX framework as if it were a "unique" parameter, using the terminology from the programming language Clean. The second argument to the parser is the initial value of the application state, the seed. The parser returns the final value of the seed, the result of a tree-induced composition of the user-supplied handlers.

`SSAX:make-parser` also accepts a number of optional handlers, which will be called when the parser encounters a processing instruction, a document type declaration, or the root element. If the optional handlers are omitted, the instantiated parser will be non-validating. `SSAX:make-parser` is actually a macro, which *integrates* the handlers into the generated parser code. We can regard `SSAX:make-parser` as a staged parser.

The semantics of `SSAX:make-parser` is the same as that of `foldts`. Both traverse a tree in a depth-first order and invoke handlers at "interesting points". Besides the traversal state `SSAX:make-parser` also maintains the list of active entities and the namespace context. The user handlers of `SSAX:make-parser` are also more complex, receiving as additional arguments the name of the current element and its attributes.

In the following section we consider several typical instantiations of `SSAX:make-parser`, with the goal of estimating SSAX complexity and comparing it with other XML parsers. The comparison will demonstrate the benefits of modeling the SSAX parser after `foldts`.

4   SSAX Examples and Comparisons

4.1   The Complexity of SSAX Parsing

The first example of using SSAX is untagging. This is a common "XML to text" translation that removes all markup from a well-formed XML document. We should point out that this is the same example as the one discussed in Section 2. Indeed, untagging is precisely determining the string-value of an XML document tree. The example in Section 2 operated on trees represented as linked data structures in memory. In this section a tree is an XML document itself. In both cases, we traverse the tree and accumulate all character data as we encounter them. As Section 2 explained, it is beneficial to accumulate the character data in a list in reverse order and join them at the very end.

The procedure to remove markup from an XML document is shown below. This is an instantiation of the SSAX parser with three handlers: `new-level-seed`

```
(define (remove-markup xml-port)
  ; Accumulate the text values of leaves in a seed, in reverse order
  (let ((result
         ((SSAX:make-parser
           NEW-LEVEL-SEED
           (lambda (elem-gi attributes namespaces expected-content seed)
             seed)

           FINISH-ELEMENT
           (lambda
               (elem-gi attributes namespaces parent-seed seed) seed)

           CHAR-DATA-HANDLER
           (lambda (string1 string2 seed)
             (let* ((seed (cons string1 seed)))
               (if (string-null? string2) seed (cons string2 seed))))
           )
          xml-port '())))
    (string-concatenate-reverse result)
    ))
```

and `finish-element` merely propagate the seed, while `char-data-handler` adds the character data to the list. Since the optional document-type and root element handlers are omitted, the remove-markup parser is non-validating. The pieces of character data are passed to `char-data-handler` in two string arguments for efficiency. The similarity of the remove-markup code with `str_value32` of Section 2 is striking. We must note however that `str_value32` relied on `foldts`, which traversed a linked structure of type `Tree` in memory. The remove-markup procedure on the other hand parses an XML document, which it reads from a given input port. When this port contains a document such as the one on Fig. 1, the procedure yields a string "01234567". To verify that remove-markup, just as `str_value32`, runs in time and space that grows only linearly with the size of XML documents, we applied the procedure to documents such as the one on Fig. 1 of increasing depth. We ran all benchmarks on a Pentium III Xeon 500 MHz computer with 128 MB of main memory and FreeBSD 4.0-RELEASE operating system. The benchmark Scheme code was compiled by a Gambit-C 3.0

```
<node><node><node><leaf>0</leaf><leaf>1</leaf></node>
            <node><leaf>2</leaf><leaf>3</leaf></node></node>
    <node><node><leaf>4</leaf><leaf>5</leaf></node>
            <node><leaf>6</leaf><leaf>7</leaf></node></node></node>
```

Fig. 1. A full binary tree as an XML document

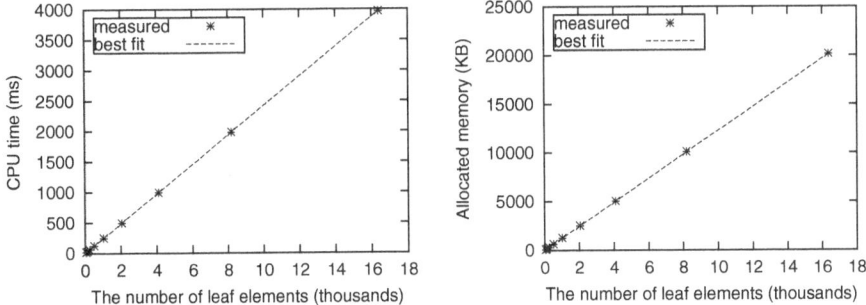

Fig. 2. Performance of the SSAX parser for documents of the form given on Fig. 1. The CPU time and the cumulative amount of allocated memory are plotted as functions of the number of leaf elements in the input XML document. Most of the allocated memory was garbage-collected

compiler. Figure 2 shows the result. The SSAX parser indeed has the linear space and time complexities. This is the *experimental* result, obtained by measuring the performance of the full-scale XML parser.

4.2   SSAX and Expat

No discussion of XML parsing can avoid Expat, which is *the* reference XML parser, written in C by James Clark [4]. Expat is a SAX, i.e., a stream-oriented parser. As the user passes it chunks of the input XML document, Expat identifies elements, character data or other entities and invokes the appropriate handler (if the user has registered one). The size of the chunks is controlled by the user; chunks can range from one byte to the whole XML document.

A tutorial article about Expat [2] explains well how Expat is supposed to be used. A user application most certainly has to have "a good stack mechanism in order to keep track of current context... The things you're likely to want to keep on a stack are the currently opened element and it's attributes. You push this information onto the stack in the start handler and you pop it off in the end handler." As an illustration, the Expat tutorial discusses a sample application `outline.c`, which prints an element outline for an XML document, indenting child elements to distinguish them from the parent element that contains them. In this case, the stack is represented by a global variable Depth, which controls the amount of indenting white space to print before the element name. The variable is incremented in a user-supplied start-element handler, and is decremented in the end-element handler. A simplified code for the two user handlers is given on Fig. 3.

```
int Depth;
void start(void *data, const char *el, const char **attr) {
int i;
for (i = 0; i < Depth; i++)
      printf("  ");
printf("%s\n", el);
Depth++; }

void end(void *data, const char *el) { Depth--; }

int main(void) {
   XML_Parser p = XML_ParserCreate(NULL);
   XML_SetElementHandler(p, start, end); /* register the callbacks */
   /* invoke XML_Parse() passing the buffer with the XML document
      or a part of it */ }
```

Fig. 3. A simplified code for the outline.c application, using Expat

It is instructive to compare the Expat application outline.c with the corresponding SSAX application, whose complete code is given on Fig. 4.

In the Expat application, the maintenance of the application state, the Depth, is split across two separate handlers. This fact increases the possibility of an error. The ssax-outline application on the other hand has no global variables or other application-specific stack to maintain. Unlike the Expat handlers, SSAX handlers can be largely decoupled and thus easily written and understood.

The function ssax-outline also illustrates the benefit of the SAX XML parsing mode. The function prints element names as they are identified and accumulates no data. It can therefore process documents of arbitrary size – far bigger than the amount of available memory. The function ssax-outline is a true stream processor, with low memory requirements and low latency.

To compare the performance of SSAX and Expat, we ran several benchmarks. We need to discuss first the difference in input modes of the two parsers. An application that uses Expat is responsible for reading an XML stream by blocks and passing the blocks to Expat, specifically noting the last block. Expat requires the calling application be able to determine the end of the XML document stream *before* parsing the stream. If an application can do that, it can read the stream by large blocks. An application can potentially load the whole document into memory and pass this single block to Expat. Expat uses shared substrings extensively, and therefore is specifically optimized for such a scenario. If we take a document from a (tcp) pipe, it may be impossible to tell offhand when to stop

```
(define (ssax-outline xml-port)
  ((SSAX:make-parser
    NEW-LEVEL-SEED
    (lambda (elem-gi attributes namespaces expected-content seed)
      (display seed)                  ; indent the element name
      (display elem-gi) (newline)  ; print the name of the element
      (string-append " " seed))    ; advance the indent level

    FINISH-ELEMENT                       ; restore the indent level
    (lambda
        (elem-gi attributes namespaces parent-seed seed) parent-seed)

    CHAR-DATA-HANDLER
    (lambda (string1 string2 seed) seed)
    )
    xml-port ""))
```

Fig. 4. The complete code for the outline application, using SSAX. The seed describes the depth of an element relative to the root of the tree. To be more precise, the seed is the string of space characters to output to indent the current element

reading. Furthermore, if we unwittingly try to read a character past the logical end of stream, we may become deadlocked. SSAX reads ahead by no more than one character, and only when the parser is positive the character to read ahead must be available. SSAX does not need to be told when the document is ended. On the contrary, SSAX will tell us when it has finished parsing a root (or other) element. SSAX can therefore safely read from pipes, can process sequences of XML documents without extra delimiters, and can handle selected parts of a document.

The performance benchmarks are based on the code to remove markup from an input XML document. This task, which was described in the previous section, simulates a typical Web service reply processing. Two input documents are XML encodings of full binary trees of depth 15 and 16. The documents are similar to the one on Fig. 1. The documents contain more markup than character data and, in addition, exhibit deeply nested elements. Overall the benchmark task is a good exercise of XML parsing engines. The first benchmark application, string-value.c, implements the most favorable to Expat scenario: it reads the whole document into memory, passes it to Expat and asks the parser to remove the markup. The second benchmark application, string-value-by-one.c, also uses Expat and also loads the whole document into memory first. The application however passes the content of that buffer to Expat one character at a time. This simulates the work of the SSAX parser. Finally, a SSAX benchmark string-value-ssax.scm likewise loads an XML document first, opens the memory buffer as a string port and passes the port to SSAX. The complete benchmark code is a part of the SSAX project [7]. The results are presented in Table 1.

Table 1. User/system times, in seconds, for running three benchmarks on two
sample XML documents. The timing results were obtained from a precise virtual clock and reproduce within 3%. Platform: FreeBSD 4.0-RELEASE system,
Pentium III Xeon 500 MHz, Bigloo 2.4a Scheme compiler. The numbers above
reflect activities that occur entirely in memory. There was no i/o of any kind,
there were no page faults

benchmark	XML-tree-depth-15	XML-tree-depth-16
string-value.c	0.105/0.016	0.213/0.022
string-value-by-one.c	0.747/0.014	1.494/0.012
string-value-ssax.scm	1.092/0.024	2.170/0.095
File size, bytes	884,723	1,769,459

The most notable result of the benchmarks is that a Scheme application is
only 1.4 times slower than a comparable well-written C application, `string-
value-by-one.c`. SSAX seems quite competitive in performance, especially
keeping in mind that the parser and all of its handlers are referentially transparent. The ability to read from pipes and streams whose end is not known ahead
of parsing costs performance. We do think however that the feature is worth
the price. Shared substrings, present in some Scheme systems (alas not in the
compiler used for benchmarking) will mitigate the trade-off.

4.3 FXP, the Functional Equivalent to Expat, and SSAX

The closest to SSAX XML parser is FXP [10], which is a purely functional, validating XML parser "shell" with a functional variant of the event-based interface.
FXP is written in SML. Both SSAX and FXP invoke user-supplied handlers
(called "hooks" in FXP) at "interesting" moments during XML parsing. The
hooks receive an application state parameter and must return a possibly new
state. The ways SSAX and FXP frameworks are instantiated to yield a specific
XML processing application are also surprisingly similar, modulo static/dynamic
typing. FXP "vitally relies" on SML's parameterized modules for customization
while SSAX depends on Scheme's macros.

The most notable difference between SSAX and FXP is the interface between
the parsing engine and the event handlers (hooks). SSAX is based on `foldts`,
whereas the interface of FXP seems to be a pure functional analogue of Expat's
application interface. The difference between the SSAX and FXP interfaces is
important and instructive. A sample FXP application discussed at the end of the
FXP API documentation [10] is a good example to illustrate that difference. The
application converts an XML document to an abstract syntax tree form, which
is not unlike the `Tree` datatype from Section 2. A SSAX distribution includes a
similar function `SSAX:XML->SXML`. It is instructive to compare event handlers of
the two applications. In both cases the event handlers are pure functional; they

receive from the parsing engine recognized pieces of markup or character data
and accumulate them in a parse tree.

In the FXP application, the application data – the seed, in SSAX terminology – represent the partial document tree constructed so far. As the FXP
documentation describes it, the seed has two components – a stack and the
content. At any point the stack holds all currently open start-tags along with
a list of their left siblings. The content component accumulates the children of
the current element that are known so far. In the initial state, both components
are empty. Character data event handlers add the identified character data to
the content of the current element. The hook for a start-tag pushes that tag
together with the content of the current element onto the stack. The element
started by that tag becomes the current element. The end-tag hook reverses the
content of the current element, pops the tag of the current element off the stack
and combines it with its content. The constructed tree is then prepended to the
content of the parent element which now becomes the current element.

The code for the comparable SSAX application is given on Figure 5. The
code does correspond to the description of the FXP application to a certain
extent. However, `simple-XML->SXML` is notably simpler. Whereas FXP application's state is comprised of a stack and the content, `simple-XML->SXML`'s state is
a regular list. The list contains the preceding siblings of the current element or a
piece of character data, in reverse document order. Maintenance of FXP's stack
was split across two separate hooks: the handlers for the start and the end tags.
The FXP handlers have to detect possible stack underflow errors. In contrast,
the handlers of `simple-XML->SXML` are relieved of any stack maintenance and
error handling responsibility: The function `simple-XML->SXML` does not have
any stack. As Figure 5 shows, `simple-XML->SXML` handlers hardly do anything
at all. The handler `new-level-seed` is particularly trivial; `finish-element` is
not more complex either. The simpler the handlers are, the easier it is to write
them and to reason about them.

We should point out that not only `simple-XML->SXML` lacks a stack, the
SSAX parsing engine itself does not have an explicit stack of currently open
XML elements. The traversal stack is implicit in activation frames of a recursive
procedure `handle-start-tag` of the SSAX framework. If there is no explicit
stack, there can be no stack underflow errors. Thus the comparison between
FXP and SSAX indicates that the SSAX framework provides a higher level of
abstraction for SAX XML parsing. This is the direct consequence of building
SSAX around the `foldts` tree traversal combinator.

4.4   Other XML Parsers Written in Functional Languages

There are several other XML parsers implemented in functional languages: CL-
XML (written in Common Lisp), XISO (written in Scheme), Tony (in OCaml),
and HaXml (in Haskell). They are all DOM parsers. Neither of these parsers can
process an XML document "on the fly," in a stream-like fashion.

Parser CL-XML [1] is the most thorough of the group. It checks all well-
formedness and most of the validation constraints given in the XML Recom-

mendation. It is the only parser among those considered in this paper (besides SSAX and Expat) that supports XML namespaces, XML whitespace handling, general entity expansion, attribute value normalization, and the proper handling of CDATA sections. CL-XML is the least functional-style parser: it is written in imperative style, with extensive reliance on global and dynamic-scope variables.

XISO [9] is a mostly-functional parser implemented in Scheme. It is a pure DOM, non-validating parser. It is does not check many of XML well-formedness constraints either. Another parser of the similar quality is Tony [8], which is written in OCaml. It is not a pure functional parser: the parsing state and a character data accumulator are mutable. Like XISO, Tony does not detect or expand entity references, does not handle CDATA sections, does not support namespaces – it does not even handle newlines in attribute values.

One component of HaXml [12], a collection of utilities for using Haskell and XML together, is an XML parser. The parsing component includes a hand-written XML lexer, which produces a token stream for the parser proper. The latter is based on a slightly extended version of the Hutton/Meijer parser combinators. The HaXml parser does not do the normalization of attribute values and does not support XML namespaces. It does not detect many well-formedness let alone validation errors. The separation between the lexing and the proper parsing stages in HaXml is a principal weakness as tokenizing an XML document heavily depends on the parsing context. The weakness manifests itself, for example, in parser's failure to handle newlines and special characters within quoted strings.

The HaXml parser is a DOM parser. An XML document is first tokenized, then it is converted into a parse tree representation, which is handed over to

```
(define (simple-XML->SXML port)
  (reverse
    ((SSAX:make-parser
       NEW-LEVEL-SEED
       (lambda (elem-gi attributes namespaces expected-content seed)
         '())

       FINISH-ELEMENT
       (lambda (elem-gi attributes namespaces parent-seed seed)
         (cons (cons elem-gi (reverse seed)) parent-seed))

       CHAR-DATA-HANDLER
       (lambda (string1 string2 seed)
         (if (string-null? string2) (cons string1 seed)
             (cons* string2 string1 seed)))
    )
    port '()))))
```

Fig. 5. A simplified SSAX:XML->SXML function from the SSAX distribution

a user application. Because Haskell is a non-strict language however, the lexer does not generate new tokens until they are required by the parser. The parser does not make a new node of the parse tree until this node is accessed in the user application code. Thus the HaXml framework *could* act similar to a SAX parser despite its multi-phase processing. This potential is not realized as HaXml eagerly loads the whole document into a string, to let the lexer backtrack or look-ahead by arbitrary amount. In contrast, SSAX never backtracks a character and never looks more than one character ahead. Therefore SSAX can handle (sequences of) documents from a TCP pipe or other stream.

5   Conclusions

In this paper we have shown an example of a principled construction of a SAX XML parser. The parser is based on a view of XML parsing as a depth-first traversing of an input document considered as a spread-out tree. We have considered the problem of efficient functional traversals of abstract trees and of capturing the pattern of recursion in a generic and expressive control structure. We have found such efficient and generic higher order operator: `foldts`. Unlike the regular tree fold, `foldts` permits space- and time-optimal accumulating tree traversals.

The `foldts` operator became the core of SSAX, a SAX parser that walks an XML document and invokes user-supplied handlers when it identified elements, processing instructions, character data and other entities. The SSAX parsing engine effectively abstracts the details of the XML document tree; the engine makes it unnecessary for user handlers to maintain their own stack of open elements; the engine reduces the amount of application state shared among the user handlers to the bare minimum. The comparison with other SAX parsers (the reference XML parser Expat and its functional analogue FXP) shows that SSAX provides a higher-level abstraction for SAX XML parsing. The user-handlers of SSAX are referentially transparent, are less error-prone to write and to reason about.

The SSAX parser is a full-featured, pure-functional, stream-oriented, algorithmically optimal SAX parser, which also makes user handlers easier to write and thus removes whole classes of possible bugs. The combination of these features distinguishes SSAX among other XML parsers. The features are the effect of the principled SSAX construction, in particularly, of the `foldts` traversal operator.

Acknowledgments

I would like to thank Shriram Krishnamurthi for valuable discussions, detailed comments and suggestions. This work has been supported in part by the National Research Council Research Associateship Program, Naval Postgraduate School, and the Army Research Office under contracts 38690-MA and 40473-MA-SP.

References

1. Anderson, J.: Common Lisp support for the 'Extensible Markup Language' (CL-XML). Version 0.906, June 2, 2001.
   http://homepage.mac.com/james_anderson/XML/documentation/cl-xml.html 221
2. Cooper, C.: Using Expat. *xml.com*, September 1, 1999.
   http://www.xml.com/pub/a/1999/09/expat/index.html 217
3. Dunford, M.: DOM XML: An Alternative to Expat.
   http://www.phpbuilder.com/columns/matt20001228.php3 210
4. Expat XML Parser. Version 1.95.1, October 21, 2000.
   http://sourceforge.net/projects/expat 210, 217
5. Hutton, G.: A tutorial on the universality and expressiveness of fold. Journal of Functional Programming, 9(4):355-372, July 1999. 211, 213
6. Gibbons, J., Jones, G.: The Under-appreciated Unfold. Proc. Intl. Conf. Functional Programming, pp. 273-279, Baltimore, Maryland, September 27-29, 1998. 211, 213
7. Kiselyov, O.: Functional XML parsing framework: SAX/DOM and SXML parsers with support for XML Namespaces and validation. Version 4.9, September 5, 2001.
   http://pobox.com/~oleg/ftp/Scheme/xml.html#XML-parser 210, 219
8. Lindig, C.: Tony - a XML Parser and Pretty Printer. Version 0.8.
   http://www.gaertner.de/~lindig/software/tony.html 222
9. van Mourik, H.: XML parser in Scheme. Version: 0.9.23, June 2, 1998.
   http://student.twi.tudelft.nl/~tw585306/ 222
10. Neumann, A.: The Functional XML Parser. Version 1.4.4, October 30, 2000.
    http://WWW.Informatik.Uni-Trier.DE/~aberlea/Fxp/ 209, 220
11. Sheard T., Fegaras, L.: A fold for all seasons. Proc. Conf. on Functional Programming and Computer Architecture (FPCA'93), pp. 233-242, Copenhagen, Denmark, June 1993. 213
12. Wallace M., Runciman, C.: HaXml. Version 1.02 release, May 3, 2001.
    http://www.cs.york.ac.uk/fp/HaXml/ 222
13. World Wide Web Consortium. Extensible Markup Language (XML) 1.0 (Second Edition). W3C Recommendation October 6, 2000.
    http://www.w3.org/TR/REC-xml 209, 210
14. World Wide Web Consortium. XML Information Set. W3C Candidate Recommendation. May 14, 2001.
    http://www.w3.org/TR/xml-infoset 211

Functional Approach to Texture Generation

Jerzy Karczmarczuk

University of Caen, France
karczma@info.unicaen.fr

Abstract. We show the applicability of pure functional programming for the construction of modules which create procedural textures for image synthesis. We focus our attention to the construction of *generic* combinators and transformers of textures, which permit to write texture generators of substantial complexity in a very compact and intuitive manner. We present a concrete package implemented in Clean.

Keywords: images, combinators, noise, tesselations, Clean

1 Introduction

1.1 What Are Textures

Generation of graphical objects by programs is the essence of image synthesis. Since those objects correspond often to data structures manipulated using regular, often generic procedures such as rotations, interpolations, unions, hierarchic embedding, etc., computer graphics is a wonderful training field for functional programming, with its higher-order functions, ubiquitous recursion, and declarative style. The literature is very rich. Already Henderson [1] shows how to *compose functionally* graphic objects, and more recent works show the applicability of Scheme, CAML [2] and Haskell [3] to picture generation. In [4] we described functional methods to model parametric surfaces in 3D. But that papers focus on modelling and *drawing* of graphical objects, i.e., choosing the region where a given figure: a polygon, a zone filled with a colour gradient, etc. will be placed. These programs operate usually upon discrete data structures.

But the decorations of surfaces need often the implementation of another process: the *texturing*, quite different from drawing techniques. There is no destination place the texturing module can *choose*, it gets the coordinates of the *current point* from the rendering engine, e.g., a ray tracer or a scan-line projector, and decides which colour assign to this point, after a possible transformation from the scene/model to the intrinsic texture space (inverse texture mapping), and after analyzing the lighting conditions. Thus, for the texturer the size of its working area is irrelevant. It occupies the whole of the coordinate space, possibly infinite. If we forget the lights, and the coordinate mapping (e.g. the projections), we may say that *textures are functions*: ***Point*** $\rightarrow$ ***Colour***, where ***Point*** is a 2-dimensional point of the texture space. They are "continuous objects", and their assembly from some primitives, transformations and compositions follow different rules than drawing of polygons, etc. Textures may be bitmap images, but

S. Krishnamurthi, C. R. Ramakrishnan (Eds.): PADL 2002, LNCS 2257, pp. 225–242, 2002.

the creation of patterns which simulate natural surfaces, geometrically regular or random decorations, is better done algorithmically. The *procedural texturing* has a long history, the reader will find all the information in the book [5], or in other documents available through the Web, e.g., [6,7]. The importance of *shaders* — user programmable modules which supply textures for ray tracers or other rendering engines increases every year, more and more rendering packages include programmable shaders. The history of functional methods in the realm of procedural texturing is also rather long. Karl Sims [8] used Lisp, and automatically generated compositions and transformations of symbolic expressions to generate exquisite patterns. One of our primary sources of inspiration was the package PAN of Conal Elliott [9], based on Haskell. (See also Pancito of Andrew Cooke [10].)

But despite the fact that the construction of textures is static, dominated by structuring of data, and some quasi-analytic operations, such as the computation of gradients, or filtering, and the concept of modifiable state doesn't need to play any significant role (mainly some dull reassignments of variables, and accumulating loops), the only widely spread procedural texturing language is imperative (very close to a truncated "C"): the RenderMan shading language, see the book [11], the documentation of the package BMRT [12], or the Web site of Pixar [13]. Other approaches to procedural shading, notably the work of Pat Hanrahan [14] also use "imperative" languages, similar in style to RenderMan (although Hanrahan began with a Lisp-style approach, and moreover his language is designed to code *very* fast programs, exploiting directly the hardware pipelines, so his shaders are rather declarative,dataflow style stream processors than imperative procedures. . .). Reading the shaders' codes give a strange impression: *the essence of shaders is declarative*, the coding is "C" like. . . It can and it should be coded in a more proper style, if only for pedagogical purposes.

1.2   Objectives and Structure of This Work

We show here the naturalness and the ease of texture construction using Clean [15]. We constructed a library called ***Clastic***, useful for experimentation in texturing. Higher-order functions and overloading of arithmetic operations to functional objects make it possible to design a decent set of combinators and transformers in an very compact way. We may code simply and universally not only the texture generators, but also the typical bitmap image manipulations available in known image processing packages, and in interactive texture designers, e.g., SynTex [16].

The aim of this work is mainly methodological and pedagogical. Clastic has been used to teach image synthesis, and it is a fragment of a bigger pedagogical project — the construction of a purely functional ray tracer (another nice field for declarative programming) equipped with dynamic shading modules. The texturing library is available separately. It has not been optimized (yet) for speed. Our main leitmotif was to identify useful *high-level abstractions*, and to show how to construct complex textures in a *regular* way, using standard functional composition techniques, and exploiting the geometrical invariance of graphical objects as far as possible.

The structure of the paper is the following. After the introduction we describe the geometric framework of the package, the primary building blocks, and simple texture combinators and transformations. We show how to construct random patterns (various "noise" textures), and also how to generate tesselations possessing non-trivial symmetries. The examples of programmed textures have been chosen to show the specificity of abstract functional coding, not always optimal; some functions within Clastic are coded in a more efficient way.

We will abuse the language, and call *textures* the final rendered bitmap images as well. For definitness and for testing we use simple Cartesian coordinates, a Clean data structure V2 x y represents a 2D point with real x and y, and a record {tr,tg,tb} belonging to the type RColour with real components in $[0 - 1]$ is a RGB colour[1]. We underline the fact that both types belong to a class of *vectors*, with all standard operations thereupon, e.g., an overloaded operator *> multiplies a point or a colour by a scalar, we can subtract them, etc. This is needed for generic interpolation procedures.

The functional layer of Clastic is platform-independent, but the interface used for the generation of examples works under the Windows Clean IO system. It permits the creation of some rendering windows in their "virtual" Cartesian coordinate systems, and launches iterators which fill the Windows *Device-Independent Bitmaps*, unboxed arrays of pixels, whose display is ensured by the Clean IO system. The interface permits also to read BMP files, to convert them into texturing functions, and to save the rendered images. We show here only the definitions of texturing functions, they are the only entities which have to be programmed by the user. The examples are simple, since our main presentation objective is to show *how* to make them from basic blocks, in a didactic environment. In order to follow the examples the reader should be able to read code written in a typical modern functional language. Some Clean particularities should be explained, especially for readers acquainted with Haskell. The sharp (#) symbol introduces a local definition (like let). The functional composition operator is o, and the unary minus sign is denoted by ~. Bars: "|" introduce alternative clauses, as in Haskell, but the default clause "| otherwise = ..." can be shortened to "=".

2 Primary Textures

Almost any reasonable *real* function on points can be used as the heart of a texture generator. Such simple function: radGrad p = norm p *> RWhite constructs a radial, linear gradient of intensity, and angCol p = hsvtorgb (angle p) 1.0 1.0 — an "azimuthal rainbow" shown on Fig. (1:A). Clastic defines several useful vector and colour functions, such as norm computing $\sqrt{x^2 + y^2}$, angle yielding atan2(y, x), or hsvtorgb converting the set Hue-Saturation-Value into a RColour record. Figure (1:B) visualizes the function

---

[1] The Clean library defines the type Colour with components in $[0–255]$

```
tacks = cmix RGrey RBlue (sscaled 0.1 tck)
 where
  tck (V2 x y) = floor(sin(x+sin(y+sin x))) -
                 floor(sin(y+sin(x+sin y)))
```

where `cmix` is a linear interpolator of colours (with its third argument usually in $[0 - 1]$), and `sscaled` is a uniform scaling transformer of a texture function. We note immediately that although such functions can be used to generate interesting tilings, texture *design* needs simpler, regular methods, not requiring an impossible mathematical insight. It is not obvious that the texture `polyg k` (Boolean, needing some colour mapping for its visualization) given by

```
polyg k (V2 x y)
 # kd = Dpi/fromInt k                    Dpi = 2π
 # kdj= kd * floor (atan2 y x / kd)
 # skdj=sin kdj; ckdj=cos kdj
 = (x-ckdj)*(sin(kdj+kd)-skdj)-(cos(kdj+kd)-ckdj)*(y-skdj)<=0.0
```

represents a ***regular polygon with k vertices***. The interested reader will find more textures of this kind in [17], and in the gallery of PAN images. But we see also that the symmetry and the periodicity of the texture generator makes definitions very compact, and this will be the main leitmotif of this section: if possible, avoid decisional structures (e.g., conditionals) in composite textures; replace the relation "belongs to W" by the characteristic function of W; exploit directly the primitive function symmetries. In such a way the texture becomes more an ordinary function than a piece of program, and may be more easily designed and composed. Such primitives as the polygon, a regular star and many others are built into Clastic.

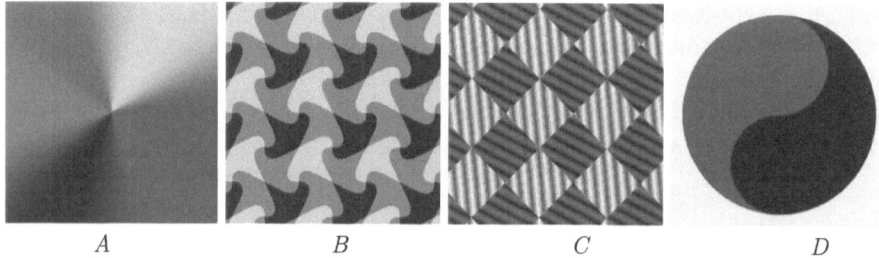

A   B   C   D

Fig. 1. Simple geometric patterns

The most typical functional texture is a binary filtering relation, say, $H(x,y) > 0$, which separates the space in two zones, the interior and the exterior of an object. The Boolean value of the relation may be transformed into one of two colours, or used as a mask for other textures, as shown on Fig. (1:C). This checkerboard mask is just $\sin(x) - \cos(y) > 0$.

2.1   Basic Building Blocks, Overloading, and Combinators

The basic abstraction which replaces the relation $r > 0$ is the function θ of Heaviside, which may be defined as `step x = if (x<0.0) 0.0 1.0`. In fact, Clastic uses *very heavily* the overloading, and our `step` is applicable to other domains as well. The real definition is:

```
step :: !a -> a | <, zero, half, one a
step x | x<zero = zero
       | x>zero = one
       = half
```

i.e., it is a strict function on a type which may be ordered, and contains the overloaded constants `zero`, `one`, and `half`, whose meaning is evident. This is an important point, several texture generators in Clastic are written in a way enabling the application of the Automatic Differentiation machinery, which permits to compute gradients of functions, precisely and easily, but those functions must be defined on entities which generalize real numbers. The details cannot be discussed here. Moreover, we have overloaded the arithmetic operations on functional objects, which permits to define several functions in a combinatoric style, without explicit parameters, e.g., `f = one + sin`. For simplicity, where this overloading is not explicitly needed, we shall write 0, 1, etc.

Thus, the checkerboard (real valued) mask above may be defined as `chkb (V2 x y) = step (sin x - cos y)`. Masking out the (real) texture `tx` outside the unit disk can be written "normally" as `f p = step (1-norm p) * tx p`, or as `f = step o (one-norm) * tx`. From `step` we may construct by subtraction the function `pulse`, equal to 1 between 0 and 1, and zero outside.

```
pulse = (id - translated one) step   where
translated a f x = f (x-a)
```

and use it to construct bands by applying it to x and ignoring y. Product of two orthogonal, scaled pulses creates a rectangle. Such elementary blocks are frequent in RenderMan shaders which make geometric patterns, and they belong to the standard panoply of builders of signal processing algorithms.

We need also several filtered (smoothed) primitives, e.g. the `ramp` function, going linearly from 0 to 1, often used for clamping the colour components, or `smoothstep` which interpolates between 0 and 1 using the Hermite cubic $h(x) = 3x^2 - 2x^3$, and ensures smooth, differentiable transitions between distinct areas. We complete the collection by various *replicators*, which are simply periodic functions permitting to reduce the coordinates of a point to the periodicity interval of the replicator. Most common is the function `frac` which returns the fractional part of a number, reducing it to $[0-1]$. Below we see some plots of primitive blocks, and periodicity generators. Such functions are usually constructed *ad hoc*. A variant of `smoothpulse` was used in our woven patterns, see Fig. (14:A, B), and `symteeth` generated the stripe patterns on Fig. (1:C).

`ramp = max zero o min one`	
`sawtooth = pulse*id`	
`filteredpulse`	
`smoothstep = pulse*hermite +translated one step`	
`smoothpulse`	
`trainpulse`	
`symteeth = symtrain abs`	

2.2 Combination of Shapes

Inequalities $H(p) > 0$ specifiying "solid" objects: polygons, disks, etc., make up their *implicit representation*, well known in the domain of 3D synthesis also, see [18]. The construction of unions or intersections of such objects is easy, with the usage of masking or arithmetic combinations, e.g., if two zones are given by $H_1(p) > 0$ and $H_2(p) > 0$, the function $\max(H_1(p), H_2(p))$ yields their union, and min — the intersection. The negation is the complement. In the space of characteristic functions, the intersection of A and B is their product, and the union is given by $A + B - A \cdot B$. In order to cover one texture by another, we have the masking operator, which has been used to create the Fig. (1:C):

```
fmask h f g = \x -> if (h x <> 0) (f x) (g x)
```

We leave to the reader the construction of Fig. (1:D) by a combination of a unit disk, two smaller and translated disks, and a half-plane (`step x`). In fact, one may create only yin, and obtain yang by a half turn.

Boolean operations (2D Constructive Solid Geometry) and masking, are not the only combinations possible, we end this section by showing another, non-trivial combination: the halftoning, where one texture modulates another. If we take the interior of the disk $x^2 + y^2 < 25$, and put inside a variable grey level: $g = 0.8 - 1/14\sqrt{(x + 3.5)^2 + (y - 2.8)^2}$, we obtain a simulation of a mat sphere. Very often such colour gradients are used to augment some 2D graphics by cheap 3D effects. But g may be used as a specific mask of a periodic function: $h = 1 - \theta(\sin(\omega x) - \cos(\omega y) + 2.0 - 4.0g)$ with a sufficiently high frequency ω. Higher g means greater statistical chance to obtain $h = 1$. The result is displayed on Fig. (2:A). The Figure (2:B) is another variant of this technique, but here the modulating density is reconstructed from a bitmap image transformed by Clastic into a texture, and the modulated pattern is a "white noise", a high-frequency random function (so, it is rather dithering than halftoning).

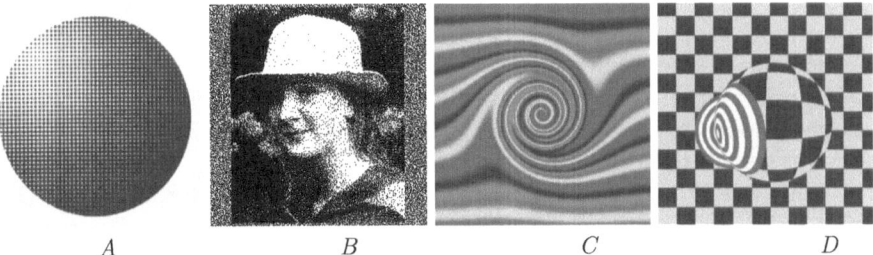

A B C D

Fig. 2. Texture combinations and deformations

3   Transformations and Deformations

Since textures are functions $\eta :: \textbf{\textit{Point}} \rightarrow \textbf{\textit{Something}}$, where $\textbf{\textit{Something}}$ is usually a geometric scalar (a real, a colour, etc.) they may be "post"-transformed by acting on their co-domain space: $\tilde{\eta}(\boldsymbol{p}) = \mathbb{T}(\boldsymbol{p}, \eta(\boldsymbol{p}))$. We may change the colours, multiply one texture by another, etc. But the textures may also undergo a global, or a local geometric transformation in the domain space, and this is the essence of all deformations.

Textures, as other implicit graphical objects transform *contravariantly*. Suppose that ζ is a texture (function), and that we have a transformation $\mathbb{R}$ (a rotation, a translation, a local warp, etc.) acting on points, moving them. We want to find the *representation* $\mathbf{T}_R$ of $\mathbb{R}$ acting on ζ. The fundamental property of a representation is that it constitutes a group homomorphic to the original: $\mathbb{R}_1\mathbb{R}_2$ generates $\mathbf{T}_{R_1 R_2} = \mathbf{T}_{R_1}\mathbf{T}_{R_2}$, and $\mathbb{R}^{-1} \rightarrow \mathbf{T}_{R^{-1}} = (\mathbf{T}_R)^{-1}$. It is easy to prove that the *definition* of $\zeta' = \mathbf{T}_R\zeta$ as $\zeta'(p) = \zeta(\mathbb{R}^{-1}p)$, gives a correct representation. For simple affine transformations Clastic define the texture transformers using directly the inverse operations:

```
translated a f = \p -> f (p-a)
scaled c f = \p -> f (p/c)

rotated a = rotated_cs (cos a) (sin a)    where
rotated_cs co si f = \(V2 x y) -> f (V2 (co*x+si*y) (co*y-si*x))
```

(Note the signs in the last line.) The scaling may be non-uniform; we have overloaded the multiplication and the division for vectors (element-wise), which is useful, even if mathematically a bit bizarre...

Clastic implements many other operations: symmetries, transpositions, replications (coordinate reduction), etc. But in general case if the user wants a specific, complicated, especially *local* (point-dependent) transformation, he must know how to construct its inverse, and this may be very difficult. At any rate this *must* be provided. Then, the package uses a simple generic combinator-deformer `transf` which acts on textures in the following way:

```
transf trf txtr = txtr o trf
```

(or: `transf = flip (o)` for combinatoric maniacs...) with `trf` being the inverse transformation. The properties of deformers are not always obvious, e.g., it is easy to forget the contravariance which implies that (`transf f1 o transf f2`) `tx` yields the texture `tx o f2 o f1`.

If this function computes only the *displacement* ("warping") of the current point, the appropriate deformer is `displace trfun txtr = txtr o (id+trfun)`. Random displacements, especially turbulent ones are particularly useful to generate irregular wood grain, distorted marble veins, etc.

The notorious eddy shown on Fig. (2:C) is the result of applying a deformer

```
eddy ampl damp p
  # (r,phi) = topolar p
  # nphi = phi + ampl*exp(~damp*r*r)
  = V2 (r*cos nphi) (r*sin nphi)
```

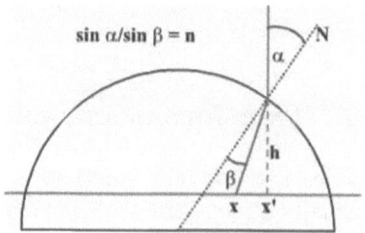

and the "lense" effect on Fig. (2:D) is an exercise in optics as shown on Fig. 3.

Fig. 3. The lense effect

The package contains several exemplary deformers, including more "physical" vortices useful for simulating whirling cloud patterns, such as on Fig. (4:A), and also some standard 3D mappings/projections discussed in the next section.

But suppose that we want to apply our "eddy" deformer to different zones of the texture space, and generate the celtic pattern on Fig. (4:B), or creating displaced and deformed lenses which would simulate water droplets on another surface. We will see that we must operate with both, direct and inverse operation, so technically the problem may be nasty. Composing global transformation is not difficult, for example it is obvious that a rotation of a texture about an *arbitrary* point may be realized in 3 stages: shifting the rotation centre to zero, rotating, and translating the texture back. Clastic defines:

```
rotatedAbout p0 angle                       of a texture
 = translated p0 o rotated angle o translated (~p0)
```

For general warping, e.g. a composition of local translations shown on Fig. 4 (C), the situation is more complicated. A function $\mathbb{G}$ of type **Point** $\to$ **Point** which undergoes the geometric transformation $\mathbb{R}$ is a composition $\mathbb{R}\mathbb{G}\mathbb{R}^{-1}$, and the appropriate representation in the domain of textures is $\zeta\left(\mathbb{R}^{-1}\mathbb{G}^{-1}\mathbb{R}p\right)$. Clastic implements three simple, generic deformer modifiers, its translation and rotation:

```
trfshift p0 deformer = ((+) p0) o deformer o ((+) (~p0))
trfturn ang deformer = rot2 ang o deformer o rot2 (~ang)
```

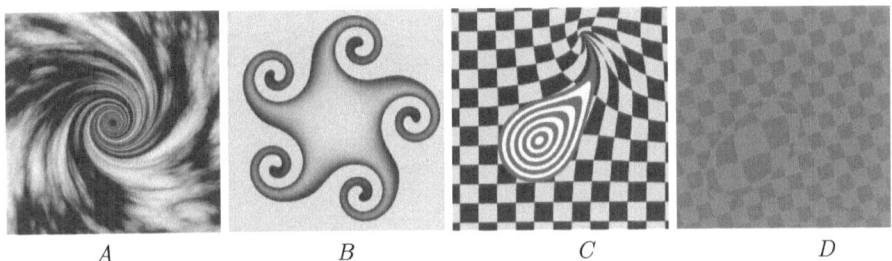

Fig. 4. More complicated mappings

where `rot2` rotates a vector, and of course the scaling. The "pentapus" on Fig. (4:B) is obtained by applying to the unit disk a 5-fold rotated and shifted `eddy` deformer. See also the Fig. (4:D). But suppose we want to translate a region near $(0,0)$ using the transformation $x' = x + \exp(-\alpha|x|)a$. This is not only non-invertible directly, but if a is too big with respect to the warping range α, the texture may fold disgracefully over itself, with a loss of structural information. The package contains a Newton solver for such equations (for small a), and a procedure which iterates (using `foldl`) small warping steps over a list representing a curve. The main purpose of this section was to show that such transformations can be *abstracted*, used generically, and easily composed, which makes their coding sometimes an order of magnitude shorter than the equivalent "classical", imperative approach.

3.1 3D Textures

Texturing of surfaces in 3D is also a geometric transformation, and Clastic offers many basic tools for such manipulations. It implements the 3D vector algebra, and includes a simple, non-recursive ray tracer able to render spheres, cubes, and cylinders (and anything the user may wish to implement himself; for us this is just a part of testing interface). The viewport is attached to a virtual camera, the appropriate procedures generate a ray through the rendered pixel, find the intersection with the object, and compute the normal to the surface. The user has only to submit a texture function with *Points* belonging to the 3D space. If the user wants to cover the surface with a "wallpaper", an external image, as shown on Fig. (5:A) which presents the True Face of our Moon, Clastic may lift the 2D texture, e.g. a planet surface projection parameterized by (ϑ, φ), into a function of (r, ϑ, φ). The rendering is trivial, and appropriate functions are extremely short, the only interesting problems come from the lighting of such textures, but we cannot discuss this issue here. The remaining pictures on Fig. (5) show a marble sphere, another one covered with a bump-map, showing the interplay between 3D and 2D texturing processes, and a "wooden" cylinder. These constructions need a reasonably complete set of *random noise* generators.

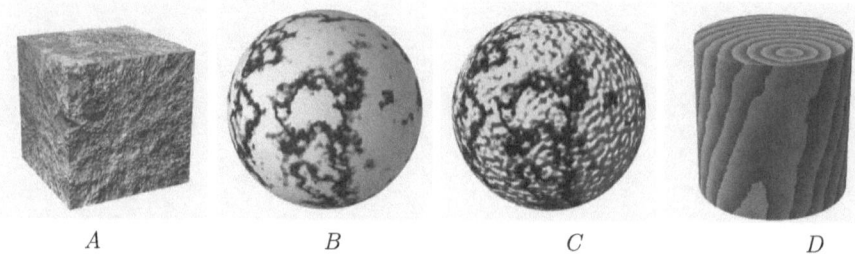

A B C D

Fig. 5. 3-dimensional texturing

4   Random Textures

Since all "natural" surfaces possess some randomness, a rich collection of *noise* generators belongs to a standard panoply of shaders. In this section we will treat a few generic techniques, random textures are functions as any other generator, and to prevent all confusion: they *must* be state-less, deterministic functions which appear random, but which yield always the same value for the same argument. It is not possible to use a typical (even very good, such as Mersenne Twister), seed-propagating random generator during the texture generation, the results would depend on order of operations. The subject is known, and well covered by the literature, e.g., by the book [5]. See also a very instructive site of Ken Perlin [19] and the tutorial pages of Hugo Elias [20].

4.1   Basic Generators

Perlin based his famous noise on the interpolation of random values stored *once* in an array. Those values were supplied before the rendering, using some standard random sequence generator. In a functional approach it is not very natural, the alternative is to use *directly* a pure function, as advocated already by Ward [21]. A typical example of such a function, of type **Integer** $\rightarrow$ **Real** may be

```
ergodic n
 # n = (n<<13) bitxor n
 = toReal((n*(n*n*15731+789221)+1376312589))/2147483648.0
```

adapted to 32 bit integers and returning a real in $[-1 : 1]$. We call such functions *ergodic* (rather than "random"), because they are stationary, unstable, returning results without visible correlations even for neighbouring arguments. (Ergodicity is a physical term, computer scientists use to call such mappings *hashing functions...*) Other parametrisations are also used in our package. In order to produce 2-dimensional distributions we may combine the arguments, e.g., defining `ergxy ix iy = ergodic (173 + (13*ix) bitxor (37*iy))`, as suggested by Ward in Graphic Gems.

Real (scalar) random distributions in the space of real (x, y) are based on a gradient version of Perlin noise visualized (specially) on Fig. (6:A) with the viewport size ≈ 12. It is generated by the classical algorithm: the points with integer coordinates q are attributed a random vector g — a pair of numbers in $[-1 : 1]$. Then, for a point p neighbouring 4 nodes q_i we compute $\xi_i = (p - q_i) \cdot g_i$, and finally a bi-Hermite (or better) interpolation combines these four contributions. Clastic contains also generators for vector noise in 2 and 3 dimensions.

4.2 Noise Functions

The rest is relatively trivial, and consists in applying the already described techniques of functional compositions and transformations, but since this is an application paper, we discuss shortly what Clastic can do with the basic noise generators.

First, as shown on Fig. (6:A), and on Fig. (5:C) a noise can be interpreted as a height field, and after computing its gradient (for which Clastic has appropriate tools), it may be used as a bump-map.

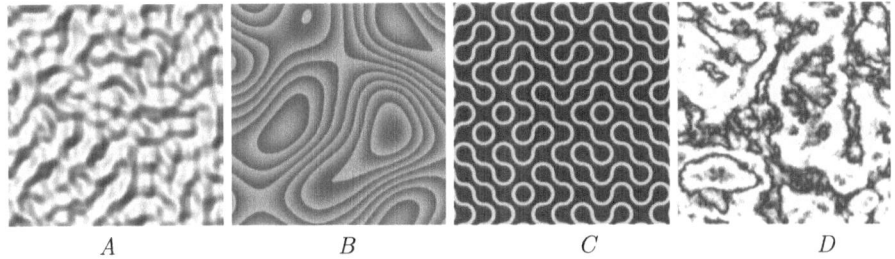

A B C D

Fig. 6. Some random textures

Even a dull, apparently featureless basic noise instance over a region of size $1 - 2$ may be useful, if an appropriate colour map is used, see Fig. (6:B). There is nothing original here, the only advantage of Clastic is that such transformations are 1-line programs, not by specific obfuscate tricks, but by the genericity of the whole design. Even the basic discrete noise on integer nodes is useful for random tesselations, such as the Truchet pattern shown on Fig. (6:C) where the discrete noise is used to choose one of two elementary cell patterns.

Clastic contains some accumulating functionals permitting to construct wide-spectrum "fractal noise" and "turbulence" patterns by summing appropriately scaled and weighted basic noise instances: $\sum_{i=0}^{n} (1/2)^{i\kappa} g \left(f_0 2^i p \right)$, where κ is usually of the order 1, and the number of octaves n varies typically between 3 and 9. If composed with a sawtooth replicator, it may generate marble-like patterns like that on Fig. (6:D)

If g is the base noise we obtain Fig. (7:A), and if we sum its absolute value, we obtain the notorious turbulence pattern on Fig. (7:B), containing interesting filamentary structures. Applying to the turbulence some nonlinear transform and thresholding (1 line of code):

```
clouds p=1.0-exp(~4.0*max 0.0 (0.25+fractsum 7 1.1 0.6 p))
```

generates the clouds used to generate the tornado on Fig. (4:A).

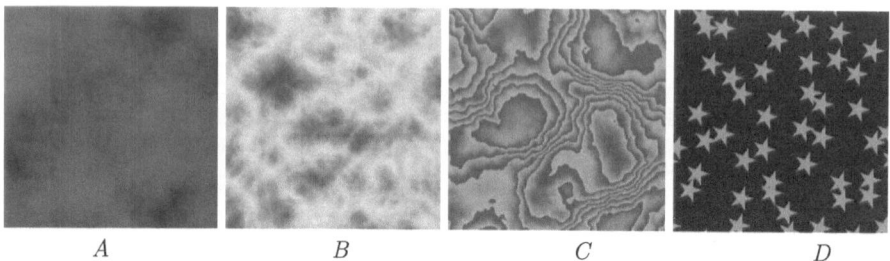

A   B   C   D

Fig. 7. Other random variants

4.3   Random Deformations, and Random Placement of Textural Objects

Even more interesting are transformations of some geometric patterns, with noise functions (especially turbulent) used as deformers. One noise can perturb another one, as shown on Fig. (7:C) If a 3-dimensional cylindrical gradient $f(x, y, z) = \sqrt{x^2 + z^2}$ is deformed by random vector fractal sum displacement, rotated and cut by a surface, in a very few lines of code we obtain the generator which yields the Fig. (5:D).

If the basic noise is scaled so that every pixel has integer coordinates, the result is a random "white noise" pattern, which may be used e.g. to dither other textures. But random spreading of bigger objects, known as "bombing", such as shown on Fig. (7:D), is more difficult. This problem is discussed in [5], and we recognize that in a point-wise, implicit texture generation framework, the solutions are not natural. One possibility is to construct a union of placed objects, with random shift attributed to each of them. This may be very costly.

We present here the "jittering" method, which uses only the standard noise. The technique is similar to those applied to generate the Truchet pattern on Fig. (6:C). An object (here: a star) occupies a unit cell, with intrinsic coordinates between 0 and 1. The (integer) cell coordinates feed the `ergxy` generator, which supplies the shift of the object inside the cell (and it might serve also to change its colour, size, or to disallow its rendering). The fractional part of the point coordinates are used normally for rendering inside the cell.

If the object approaches the cell boundary, it may get truncated, so a more robust algorithm analyses also the cell neighbours. As we see, Clastic handles gracefully this problem.

5   Symmetries and Tesselation

Pavements, wallpaper, rugs... — the necessity to generate textures possessing tiled symmetric patterns is obvious. Texturing does not "redraw" them. In order to replicate a shape, the argument p of the generator must be appropriately *reduced*. The details of the reduction depend so strongly on the result the user wants to obtain, that a method which would be universal is a dream. General tesselations in our functional texturing framework will be discussed elsewhere, here we discuss some simple techniques which produce such tiles as on Fig. (8:B), starting with any motif (Fig. (8:A)) placed near the origin of the coordinate system. *The main objective of this section is to extract some useful, generic abstractions* .

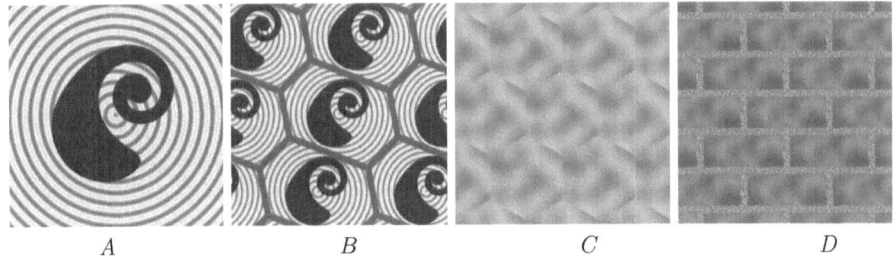

A B C D

Fig. 8. Simple (and less so) tesselations

The first concept which must be understood is the *symmetry* of the design, the set of transformations which *leave the texture invariant*. We know that there are 17 so called "wallpaper groups", containing translations together with rotational, reflective and glide-reflective (combination of an axial reflection and a translation along the axis) symmetries, see [22,23,24], or dozens of other books, e.g. [25], and references available on Internet. We have to distinguish between three distinct entities:

1. The *Unit Cell* (UC), the basic fragment of the "crystallographic", translational lattice. Its translations fill the entire plane. IF UC is rectangular, the tesselation is trivial, this is what we see as typical background motifs on windowing systems, Web pages, etc.
2. The *Fundamental Region* (FR) (usually a fragment of the Unit Cell), which generates the plane through all its symmetry operations.
3. The *Motif Region* (MR), which *does not need* to cover any of the above.

A non-trivial FR-Motif combination is shown on Fig. (9), a tribute to Escher.

5.1   Translational Tiling

Translations are handled universally, independently of other symmetries, and they are always present if the texture occupies the entire plane.

Fig. 9. Escher reptiles

Clastic defines a special data structure, `UnitCell` constructed by the specification of its two non-Cartesian axes, S and T. It contains all the conversion procedures permitting to decompose the current point (vector) in local coordinates, to *reduce these coordinates*, and to reconstruct the reduced cartesian vector. For the simplest symmetry, called P1, for which

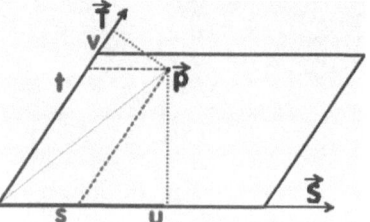

Fig. 10. Unit Cell attributes

FR and UC are identical (it is a parallelogram) nothing else is needed, unless the Motif is shared between neighbouring cells.

The Figure (11) shows that UC must be cut into 4 pieces in order to reconstruct the hexagonal design. The user must supply the motif definition and its location. So, in which sense the genericity of Clastic may be helpful here?

- The reduction of the Motif area *within* the UC is the only thing to do.
- It is easy to define some universal clichés; Clastic has a universal generator

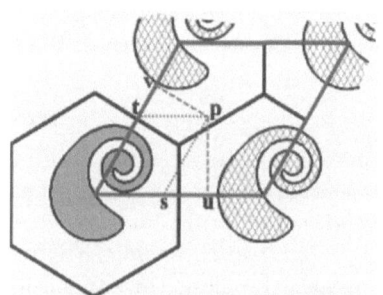

Fig. 11. Hexagonal, P1 tiling

of all hexagonal patterns, the user specifies only two (corner) points inside the UC, the rest is unambiguously constrained.
- The reducing procedure is sensible to the distance of a point to the UC edge, and as a "free bonus" it may add some "mortar" texture to the basic repetitive filling.

All is composable and deformable, and seeing that the classical brick wall has a hexagonal topology, we needed just a few lines to generate the textures on Figs. (8:B, C, and D). One more comment seems useful. The coordinate reducers are functions **Point** → **Point**, and they behave as deformers. Their composition requires some attention in order not to distort, or to break the texture inside.

5.2   Rotational Symmetry; Group P3

Our second example is the group describing a rotational symmetry of order 3, which generates Echer reptiles.

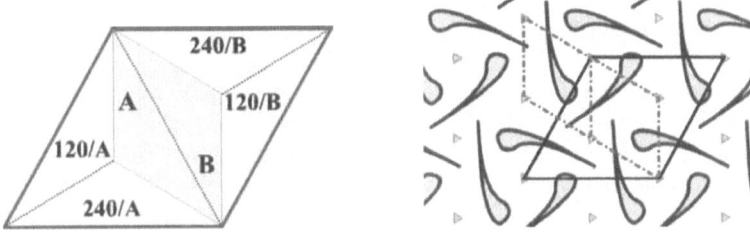

Fig. 12. P3 group: UC, FR, and a pattern with two different FRs

The Unit Cell is a rhombus with 60 and 120 degrees. Only one third of it, the central smaller rhombus, is the FR, the remaining parts are obtained by rotations (to which we attached some colour changing procedures while generating the reptile tiling).

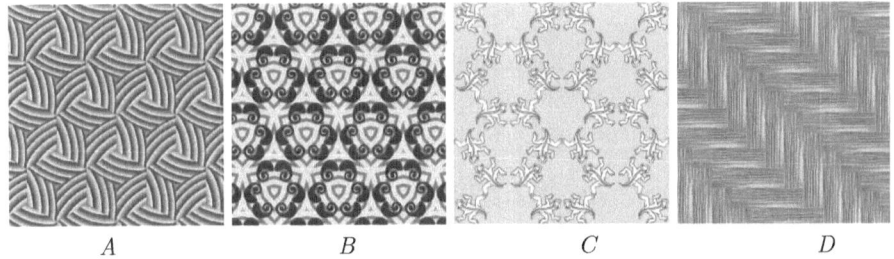

Fig. 13. More tesselations

The relation between the Motif and the Fundamental Region is not universal, and the generation of the Fig. (13:A) ignores this. If the Motif occupies the FR, the reducing procedure for P3 is extremely simple, less than 10 lines: it applies already known `rotatedabout` transformer, using as pivots the corners of FR which are inside UC, and thus filling the Unit Cell. In more complicated cases, such as typical Escher patterns, the human insight is necessary, although there are papers which deal with automatic "Escherization" of arbitrary shapes.

5.3 More "Wallpaper" Symmetries...

Clastic implements a subset of all wallpaper groups, this work is still in progress. But no new techniques are needed, everything is reused. We had just to add a few primitive reducers for 4- and 6-fold rotations, mirrors, and glide-reflections, and again, in a few lines it was possible to construct the reducers for the P6ML ("kaleidoscopic") group, depicted on Fig. (13:B,C), and a generic (arbitrary proportions, arbitrary filling) classical parquet generator, whose boundary has the symmetry PGG, containing some glide-reflections (about diagonal axes, not immediate to see...)

6 Woven Patterns

Tiling is not the only generic method to produce repetitive patterns. Another technique is weaving, knitting, etc., the interlacing of linear objects is also omnipresent (and several programming applications helping to design fabrics are available commercially).

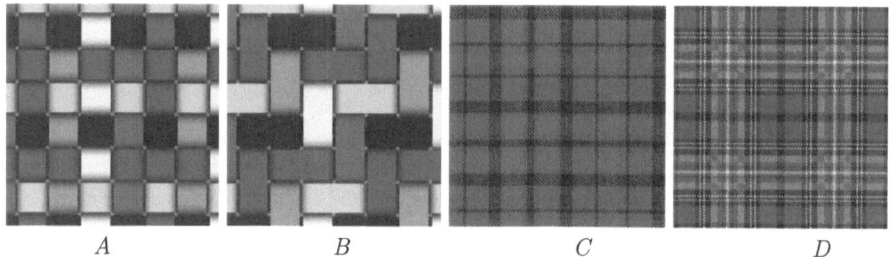

A B C D

Fig. 14. Woven patterns

We added to Clastic a small subpackage which can generate the patterns shown on Fig. (14). The user specifies his "sett", the sequence of thread colours and their width, and the virtual "loom" driving protocol: a Boolean function on (x, y) (Integers!) which tells the texturing function whether at a given point the horizontal thread masks the vertical or *vice-versa*. The darkening decoration needed just a variant of `smoothpulse` as a mask.

This work is not complete, manufacturing baskets, rustic chairs, ring armours, etc. with hexagonal or octogonal symmetry may be technically more involved, requiring some symmetry considerations, but Clastic is prepared to deal with such problems.

7 Further Work and Conclusions

Our texturing library belongs to a broader pedagogical project: teaching of image synthesis with the aid of functional methods. Clastic is less suitable for those who just need a few textures, more for those who want to learn how to do them, and how to build texturing applications, with better interfaces, and well tuned generators of regular patterns and noise. It contains a rich collection of utilities, including some bitmap processing routines, noise generators, geometric tools, and equation solvers. The advantage of the presented functional methods with respect to, say, the Renderman shading language, is twofold.

Universal functional languages are rich enough to write *complete* rendering applications. Their data abstraction facilities make it easy to implement recursive ray tracers, and also to exploit them as the *scene description* languages, with the definition of objects, cameras, light sources, etc. Their genericity: overloading based on a system of type classes, and the possibility to use partial applications and other higher-order functional objects, facilitates the implementation of reusable building blocks and transformers for all kind of graphical objects. The texturing is just a concrete application of this methodology.

Textural functional objects are convenient for teaching. Some informal specifications as "shifted threshold", or "filtering out the Blue component of the texture A by a chessboard pattern" have **almost direct**, very short, (often one line) concrete implementations. Image synthesis involves geometry, numerics, some knowledge of optics, etc., and requires many test runs. Even if the impatience of students makes them often looking for speed in order to economise computer time instead of their own, the possibility to transform an abstract specification in an algorithm, and to debug it fast before converting it into an optimized version, is very important.

Only part of this work is reported here. The tesselation sub-package will be presented elsewhere. We have omitted also the discussion of the Automatic Differentiation subpackage: a generalization of the functional differentiation framework described in [26] to general vector structures, permitting an easy and precise computation of gradients (in x and colour spaces), and useful for the construction of bump maps, contours of implicitly defined areas, etc. This issue is discussed in the Clastic tutorial available from the author. The interface to a ray tracer could not be discussed either. Complete shaders need not only a point in the texture space, but are provided by the rendering engine with the actual surface point in the scene space, the normal to the surface, the parameters of light sources, the pixel resolution (e.g. for the anti-aliasing) etc. While functional methods permit elegant and natural coding of these features, they remain outside the aims of this paper.

Acknowledgments

We are indebted to Conal Elliott for his work and interesting discussions. We thank also one of the Reviewers for pointing out missing references.

References

1. Peter Henderson, *Functional Programming, Application and Implementation*, Prentice-Hall, (**1980**). Also: *Functional Geometry*, Symposium on Lisp and Functional Programming, (**1982**). 225
2. Emmanuel Chailloux, Guy Cousineau, *Programming Images in ML*, ACM SIGPLAN Workshop on ML and its Applications (**1992**). 225
3. Simon Peyton Jones, S. Finne, *Pictures: a Simple Structured Graphic Model*, Preoceedings, Glasgow Functional Programming Workshop, (**1996**). 225
4. Jerzy Karczmarczuk, *Geometric Modelling in Functional Style*, Proc., III Latino-Americal Conf. on Functional Programming, Recife, Brazil, (**1999**). 225
5. David S. Ebert, F. Kenton Musgrave, Darwyn Peachey, Ken Perlin, Steven Worley, *Texturing and Modeling. A Procedural Approach*, AP Professional, (**1998**). 226, 234, 236
6. B. Gibson-Winge, *Texture Synthesis*, www.threedgraphics.com/texsynth. 226
7. John C. Hart, *Procedural Texturing*, Web course, available from the site graphics.eecs.wsu.edu/cpts548/procedural/sld0001.htm. 226
8. Karl Sims, *Artificial Evolution for Computer Graphics*, Comp. Graphics **25**(4), pp. 319–328, (**1991**). See also the site genarts.com/karl/papers/siggraph91.html. 226
9. Conal Elliott, *Functional Images*, research.microsoft.com/~conal/Pan with references, plenty of additional documentation and examples. 226
10. Andrew Cooke, *Pancito*, site www.acooke.org/jara/pancito. 226
11. Steve Upstill, *The RenderMan Companion: A Programmer's Guide to Realistic Computer Graphics*, Addison-Wesley, (**1990**). 226
12. Larry Gritz, *Blue Moon Rendering Tools*, Exluna Inc., www.exluna.com/bmrt/. 226
13. Web site www.pixar.com. 226
14. Pat Hanrahan, Kekoa Proudfoot, William R. Mark, Svetoslav Tzvetkov, *A Real-Time Procedural Shading System for Programmable Graphics Hardware*, SIGGRAPH, (**2001**). See also graphics.stanford.edu/projects/shading. 226
15. Rinus Plasmaijer, Marko van Eekelen, *Concurrent Clean Language Report, Version 1.3*, HILT B. V. and University of Nijmegen, (**1998**). See also www.cs.kun.nl/~clean. 226
16. Sean Gibb, Peter Graumann, *SynTex*, Synthetic Realms, Calgary, Canada. Web site www.SyntheticRealms.com. 226
17. Pedagoguery Software Inc., *GrafEq*, www.peda.com/grafeq. 228
18. Jules Bloomenthal (ed.), *Introduction to Implicit Surfaces*, Kaufmann, (**1997**). 230
19. Ken Perlin, www.noisemachine.com , see also mrl.nyu.edu/perlin. 234
20. Hugo Elias, tutorial, freespace.virgin.net/hugo.elias. 234
21. G. Ward, A recursive Implementation of the Perlin Noise Function, in *Graphic Gems II*, ed. James Arvo, AP PROFESSIONAL, pp. 396–401, (**1991**). 234
22. Doris Schattschneider, *The Plane Symmetry Groups: Their recognition and notation*, American Math. Monthly. **85**, pp. 439–450, (**1978**). 237
23. Xah Lee, *The Discontinuous Groups of Rotation and Translation in the Plane*, Web pages www.best.com/~xah/. Contains a good overview of literature. 237
24. David E. Joyce, *Wallpaper Groups (Plane Symmetry Groups)*, tutorial. Web site aleph0.clarku.edu/~djoyce/home.html. 237
25. A. Shubnikov, V. Koptsik, *Symmetry in Science and Art*, Plenum, (**1974**). 237
26. J. Karczmarczuk, *Functional Differentiation of Computer Programs*, Journal of Higher Order and Symbolic Computing **14**, (**2001**). 241

Abstract Interpretation over Non-deterministic Finite Tree Automata for Set-Based Analysis of Logic Programs

John P. Gallagher[1] and Germán Puebla[2]

[1] University of Bristol, Dept. of Computer Science
BS8 1UB Bristol, UK
john@cs.bris.ac.uk
[2] Universidad Politécnica de Madrid, Facultad de Informática
E-28660 Boadilla del Monte, Madrid
german@fi.upm.es

Abstract. Set-based program analysis has many potential applications, including compiler optimisations, type-checking, debugging, verification and planning. One method of set-based analysis is to solve a set of *set constraints* derived directly from the program text. Another approach is based on abstract interpretation (with widening) over an infinite-height domain of regular types. Up till now only deterministic types have been used in abstract interpretations, whereas solving set constraints yields non-deterministic types, which are more precise. It was pointed out by Cousot and Cousot that set constraint analysis of a particular program P could be understood as an abstract interpretation over a finite domain of regular tree grammars, constructed from P. In this paper we define such an abstract interpretation for logic programs, formulated over a domain of non-deterministic finite tree automata, and describe its implementation. Both goal-dependent and goal-independent analysis are considered. Variations on the abstract domains operations are introduced, and we discuss the associated tradeoffs of precision and complexity. The experimental results indicate that this approach is a practical way of achieving the precision of set-constraints in the abstract interpretation framework.

1 Introduction

Recursively defined sets of terms are familiar to us as approximations of the runtime values of program variables. For example, the expression $intlist ::=$ [ ]; $[int|intlist]$ defines a set called *intlist* containing all lists of integers, where *int* denotes the set of integers. Such expressions are sometimes used by the programmer to restrict the values that an argument or variable is allowed to take, but in this paper we are concerned with deriving such descriptions statically, rather than prescribing them.

Derivation of set expressions such as these has many applications including type inference [16,8], debugging [24], assisting compiler optimisations [25,34], optimising a theorem prover [14], program specialisation [20], planning [4] and

S. Krishnamurthi, C. R. Ramakrishnan (Eds.): PADL 2002, LNCS 2257, pp. 243–261, 2002.

verification [8]. The first work in this area was by Reynolds [33]; other early research was done by Jones and Muchnick [27,26]. In the past decade two different approaches to deriving set expressions have been followed. One approach is based on abstract interpretation [25,34,19,13,30], and the other on solving set constraints derived from the program text [22,16,21,2,1,28,9,32]. In abstract interpretation the program is executed over an abstract *type domain*, program variables taking on abstract values represented by types rather than standard values. In set-constraint analysis, program variables are also interpreted as taking on sets of values, but a set of inclusion relations is derived from the program text and then solved.

Cousot and Cousot pointed out [13] that set constraint solving of a particular program P could be understood as an abstract interpretation over a finite domain of tree grammars, constructed from P. Set constraint analysis can be seen as one of a range of related "grammar-based" analyses. One practical advantage of seeing set constraint solving as abstract interpretation (noted by Cousot and Cousot) is that set-constraint-based analysis can be combined with other analysis domains, using well established principles. A second advantage is that various tradeoffs of precision against efficiency can be exploited without departing from the abstract interpretation framework.

In this paper we pursue the idea of an abstract interpretation corresponding to set constraints in more depth. After reviewing the basic notions of non-deterministic finite tree automata in Section 2, we construct an abstract domain for a given logic program in Section 4. In Section 5 we construct abstract interpretations for logic programs over this domain. These include two variants that we call the variable-based and the argument-based interpretations. We also consider both goal-dependent and goal-independent interpretations. Our implementation is described in Section 6 and the results of experiments in Section 7. The results are discussed in Section 8.

2   Preliminaries

Let Σ be a set of ranked function symbols. We refer to elements of Σ as $f_j^{n_j}$ where $n_j \geq 0$ is the rank (arity) of function symbol (functor) f_j. If $n_j = 0$ we call f_j a *constant*. The set of *ground terms* (or *trees*) Term_Σ associated with Σ is the least set containing the constants and all expressions $f_j^{n_j}(t_1, \ldots, t_{n_j})$ such that $t_1, \ldots, t_{n_j}$ are elements of Term_Σ.

Finite tree automata provide a means of finitely describing possibly infinite sets of ground terms, just as finite automata describe sets of strings. A non-deterministic finite tree automaton (NFTA) is defined as a quadruple $\langle Q, q_0, \Sigma, \Delta \rangle$, where Q is a finite set of *states*, $q_0 \in Q$ is called the accepting state, Σ is a set of ranked function symbols and Δ is a set of *transitions*. Each element of Δ is of the form $f_j^{n_j}(q_1, \ldots, q_{n_j}) \rightarrow q$, where $f_j^{n_j} \in \Sigma$ and $q, q_1, \ldots, q_{n_j} \in Q$.

Let $R = \langle Q, q_0, \Sigma, \Delta \rangle$ be an NFTA; a *derivation* in R is a labelled tree τ such that each node of τ is labelled with a term from Term_Σ and a state from Q, satisfying the following condition. The state labelling the root node is q_0, and if any node p is labelled with term $f_j^{n_j}(t_1, \ldots, t_{n_j})$ and state q then there is a transition $f_j^{n_j}(q_1, \ldots, q_{n_j}) \to q \in \Delta$ and p has n_j children $p_1, \ldots, p_{n_j}$ labelled with terms $t_1, \ldots, t_{n_j}$ and states $q_1, \ldots, q_{n_j}$ respectively. In particular, if p is a leaf node, then p is labelled with a constant f_j^0 and some state q, and there is a transition $f_j^0 \to q$.

We say that a term t is *accepted* by automaton R if there is a derivation in R whose root node is labelled with t. The set of all terms accepted by automaton R is called the *(tree) language* of R, denoted $L(R)$. Two automata R_1, R_2 are *equivalent*, written $R_1 \cong R_2$, iff $L(R_1) = L(R_2)$. empty(R) is true iff $L(R)$ is empty, and nonempty(R) is the same as $\neg$empty(S). An automaton R_1 is contained in automaton R_2, written $R_1 \preceq R_2$ iff $L(R_1) \subseteq L(R_2)$.

An automaton with transitions Δ is called (top-down) deterministic if there are no two transitions in Δ with both the same right-hand-side q and the same function symbol $f_j^{n_j}$ on the left. Deterministic automata are less expressive than NFTAs in general, unlike finite automata for string languages. There are NFTAs for which there is no equivalent deterministic finite tree automaton.

Let $R_1 = \langle Q_1, q_1, \Sigma, \Delta_1 \rangle$ and $R_2 = \langle Q_2, q_2, \Sigma, \Delta_2 \rangle$ be NFTAs. The *product* automaton $R_1 \times R_2$ is defined as the automaton $\langle Q_1 \times Q_2, (q_1, q_2), \Sigma, \Delta_1 \times \Delta_2 \rangle$ where

$$\Delta_1 \times \Delta_2 = \{ f_j^{n_j}((q_1, q_1'), \ldots, (q_{n_j}, q_{n_j}'))) \to (q, q') \mid$$
$$f_j^{n_j}(q_1, \ldots, q_{n_j}) \to q \in \Delta_1$$
$$f_j^{n_j}(q_1', \ldots, q_{n_j}') \to q' \in \Delta_2 \}$$

The language accepted by $R_1 \times R_2$ is $L(R_1) \cap L(R_2)$.

NFTAs can be extended to allow ϵ-transitions, without altering their expressive power. An ϵ-transition is of the form $q \to q'$. Such transitions can be removed from Δ, after adding all transitions $f_j^{n_j}(q_1, \ldots, q_{n_j}) \to q'$ such that there is a transition $f_j^{n_j}(q_1, \ldots, q_{n_j}) \to q$ in Δ, and q' is reachable from q using only ϵ-transitions. Given a set of transitions Δ containing ϵ-transitions, the result of eliminating them will be called $\mathsf{elim}_\epsilon(\Delta)$.

NFTAs are quite expressive, as we will see from examples, yet key properties are decidable. It is decidable whether an automaton is empty, and whether a given term is accepted by an automaton. Containment, and hence equivalence, is also decidable.

We will use the following shorthand notation. If we name an automaton R_{q_0} then q_0 is its accepting state. If two automata R_{q_1} and R_{q_2} appear in the same context, we mean that they differ only in their accepting state.

If R_q contains two transitions $f_j^{n_j}(q_1, \ldots, q_{n_j}) \to q$ and $f_j^{n_j}(q_1', \ldots, q_{n_j}') \to q$, and $R_{q_k} \preceq R_{q_k'}$ for $1 \leq k \leq n_j$, then the transition $f_j^{n_j}(q_1, \ldots, q_{n_j}) \to q$ is *redundant*. Clearly we can remove redundant transitions from an automaton without altering its language.

As we will be applying NFTAs in the context of logic programming, it will be convenient to adopt the notation of *regular unary logic (RUL) programs* to describe NFTAs. An RUL clause is a formula of the form $q(f(x_1, \ldots, x_n)) \leftarrow q_1(x_1), \ldots, q_n(x_n)$ where $x_1, \ldots, x_n$ are distinct variables. An NFTA $\langle Q, q_0, \Sigma, \Delta \rangle$

can be translated to an RUL program where Q is a set of unary predicate symbols, and each transition $f_j^{n_j}(q_1, \ldots, q_{n_j}) \to q \in \Delta$ is represented as the RUL clause $q(f_j^{n_j}(x_1, \ldots, x_{n_j})) \leftarrow q_1(x_1), \ldots, q_{n_j}(x_{n_j})$. Thus in this representation, Δ is an RUL program. There is then a straightforward correspondence between derivations and acceptance in NFTAs and logic program computations. In particular, the term t is accepted by the automaton R_q iff $\Delta \cup \{\leftarrow q(t)\}$ has an SLD refutation, where Δ is the set of transitions of R.

Further details on NFTAs and their properties can be found elsewhere [12].

3   Core Semantics

In this section we develop bottom-up semantics for definite logic programs, parameterised by a domain of interpretation, and certain operations on that domain. Thus we follow the established method in abstract interpretation of providing *core semantics* that can be instantiated to yield either the standard (concrete) semantics, or some other abstract semantics.

We start from the familiar T_P operator associated with a definite program P. We write the definition of T_P as follows, introducing operators project, reduce and $\bigsqcup$ that will be abstracted later on.

$$T_P(I) = \bigsqcup_P \{\text{project}(H, \theta) \mid H \leftarrow B \in P, \ \theta \in \text{reduce}(B, I)\}$$

Let B_P be the Herbrand base of P, and $D_P = 2^{B_P}$. The concrete domain $(D_P, \subseteq, \emptyset, B_P)$ is a complete lattice. In the concrete semantics, $I \in D_P$, $\text{reduce}((B_1, \ldots, B_k), I)$ is the set of all ground substitutions θ, whose domain is $\text{vars}(B_1, \ldots, B_k)$ and range is the Herbrand universe of P, such that $\{B_1\theta, \ldots, B_k\theta\} \subseteq I$. $\text{project}(H, \theta)$ is $H\theta$, and $\bigsqcup_P(S)$ set of ground instances (over the Herbrand universe of P) of elements of S.

This can easily be seen to be equivalent to the more familiar presentation of T_P [29], and we have the well known result that the least fixed point (lfp) of T_P (with respect to the partial order on D_P) is the least Herbrand model of P, $M[P]$. The least fixed point is the limit of the sequence $\{T_P^n(\emptyset)\}$, $n = 0, 1, \ldots$.

In the following sections, we will develop abstract instances of the core semantics. We start by defining abstract domains, and then we define the abstract versions of reduce, project and $\bigsqcup$.

4   Abstract Domains of NFTAs

Let P be a definite logic program and $M[P]$ its minimal Herbrand model. Consider the set of *occurrences* of subterms of the heads of clauses in P, including the heads themselves; call this set headterms(P). headterms(P) is the set of program points that we want to observe. We are interested in analysing the set of terms that can occur at each of these positions in instances of clauses satisfied by $M[P]$.

A function S will be defined from headterms(P) to a set of identifiers. The states of an NFTA will be constructed from these identifiers in Section 4; in fact, an automaton state will correspond to a set of identifiers. For instance, we might assign an identifier, say q_X, to an occurrence of a variable X in some clause head. The set of terms accepted at state $\{q_X\}$ in the automaton that is produced (Section 5) will approximate the set of terms that could appear as instances of X at that position. There will be one or more transitions in the automaton of the form $f(Q_1, \ldots, Q_k) \rightarrow \{q_X\}$, where $Q_1, \ldots, Q_k$ are themselves sets of identifiers.

Thus if S maps two distinct elements of headterms(P) to the same state, then we will not be able to distinguish the sets of terms that occur at the two positions. We will consider two variants of the mapping, called S^P_{var}, the *variable-based* mapping, and S^P_{arg}, the *argument-based* mapping, which differ in the degree to which they distinguish different positions.

The S mapping is built from several components, representing the mappings of arguments, variables, and other terms that occur in the clause heads. Let Q, Args and V be disjoint infinite sets of identifiers. The mapping id_P is chosen to be any injective mapping headterms(P) $\rightarrow$ Q. The set of *argument positions* is the set of pairs $\langle p, j \rangle$ such that p is an n-ary predicate of the language and $1 \leq j \leq n$. The function argpos is some injective mapping from the set of argument positions to Args, that is, giving a unique identifier to each argument position. Let varid be an injective mapping from the set of variables of the language to V. Let type and any be distinguished identifiers not in Q $\cup$ Args $\cup$ V.

We will assume for convenience that the clauses of programs have been *standardised apart*; that is, no variable occurs in more than one clause. The following definitions define two different mappings from clause head positions to states.

Definition 1. S^P_{var}

Let P be a definite program. The function S^P_{var} : headterms(P) $\rightarrow$ Q $\cup$ V $\cup$ {type} *is defined as follows.*

$\mathsf{S}^P_{var}(t) = $ *if t is a clause head, then* type
else if t is a variable, then varid(t)
else $\mathrm{id}_P(t)$

Definition 2. S^P_{arg}

Let P be a definite program. The function S^P_{arg} : headterms(P) $\rightarrow$ Q $\cup$ Args $\cup$ V $\cup$ {type} *is defined as follows.*

$\mathsf{S}^P_{var}(t) = $ *if t is a clause head, then* type
else if t occurs as argument j of predicate p, then argpos($\langle p, j \rangle$)
else if t is a variable, then varid(t)
else $\mathrm{id}_P(t)$

Example 1. Let P be the *append* program.

$$append([\,], A, A) \leftarrow true \qquad append([B|C], D, [B|E]) \leftarrow append(C, D, E)$$

Taking them in textual order headterms(P) is the following set. We can imagine the different occurrences of the same term (such as A) to be subscripted to indicate their positions, but we omit this extra notation.

$\{append([\,], A, A), [\,], A, A, append([B|C], D, [B|E]), [B|C], B, C, D, [B|E], B, E\}.$

Let $Q = \{q_1, q_2, \ldots\}$; let id_P map the ith element of $\mathsf{headterms}(P)$ (in the given order) to q_i; let $\mathsf{Args} = \{app_1, app_2, app_3\}$ and let argpos be the obvious mapping into this set; let $\mathsf{V} = \{a, b, c, d, \ldots\}$, and let $\mathsf{varid}(A) = a, \mathsf{varid}(B) = b$ etc. Then S^P_{var} is the following mapping.

$append([\,], A, A) \mapsto \mathsf{type}$ $append([B|C], D, [B|E]) \mapsto \mathsf{type}$ $D \mapsto d$
$[\,] \mapsto q_2$ $[B|C] \mapsto q_6$ $[B|E] \mapsto q_{10}$
$A \mapsto a$ $B \mapsto b$ $B \mapsto b$
$A \mapsto a$ $C \mapsto c$ $E \mapsto e$

The mapping S^P_{arg} is given as follows.

$append([\,], A, A) \mapsto \mathsf{type}$ $append([B|C], D, [B|E]) \mapsto \mathsf{type}$ $D \mapsto app_2$
$[\,] \mapsto app_1$ $[B|C] \mapsto app_1$ $[B|E] \mapsto app_3$
$A \mapsto app_2$ $B \mapsto b$ $B \mapsto b$
$A \mapsto app_3$ $C \mapsto c$ $E \mapsto e$

It can be seen that S^P_{var} distinguishes more states than S^P_{var}, and hence will lead to a finer-grained analysis.

4.1   The Abstract Domains

We now define two sets of NFTAs. The variable-based domain is the more fine-grained, and is intended to capture a separate set of terms for each position in each clause head. The argument-based domain only captures one set corresponding to each argument of a predicate.

Define $\Delta^{\Sigma}_{\mathsf{any}}$ to be the set of transitions $\{f^{n_j}_j(\{\mathsf{any}\}, \ldots, \{\mathsf{any}\}) \to \{\mathsf{any}\} \mid f^{n_j}_j \in \Sigma\}$, where Σ is a finite set of function symbols. Every element in Term_{Σ} is accepted by the NFTA $\langle \{\mathsf{any}\}, \{\mathsf{any}\}, \Sigma, \Delta^{\Sigma}_{\mathsf{any}} \rangle$. The state $\{\mathsf{any}\}$, though it can be regarded as if it were an ordinary state, is treated specially for efficiency reasons. In particular, we do not eliminate ϵ-transitions of the form $\{\mathsf{any}\} \to q$.

Definition 3. *Variable-Based and Argument-Based Domains*

Let P be a definite logic program, and let Σ be the set of function and predicate symbols in P. Let $R^P_d = \mathsf{range}(S^P_d)$, $d \in \{var, arg\}$ and let $Q^P_d = 2^{R^P_d}$. Let Δ^P_d be the set of transitions $\{f^{n_j}_j(q_1, \ldots, q_{n_j}) \to q \mid f^{n_j}_j \in \Sigma, \{q_1, \ldots, q_{n_j}, q\} \subseteq Q^P_d\}$. Note that the states $q_1, \ldots, q_{n_j}$, and q are not elements of $\mathsf{range}(S^P_d)$, but rather sets of elements.

Then the variable-based *domain for P, called D^{var}_P is the following set of automata.*

$$\{\langle Q^P_{var}, \{\mathsf{type}\}, \Sigma, \Delta' \cup \Delta^{\Sigma}_{\mathsf{any}} \rangle \mid \Delta' \subseteq \Delta^P_{var}\}$$

The argument-based *domain for P, called D^{arg}_P is the following set of automata.*

$$\{\langle Q^P_{arg}, \{\mathsf{type}\}, \Sigma, \Delta' \cup \Delta^{\Sigma}_{\mathsf{any}} \rangle \mid \Delta' \subseteq \Delta^P_{arg}\}$$

In the above definition, it can be seen that the two domains D_P^{var} and D_P^{arg} differ only in the choice of the set of states of the automata, which are determined by the range of the S_{var}^P and S_{arg}^P functions respectively. Note that range(S_{var}^P) and range(S_{arg}^P) are finite, and hence the domains D_P^{var} and D_P^{arg} are finite.

Let $R_1 = \langle Q, \{\mathsf{type}\}, \Sigma, \Delta_1 \rangle$ and $R_2 = \langle Q, \{\mathsf{type}\}, \Sigma, \Delta_2 \rangle$ be two elements of D_P^d, $d \in \{var, arg\}$. We have a partial order $\sqsubseteq$ such that $R_1 \sqsubseteq R_2$ iff $\Delta_1 \subseteq \Delta_2$. The minimal element R_d^{min} is $\langle Q_d^P, \{\mathsf{type}\}, \Sigma, \emptyset \rangle$, and the maximal element R_d^{max} is $\langle Q_d^P, \{\mathsf{type}\}, \Sigma, \Delta_d^P \cup \Delta_{\mathsf{any}}^\Sigma \rangle$, $d \in \{var, arg\}$, and we have complete lattices $(D_d^P, \{\mathsf{type}\}, R_d^{min}, R_d^{max})$.

Define the concretisation functions $\gamma_d : D_P^d \rightarrow D_P$, $d \in \{var, arg\}$, as $\gamma_d(R) = L(R)$, where $L(R)$ is the language of the NFTA R. γ_d is monotonic with respect to the partial orders on D_P^d and D_P.

States that are sets containing more than one identifier represent products. For instance, in the transition $f(\{q_1, q_2\}, \{q_3\}) \rightarrow \{q\}$, the state $\{q_1, q_2\}$ represents the product state. The set of terms accepted by $R_{\{q_1, q_2\}}$ is the product of $R_{\{q_1\}}$ and $R_{\{q_2\}}$. When representing an automaton, we write down only the transitions whose right hand side is a singleton, and the transitions for the products are not explicitly included. For convenience we will often refer to a singleton state $\{q\}$ simply as q, especially in examples.

5   Abstract Semantic Operations

We now proceed to define the operations reduce, project, and $\bigsqcup$ for the variable-based and argument-based interpretations. As for the abstract domains, we define operations parameterised where necessary by a variable d that stands for either var or arg.

The reduce operation takes a clause body B and an element R of D_P^d. For convenience in presenting the operation, we use the RUL representation of R, that is, a transition $f(q_1, \ldots, q_{n_j}) \rightarrow q$ in R is represented in the form $q(f_j^{n_j}(x_1, \ldots, x_{n_j})) \leftarrow q_1(x_1), \ldots, q_{n_j}(x_{n_j})$. Let B be a clause body $p_1(\bar{t}_1), \ldots, p_m(\bar{t}_m)$: then $\mathsf{type}(B)$ is the conjunction $\mathsf{type}(p_1(\bar{t}_1)), \ldots, \mathsf{type}(p_m(\bar{t}_m))$.

Definition 4. reduce

Let P be a definite program, B be a clause body in P, and $R \in D_P^d$ be an NFTA, with transitions Δ represented as an RUL program. Let τ be an SLD-tree for $\Delta \cup \{\leftarrow \mathsf{type}(B)\}$. Then define $\mathsf{reduce}(B, R) = \{E_1, \ldots, E_r\}$, where $\leftarrow E_1, \ldots, \leftarrow E_r$ is the set of all goals from τ, satisfying the conditions that

(i) $\leftarrow E_i$ is the first goal on its branch of τ that contains no function symbols, for $0 \leq i \leq r$;

(ii) for each set of predicates in E_i all of which have the same argument, say $\{q_1', \ldots, q_p'\}$, nonempty($R_{\bar{q}}$) holds, where $\bar{q} = q_1' \times \cdots \times q_p'$, for $0 \leq i \leq r$.

The idea of reduce is to "solve" a clause body with respect to an NFTA. We can think of it as "partially evaluating" the clause body (after transforming it by the type operation) using the transitions of the NFTA, until all the predicate and function symbols in B have been eliminated. The order of selection of literals in the construction of the SLD tree does not affect the values of $\{E_1, \ldots, E_r\}$. If there are k function symbols in B, then exactly k resolution steps are required to remove them, since each transition (RUL clause) contains exactly one function symbol in its left hand side, and no function symbol can be introduced by a resolution step, since all the head variables of RUL clauses are distinct, and each head variable occurs exactly once in the body. We then have to perform an emptiness check on the product of the automata corresponding to repeated variables.

The project$_d$ operation ($d \in \{var, arg\}$) takes a clause head H and one of the conjunctions E returned by the reduce operation. It returns a set of transitions.

Definition 5. project$_d$

Let P be a definite program, $H \leftarrow B$ be a clause in P, $R \in D_P^d$ be an NFTA, and $E \in$ reduce(B, R). Then project$_d(H, E)$ is a set of transitions defined as follows.

project$_d(H, E) =$

$$\{f(\{q_1\}, \ldots, \{q_n\}) \rightarrow \{q\} \mid f(t_1, \ldots, t_n) \text{ is a subterm of } H,$$
$$S_d^P(f(t_1, \ldots, t_n)) = q,$$
$$S_d^P(t_i) = q_i, 1 \le i \le n\}$$

$$\bigcup$$
$$\{q' \rightarrow \{q\} \mid \qquad\qquad x \text{ is a variable in } H,$$
$$S_d^P(x) = q,$$
$$q' = \text{restrict}(E, x)\}$$

The subsidiary function restrict(E, x) returns $\{any\}$, if x does not occur in E, otherwise it returns $\{q_1, \ldots, q_m\} \setminus \{any\}$, if $q_1(x), \ldots, q_m(x)$ are the occurrences of predicates with argument x in E.

The abstract interpretation is completed by defining $\bigsqcup_P^d(S)$ (where S is a set of sets of transitions) to be the NFTA $\langle Q_d^P, \{type\}, \Sigma, \Delta \rangle$ where $\Delta = \text{elim}_\epsilon(\bigcup S) \cup \Delta_{any}^\Sigma$. Thus the result of $\bigsqcup_d^P(S)$ is an element of D_P^d. Finally, define the abstract interpretation to be $\text{lfp}(T_P^d)$, where

$$T_P^d(R) = \bigsqcup_P^d\{\text{project}_d(H, \theta) \mid H \leftarrow B \in P, \theta \in \text{reduce}(B, R)\}.$$

As noted as the end of Section 4, we do not represent product automata explicitly. However, when eliminating ϵ-transitions of the form $\{q_1, \ldots, q_n\} \rightarrow \{q\}$, we have to calculate the product corresponding to $\{q_1, \ldots, q_n\}$, in order to derive the transitions with right hand side $\{q\}$.

Example 2. Let P be the *append* program. In the first application of T_{var}^P we have:

$$\text{reduce}(true, R_{min}) = \{true\} \qquad \text{reduce}(append(C, D, E), R_{min}) = \emptyset.$$

For the first clause, project$_{var}(append([\,], A, A)$ gives these transitions.

$$append(q_2, a, a) \rightarrow type \qquad [\,] \rightarrow q_2 \qquad any \rightarrow a$$

No transitions are returned from the second clause. On the second iteration, the first clause returns the same result. reduce applied to $append(C, D, E)$ returns the conjunction $(q_2(C), a(D), a(E))$, since we can unfold $append(C, D, E)$ using the transition (in RUL form) $\mathsf{type}(append(X, Y, Z)) \leftarrow q_2(X), a(Y), a(Z)$ obtained on the first step. Thus project gives the following transitions for the second clause head.

$$append(q_6, d, q_{10}) \rightarrow \mathsf{type} \qquad [b|c] \rightarrow q_6 \qquad [b|e] \rightarrow q_{10} \qquad q_2 \rightarrow c$$
$$a \rightarrow d \qquad\qquad\qquad\qquad a \rightarrow e \qquad\quad \mathsf{any} \rightarrow b$$

Adding these to the results of the first iteration and eliminating ϵ-transitions we obtain the following.

$$append(q_6, d, q_{10}) \rightarrow \mathsf{type} \qquad [b|c] \rightarrow q_6 \qquad [b|e] \rightarrow q_{10} \qquad [\,] \rightarrow c$$
$$\mathsf{any} \rightarrow d \qquad\qquad\qquad \mathsf{any} \rightarrow e \qquad \mathsf{any} \rightarrow b$$

The third iteration yields the following new transitions, after eliminating ϵ-transitions.

$$[b|c] \rightarrow c \qquad [b|e] \rightarrow e$$

No new transitions are added on the fourth iteration, thus the least fixed point has been reached.

The argument-based approximation generates the following sequence of results: (only the new transitions on each iteration are shown).

(1) $append(app_1, app_2, app_3) \rightarrow \mathsf{type}$ $[\,] \rightarrow app_1$ $\quad \mathsf{any} \rightarrow app_2$ $\mathsf{any} \rightarrow app_3$
(2) $[b|c] \rightarrow app_1$ $\qquad\qquad\qquad [\,] \rightarrow c \qquad [b|e] \rightarrow app_3 \quad \mathsf{any} \rightarrow e \qquad \mathsf{any} \rightarrow b$
(3) $[b|c] \rightarrow c$ $\qquad\qquad\qquad\; [b|e] \rightarrow e$

Considering the first argument of $append$, we can see that the variable-based analysis is more precise. For instance, the term $append([a], [\,], [\,])$ is accepted by the second automaton but not by the first. This is because the two clauses of the $append$ program are distinguished in the first, with two states (q_2 and q_6) describing the first argument in the two clauses respectively. A single state app_1 describes the first argument in the argument-based analysis. However, in this case (though not always), the precision of the variable-based analysis could be recovered from the argument-based analysis. We will discuss this further in Section 8. Further, note that the derived automata are not minimal in the number of states. For example the states c and e could be eliminated in the argument-based analysis, giving an equivalent more compact result.

$$append(app_1, app_2, app_3) \rightarrow \mathsf{type} \quad [\,] \rightarrow app_1 \qquad\quad \mathsf{any} \rightarrow app_2 \;\; \mathsf{any} \rightarrow app_3$$
$$[b|app_1] \rightarrow app_1 \qquad\qquad\qquad [b|app_3] \rightarrow app_3 \;\; \mathsf{any} \rightarrow b$$

5.1 Soundness of the Abstract Interpretations

The convergence of the sequence depends on the monotonicity of T_P^{var} and T_P^{arg} respectively, and the finiteness of the domains D_P^{var} and D_P^{arg}. Space does not permit a detailed proof of monotonicity, but it follows from the monotonicity of reduce in its second argument.

To show the soundness of the analyses requires proving that $\mathsf{lfp}(T_P) \subseteq \gamma_d(\mathsf{lfp}(T_P^d))$, $d \in \{var, arg\}$. Again, only a brief justification can be given here. The result follows in the framework of abstract interpretation [13] after showing that for all $R \in D_d^P$, $T_P(\gamma_d(R)) \subseteq \gamma_d(T_P^d(R))$. Informally, if t can be "generated" by applying T_P to the set of atoms accepted by automaton R (that is, $\gamma_d(R)$), then we can show that t is accepted by the automaton "generated" by applying T_P^d to R.

6   Implementation Aspects

We have implemented both the variable-based and the argument-based analyses. They share the same core semantics, and the code differs only in the part implementing the project operators, which takes into account the different relationships between program points and automata states.

6.1   Domain-Independent Optimisations

The presentation in Section 5 is naive from the implementation point of view, as it suggests that the sequence of approximations converging to the fixed point is computed by applying T_P^{var} (or T_P^{arg}) repeatedly to the complete accumulated result.

Various domain-independent optimisations are well known and have been applied in our implementation. We followed the pattern of our previous work on bottom-up analysis of logic programs [19,18,17]. The most important optimisations are the decomposition into strongly connected components (SCCs) of the predicate dependency graph of the program being analysed, and a variant of the "semi-naive" optimisation.

There are other domain-independent optimisations that could be included, such as the "chaotic iteration strategy" of Bourdoncle [3], and "eager evaluation" [36].

6.2   Domain-Dependent Optimisations

The operation $\bigsqcup_P$ for the two interpretations is defined as the union of sets of transitions, followed by the elimination of ϵ-transitions. This accords with the partial order on the domains, and has a conceptual simplicity. The successive applications of T_P^d simply keep on adding transitions until no new ones are generated. However, many redundant transitions can be generated, and the number of transitions is the major factor in the cost of expensive operations such as computing products of automata.

Thus in our implementation of $\bigsqcup_P$ the redundant transitions are removed from the automata. In the example in Section 5, the transition $[b|e] \to e$ can be removed from the variable-based analysis, and the transitions $[b|e] \rightarrow app_3$ and $[b|e] \rightarrow e$ from the argument-based analysis.

This optimisation implies that the sequence of automata generated in the sequence does not necessarily monotonically increase with respect to the partial order on the domain, since transitions can be removed as well as added. Convergence is still guaranteed due to the finiteness of the domain (and we take care not to introduce the same transition more than once). Soundness is obviously preserved since $\gamma_d(R) = \gamma_d(R')$ if R differs from R' only in the presence of redundant transitions. Alternatively, we could use the standard technique of constructing a domain and partial order on the domain, based on equivalence classes of automata with respect to the equivalence relation $\cong$. Clearly removing redundant transitions from an automaton yields an element of the same equivalence class.

6.3   Checking Non-emptiness of Product Automata

Our experiments show that large numbers of states and transitions can be generated from user-written programs, as can be seen from Tables 1 and 2. It is therefore essential to implement the basic domain operations as efficiently as possible. In particular, the check for emptiness within the reduce operation is critical. Non-emptiness of an automaton can be checked in time linear in the size of the automaton, but we are required to check the emptiness of product automata, which is EXPTIME-complete [12].

We store the non-empty products that arise during the analysis as a table of tuples $\langle q'_1, \ldots, q'_p \rangle$. Suppose that during the reduce operation we have to check nonempty($R_{\bar{q}}$) where $\bar{q} = q'_1 \times \cdots \times q'_p$. We first check to see whether $R_{\bar{q}}$ has already been shown to be non-empty, that is, whether $\langle q'_1, \ldots, q'_p \rangle$ is already tabulated. If so, then the monotonicity of T_P^d implies that it is still non-empty *even if the definitions of $q'_1, \ldots q'_p$ have changed since non-emptiness was established.* To check non-emptiness of a product that has not yet been shown to be non-empty, we must first compute the transitions in the product. However, the table of non-empty products can be exploited again. As described by Comon *et al.* the non-emptiness check involves treating each transition $f(q_1, \ldots, q_n) \rightarrow q$ as a propositional formula $q_1 \wedge \ldots \wedge q_n \rightarrow q$. Non-emptiness of an automaton R_s reduces to checking that s follows from the set of propositional Horn formulas obtained from the transitions of R_s. For each such formula derived from the product automaton we can strike out any q_j that is already known to be non-empty (since in the propositional form it is already *true*).

Example 3. The use of the table of non-empty products is illustrated by the analysis of the naive reverse program.

$$rev([\,],[\,]) \leftarrow true \qquad rev([A|B], C) \leftarrow rev(B, D), append(D, [A], C)$$

The definition of *append* is as before, and assume that it has already been analysed (as the lowest SCC component) using the argument-based interpretation.

The first iteration on rev yields transitions

$$rev(rev_1, rev_2) \rightarrow \mathsf{type} \qquad [\,] \rightarrow rev_1 \qquad [\,] \rightarrow rev_2$$

The next iteration applies reduce to the body of the second clause for rev. This requires checking the non-emptiness of the product $rev_2 \times app_1$ due to the repeated variable D. Computing the product of rev_2 and app_1 we obtain the propositional formula $true \rightarrow (rev_2 \times app_1)$, hence $rev_2 \times app_1$ is non-empty. Thus the following transitions are generated.

$$[a|b] \rightarrow rev_1 \qquad \mathsf{any} \rightarrow rev_2 \qquad \mathsf{any} \rightarrow a \qquad [\,] \rightarrow b$$

On the third iteration, we again must check non-emptiness of $rev_2 \times app_1$ but since it is already known to be non-empty we do not need to recompute the product. Note that the product is in fact larger than on the first iteration. The final transition to be added is $[a|b] \rightarrow b$.

We use a balanced 2-3-4 tree structure (that is, a B-tree of order 4) to store the transitions and the table of non-empty products. In the tree of transitions, the primary key is the state on the right-hand-side of the transition; within each record we use the function symbol on the left of the transition as a secondary key.

The elimination of unnecessary states, as illustrated in Example 2, trades off in general with an increase in the number of transitions. The choice of whether to eliminate is thus in general a heuristic matter. We adopt the following strategy. Any state $\{q\}$ that is defined by a single ϵ-transition $q' \rightarrow \{q\}$ (before the elimination of ϵ-transitions in the $\bigsqcup$ operation) is eliminated and replaced by q' wherever it occurs. Thus we eliminate states without increasing the number of transitions. We can keep a list of such eliminated states during the analysis, in case we need to access information about the program point (which will always be a variable in a clause head) represented by $\{q\}$. The analysis results given by q' can be applied to that program point.

For goal-dependent analysis we used "query-answer" transformations, related to "magic-set" transformations, to achieve a goal-dependent analysis in a bottom-up semantic framework [11,15,19]. This is a fairly crude but easily implemented technique for goal-directed analysis. Techniques such as "induced magic" [10] would doubtless improve performance.

7   Experiments

Some of the potential applications of set-constraint-based analysis were mentioned in Section 1. Our experiments were selected to show a range of different kinds of analysis, ranging from goal-independent type inference to planning and verification problems.

The implementation was developed in Ciao-Prolog [5]. The experiments were run in SICStus Prolog v. 3.8.6 under Solaris using a machine with two Ultrasparc processors running at 200 MHz.

Table 1. Results for Goal-Independent Analysis

Program	Clauses	Preds	Variable-Based		Argument-Based	
			Transitions	Time (secs)	Transitions	Time (secs)
cs_r	109	37	462	0.56	245	0.26
disj_r	80	43	220	0.23	132	0.17
gabriel	45	20	165	0.18	82	0.08
kalah	88	45	297	0.30	176	0.19
peep	227	22	832	1.19	279	0.57
pg	18	10	62	0.07	32	0.04
plan	29	16	118	0.09	67	0.08
press	155	50	627	0.97	302	0.35
qsort	6	3	31	0.04	11	0.01
queens	9	5	29	0.03	15	0.02
read	161	43	438	0.55	186	0.42
aquarius	4192	1471	20075	41.46	7464	14.30
odd_even	4	3	8	0.01	5	0.01
wicked_oe	5	4	10	0.01	10	0.01
appendlast	5	3	22	0.01	16	0.01
reverselast	5	3	17	0.02	13	0.01
nreverselast	7	4	30	0.03	21	0.02
schedule	13	7	62	0.04	40	0.05
multisetl	6	4	14	0.02	11	0.01
multiseto	8	2	13	0.02	8	0.02
blockpair2o	16	4	88	0.04	77	0.05
blockpair3o	16	4	105	0.07	55	0.06
blockpair2l	15	6	117	0.07	104	0.02
blockpair3l	15	6	134	0.11	112	0.06
blocksol	14	6	109	0.07	98	0.05

Table 1 shows the results for goal-independent analysis, and Table 2 gives the results of analysing the program with respect to a goal. The first group of benchmarks consists of a standard set of test programs widely available. To these we added the Aquarius compiler of Van Roy [35]. The second set of benchmarks are planning programs, which we obtained from [4]. For these, there is a given goal, and the aim of the analysis is to show that the goal has no solution. For these, an indication is provided ($\sqrt{}$) as to whether the analysis did prove the failure of the goal (the "F" column in Table 2). The variable-based analysis is more precise over these examples, showing failure in several cases where the argument-based analysis cannot.

The programs in the first group of benchmarks do not always have a clear entry point, and sometimes contain dead code with respect to the apparent entry point, so the significance of the goal-dependent analyses is variable. The goal-dependent result for the Aquarius compiler in particular seems meaningless.

Table 2. Results for Goal-Dependent Analysis

Program	Clauses	Preds	Variable-Based			Argument-Based		
			Transitions	Time (secs)		Transitions	Time (secs)	F
cs_r	225	74	971	3.29		372	1.03	
disj_r	154	86	360	1.18		254	0.89	
gabriel	83	40	203	0.50		108	0.29	
kalah	171	90	67	0.27		50	0.28	
peep	318	44	888	2.91		393	1.1	
pg	34	20	88	0.36		74	0.17	
plan	58	32	152	0.37		57	0.16	
press	278	100	838	4.16		554	1.93	
qsort	13	6	47	0.10		16	0.04	
queens	18	10	40	0.06		24	0.07	
read	352	86	236	1.23		125	0.98	
aquarius	9122	2942	129	23.21		32	25.38	
					F			F
odd_even	9	6	14	0.02	$\checkmark$	9	0.02	$\checkmark$
wicked_oe	13	8	15	0.03	$\checkmark$	15	0.03	$\checkmark$
appendlast	10	6	25	0.03	$\checkmark$	18	0.02	$\checkmark$
reverselast	10	6	31	0.05	$\checkmark$	23	0.03	$\times$
nreverselast	14	8	48	0.08	$\times$	36	0.06	$\times$
schedule	25	14	62	0.16	$\checkmark$	47	0.13	$\checkmark$
multisetl	12	8	23	0.04	$\checkmark$	20	0.07	$\times$
multiseto	16	4	67	0.26	$\checkmark$	36	0.12	$\checkmark$
blockpair2o	62	14	-	-	$\times$	-	-	$\times$
blockpair3o	62	14	-	-	$\times$	-	-	$\times$
blockpair2l	26	12	276	2.4	$\checkmark$	250	1.12	$\times$
blockpair3l	26	12	223	2.62	$\checkmark$	258	1.11	$\times$
blocksol	24	12	223	1.85		206	0.65	

They are all included for completeness. A "-" indicates that the analysis did not terminate in the resources available.

The results show that the argument-based interpretation is faster than the variable-based interpretation. Both execution time and the number of transitions in the final result is typically approximately halved in the argument-based interpretation.

8   Discussion and Conclusions

The results in Section 7 show that the argument-based interpretation is faster than the variable-based interpretation. Although there is a loss of precision associated with the argument-based interpretation, it can often be regained. Simply apply the T_P^{var} function to the result of the argument-based analysis. That is, compute $T_P^{var}(\mathsf{lfp}(T_P^{arg}))$. This projects the results of the argument-based analysis onto the domain of the variable-based analysis, producing a separate result for each position in the clause heads. In general, $\mathsf{lfp}(T_P^{var}) \subseteq T_P^{var}(\mathsf{lfp}(T_P^{arg}))$, but we have not yet made a detailed comparison of the relative precision of the two analyses. For many programs, the two are identical. To increase precision further, we could compute the limit (or any finite prefix) of the finite decreasing sequence $A, T_P^{var}(A), T_P^{var}(T_P^{var}(A)), \ldots$, where $A = \mathsf{lfp}(T_P^{arg}))$.

8.1   Comparison with Type Inference by Abstract Interpretation

Comparing our analyses with other abstract interpretations over type domains [25,34,19,13,30], the main difference is that all previous work is based on deterministic types. That is, a type may have have at most one "case" for each function symbol. These correspond roughly to deterministic finite tree automata, and as noted in Section 2, these have less expressive power than NFTAs. For example, it is not possible to represent the set of lists terminating in the element a using deterministic automata. The relative precision non-deterministic regular types compared to deterministic ones is discussed by Podelski and Charatonik [7]. The other aspect of existing type analyses based on abstract interpretations is that they are defined on an infinite domain, and so require a widening in order for the analysis to terminate. Mildner [30] has made a detailed comparison of various widenings in the literature.

The use of an infinite domain of NFTAs along with a widening is in principle more precise than our approach, since widening can be delayed an arbitrary number of iterations. The widenings that appear in the literature do not give more precision; our goal-dependent analysis produces the same accuracy as the examples discussed by Van Hentenryck *et al.*, including those "that require the widening to be rather sophisticated" [34]. However, existing abstract interpretations are based on deterministic types; the combination of non-deterministic types and widening has not been investigated, to our knowledge.

In summary, the method we presented seems to compare favourably, both in precision and efficiency, to all other type inference abstract interpreters known to us. For applications such as planning and verification, the extra precision of non-deterministic types over deterministic ones is significant.

8.2   Comparison with Set-Constraint Analysis

The variable-based analysis can be compared with set-constraint analysis [22,21] via the monadic approximation of a program presented by Frühwirth *et al.* [16]. The minimal model of the monadic program is equivalent to the solution of the set-constraints for the program. Our project$_{var}$ operator can be seen as performing the monadic transformation dynamically during the analysis. We claim that our variable-based analysis computes the minimal model of the corresponding monadic program (our project$_{var}$ operator mimics the monadic transformation), and thus can be seen as a method of solving set-constraints for logic programs.

The monadic transformation is attractive from the point of view of presenting set-constraint analysis, but direct use of the monadic transformation in the implementation of the analysis seems to be inadvisable. The transformation produces one copy of each clause body for every variable in its head. Solving these separately would be very inefficient. The somewhat awkward "pretend" variable, that is introduced in the monadic transformation of clauses with ground heads, is avoided in our approach.

We do not have an implementation of set-constraint solving against which to compare our implementation. Judging by our experiments and results reported in the literature, our approach is a practical alternative to set-constraint-solving algorithms. However, it does not seem likely that there are any inherent advantages in our approach to solving set-constraints. The main interest comes from combining set constraints with other analyses, in the framework of abstract interpretation.

8.3   Complexity and Scalability

Charatonik and Podelski remark that the worst-case complexity of set-based analysis is seldom encountered since types in user-written programs tend to be relatively small [7]. This does indeed seem to be true for "type analysis" applications of set constraints. However, for verification and planning problems, the types can grow very large since they can be combinatorial combinations of initial states present in the top goal. For instance, some of the planning problems discussed by Bruynooghe et al. [4] contain a procedure for checking equality of multisets. The procedure generates all permutations of the elements of one of the multisets. Set-based analysis is precise enough to generate a type containing all the permutations too, when the input sets are given. The two planning problems "blockpair2o" and "blockpair3o" were too complex for our implementation and ran out of memory. In summary, the precision of set-based analysis is sometimes too good to be practical, and coarser domains or widening operators may be needed in the abstract interpretations. A coarser domain, such as one containing deterministic automata only, could be used for more intractable examples. Introduction of widenings is arguably more systematic and conceptually easier in the abstract interpretation approach than in the original framework of set constraints. The generic correctness conditions for widening operators are established, and the invention of widenings follows a pattern of identifying invariant parts of the approximations from one iteration to the next.

8.4   Future Work

An advantage of our approach to set constraint analysis is that it can be incorporated into existing abstract interpretation frameworks such as PLAI [6,31] which forms part of the Ciao-Prolog pre-processor [24]. The aims of integrating set-constraint analysis into PLAI are to allow combination with other abstract domains, especially numerical approximations like convex hulls, and to have access to features of PLAI such as incremental analysis [23]. The pre-processor already includes a type analyser, and the greater precision available from set-based-analysis would increase its scope. To implement an abstract interpretation for a given domain in PLAI, a small number of domain-dependent operations have to be provided, such as abstract unification and projection. The transitions of the automata would be carried around the AND-OR tree of PLAI as "abstract substitutions". We can see no difficulty in principle in performing the integration, and this is the next stage in our research.

In conclusion, we have demonstrated that abstract interpretation over NF-TAs for set-based analysis of logic programs is feasible, and we argue that there are conceptual and practical advaantages in following this approach. Future research will focus on integrating the analysis into a generic abstract interpretation framework, combining it with other abstract interpretations.

Acknowledgements

This work was performed while the first author was on study leave at the Universidad Politécnica de Madrid. The second author is supported in part by Spanish CICYT project TIC 99-1151 "EDIPIA". Some of the ideas presented here (in particular the tabulation of the non-empty products) were originally inspired by discussions between the first author and Andreas Podelski in January 1998. We thank Julio Peralta and the anonymous referees for their helpful comments.

References

1. A. Aiken. Set constraints: Results, applications, and future directions. In A. Borning, editor, *Principles and Practice of Constraint Programming (PPCP 1994)*, volume 874 of *Springer-Verlag Lecture Notes in Computer Science*, pages 326–335. Springer Verlag, 1994. 244

2. A. Aiken and E. L. Wimmers. Solving systems of set constraints (extended abstract). In *IEEE Symposium on Logic in Computer Science (LICS 1992)*, pages 329–340, 1992. 244

3. F. Bourdoncle. Efficient chaotic iteration strategies with widenings. In *Formal Methods in Programming and their Applications*, volume 735 of *Springer-Verlag Lecture Notes in Computer Science*, pages 123–141, 1993. 252

4. M. Bruynooghe, H. Vandecasteele, D. A. de Waal, and M. Denecker. Detecting unsolvable queries for definite logic programs. *Journal of Functional and Logic Programming*, Special Issue 2, 1999. 243, 255, 258

5. F. Bueno, D. Cabeza, M. Carro, M. Hermenegildo, P. López-García, and G. Puebla. The Ciao prolog system. reference manual. Technical Report CLIP3/97.1, School of Computer Science, Technical University of Madrid (UPM), August 1997. Available from http://www.clip.dia.fi.upm.es/. 254

6. F. Bueno, M. G. de la Banda, and M. Hermenegildo. Effectiveness of Abstract Interpretation in Automatic Parallelization: A Case Study in Logic Programming. *ACM Transactions on Programming Languages and Systems*, 21(2):189–238, March 1999. 258

7. W. Charatonik and A. Podelski. Directional type inference for logic programs. In G. Levi, editor, *Proceedings of the International Symposium on Static Analysis (SAS'98), Pisa, September 14 - 16, 1998*, volume 1503 of *Springer LNCS*, pages 278–294. Springer-Verlag, 1998. 257, 258

8. W. Charatonik and A. Podelski. Set-based analysis of reactive infinite-state systems. In B. Steffen, editor, *Proc. of TACAS'98, Tools and Algorithms for Construction and Analysis of Systems, 4th International Conference, TACAS '98*, volume 1384 of *Springer-Verlag Lecture Notes in Computer Science*, 1998. 243, 244

9. W. Charatonik, A. Podelski, and J.-M. Talbot. Paths vs. trees in set-based program analysis. In T. Reps, editor, *Proceedings of POPL'00: Principles of Programming Languages*, pages 330–338. ACM, ACM Press, January 2000. 244

10. M. Codish. Efficient goal directed bottom-up evaluation of logic programs. *Journal of Logic Programming*, 38(3):355–370, 1999. 254

11. M. Codish and B. Demoen. Analysing logic programs using "Prop"-ositional logic programs and a magic wand. In D. Miller, editor, *Proceedings of the 1993 International Symposium on Logic Programming, Vancouver*. MIT Press, 1993. 254

12. H. Comon, M. Dauchet, R. Gilleron, F. Jacquemard, D. Lugiez, S. Tison, and M. Tommasi. *Tree Automata Techniques and Applications.* http://www.grappa.univ-lille3.fr/tata, 1999. 246, 253

13. P. Cousot and R. Cousot. Formal language, grammar and set-constraint-based program analysis by abstract interpretation. In *Proceedings of the Seventh ACM Conference on Functional Programming Languages and Computer Architecture*, pages 170–181, La Jolla, California, 25–28 June 1995. ACM Press, New York, NY. 244, 252, 257

14. D. de Waal and J. Gallagher. The applicability of logic program analysis and transformation to theorem proving. In *Proceedings of the 12th International Conference on Automated Deduction (CADE-12), Nancy*, 1994. 243

15. S. Debray and R. Ramakrishnan. Abstract Interpretation of Logic Programs Using Magic Transformations. *Journal of Logic Programming*, 18:149–176, 1994. 254

16. T. Frühwirth, E. Shapiro, M. Vardi, and E. Yardeni. Logic programs as types for logic programs. In *Proceedings of the IEEE Symposium on Logic in Computer Science, Amsterdam*, July 1991. 243, 244, 257

17. J. Gallagher. A bottom-up analysis toolkit. In *Proceedings of the Workshop on Analysis of Logic Languages (WAILL); Eilat, Israel; (also Technical Report CSTR-95-016, Department of Computer Science, University of Bristol, July 1995)*, June 1995. 252

18. J. Gallagher, D. Boulanger, and H. Sağlam. Practical model-based static analysis for definite logic programs. In J. W. Lloyd, editor, *Proc. of International Logic Programming Symposium*, pages 351–365, 1995. 252

19. J. Gallagher and D. de Waal. Fast and precise regular approximation of logic programs. In P. Van Hentenryck, editor, *Proceedings of the International Conference on Logic Programming (ICLP'94), Santa Margherita Ligure, Italy*. MIT Press, 1994. 244, 252, 254, 257

20. J. P. Gallagher and J. C. Peralta. Using regular approximations for generalisation during partial evaluation. In *Proceedings of the 2000 ACM SIGPLAN Workshop on Partial Evaluation and Semantics-Based Program Manipulation (PEPM'2000), Boston, Mass., (ed. J. Lawall)*, pages 44–51. ACM Press, January 2000. 243

21. N. Heintze. Practical aspects of set based analysis. In K. Apt, editor, *Proceedings of the Joint International Symposium and Conference on Logic Programming*, pages 765–769. MIT Press, 1992. 244, 257

22. N. Heintze and J. Jaffar. A Finite Presentation Theorem for Approximating Logic Programs. In *Proceedings of the 17th Annual ACM Symposium on Principles of Programming Languages, San Francisco*, pages 197–209. ACM Press, 1990. 244, 257

23. M. Hermenegildo, G. Puebla, K. Marriott, and P. Stuckey. Incremental Analysis of Constraint Logic Programs. *ACM Transactions on Programming Languages and Systems*, 22(2):187–223, March 2000. 258

24. M. V. Hermenegildo, F. Bueno, G. Puebla, and P. López. Program analysis, debugging, and optimization using the Ciao system preprocessor. In D. De Schreye, editor, *Proceedings of ICLP 1999: International Conference on Logic Programming, Las Cruces, New Mexico, USA*, pages 52–66. MIT Press, 1999. 243, 258

25. G. Janssens and M. Bruynooghe. Deriving descriptions of possible values of program variables by means of abstract interpretation. *Journal of Logic Programming*, 13(2-3):205–258, July 1992. 243, 244, 257

26. N. Jones. Flow analysis of lazy higher order functional programs. In S. Abramsky and C. Hankin, editors, *Abstract Interpretation of Declarative Languages*. Ellis-Horwood, 1987. 244

27. N. D. Jones and S. S. Muchnick. A flexible approach to interprocedural data flow analysis and programs with recursive data structures. In *Conference Record of the Ninth Symposium on Principles of Programming Languages*, pages 66–74. ACM Press, 1982. 244

28. D. Kozen. Set constraints and logic programming. *Information and Computation*, 143(1):2–25, 1998. 244

29. J. Lloyd. *Foundations of Logic Programming: 2nd Edition*. Springer-Verlag, 1987. 246

30. P. Mildner. *Type Domains for Abstract Interpretation: A Critical Study*. PhD thesis, Department of Computer Science, Uppsala University, 1999. 244, 257

31. K. Muthukumar and M. Hermenegildo. Compile-time Derivation of Variable Dependency Using Abstract Interpretation. *Journal of Logic Programming*, 13(2 and 3):315–347, July 1992. 258

32. A. Podelski, W. Charatonik, and M. Müller. Set-based failure analysis for logic programs and concurrent constraint programs. In S. D. Swierstra, editor, *Programming Languages and Systems, 8th European Symposium on Programming, ESOP'99*, volume 1576 of *LNCS*, pages 177–192. Springer-Verlag, 1999. 244

33. J. C. Reynolds. Automatic construction of data set definitions. In J. Morrell, editor, *Information Processing 68*, pages 456–461. North-Holland, 1969. 244

34. P. Van Hentenryck, A. Cortesi, and B. Le Charlier. Type analysis of prolog using type graphs. *Journal of Logic Programming*, 22(3):179–210, 1994. 243, 244, 257

35. P. Van Roy and A. M. Despain. High-performance logic programming with the Aquarius Prolog compiler. *IEEE Computer*, 25(1):54–68, 1992. 255

36. J. Wunderwald. Memoing evaluation by source-to-source transformation. In M. Proietti, editor, *Logic Program Synthesis and Transformation (LOPSTR'95)*, volume 1048 of *Springer-Verlag Lecture Notes in Computer Science*, pages 17–32, 1995. 252

A High-Level Generic Interface to External Programming Languages for ECLiPSe

Kish Shen, Joachim Schimpf, Stefano Novello, and Josh Singer

IC-Parc, Imperial College
London SW7 2AZ, UK
{K.Shen,J.Schimpf}@icparc.ic.ac.uk
{stefano.novello,josh.singer}@parc-technologies.com

Abstract. This paper addresses an important but rarely discussed practical aspect of programming in a declarative language: its interface to other programming languages. We present the high-level, generic interface of ECL^iPS^e, and discuss the reasons for our design choices. The main feature of the interface is that it cleanly separates the code for ECL^iPS^e from that of the external language, allowing the interface to be used for different languages. We believe that many of the concepts developed for this interface can be applied to other declarative languages, especially for other Prolog systems.

Keywords: Logic Programming, language interfaces, implementation, application development

1 Introduction

An important practical aspect of a high-level programming language such as Prolog is its interface to other programming languages. In a large scale programming setting, it is unlikely that any one programming language will be used exclusively. In particular, the strengths of Prolog which make it ideal for expressing and solving complex problems also means it is not well suited for non-logical tasks such low-level programming and providing a graphical user interface (GUI) to applications. Thus, it is important to provide means to interface Prolog to other programming languages that are more suited to such tasks.

Many Prolog systems have interfaces to other programming languages, these generally allow Prolog code to invoke commands/procedures written in another programming language (which we will refer to as the *external language*), and/or for code in the external language to invoke Prolog predicates (if both directions are possible, the interface is said to be bi-directional). The interfaces can be broadly classified into two categories by the level of access to the internals of the Prolog system:

Low-level interfaces these provide the external language with direct access to the memory areas and low level representation of data structures of the Prolog system. The external language is thus tightly coupled to the Prolog

S. Krishnamurthi, C. R. Ramakrishnan (Eds.): PADL 2002, LNCS 2257, pp. 262–279, 2002.

system, and able to manipulate the Prolog data structures and machine state. In fact, some form of such an interface is normally used in the implementation of the Prolog system itself, as the interface between Prolog and the language it is implemented in, which is usually C. Because of the low-level nature of the interface, it is very system specific, and is usually restricted to interfacing to the one language.

Allowing the Prolog data structures to be directly manipulated can be powerful and efficient, but at the same time, it can be dangerous. It also requires the programmer to have a reasonable knowledge of the Prolog system.

High-level interfaces these provide the external language with a less direct access to the Prolog side. In particular, the external language is not able to directly access or manipulate the Prolog data structures.

For many purposes, such as providing a GUI, low-level access to the Prolog state is not required or even desirable. Furthermore, some programming languages (e.g. script-based languages such as Tcl/Tk or Perl) are unsuitable for manipulating the raw Prolog data structures in any case. In these cases, the data communicated between the two sides often have their own, separate, representations, and manipulating the data on one side does not directly affect the other side.

There are of course many different programming languages, and different ways they can be interfaced to Prolog. Many issues are involved in the design of such an interface, and various interfaces have been developed for various Prolog systems to various programming languages. However, there has been little or no discussion in the published literature about the reasons and issues behind the design of the interfaces. We feel that there are common issues that are worth discussing, and in this paper, we present our experience with developing a high-level interface for several external languages with ECL^{i}PS^e.

ECL^{i}PS^e is a constraint logic programming system being developed at IC-Parc. It is used at IC-Parc, and its spin-off company, Parc Technologies, as the core for developing industrial scheduling and planning applications. In the design of our external language interface, we needed to meet the commercial demands of Parc Technologies, and this strongly influenced some of our design decisions, which will be discussed in this paper.

ECL^{i}PS^e has both a low-level, bi-directional, interface to C, and a high-level, also bi-directional, interface to Java, Tcl/Tk and Visual Basic. In this paper, we concentrate on the high-level interface because it involves issues which apply to other Prolog/Logic Programming systems (and perhaps other declarative languages as well). This interface was first introduced in version 4.1 of ECL^{i}PS^e, released early in 1999, and evolved to its current form described here.

2   Motivation and Objective

Our main motivation for the development of a new external interface was to allow our ECL^{i}PS^e applications to be used within larger applications written in different languages. We also wanted to implement a robust development GUI for ECL^{i}PS^e, and provide a stable basis for a multitude of GUIs for various ECL^{i}PS^e applications in the future.

From experience with previous external language interfaces and requirements for our applications, we had several issues and objectives in mind while we were developing the interface:

Language Generic We did not want an interface that was specific to a particular language. Developments in programming languages mean that a language in favour today may no longer be so in the future. Also, in commercial settings, there may be specific requirements to use a particular language, e.g. a client for one of our commercial applications explicitly required Visual Basic as the external interface language, while at the time we provided a Tcl/Tk interface.

We wanted an interface that is generic in the sense that the ECL^{i}PS^e side is independent of the languages used on the external side. Thus an agent written in a different programming language can be substituted on the external side without changing any code on the ECL^{i}PS^e side of the interface. In addition, while the syntax on the external side would certainly differ from language to language, they should all implement the same concepts, so it should be easy to move from using the interface in one language to another.

Maintenance We wanted to minimise the development/maintenance overheads to support a new language via the interface. Thus, when interfacing to a new language is required, we can rapidly develop the interface required.

Control When ECL^{i}PS^e is interfaced to an external language, we often need to mesh the very different control regimes of the two languages: ECL^{i}PS^e is non-deterministic and single-threaded, and the external language tend to be deterministic and multi-threaded. We wanted to avoid complex control flow between the two languages, as this can easily lead to unmanageable nesting and interactions between the two languages.

Syntax We wanted to avoid any conflicts in syntax between ECL^{i}PS^e and the external language, which could happen if commands or data structures in the external language can occur in their native syntax within the ECL^{i}PS^e side and vice-versa. Allowing syntax of one language to appear in another is always error prone, especially for quoting of special characters (which are likely to be different in the languages), and when the command may be assembled dynamically during execution.

Uniform Usage We wanted to have a uniform interface, no matter whether ECL^{i}PS^e was used as a library (embedded into an external language host program) or as a server (in a separate process, possibly on a remote machine).

2.1   Conceptual Model

We developed a message-based, data-driven interface, as shown in Figure 1. The interface connects one agent written in ECL^{i}PS^e with one or more agents written in external languages.

The main conceptual points of the interface can be summarised by:

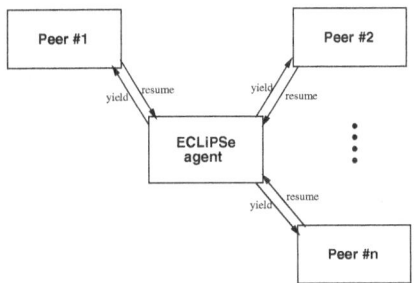

Fig. 1. The Generic External Interface with Multiple Peers

Multiple agents Multiple external agents can be connected to an ECL^{i}PS^e agent via the interface, and the connection itself may be by different methods. The interface provides the concept of *peers* to allow these external sides to be accessed in a uniform way. A peer is any external side (i.e. the external agent and its connecting peer queues).

Data-driven queues The two sides are connected by I/O queues with data-driven handlers, called *peer queues*. The interface provides operations to set up peer queues that connect the two sides. These are I/O queues that can send messages between the two sides in one direction. If the direction of data flow is from ECL^{i}PS^e side to the external side, the queue is called a *from*-ECL^{i}PS^e queue; if the data flow is from the external side to ECL^{i}PS^e, it is called a *to*-ECL^{i}PS^e queue.

For each peer queue, a *handler* can be defined to handle the data transfer. These are procedures (or predicates in ECL^{i}PS^e) which are invoked to handle the transfer of data. The handler can either be a *data provider*, which supplies data to the other side when requested (when the other side reads from the queue and no data is available); or be a *data consumer*, which consumes data arriving on a queue. The execution of the handler for a queue is thus driven by the data transfer on that queue.

Structured messages To allow for platform and language independent interchange of typed data on the queues connecting the two sides, an ECL^{i}PS^e external data representation (EXDR) format was defined. EXDR allows the representation of a large subset of ECL^{i}PS^e's data types, including lists and nested structures. EXDR was inspired by Sun Microsystem's XDR format [7], however, unlike XDR, every EXDR term also includes its own type information.

Synchronous control flow Conceptually, there is a single thread of control flow between the external and ECL^{i}PS^e sides. At any time, one side has control, and only it can initiate the transfer of data on the queues (i.e. either sending data to the other side, or requesting data from the other side). On the ECL^{i}PS^e side, execution is suspended while the external side has control. Execution on the external side may or may not be suspended[1] while ECL^{i}PS^e side has control, depending on the programming language and/or the platform.

ECL^{i}PS^e remote predicate call (ERPC) The queue handlers already provide all the means for invoking actions in both directions. For convenience, and because an external side is always interfaced to an ECL^{i}PS^e agent, a form of Remote Procedure Call [1], which we call ECL^{i}PS^e Remote Predicate Call (ERPC) is always provided. It allows an external agent to conveniently invoke deterministic ECL^{i}PS^e predicates and retrieve their results.

3 Design Details

3.1 Peers

In the conceptual view of the interface, the way an external agent is connected to an ECL^{i}PS^e agent is not important, only that the two sides can communicate via data-driven peer queues. Thus, different concrete realisations of the interface are possible. We have provided two: an **embedded** variant, where the ECL^{i}PS^e agent and the external agent are in the same process (communicating through main memory); and a **remote** variant, where the ECL^{i}PS^e and remote agents are separate processes (connected by TCP/IP sockets). In the latter case, as the connections are sockets, the two agents can be located on different machines.

An ECL^{i}PS^e agent can be embedded into only one external agent. Multiple remote connections (perhaps to agents of different external languages) can be made, and any ECL^{i}PS^e agent can be connected, including one that is already embedded, i.e. an ECL^{i}PS^e agent can have at most one embedded peer, but multiple remote peers.

The differences between the embedded and remote interface variants are largely abstracted away by the unified conceptual view and the concept of peers. From the programmer's point of view, the remote and embedded variants can be largely used in the same way, and code written for one can be reused for the other. This is achieved by providing the same predicate/procedure names/methods interface calls with both variants on both the ECL^{i}PS^e and external sides.

The one main difference visible to the programmer is the process of initialising and terminating the connection with the two interfaces. With the embedding interface, the ECL^{i}PS^e agent is started from within the external agent (the agent loads ECL^{i}PS^e as a library), and the connection terminated by terminating the ECL^{i}PS^e agent. With the remote interface, the external agent has to be explicitly *attached* to the ECL^{i}PS^e agent for the connection, and detached for the termination. Attachment establishes an initial control connection between the two sides, along with some initial exchange of information. The control connection is used to co-ordinate and synchronise subsequent actions.

---

[1] If execution is not suspended, then it cannot initiate data transfer to the ECL^{i}PS^e side.

As an example of the use of both variants, the TkECL^{i}PS^e development tools (a set of development tools including debugger and state browsers), which were originally written to be used in an embedded setting together with the TkECL^{i}PS^e toplevel GUI, runs in the remote setting with very few modifications, even though the bulk of the code was developed before the conception of the remote interface. In terms of code sizes, there is about 4260 lines of Tcl and 1750 lines of ECL^{i}PS^e code that are shared. The specific code for starting the tools with the remote interface is about 200 lines of Tcl code and 60 lines of ECL^{i}PS^e code. About 30 lines of Tcl code and no ECL^{i}PS^e code would be needed to start the development tools with the embedding interface.

3.2 Peer Queues

The peer queues are implemented differently in the embedded and remote setting. In the embedded case the queues are shared memory buffers, while in the remote case the queues are implemented with sockets connecting the two sides.

To a user, a peer (once it is set up), whether remote or embedded, can be treated in the same way. Information is transferred between the two sides via the peer queues, which are created in a uniform way. The creation can be initiated from either the ECL^{i}PS^e or the peer side. From the ECL^{i}PS^e side, the difference between a remote peer queue and an embedded peer queue is hidden by providing the same predicate to create the queue – the user just specifies which peer the queue is for, and then the appropriate queue is created.

3.3 Typed EXDR Messages

The EXDR encoding is instrumental in providing language and architecture independence for the interface. Similar to XML [11], and unlike XDR, EXDR data includes type information. This is implemented in a very compact way by tagging each data item with a byte that identifies the particular data type. This allows the type of the data sent to be dynamically determined when the data is sent, rather than being statically fixed, and is particularly useful for a dynamically typed language like Prolog.

The data types that are available in this format are listed in Figure 2. The idea is to represent that subset of ECL^{i}PS^e types which has a meaningful mapping to many other languages' data types. Apart from the basic types, lists and nested structures are available and are mapped to meaningful types in many external languages. The main restriction is that logical variables (which have no equivalent in most other languages) are not allowed in their general form. However, singleton occurrences are allowed and useful to serve as place-holders, e.g. for result arguments in ERPCs (see section 3.7)

A small difficulty arises with a language like Tcl whose type system is too weak to distinguish between all the EXDR types: different EXDR types map to the same string in Tcl. While this is usually no problem when Tcl receives data, we have augmented the Tcl send primitive to take an additional argument which specifies the EXDR type into which a given string should be encoded.

EXDR type	ECLiPSe type	Tcl type	VB type	Java type
Integer (32bit)	integer	int	Long	java.lang.Integer
Long (64bit)	integer	string	n/a	java.lang.Long
Double	float	double	Double	java.lang.Double
String	string	string	String	java.lang.String
List	./2	list	Collection of Variant	java.util.Collection
Nil	[ ] /0	string ""	Collection of Variant	java.util.Collection
Struct	compound	list	Array of Variant	CompoundTerm
Placeholder	anon variable	string "_"	Empty Variant	null

Fig. 2. EXDR types with some language mappings

The complete specification including the concrete physical encoding for the EXDR format is given in [6] and appendex A. As part of the external side of the interface for a particular external language, the mapping of EXDR data types into that language must be defined.

3.4   Control Flow

The control flow between the two sides is based on the synchronous yield/resume model: Control is transferred from ECL^{i}PS^e to the external side when ECL^{i}PS^e *yields* to the external side. Control is transferred from the external side back to ECL^{i}PS^e by *resuming* ECL^{i}PS^e. For example, when data is transferred from ECL^{i}PS^e to the external side on a peer queue, ECL^{i}PS^e will yield to the external side to allow the external side to process the data (via a handler for the queue). When the external side completes the processing, control is returned to the ECL^{i}PS^e by resuming ECL^{i}PS^e.

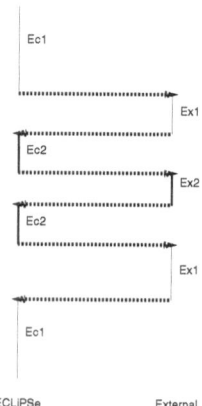

Fig. 3. Nesting of Handlers

Note that handler execution on the two sides can be nested. An example of this is shown in Figure 3. In the figure, time advances down the page, and the figure shows the transfer of control between the ECL^{i}PS^e and remote sides. A vertical line shows that a particular side has control, and the horizontal arrows shows the transfer of control. Initially, the ECL^{i}PS^e handler Ec1 is executing, and ECL^{i}PS^e has control. At some point, control is transferred to the external language, and the external handler Ex1 is invoked. This transfers control back to ECL^{i}PS^e, starting a new handler Ec2 (the line is thicker to more readily distinguish it from Ec1), which in turn invokes an external handler Ex2. When Ex2 completes, control is returned to ECL^{i}PS^e and the execution of Ec2 continues until it also completes and returns to the remote side, where Ex1 continues and completes, returning control to ECL^{i}PS^e, which continues the execution of Ec1. Thus, Ex2 is nested within the execution of Ec2, which is nested within Ex1, which is nested within Ec1. This nesting allows the implementation of the equivalent of the 'call back' functionality of traditional RPCs.

The thread-based control flow limits the complexity of interactions between the two sides. As ECL^{i}PS^e has only a single thread of execution, it would not be sensible to allow the external side to request execution of other goals while ECL^{i}PS^e side has control and is executing a goal. Note that the external side is not limited to being single threaded (and in fact neither Java or Tcl are single threaded).

The topology for transferring control with multiple peers is always a star shape with the ECL^{i}PS^e agent in the middle: control is handed over from the ECL^{i}PS^e agent to a peer, which can then only hand back control to that ECL^{i}PS^e agent. This is shown in Figure 1.

3.5 Generic Invocation of Action

We achieve language independence in our interface by using the generic concept of queues over which messages in the language independent EXDR format are transferred. We did not provide any built-in method to directly execute commands of the external language from within ECL^{i}PS^e. Nevertheless, ECL^{i}PS^e can cause actions to take place on the external side. The idea is that instead of making a procedure call directly, data transfers on a queue are used to invoke the handler for the queue. The data transferred specifies how the procedure should be invoked. The ECL^{i}PS^e side can thus regard the remote side as a black box, where the programming of a particular queue just involves specifying the protocol for transferring data and what the data is for. None of the details of *how* the data would be processed need to be known on the ECL^{i}PS^e side – all the code for doing this remains on the remote side. In particular, a different language can be substituted on the remote side, and as long as the handler for the queue obeys the same protocol, nothing on the ECL^{i}PS^e side is affected by the change.

3.6   Generic Interface within the External Language

The key abstractions of peer and of a peer queue allow natural counterpart abstractions on the external side, which can give a highly flexible underlying architecture. Abstraction is a strong element of object-oriented language such as Java, and our Java side of the interface demonstrates this. Just as a peer is a generic interface to an external side of any kind, the *EclipseConnection* interface in our Java code is implemented by different classes providing a connection to an ECL^{i}PS^e engine. For example *EmbeddedEclipse* implements *EclipseConnection* in the embedded variant of the interface; and *RemoteEclipse* class on the other hand implements *EclipseConnection* in the remote variant. Just as a peer queue allows communication between ECL^{i}PS^e and any kind of peer, so the Java classes *FromEclipseQueue* and *ToEclipseQueue* are provided by any class implementing *EclipseConnection*.

3.7   ERPC

The ERPC mechanism is provided for ease of programming. It is implemented on top of a pair of peer queues (to- and from-ECL^{i}PS^e), with the handler for the to-ECL^{i}PS^e queue reading the goal (in EXDR format), executing it, and returning the resulting goal to the external side. The handler essentially looks like:

```
erpc_handler :-
    read_exdr(rpc_in, Goal), once(Goal), write_exdr(rpc_out, Goal).
```

The actual ERPC handler code deals with failures and exceptions as well. These queues and the handler are pre-defined by the ECL^{i}PS^e-side of the interface, along with the handler.

Since we are interfacing to a variety of different external languages, none of which have concepts of logical variables, backtracking or goal suspension, the kind of ECL^{i}PS^e goals that can be called through the interface must be restricted. The abstraction of an ECL^{i}PS^e goal which the interface provides to the external language is that of a procedure with input arguments and output arguments which expect/return data of certain EXDR types.

On the ECL^{i}PS^e side that means that (i) externally callable goals are limited to return only one solution by committing to the first one, (ii) all variables in input arguments will be singleton variables and can only be used to return results, (iii) results cannot contain shared variables. It is in the responsibility of the ECL^{i}PS^e programmer to provide callable predicates that observe these restrictions. In practice that means that e.g. difference lists need to be transformed into standard lists, and multiple solutions can be either collected and returned in a list, or alternatively returned incrementally via a dedicated, application-specific peer queue (as demonstrated in the map coloring example of section 5).

Since the external languages have different, incompatible argument passing conventions, especially for output arguments, we decided on an ERPC protocol that is at least natural and easy to implement on the ECL^{i}PS^e side: the goal is sent as a compound term, which may contain one or more singleton variables as placeholders for the output arguments. To return the result after successful execution, we send back the complete original goal, but with the former variables replaced by result values. This method avoids the need for a complex return-result protocol involving variable-handles or identifiers. It does however requires the external side to extract the results from the goal term. This protocol is suitable for most rpcs except those that have very large input arguments. In this latter case, the programmer would set up a queue for sending the input separately.

4   Discussion

4.1   Separation of ECL^{i}PS^e and External Code

The interface clearly separates the code for ECL^{i}PS^e and the code for the external language. This means that the ECL^{i}PS^e code and the external code can be developed separately with just the interchanges between the two languages clearly specified. In particular, it means that

- Any problems with incompatibilities between the syntax of ECL^{i}PS^e and the remote language is avoided.
- The same ECL^{i}PS^e side of the interface can be used for different languages. There is no need to learn to use a different interface if the external language is changed.
- The development of the interface for a new external language means only a new external side of the interface has to be developed.
- The programmers on one side need not have much knowledge about the other programming language. In the case of Parc Technologies, this means that GUI and Java programmers can be hired without requiring them to either already know or undergo extensive training in ECL^{i}PS^e or Prolog.
- The converse is also true: ECL^{i}PS^e and CLP programmers do not need expertise or knowledge in GUI or Java programming.
- Each language is left to do the tasks they are most suited for. We do not need to 'enhance' ECL^{i}PS^e to provide features for tasks it is not suited for. For example, to properly support GUIs, a language needs to support some notion of multi-threading or an event-loop to cope with the inherently reactive nature of the task. As none of this management of the GUI is done on the ECL^{i}PS^e side, there is no need to introduce such features to ECL^{i}PS^e.
- Where the external language is used for providing a GUI, then the core part of the ECL^{i}PS^e code can often be easily detached from the interface and used separately. This is particularly convenient for both development and unit-testing of the ECL^{i}PS^e code.

4.2   Supporting a New External Language

The ECL^{i}PS^e side and the external side are loosely coupled, and have few dependencies on the low-level workings of either ECL^{i}PS^e or the external language.

To implement the embedded variant of the interface, the external language system must be able to load ECL^{i}PS^e as a library and to invoke a subset of the functions provided by ECL^{i}PS^e's C/C++ interface. These are the functions needed to initialise and finalise the ECL^{i}PS^e engine and to access the memory queue buffers.

For the remote variant of the interface, the remote side of the interface protocol has to be implemented, i.e. sending the appropriate message at the appropriate time, and performing the right actions on receiving messages from the ECL^{i}PS^e side. The protocol is specified in the ECL^{i}PS^e Embedding and Interfacing manual. This code should be straightforward to write and basically requires that sockets can be programmed in the language.

Both interfaces also need to provide support for the EXDR format, i.e. encoding/decoding native data into/from EXDR format. Depending on the external language, this may need to be supported at the C level (for example, in Tcl this is done in C, in Java this is done in Java).

Our experience so far is positive: the interface was initially developed mainly for use with Tcl/Tk for the development of the GUI for ECL^{i}PS^e itself. Since then, Parc Technologies have decided to standardise on using Java for all their GUI (and any other non-ECL^{i}PS^e) development, and support through this interface for Java was rapidly developed, both in the embedded and remote variants.

We could also confirm the reusability of the ECL^{i}PS^e side code with different external languages: parts of the ECL^{i}PS^e development GUI that was written in Tcl originally have been successfully replicated in Visual Basic or Java. However, with the introduction of the peer concept, this replication is now rarely necessary, as GUI components can be written in different languages.

4.3   Synchronous Control Flow

In our interface, the interaction between the external and ECL^{i}PS^e sides is synchronous. We deliberately avoided the complexity of a general message passing system, which would be difficult to combine with the already complex control flow in a constraint programming system.

As control is transferred for each exchange of data, and when the external side has control, ECL^{i}PS^e execution is suspended, there might be a problem with efficiency. However, as discussed in section 2.1, the execution of the external agent is not necessarily suspended while ECL^{i}PS^e side has control. In a multi-threaded external language like Java, the data can be read by the Java side and control returned to ECL^{i}PS^e side quickly while the Java side then processes the data concurrently.

With our current main area of application, the provision of GUIs, efficiency does not seem to be a problem. Asynchronous communications can be programmed separately, using standard sockets, if necessary.

4.4 Scope of Applicability

The high-level interface is a general interface to an external language, and is of course not limited to allowing the external language to providing GUIs for ECL^{i}PS^e applications.

The different strengths of the embedding and remote variants of the interface makes them suitable for different uses. Some of the issues to consider are efficiency, flexibility, security and fault tolerance.

Efficiency The memory buffers of the embedded interface offer faster communications between the two sides than the socket connections of the remote variant. With the remote interface, data sent from one side needs to be physically transmitted (via sockets) to the other side, perhaps with buffering on both sides. TCP/IP also imposes an overhead on each transmission of data, such that it takes tens of milliseconds per transmission, regardless of the size of data transmitted, even when the two sides are on the same machine. This means that for applications where there are frequent exchanges of data, the process can be noticeably slowed by the interface. In some situations, it might be possible to reduce the number of times the control is transferred by pooling the updates and sending them in batches.

Flexibility The flexibility of connecting to multiple external agents via the remote interface is quite useful. For example, Parc Technologies decided to standardise on using Java for all its non-ECL^{i}PS^e coding, while the ECL^{i}PS^e graphical development tools are written in Tcl/Tk. With the initial embedding interface, these tools were only available to programs which also used Tcl/Tk for their GUI, but the remote interface allows these tools to be used in conjunction with a Java agent, making the process of development much easier. The multiple agents approach will also allow new tools to be developed in Java, without needing to recode all the existing development tools into Java.

The remote interface allows an ECL^{i}PS^e agent to be run remotely, on any machine that can be reached via the internet. One use for this is to allow an ECL^{i}PS^e program to be debugged remotely.

A practical advantage for the remote interface that we did not initially foresee is that the memory and other resources are not shared between the ECL^{i}PS^e and external agents. In the embedding interface, our experience with programming large applications in Java, ECL^{i}PS^e and also other software systems such as an external Mixed Integer Programming solver, all doing their own memory management and all interacting as a single process, non-repeatable problems (perhaps due to some memory leak) do occur that are difficult to track down. In the remote interface, bugs caused by the interaction of different memory management are less likely to occur, and any bugs which do occur are easier to track down.

Security Potentially, because the remote interface allows connections from any-where reachable on the network, the remote side can be 'hijacked' by an imposter, and once attached, it has full access to the ECL^{i}PS^e side through ERPC, and hence to the ECL^{i}PS^e side's file space. The remote protocol implements a 'pass-term' check, where an ECL^{i}PS^e term is transmitted from the remote side to the ECL^{i}PS^e side and checked before the socket connection for the ERPC is allowed. Another method to limit access is to allow attachment on the local machine only via the loopback address. Further security can be imposed by the programmer, e.g. encryption of the data transmitted on the queues.

Fault-Tolerance With the remote variant, there is the possibility that the connection between the two sides may be lost unexpectedly, either because of some network problems, or because one side dies unexpectedly. In such cases, the peer queues will be disconnected, and when one side detects this, a unilateral detachment will be performed by the remote protocol, and control is returned to the programmer to deal with this unexpected situation. In the embedded variant, the two sides are in the same process, so the problem does not arise.

5 An Example – Map Colouring

In the ECL^{i}PS^e distribution, there is an example illustrating the use of the interface. Currently Tcl/Tk is used as the external language, providing a GUI for the main ECL^{i}PS^e code, which solves the standard map colouring problem where a map of countries should be coloured with four colours such that no neighbouring countries share the same colour.

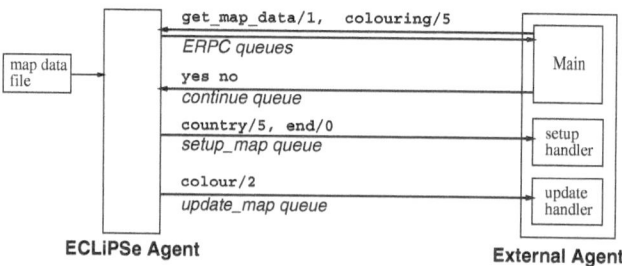

Fig. 4. Structure of Map Colouring Program

The overall structure of the program is shown in Figure 4. In brief, the ECL^{i}PS^e agent can colour a map by several different methods, using the map data specified in a map data file. The external agent provides the GUI for the user to select the map, and how many countries from the map, should be coloured; method of colouring the map, and also for displaying the map as it is being coloured by the ECL^{i}PS^e agent. Finally, when the map is successfully coloured, the external agent allows the user to ask for more solutions.

The two sides communicate via ERPCs, and three peer queues:

setup_map : this from-ECL^{i}PS^e queue transmits the shape and position information of a map to the external side, which uses the information to construct the map.

update_map : this from-ECL^{i}PS^e queue transmits the information for updating the map as it is being coloured by the ECL^{i}PS^e program.

continue : this to-ECL^{i}PS^e queue transmits the request for further solutions once the map is coloured.

The ECL^{i}PS^e code consists of two main components: the setting up of the map for the external side in get_map_data/1, and the colouring of the map in colouring/5. The abstract outline of the code relevant to the interface is as follows:

```
get_map_data(Size) :-
    ....
    write_exdr(map_data, country(C,X1,Y1,X2,Y2)),
    ....
    write_exdr(map_data, end)

colouring(Type, Select, Choice, Size, Time) :-
    ....
    ( write_exdr(update_map, colour(C, Colour)
    ; write_exdr(update_map, colour(C, gray)
    ),
    ....
    read_exdr(continue, Continue),
    Continue == no.
```

get_map_data/1 sends the data for the map to be coloured to the external side. The full map has been read into the ECL^{i}PS^e side earlier by another predicate (not shown here). Size specifies how many countries from the full map are to be coloured: configuration information on Size countries are sent to the external side. This information is sent in a loop, consisting of a series of country/5 terms, terminating in a end term.

colouring/5 does the actual colouring of the map. The first four arguments specify various options, and the last argument Time is an output argument for returning the cpu time consumed for colouring the map. When a country C is set to a particular colour Colour during the colouring process, this information is sent to the external side via the update_map queue; a choice-point is created so that the colour can be reset (to gray) when it is backtracked over. Finally, when the map is successfully coloured, the program reads from the continue peer queue. This hands control over to the external side, where the user can specify via the GUI if the program should continue and return another solution or not.

By clicking on the appropriate widget, either yes or no is sent via the continue queue to the ECL^{i}PS^e side, and read_exdr/2 on the ECL^{i}PS^e side returns. The execution then either backtracks to get the next solution or finishes.

Both predicates are called from the external side via ERPC calls, with the ERPC invoked when the user clicks on the appropriate widget in the GUI.

This example shows the generic nature of the interface concretely: the ECL^{i}PS^e side of the code does not depend on the external side being Tcl. Another external language can be used to provide the GUI, as long as the implementation follows the protocol defined above. The actual example program in the distribution can also be run either embedded or remotely.

For illustration, we outline the Tcl code for handling the map colouring:

```
proc run {} {
    ....
    ;# calling colouring/5, followed by the type information
    ec_rpc [list colouring $solver $select $choice $mapsize _] (()()()I_)
    ....
}

proc update_map {...} {
    ....
    ;# read the colour/2 term
    set info [ec_read_exdr update_map]
    ;# extract the country and colour from the data and display it
    set country [lindex $info 1]
    set colour  [lindex $info 2]
    ....
}

proc continue_colouring {continue_queue} {
    global continue_state
    ....
    ;# wait for user to decide if more solution is wanted
    tkwait variable continue_state
    ....
    ;# send decision to ECLiPSe
    ec_write_exdr $continue_queue $continue_state ()
    ....
}
```

run is a procedure invoked by pressing a 'Run' button which starts the colouring process. This procedure makes an ERPC call. As discussed previously, for a weakly typed language like Tcl, type information has to be specified (the (()()()I_) string, see the manual [6] for more details).

While colouring/5 is running, it sends the colour information as described above. On the Tcl side, this invokes the handler update_map, which reads the information from the update_map queue and displays it.

continue_colouring is the handler procedure for the continue queue. When ECL^{i}PS^e reads from the queue, this procedure is invoked on the Tcl side. The Tcl code waits for the continue_state variable to be set by the appropriate widgets (buttons that the user clicks to specify if another solution is wanted). This variable is set to either yes or no, and the information is returned to the ECL^{i}PS^e side.

6   Related Work

Many existing Prolog systems provide some form of external language interface. Most of the earliest are 'low-level' interfaces to C. Interfaces to Tcl/Tk and, more recently, to Java and Visual Basic have been developed. For script languages such as Tcl/Tk, the interface is usually high-level, because Tcl itself cannot represent or manipulate the raw representation of Prolog data structures. On the other hand, Java interfaces can be either high-level or low-level.

Examples of high-level interfaces include the old ProTcXl [5] of ECL^{i}PS^e; the Tcl/Tk and Visual Basic interfaces of SICStus [8]; the Tcl/Tk and Java interfaces of Ciao [2]; the Tcl/Tk interface of BinProlog and ProLog by BIM [9].

Most of these interfaces are not generic; for example, the Visual Basic, Tcl/Tk and Java interfaces of SICStus are very different from each other, and so are the Tcl/Tk and Java interfaces of Ciao. In fact, Java interfaces can be low-level like C interfaces, allowing the Java program to directly access the Prolog data. An example of this is Jasper, the Java interface of SICStus. Foreign language interfaces tend to be complex (this can be seen by simply looking at the amount of documentation that the manuals need to dedicate to their description). We hope that having a generic interface will significantly reduce the learning curve for the user.

The design of our interface was motivated partly by our experience with ProTcXl, an earlier interface for ECL^{i}PS^e to Tcl/Tk, which we abandoned in favour of starting afresh with the generic interface. We designed the new interface to overcome some of the problems of ProTcXl: it was Tcl specific, had a complex control scheme that inexperienced programmers often got wrong, allowed Tcl commands in Tcl-syntax to be assembled and called within the ECL^{i}PS^e code, which often lead to incorrect parsing by the Tcl interpreter. In contrast, the new interface is not Tcl specific, has a much simpler control flow, and does not provide for executing Tcl commands directly within the ECL^{i}PS^e code. In addition, there are less low-level 'glue' code, so maintenance and portability should be easier.

Our interface avoided the problem of syntax conflicts between the external language and Prolog by avoiding the specification of external procedures from within Prolog code. Other ways of avoiding this problem are:

- Wrapping the components of a command with 'type-wrappers' so that they would not be mis-identified. An example of this is Ciao's Tcl/Tk interface.
- Specifying the external command in Prolog syntax, and perform on-the-fly translation into the external language. This was the approach taken with

BinProlog's Tcl/Tk interface. It offers the possibility that the command may be executed in a different external language with a different translator. However, this approach may have some problems with statically and strongly typed languages.

The Ciao Java interface has some interesting similarities to ours. The two sides are also connected via sockets, and a serialised representation of Prolog terms and Java object references is used to transport data between the two sides. Actions on both sides can be invoked via event handlers. One main difference from our interface is that the interaction between the Prolog and Java sides appear more complex than in our scheme, and requires the Prolog side to be multi-threaded. With our more simple control scheme, we do not need threads.

An alternative to providing external interfaces directly might be to use a 'middle-ware' layer like Corba [10], which will allow RPC calls, but at the price of an additional software layer, and an unnatural match of the object oriented aspects of Corba and ECL^{i}PS^e (which currently does not have an interface to Corba). The main difference between an interface specified in Corba IDL versus one in ECL^{i}PS^e EXDR would be that the IDL typing is more rigid and does not offer such a natural match with ECL^{i}PS^e/Prolog data types. Another concern is that Corba is mainly designed for network interoperability, and having unified embedded and remote versions would require the definition of a suitable subset.

Of course, there is nothing inherent in our interface that would limit it to a Logic Programming language. It should be equally applicable to Functional Programming languages. We are not aware of any direct equivalent in Functional Programming languages: although foreign language interfaces also exist for Functional Programming languages, many such interfaces seem to be targeted to C. HaskellDirect [3] allows Haskell to be interfaced to an external language, generating the necessary code to make function calls (and be called from an external language) by specifying the 'signatures' for functions in an Interface Definition Language, which is then compiled by HaskellDirect. Although it can be used to interface to different languages, it seems to be mainly targeted for C. Unlike our interface, function calls are to be made directly in the language, instead of just passing the data. An example of a non-C foreign language interface is sml_tk [4], which is an interface to Tcl/Tk for Standard ML. This interface is quite tightly coupled to Tcl/Tk, and probably cannot be used to interface to another language.

7   Conclusion

We have presented the ECL^{i}PS^e high level external language interface. Since its initial development two years ago, this interface has been used extensively by us. The Java interface is being used for all the commercial applications that Parc Technologies is developing. The interface has also been used for a development GUI toplevel for ECL^{i}PS^e, and a set of development tools that can be accessed from the toplevel and other ECL^{i}PS^e applications that use the embedded Tcl/Tk interface, and through the remote interface, the development tools can be used with any ECL^{i}PS^e process. The Tcl/Tk interface was also used in an application that IC-Parc was developing for a customer.

We believe that the interface offers advantages over previous external language interfaces in that it cleanly separates the ECL^{i}PS^e (Prolog) and the external code. This allows the interface to be generic and eases our development and maintenance efforts.

Acknowledgements

The authors gratefully acknowledge the invaluable help that our colleagues at IC-Parc and Parc Technologies for their feedback and discussions on the development of the interface. We also thank Mark Wallace for his quick feedback and comments on this paper. We also thank the referees for their comments.

A   The EXDR Format Specification

```
ExdrTerm ::= 'V' Version Term          Struct    ::= 'F' Arity String Term*
Term     ::= (Integer|Double|String|List   Variable  ::= '_'
             |Nil|Struct|Variable)     Length    ::= XDR_int
Integer  ::= 'I' XDR_int | 'J' XDR_long   Arity     ::= XDR_int
Double   ::= 'D' XDR_double             Version   ::= <byte>
String   ::= 'S' Length <byte>*         XDR_int   ::= <4 bytes, msb first>
List     ::= '[' Term (List|Nil)        XDR_long  ::= <8 bytes, msb first>
Nil      ::= ']'                        XDR_double ::= <ieee double, exponent first>
```

References

1. A. D. Birrell and B. J. Nelson. Implementing Remote Procedure Calls. *ACM Transactions on Computer Systems*, 2(1), Feb. 1984. 266
2. F. Bueno, D. Cabeza, M. Carro, M. Hermenegildo, P. López, and G. Puebla. *The Ciao Prolog System Reference Manual*, 2000. 277
3. S. Finne, D. Leijen, and E. Meijer. Calling Hell from Heaven and Heaven from Hell. In *Proceedings of the International Conference on Functional Programming*. ACM Press, 1999. 278
4. C. Lüth and B. Wolff. *sml_tk: Functional Programming for Graphical User Interfaces, Release 3.0.* 278
5. M. Meier. *ProTcXl 2.1 User Manual*, 1996. 277
6. S. Novello, J. Schimpf, J. Singer, and K. Shen. *ECLiPSe Embedding and Interfacing Manual, Release 5.2*, 2001. 268, 276
7. R. Srinivasan. *XDR: External Data Representation Standard.* Request for Comments (RFCs) 1832. The RFC Editor, Sun Microsystems, Inc., 1995. 265
8. Swedish Institute of Computer Science. *SICStus Prolog User's Manual*, 1995. 277
9. P. Tarau and B. Demoen. Language Embedding by Dual Compilation and State Mirroring. In *Proceedings of the 6-th Workshop on Logic Programming Environments, ICLP94*, 1994. 277
10. S. Vinoski. CORBA: Intergrating Diverse Applications Within Distributed Hetrogeneous Environments. *IEEE Communications*, Feb. 1997. 278
11. W3C. *Extensible Markup Language (XML) 1.0 (Second Edition)*, 2000. available at url: http://www.w3.org/YR/2000/REC-xml-20001006. 267

A Debugging Scheme for Declarative Equation Based Modeling Languages

Peter Bunus and Peter Fritzson

Department of Computer and Information Science, Linköping University
SE 581-83, Linköping, Sweden
{petbu,petfr}@ida.liu.se

Abstract. This paper concerns the static analysis for debugging purposes of programs written in declarative equation based modeling languages. We first give an introduction to declarative equation based languages and the consequences equation based programming has for debugging. At the same time, we examine the particular debugging problems posed by Modelica, a declarative equation based modeling language. A brief overview of the Modelica language is also given. We also present our view of the issues and solutions based on a proposed framework for debugging declarative equation based languages. Program analysis solutions for program understanding and for static debugging of declarative equation based languages, based on bipartite graph decomposition, are presented in the paper. We also present an efficient way to annotate the underlying equations in order to help the implemented debugger to eliminate the heuristics involved in choosing the right error fixing solution. This also provides means to report the location of an error caught by the static analyzer or by the numeric solver, consistent with the user's perception of the source code and simulation model.

Keywords: Declarative equation based language, modeling languages, bipartite graphs, graph decomposition techniques, static analysis, debugging, Modelica

1 Introduction

Simulation models are increasingly being used in problem solving and in decision making since engineers need to analyze increasingly complex and heterogeneous physical systems. In order to support mathematical modeling and simulation, a number of object-oriented and/or declarative acausal modeling languages have emerged. The advantage of such a modeling language is that the user can concentrate on the logic of the problem rather than on a detailed algorithmic implementation of the simulation model.

Equation based declarative programming presents new challenges in the design of programming environments. In order for declarative equation based modeling languages to achieve widespread acceptance, associated programming environments and development tools must become more accessible to the user.

S. Krishnamurthi, C. R. Ramakrishnan (Eds.): PADL 2002, LNCS 2257, pp. 280–298, 2002.

A significant part of the simulation design effort is spent on detecting deviations from the specifications and subsequently localizing the sources of such errors. Employment of debugging environments that control the correctness of the developed source code has been an important factor in reducing the time and cost of software development in classical programming languages. Currently, few or no tools are available to assist developers debugging declarative equation based modeling languages. Since these languages usually are based on object-orientation and acausal physical modeling, traditional approaches to debugging are inadequate and inappropriate to solve the error location problem. To begin to address this need, we propose a methodology for implementing an efficient debugging framework for high level declarative equation based languages, by adapting graph decomposition techniques for reasoning about the underlying systems of equations. Detecting anomalies in the source code without actually solving the underlying system of equations provides a significant advantage: the modeling error can be corrected before embarking on a computationally expensive numerical solution process provided by a numerical solver. The errors detected by the numerical solvers are usually reported in a way which is not consistent with the user's perception of the declarative source code.

This paper is organized as follows: Section 2 provides a very brief description of Modelica, a declarative equation based modeling language. Section 3 give some explanations why is hard to debug declarative equation based languages and in Section 4 related work is briefly surveyed. In Section 5 a simple simulation model together with the underlying declarative specification is presented. Then we present several graph decomposition techniques and our algorithmic debugging approach based on those techniques. Section 7 provides some details about the structures used to annotate the underlying equations of the simulation model, in order to help the debugger to eliminate the heuristics when multiple choices are available to fix an error. In Section 8 explanations about debugging of an over-constrained system are given. Implementation details of the debugger are given in Section 9. Finally, Section 10 concludes and summarizes the work.

2   Modelica, a Declarative Modeling Language

Before describing the difficulties of debugging a declarative equation based language, we will acquaint the reader with Modelica, a declarative equation based modeling language. This part of the paper will briefly describe the Modelica language by presenting some language features which are necessary to understand the ideas presented in the paper. Modelica is a new language for hierarchical object-oriented physical modeling which is developed through an international effort [10,7]. The language unifies and generalizes previous object-oriented modeling languages. Modelica is intended to become a *de facto* standard. The language has been designed to allow tools to generate efficient simulation code automatically with the main objective to facilitate exchange of models, model libraries and simulation specifications. It allows defining simulation models in a declarative manner, modularly and hierarchically and combining various formalisms expressible in the more general Modelica formalism. The multidomain capability of Modelica gives the user the possibility to combine electrical, mechanical, hydraulic, thermodynamic, etc., model components within the same application model. Compared to other modeling languages available today, Modelica offers four important advantages from the simulation practitioners point of view:

- Acausal modeling based on ordinary differential equations (ODE) and differential algebraic equations (DAE). There is also ongoing research to include partial differential equations (PDE) in the language syntax and semantics [20].
- Multi-domain modeling capability, which gives the user the possibility to combine electrical, mechanical, thermodynamic, hydraulic etc., model components within the same application model.
- A general type system that unifies object-orientation, multiple inheritance, and generics templates within a single class construct. This facilitates reuse of components and evolution of models.
- A strong software component model, with constructs for creating and connecting components. Thus the language is ideally suited as an architectural description language for complex physical systems, and to some extent for software systems.

The reader of the paper is referred to [17,18] and [22] for a complete description of the language and its functionality from the perspective of the motivations and design goals of the researchers who developed it. Those interested in shorter overviews of the language may wish to consult [10] or [7].

2.1 Modelica Acausal Modeling

At the lowest level of the language equations are used to describe the relations between the quantities of a model. As it was mentioned before, one of the distinctive features of Modelica is the acausal programming model. The equations should be stated in a neutral form without consideration of order of elements evaluation in the model. Modelica computation semantics does not depend on the order in which equations are written. However, this property complicates the debugging process. The acausality makes Modelica library classes more reusable than traditional classes containing assignment statements where the input-output causality is fixed, since Modelica classes adapt to the data flow context in which they are used. The data flow context is defined by telling which variables are needed as outputs and which are external inputs to the simulated system. From the simulation practice point of view this generalization enables both simpler models and more efficient simulation. The declarative form allows a one-to-one correspondence between physical components and their software representation.

2.2 Modelica Classes

Modelica programs are built from classes, like in other object-oriented languages. The main difference compared with traditional object-oriented languages is that instead of functions (methods) equations are used to specify the behavior. A class declaration contains a list of variable declarations and a list of equations preceded by the keyword `equation`. The following is an example of a low pass filter in Modelica taken from [17].

```
class LowPassFilter              class FilterInSeries
   parameter Real T=1;              LowPassFilter F1(T=2), F2(T=3);
   Real u, y (start=1);          equation
equation                            F1.u = sin(time);
   T*der(y) + y = u;                F2.u = F1.y;
end LowPassFilter;               end FilterInSeries;
```

A new class FilterInSeries can be created by declaring two instances of the LowPassFilter class (`F1` and `F2`) with different time constants and *"connecting"* them together by an equation, as it is illustrated above.

2.3 Modelica Subtyping

The notion of subtyping in Modelica is influenced by the theory of objects [1]. The notion of inheritance is separated from the notion of subtyping. According to the definition, a class `A` is a subtype of a class `B` if class `A` contains all public variables declared in the class `B`, and types of these variables are subtypes of the types of corresponding variables in `B`. For instance, the class `TempResistor` is a subtype of `Resistor`.

```
class Resistor                   class TempResistor
   extends TwoPin;                  extends TwoPin;
   parameter Real R;               parameter Real R, RT, Tref;
equation                             Real T;
   v = R * i;                    equation
end Resistor;                        v = I * (R+RT * (T - Tref));
                                 end TempResistor;
```

Subtyping is used for example in class instantiation, redeclarations and function calls. If variable `a` is of type `A`, and `A` is a subtype of `B`, then `a` can be initialized by a variable of type `B`. Note that `TempResistor` does not inherit the `Resistor` class. There are different equations for the evaluation of v. If equations are inherited from `Resistor` then the set of equations will become inconsistent in `TempResistor`, since Modelica currently does not support named equations and replacement of equations. For example, the specialized equation below from `TempResistor`:

v=i*(R+RT*(T-Tref))

and the general equation from class `Resistor` v=R*i are inconsistent.

2.4   Modelica Connections and Connectors

Equations in Modelica can also be specified by using the connect statement. The statement `connect(v1, v2)` expresses coupling between variables. These variables are called connectors and belong to the connected objects. Connections specify interaction between components. A connector should contain all quantities needed to describe the interaction. This gives a flexible way of specifying topology of physical systems described in an object-oriented way using Modelica.

For example, `Pin` is a connector class that can be used to specify the external interfaces for electrical components that have pins. Each `Pin` is characterized by two variables: voltage v and current i. A connector class is defined as follows:

```
connector Pin
   Voltage v;
   flow Current i;
end Pin;
```

The `flow` prefix is required for variables which belong to instances of connector classes and specify flow quantities, e.g. current flow, fluid flow, force, etc. Such quantities obey Kirchhoff's current law of summing all flows into a specific point to zero. Connection statements are used to connect instances of connection classes. A connection statement `connect(Pin1,Pin2)`, with `Pin1` and `Pin2` of connector class `Pin`, connects the two pins so that they form one node. This implies two equations, namely:

```
Pin1.v = Pin2.v; Pin1.i + Pin2.i = 0
```

3   Arising Difficulties when Debugging Declarative Equation Based Languages

The application of algorithmic debugging techniques [21] and generalized algorithmic debugging techniques [11] to the evaluation of structural procedural languages is an approach which has found increased applicability over the past years. However, traditional approaches to debugging are inadequate and inappropriate to solve the error location problem in declarative equation based languages. The fundamental problem is that conventional debuggers and debugging techniques are based on observation of execution events as they occur.

Even nontraditional declarative debugging techniques such as the above-mentioned algorithmic debugging method, are inadequate for equation-based languages. In order to see this, consider invoking an algorithmic program debugger [22] on a functional/logic program after noticing an external symptom of a bug. The debugger executes the program and builds a trace execution tree at the function level while saving some useful trace information such as function names and input/output parameter values. In other words, the algorithmic debugging method is dependent on the use of functions and function calls in the language. In the case of declarative equation based languages, there is no clear execution tree and the inputs and outputs are not clearly stated inside the model. In conclusion we can take a look on why errors are hard to find in a declarative equation based language:

- There is a cause-effect gap between the time or space when an error occurs and the time or space when the error becomes apparent to the programmer.
- The acausality of the language eliminates the use of program traces as a debugging guide.
- The transformation process from the declarative form to the procedural form looses or obscures a lot of model structure information, which might be useful for debugging purposes.
- Even in a highly structured system, which extensively uses hierarchical and modular simulation models, surprising events may occur because the human mind is not able to fully comprehend the many conditions that can arise mainly because of the interactions of the components.
- Debugging is in some sense harder to perform because much run-time debugging must be replaced by compile-time static checking.
- The static analysis is mostly global and it is necessary to consider the whole program.

4   Related Work

Our debugging approach follows the same philosophy as does the reduction of constraint systems used for geometric modeling in [2]. In [2] the resulting algebraic equations from a geometric modeling by constraints problem are decomposed in well constrained, over and under constrained subsystems for debugging purposes. The well constrained systems are further decomposed into irreducible subsystems for speeding up the resolution in case of reductible systems.

In [4] attention is paid to the well-constrained part of the equations by proposing new algorithms for solving the structurally well-constrained problems by combining the use of numerical solvers with intelligent backtracking techniques. The backtracking of the ordered blocks is performed when a block has no solution. This approach mostly deals with so called numerical problems, which of course are due to erroneous modeling and wrong declarative specification of the problem, and requires the use of numerical solvers. In [4] an algorithm for underconstrained problems is presented which deals with the problem of selecting the input parameters that leads to a good decomposition.

Our work and the above-mentioned related work share the common goal of providing users with an effective way of debugging constraint related problems. The above-presented related work, is extended by our approach by incorporating the ordinary and differential algebraic equations into the static analysis by manipulating the system of equations to achieve an acceptable index [19] and linking the graph decomposition techniques and algorithms to the original source code of the declarative equational based language. To our knowledge, no existing simulation system which employ a declarative equation based modeling language performs an efficient mapping between information obtained from graph decomposition techniques and the original program source code.

5   Simulation Model Example

Obviously, each simulation problem is associated with a corresponding mathematical model. In dynamic continuous simulation the mathematical model is usually represented by a mixed set of algebraic equations and ordinary differential equations. For some complicated simulation problem the model can be represented by a mixed set of ordinary differential equations (ODEs), differential algebraic equations (DAEs) and partial differential equations (PDEs). Simulation models can become quite large and very complex in their structure sometimes involving several thousand equations.

The system of equations describing the overall model is obtained by merging the equations of all simple models and all binding equations generated by the connect statements. In Fig.1 the Modelica source code of a simple simulation model consisting of a resistor connected in parallel to sinusoidal voltage is given. The intermediate form is also given for explanatory purposes. The Circuit model is represented as an aggregation of the Resistor, Source and Ground submodels connected together by means of physical ports.

6   Graph Based Representation of the Underlying Model

Many practical problems form a model of interaction between two different types of objects and can be phrased in terms of problems on bipartite graphs. The expressiveness of the bipartite graphs in concrete practical applications has been demonstrated many times in the literature [5,3]. We will show that the bipartite graph representations are general enough to efficiently accommodate several numeric analysis methods in order to reason about the solvability and unsolvability of the flattened system of equations and implicitly about the simulation model behavior. Another advantage of using the bipartite graphs is that it offers an efficient abstraction necessary for program transformation visualization when the equation based declarative specifications are translated to procedural form.

The bipartite graph representation and the associated decomposition techniques are widely used internally by compilers when generating the procedural form from the declarative equation based description of the simulation model [8,16] but none of the existing simulation systems use them for debugging purposes or expose them visually for program understanding purposes.

In the remaining of this paragraph it is our intention to give the basic definitions and some of the notation which we shall use throughout the rest of this paper.

Definition 1: A bipartite graph is an ordered triple $G = (V_1, V_2, E)$ such that V_1 and V_2 are sets, $V_1 \cap V_2 = \emptyset$ and $E \subseteq \{\{x, y\}; x \in V_1, y \in V_2\}$. The vertices of G are elements of $V_1 \cap V_2$. The edges of G are elements of E.

Definition 2: Let G be a graph with vertex set $V(G) = \{v_1, v_2, ..., v_p\}$ and edge set $E(G) = \{e_1, e_2, ..., e_q\}$. The incidence matrix of G is the $p \times q$ matrix $M(G) = | m_{ij} |$, where m_{ij} is 1 if the edge e_{ij} is incident with vertex v_{ij} and 0 otherwise.

```
connector Pin                              Flat equations
  Voltage v;                               1.     R1.v == -R1.n.v + R1.p.v
  Flow Current i;                          2.     0 == R1.n.i + R1.pi
end Pin;
                                           3.     R1.i == R1.p.i
model TwoPin                               4.     R1.i*R1.R == R1.v
  Pin p, n;                                5.     AC.v == -AC.n.v + AC.p.v
  Voltage v;
  Current i;                               5.     0 == AC.n.i + AC.p.i
equation                                   7.     AC.i == AC.p.i
  v = p.v - n.v; 0 = p.i + n.i; i = p.i    8.     AC.v == AC.VA*Sin[2*time*AC.f*AC.PI]
end TwoPin;
                                           9.     G.p.v == 0
model Resistor                             10.    AC.p.v == R1.p.v
  extends TwoPin;                          11.    AC.p.i + R1.p.i == 0
  parameter Real R;
equation                                   12.    R1.n.v == AC.n.v
  R*i == v;                                13.    AC.n.v == G.p.v
end Resistor;
                                           14.    AC.n.i + G.p.i + R1.n.i == 0
model VsourceAC
  extends TwoPin;
  parameter Real VA=220;  parameter Real f=50;
  protected constant Real PI=3.141592;     Flat Variables
equation
  v=VA*(sin(2*PI*f*time));                 1. R1.p.v     2. R1.p.i     3. R1.n.v
end VsourceAC;
                                           4. R1.n.i     5. R1.v       6. R1.i
model Ground                               7. AC.p.v     8. AC.p.i     9. AC.n.v
  Pin p;
equation                                   10. AC.n.i    11. AC.v      12. AC.i
  p.v == 0                                 13. G.p.v     14. G.p.i
end Ground;
                                           Flat Parameters
model Circuit                              R1.R -> 10
  Resistor R1(R=10); VsourceAC AC; Ground G;   AC.VA -> 220
equation                                   AC.f -> 50
  connect(AC.p,R1.p); connect(R1.n,AC.n);
  connect(AC.n,G.p);                       Flat Constants
end Circuit;                               AC.PI -> 3.14159
```

Fig. 1. Modelica source code of a simple simulation model and the corresponding flattened systems of equation, variables, parameters and constants

We consider the bipartite graph associated to a given system of equations resulting from the flattening operation of the declarative specification. Let be V_1 the set of equations and V_2 the set of variables representing unknowns. An edge between $eq \in V_1$ and $var \in V_2$ means that the variable var appears in the corresponding equation eq. Based on this rule the associated bipartite graph of the flattened system of equation from Fig. 1 is presented in Fig.2.

6.1 Bipartite Matching Algorithms

The following definitions are given:

Definition 3: A *matching* is a set of edges from graph G where no two edges have a common end vertex.

Definition 4: A *maximum matching* is the matching with the largest possible number of edges.

Definition 5: A matching M of a graph G is *maximal* if it is not properly contained in any other matching.

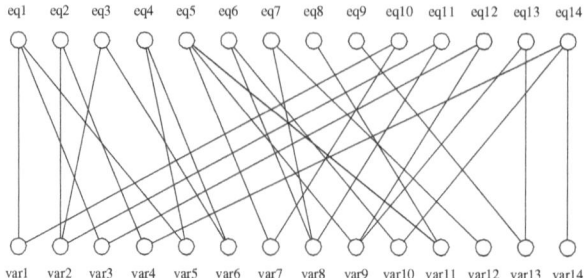

Fig. 2. The associated bipartite graph of the simple circuit model from Fig.1

Definition 6: A vertex v is *saturated* or *covered* by a matching M if some edge of M is incident with v. An *unsaturated* vertex is called a *free vertex*.

Definition 7: A *perfect matching* P is a matching in a graph G that covers all its vertices.

In Fig.3 all the possible perfect matchings of a simple bipartite graph are presented. It should be noted that a maximum matching and the perfect matching of a given bipartite graph is not unique.

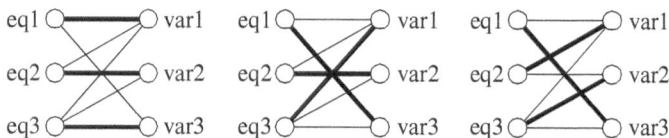

Fig. 3. An example bipartite graph with all the possible perfect matchings marked by thick lines

The equation system associated with a perfect matching is structurally well-constrained and therefore can be further decomposed into smaller blocks and sent to a numerical solver. Fig.4 illustrates the maximal matching of the associated bipartite graph to the simulation model presented in Fig.1. It is worth noting that, in this case, the maximal matching is also a perfect matching of the associated bipartite graph.

From the computational complexity point of view, the best sequential algorithm for finding a maximum matching in bipartite graphs is due to Hopcroft and Karp [13]. The algorithm solves the maximum cardinality matching problem in $O(n^{\frac{5}{2}})$ time and $O(nm)$ memory storage where n is the number of vertices and m is the number of edges.

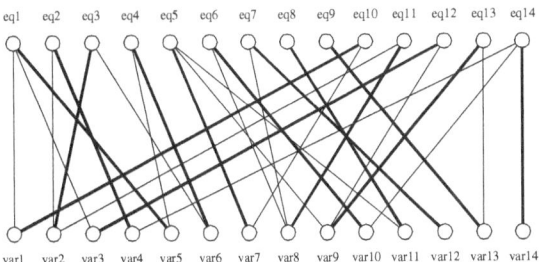

Fig. 4. One possible perfect matching of the simulation model associated bipartite graph

6.2   Dulmage – Mendelsohn's Canonical Decomposition

In this section we shall present a structural decomposition of a bipartite graph associated with a simulation model which relies on the above presented vertex coverings. The algorithm is due to Dulmage and Mendelsohn [6] and canonically decompose any maximum matching of a bipartite graph in three distinct parts: over-constrained, under-constrained, and well-constrained part.

Algorithm 1: Dulmage and Mendelsohn's canonical decomposition

---

Input Data: A bipartite graph **G**
Result: Three subgraphs: well-constrained **WG**, over-constrained **OG** and under-constrained **UG**.
begin:
    - Compute the maximum matching **MG** of **G**.
    - Compute the directed graph $\vec{\mathbf{G}}$ by replacing each edge in **MG** by two arcs and orienting all other edges from the equations to the variables.
    - Let be **OG** the set of all descendants of sources of the directed graph $\vec{\mathbf{G}}$.
    - Let be **UG** the set of all ancestors of sinks of the directed graph $\vec{\mathbf{G}}$.
    - Calculate **WG = G - OG - UG**.
end.

The *over-constrained* part: the number of equations in the system is greater than the number of variables. The additional equations are either redundant or contradictory and thus yield no solution. A possible error fixing strategy is to remove the additional over-constraining equations from the system in order to make the system well-constrained. Even if the additional equations are *soft constraints* which means that they verify the solution of the equation system and are just redundant equations, they are reported as errors by the debugger because there is no way to verify the equation solution during static analysis without explicitly solving them.

The *under-constrained* part: the number of variables in the system is greater than the number of equations. A possible error fixing strategy would be to initialize some of the variables in order to obtain a well-constrained part or add additional equations to the system.

Over and under-constrained situations can coexist in the same model. In the case of over-constrained model, the user would like to remove the over-constraining equations in a manner which is consistent to the original source code specifications, in order to alleviate the model definition.

The *well-constrained* part: the number of equations in the system is equal to the number of variables and therefore the mathematical system of equations is structurally sound having a finite number of solutions. This part can be further decomposed into smaller solution subsets. A failure in decomposing the well-constrained part into smaller subsets means that this part cannot be decomposed and has to be solved as it is. A failure in numerically solving the well-constrained part means that no valid solution exists and there is somewhere a numerical redundancy in the system.

The decomposition captures one of the many possible solutions in which the model can be made consistent. The direct solution proposed by the decomposition sometimes cannot be acceptable from the restriction imposed by the modeling language or by the modeling methodology by itself. Therefore a search through the equivalent solution space needs to be done and, check whether the equivalent solutions are acceptable.

7   Equation Annotations

For annotating the equations we use a structure which resembles the one developed in [9]. We define an annotated equation as a record with the following structure: ⟨*Equations, Name, Description, No. of associated eqs., Class name, Flexibility level, Connector generated*⟩. The values defined by annotations are later incorporated in the error repair strategies, when heuristics involved in choosing the right option from a series of repair strategies needs to be eliminated.

Table 1. An example of an annotated equation

Attribute	Value
Equation	`R1.i * R1.R == R1.v`
Name	*"eq4"*
Description	*"Ohm's Law for the resistor component"*
No. of associated eqs	1
Class Name	*"Resistor"*
Flexibility Level	3
Connector generated	no

The *Class Name* tells from which class the equation is coming. This annotation is extremely useful in exactly locating the associated class of the equation and therefore providing concise error messages to the user.

The *No. of associated eqs.* parameter specify the number of equations which are specified together with the annotated equation. In the above example the *No. of associated eqs.* is equal to one since there are no additional equations specified in the `Resistor` component. In the case of the `TwoPin` component the number of associated equations is equal to 3. If one associated equation of the component need to be eliminated the value is decremented by 1. If, during debugging, the equation `R1.i * R1.R == R1.v` is diagnosed to be an over-constraining equation and therefore need to be eliminated, the elimination is not possible because the model will be invalidated in that way (the *No. of associated eqs.* cannot be equal to 0) and therefore other solutions need to be taken into account.

The *flexibility level*, in a similar way as it is defined in [10], allows the ranking of the relative importance of the constraint in the overall flattened system of equations. The value can be in the range of 1 to 3, with 1 representing the most rigid equation and 3 being the most flexible equation. Equations, which are coming from a partial model and therefore are inherited by the final model, have a greater rigidity compared to the equations defined in the final model. For example, in practice, it turns out that the equations generated by connections are more rigid from the constraint relaxation point of view than the equations specified inside the model. Taking into account these formal rules, a maximal flexibility level will be assigned for an equation defined inside a final Modelica class. In conclusion a maximum flexibility level will be defined for the equations in the final model, followed by equations defined in partial classes and equations generated by the connect statements.

The *Connector generated* is a `Boolean` attribute which tells whether the equation is generated or not by a `connect` statement. Usually these equations have a very low flexibility level.

It is worth nothing that the annotation attributes are automatically initialized by the static analyzer, incorporated in the front end of the compiler, by using several graph representations [12] of the declarative program code.

8   Debugging of an Over-Constrained System

Let us again examine the simple simulation example presented in Fig.1 where an additional equation (`i=23`) was intentionally introduced inside the `Resistor` component in order to obtain a generally over-constrained system. The D&M canonical decomposition will lead to two parts: a well-constrained part and an over-constrained part (see Fig. 5.). Equation *"eq11"* is a non-saturated vertex of the equation set so it is a source for the over-constrained part. Starting from *"eq11"* the directed graph can be redrawn as is illustrated in Fig.6. An immediate solution of fixing the over-constrained part is to eliminate *"eq11"* which will lead to a well-constrained part and therefore the equation system becomes structurally sound. However, examining the associated annotations to the *"eq11"*:

$\langle AC.p.v == R1.pv,$ "eq11", " ", 2, "Circuit", 1, yes$\rangle$, one can note that the
equation is generated by a `connect` statement from the `Circuit` model and the
only way to remove the equation is to remove the `connect(AC.p, R1.p)` statement. But removing the above-mentioned statement will remove two equations
from the flattened model, which is indicated by the *No. of associated eqs.* =
2 parameter. One should also note the *flexibility level* of the equation is equal
to 1, which is extremely low, indicating that the equation is extremely rigid.
Therefore an another solution need to be found, namely another equation need
to be eliminated from the equation system instead of removing the equation
`AC.p.v == R1.pv`.

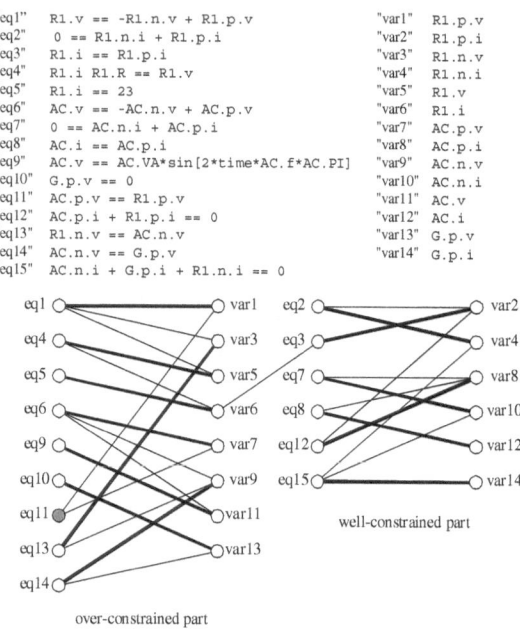

"eq1"   R1.v == -R1.n.v + R1.p.v
"eq2"   0 == R1.n.i + R1.p.i
"eq3"   R1.i == R1.p.i
"eq4"   R1.i R1.R == R1.v
"eq5"   R1.i == 23
"eq6"   AC.v == -AC.n.v + AC.p.v
"eq7"   0 == AC.n.i + AC.p.i
"eq8"   AC.i == AC.p.i
"eq9"   AC.v == AC.VA*sin[2*time*AC.f*AC.PI]
"eq10" G.p.v == 0
"eq11" AC.p.v == R1.p.v
"eq12" AC.p.i + R1.p.i == 0
"eq13" R1.n.v == AC.n.v
"eq14" AC.n.v == G.p.v
"eq15" AC.n.i + G.p.i + R1.n.i == 0

"var1"   R1.p.v
"var2"   R1.p.i
"var3"   R1.n.v
"var4"   R1.n.i
"var5"   R1.v
"var6"   R1.i
"var7"   AC.p.v
"var8"   AC.p.i
"var9"   AC.n.v
"var10" AC.n.i
"var11" AC.v
"var12" AC.i
"var13" G.p.v
"var14" G.p.i

over-constrained part

well-constrained part

Fig. 5. The decomposition of an over-constrained system

In the next step of the debugging procedure for the over-constrained system
of equations we need to introduce several definitions regarding some particular
equation subsets which have special properties from the structural analysis point
of view.

Definition 8: We call the *equivalent over-constraining equation list* associated
to a system of equations the list of equations $\{eq_1, eq_2, ..., eq_n\}$ from where eliminating any of the component equations will lead to a well constrained system
of equations.

Definition 9: We call the *reduced equivalent over-constraining equation list* the subset of equations obtained from the equivalent over-constraining equations after the language constraints have been applied.

When the size of the reduced equivalent over-constraining equation list exceeds 1, the automatic debugging is no longer available, and then the list should be output to the user by the debugger in order to solve the conflicting situation.

From the over-constrained part resulting from the D&M decomposition we can construct an algorithm to find the equivalent over-constraining list based on the associated directed graph of the over-constrained part. We describe the algorithm as follows:

Algorithm 2: Finding the equivalent over-constraining equations list

---

Input Data: An over-constrained graph **OG** resulting after D&M decomposition applied to **G**.
Result: the reduced equivalent over-constraining equation list
begin:
   - Compute the directed graph $\overrightarrow{\mathbf{OG}}$ by replacing each edge in **MG** by two arcs and orienting all other edges from the equations to the variables.
   - Find a depth-first search tree **T** in $\overrightarrow{\mathbf{OG}}$ with the root vertex being one of the sources of the directed graph $\overrightarrow{\mathbf{OG}}$.
   - Apply a strongly connected component decomposition algorithm on the undirected graph **G*** obtained by removing the last visited equation vertex in the search tree from the undirected graph **OG**.
   - **If** the number of strongly connected components is equal to 1 **then**
        add the last visited equation vertex to the reduced list.
   - Output the equivalent over-constraining equation list.
end.

An algorithm for computing the reduced equivalent over-constraining equation list is given below:

If the length of the reduced equivalent over-constraining list is equal to 1 automatic debugging of the model is possible by eliminating the equation from the simulation model without any supplementary user-intervention. Of course the history list together with the elimination is output to the user. If the length of the list is greater than 1, this means that several error fixing strategies are possible and therefore user intervention is required. The reduced list is output to the user starting with the equation which has the higher flexibility level.

In our case the set of equivalent over-constraining equations is { *"eq11"*, *"eq13"*, *"eq10"*, *"eq5"*, *"eq9"*}. *"Eq11"* was already analyzed and therefore can be eliminated from the set. *"Eq13"* is eliminated too for the same reasons as equation *"eq11"*. Analyzing the remaining equations { *"eq10"*, *"eq5"*, *"eq9"*} one should note that they have the same flexibility level and therefore they are candidates for elimination with an equal chance. But analyzing the value of the *No. of associated eqs.* parameter, equation *"eq10"* and *"eq9"* have that at-

---

Algorithm 3: Annotation based equation set reduction

Input Data: A reduced equation set taken from the output of **Algorithm 2** applied on **G**.
Result: the final reduced equivalent over-constraining equation list
begin:
    - Eliminate from the list all of the equations generated by a connect statement and for which the *No. of associated eqs.* parameter exceeds the system constraining level (no. of over-constraining equations).
    - Eliminate all the equations for which the *No. of associated eqs.* parameter is equal to 1. Add that equation to the history list.
    - Sort the remaining equations after decreasing order of flexibility level
    - Output the sorted list of equations.
end.

---

tribute equal to one, which means that they are singular equations defined inside the model. Eliminating one of these equations will invalidate the corresponding model, which is probably not the intention of the modeler. Examining the annotations corresponding to equation *"eq5"* one can see that it can be safely eliminated because the flexibility level is high and eliminating the equation will not invalidate the model since there is another equation defined inside the model. After choosing the right equation for elimination the debugger tries to identify the associated class of that equation based on the *Class name* parameter defined in the annotation structure. Having the class name and the intermediate equation form (R1.i=23) the original equation can be reconstructed (i=23) indicating exactly to the user which equation need to be removed in order to make the simulation model mathematically sound. In that case the debugger has correctly located the faulty equation in the simulation system which was previously introduced by us.

In conclusion, by examining the annotations corresponding to the set of equations which need to be eliminated, the implemented debugger can automatically determine the possible error fixing solutions and of course prioritize them. For example, by examining the flexibility level of the associated equation compared to the flexibility level of another equation the debugger can prioritize the proposed error fixing schemes. When multiple valid error fixing solutions are possible and the debugger cannot decide which one to chose, a prioritized list of possible error fixes is presented to the user for further analysis and decision. In those cases, the final decision must be taken by the user, as the debugger cannot know or doesn't have sufficient information to decide which equation is over-constraining. The advantage of this approach is that the debugger automatically identifies and solves several anomalies in the declarative simulation model specification without having to execute the system.

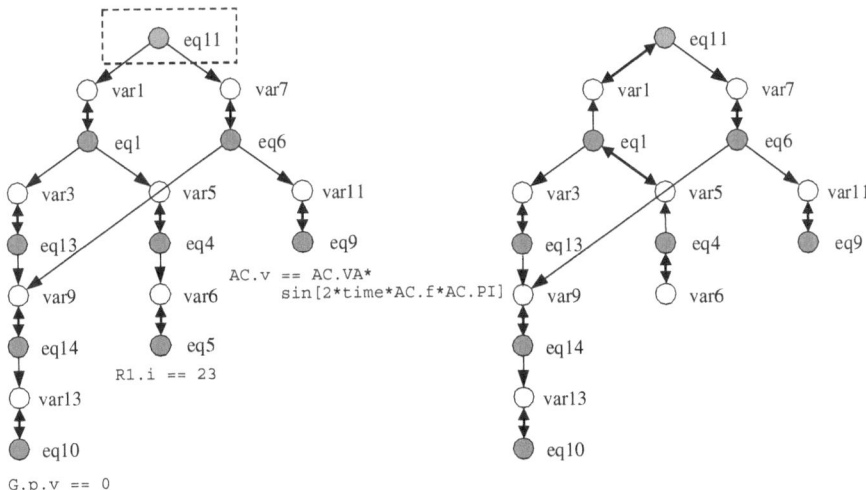

Fig. 6. An associated directed graph to the over-constrained part starting from "eq11" (left) and the fixed well-constrained directed graph by eliminating equation "eq5" (right)

9   Prototype Debugger Implementation Details

For the above presented graph decomposition techniques to be useful in practice, we must be able to construct and manage the graph representation of the declarative specification efficiently. Another important factor which must to be taken into account is the incrementality of the approach in order to accommodate incremental static analyzers to be added to the existing simulation environment of the declarative equation based language. In this section, we outline the architecture and organization of the implemented debugger attached to the simulation environment.

A prototype debugger was built and attached to the *MathModelica* simulation environment as a testbed for evaluating the usability of the above presented graph decomposition techniques for debugging declarative equation based languages. *MathModelica* is an integrated problem-solving environment (PSE) for full system modeling and simulation [14,15]. The environment integrates Modelica-based modeling and simulation with graphic design, advanced scripting facilities, integration of code and documentation, and symbolic formula manipulation provided via *Mathematica*. Import and export of Modelica code between internal structured and external textual representation is supported by *MathModelica*. The environment extensively supports the principles of literate programming and integrates most activities needed in simulation design: modeling, documentation, symbolic processing, transformation and formula manipulation, input and output data visualization.

As indicated previously, it is necessary for the compiler to annotate the underlying equations to help identify the equations and to help eliminating the heuristic involved in choosing the right solution. Accordingly, we modified the front end of the compiler to annotate the intermediate representation of the source code where equations are involved. The annotations are propagated appropriately through the various phases of the compiler, and, when an error is detected, the debugger uses them to eliminate some of the heuristics involved in the error solving process and, of course, to exactly identify the problematic equations and to generate error messages consistent with the user's perception of the source code corresponding to the simulation model. The debugger focuses on those errors whose identification would not require the solution of the underlying system of equations.

10   Summary and Conclusion

The acausality of declarative equation based languages makes many program errors hard to find. Often the error messages do not refer back to the component of the model which is the cause of the problem. The situation if further complicated by program optimizations on the source code, which eliminates or obscures a lot of the model structure information, which are useful for debugging purposes.

In this paper we have presented a general framework for debugging declarative equation based languages. The contributions of this paper are twofold: the proposal of integrating graph decomposition techniques for debugging declarative equation based languages and an efficient equation annotation structure which helps the debugger to eliminate some of the heuristics involved in the error solving process. The annotations also provides an efficient way of identifying the equations and therefore helps the debugger in providing error messages consistent with the user's perception of the original source code and simulation model. The implemented debugger helps to statically detect a broad range of errors without having to execute the simulation model. Since the simulation system execution is expensive the implemented debugger helps to greatly reduce the number of test cases used to validate the simulation model.

One extended case study, along with a number of small examples scattered throughout this paper, illustrates the main points and potential applications of the graph theory related to the proposed method for debugging of declarative equation based languages.

Acknowledgements

We thank Peter Aronsson for his contributions to the implementation of the *MathModelica* interpreter and the entire *MathModelica* team, without which this work would not have been possible. The work has been supported by *MathCore AB* and by the *ECSEL Graduate School* supported by the *Swedish Strategic Research Foundation*.

References

1. Abadi M., and Cardelli: *A Theory of Objects*. Springer Verlag, ISBN 0-387-94775-2, 1996. 283
2. Ait-Aoudia, S.; Jegou, R. and Michelucci, D. "Reduction of Constraint Systems." In *Compugraphic*, pages 83–92, Alvor, Portugal, 1993. 285
3. Asratian A. S.; Denley T. and Häggkvist R. *Bipartite Graphs and their Applications*. Cambridge University Press 1998. 286
4. Bliek, C.; Neveu, B. and Trombettoni G. "Using Graph Decomposition for Solving Continuous CSPs", *Priciples and Practice of Constraint Programming*, CP'98, Springer LNCS 1520, pages 102-116, Pisa, Italy, November 1998. 285
5. Dolan A. and Aldous J. *Networks and algorithms - An introductory approach*. John Wiley and Sons 1993 England. 286
6. Dulmage, A. L., Mendelsohn, N. S. *Coverings of bipartite graphs*, Canadian J. Math., 10, 517-534. 289
7. Elmqvist, H.; Mattsson S.E and Otter, M. "Modelica - A Language for Physical System Modeling, Visualization and Interaction." In *Proceedings of the 1999 IEEE Symposium on Computer-Aided Control System Design* (Hawaii, Aug. 22-27) 1999. 281, 282
8. Elmqvist, H. *A Structured Model Language for Large Continuous Systems*. PhD thesis TFRT-1015, Department of Automatic Control, Lund Institute of Technology, Lund, Sweden. 1978. 286
9. Flannery, L. M. and Gonzalez, A. J. *Detecting Anomalies in Constraint-based Systems*, Engineering Applications of Artificial Intelligence, Vol. 10, No. 3, June 1997, pages. 257-268. 290
10. Fritzson, P. and Engelson, V. "Modelica - A Unified Object-Oriented Language for System Modeling and Simulation." In *Proceedings of the 12th European Conference on Object-Oriented Programming* (ECOOP'98 , Brussels, Belgium, Jul. 20-24), 1998. 281, 282
11. Fritzson, P.; Shahmehri, N.; Kamkar, M. and Gyimothy, T. *Generalized algorithmic debugging and testing*. ACM Letters on Programming Languages and Systems, 1(4):303–322, December 1992. 284
12. Harrold, M.J and Rothermel, G. "A Coherent Family of Analyzable Graphical Representations for Object-Oriented Software." *Technical Report OSU-CISRC-11/96-TR60*, November, 1996, Department of Computer and Information Science Ohio State University 291
13. Hopcroft, J. E. and Karp, R. M. An $n^{\frac{5}{2}}$ algorithm for maximum matchings in bipartite graphs. SIAM Journal of Computing, 2(4):225–231, December 1973. 288
14. Jirstrand, M. "MathModelica - A Full System Simulation Tool". *In Proceedings of Modelica Workshop 2000* (Lund, Sweden, Oct. 23-24), 2000. 295
15. Jirstrand, M.; Gunnarsson J. and Fritzson P. "MathModelica - a new modeling and simulation environment for Modelica. " *In Proceedings of the Third International Mathematica Symposium* (IMS'99, Linz, Austria, Aug), 1999. 295
16. Maffezzoni C.; Girelli R. and Lluka P. *Generating efficient computational procedures from declarative models*. Simulation Practice and Theory 4 (1996) pages 303-317. 286
17. Modelica Association. Modelica - *A Unified Object-Oriented Language for Physical Systems Modeling - Tutorial and Design Rationale Version 1.4* (December 15, 2000). 282, 283

18. Modelica Association. Modelica - A Unified Object-Oriented Language for Physical Systems Modeling - Language Specification Version 1.4. (December 15, 2000). 282
19. Pantelides, C. The consistent initialization of differentialalgebraic systems. SIAM Journal on Scientific and Statistical Computing, 9(2):213–231, March 1988. 285
20. Saldamli, L.; Fritzson, P. "Object-oriented Modeling With Partial Differential Equations". In Proceedings of Modelica Workshop 2000 (Lund, Sweden, Oct. 23-24), 2000. 282
21. Shapiro Ehud Y. Algorithmic Program Debugging. MIT Press (May). 1982. 284
22. Tiller M. Michael. Introduction to Physical Modeling with Modelica. Kluwer Academic Publisher 2001. 282

Segment Order Preserving and Generational Garbage Collection for Prolog

Ruben Vandeginste[1], Konstantinos Sagonas[2], and Bart Demoen[1]

[1] Department of Computer Science, Katholieke Universiteit Leuven, Belgium
{ruben,bmd}@cs.kuleuven.ac.be
[2] Computing Science Department, Uppsala Universitet, Sweden
kostis@csd.uu.se

Abstract. We treat two important issues in heap garbage collection for
WAM-based Prolog systems. First we describe a new method for preserving the order of heap segments in a copying garbage collector. Second, we
deal with methods for (multi-)generational garbage collection; in particular we show the importance of precise maintenance of generation lines
and propose different and novel ways for its implementation. All the
methods are experimentally evaluated.

1 Introduction

High-level languages like Prolog rely heavily on heap garbage collection and a
lot of work has already been done in this area: the DEC-10 Prolog system (mid
seventies) had a garbage collector and the earliest published description of the
algorithms used in an implementation is probably [3]. An excellent account of
issues in Prolog heap garbage collection can be found in [4]. As a result, several
Prolog systems do have a heap garbage collector and it might appear that the
issue is solved completely and in a satisfactory way. However, this is not the
case: to start with, traditional heap garbage collectors are of the sliding type as
described in [3,15]. Still, there is evidence that the characteristics of a copying
collector suit Prolog better: indeed, it has been observed that the percentage
of live data in the heap is usually quite small, which makes copying a better
choice than sliding because of its intrinsic properties. On the other hand, the
first proposed copying collector for Prolog ([5]) was not *segment order preserving*
and making a copying collector also preserve the order of segments is not easy.
A heap *segment* is a part of the heap delimited by the heap pointers in two
consecutive choice points. Preserving the order of segments is desirable, as this
permits instant reclamation of a heap segment on backtracking. [9] presents an
algorithm for preserving the segment order in a copying collector: the method relies on a traversal of the stacks from old to young. Finally, although [3] describes
generational garbage collection—actually a two-generational schema—some basic problems of this schema are not discussed and moreover, lifting the schema to
multi-generational garbage collection has not been attempted nor experimented
with. In principle, the method of [9] does not combine well with generations

S. Krishnamurthi, C. R. Ramakrishnan (Eds.): PADL 2002, LNCS 2257, pp. 299–317, 2002.
© Springer-Verlag Berlin Heidelberg 2002

because of rejuvenation of heap data; see [16]. So it is worthwhile continuing research and development in the area of copying collectors that preserve the order of heap segments and that allow (multi-)generational collection.

We begin by proposing a new algorithm for preserving the segment order in a copying collector (Section 2). The characteristics of this algorithm are described and variants are discussed. An experimental evaluation is presented, by comparing it to a previously existing copying garbage collector in the context of ilProlog. We also show the advantage of preserving segment order over not doing so.

At first sight, the issues of preserving the segment order and generational garbage collection seem unrelated. However, for optimal generational collection, it is essential that generation order is preserved. In principle, generation order can be preserved without preserving segment order. A sliding algorithm keeps the order of heap cells, and *a fortiori* of segments and generations. In a copying context, preserving generation order poses the same problem as preserving the segment order. In fact, our new method for preserving segment order resulted from research in multi-generational copying collectors; see [16].

Section 3 reviews the basic two-generational schema of [3]. The problems with this approach are discussed, the need for maintaining generations more precisely is shown, and different ways to achieve this are developed. This section is largely independent of which segment order preserving method is used and thus also useful in the context of sliding collectors which are still more commonly used in Prolog systems. Small changes to the underlying abstract machine are described. This section also contains an evaluation of all the techniques and a separate account of the cost of the changes to the WAM. Section 4 concludes.

2   A New Segment Order Preserving Copying Collector

In general, a copying collector does not preserve the order of useful data. This is partly due to the fact that the root set is not ordered according to the heap pointers they contain and thus heap cells are forwarded in an *a priori* unknown order. Also, copying happens typically breadth-first (based on [7]) or depth-first with a recursive copying algorithm; neither of these algorithms retain the order of cells. This implies that a copying collector might both improve or deteriorate the locality of reference of the mutator. On the other hand, copying has the very attractive property of being linear in the size of the data to be copied, or stated in the garbage collection context: linear in the live data. In its most basic form, a sliding collector (based on [15] for instance) is linear in the size of the heap. So it follows that for a heap with a low occupancy, a copying collector performs better, unless more sophisticated techniques are used as for example in [8].

Usually, copying collectors do not have a marking phase either: by allocating a *to-space* that is as large as the *from-space*, there is the guarantee that there will be enough space to contain the copy, even in the worst case that there is no garbage. This is based on the fact that the size of a copied term is usually not larger than the original.

However, in the context of the WAM term representation, this is not true. A very simple example consists of the following goal: Y = f(X), for which in the WAM, the term Y occupies 2 cells in the heap; the self-reference X is the second one. The root set contains the variables X and Y. Assume X is copied first, and only later Y; then the total copy will contain 3 heap cells. [5] proposes a solution for this problem: start the collection with a traditional marking phase and during the copy phase forward contiguous blocks of marked heap cells together. That way, one avoids the undesirable situation that the copy is larger than the original.[1]

Since marking is needed, we might as well exploit it to our advantage. The method in [9] proposes to *count* the number of marked cells during the marking phase and use this number to reduce the memory needs: the to-space used for copying can actually be allocated only on demand and needs only be as large as to contain the surviving cells. Rather than swapping the two semi-spaces— which in many systems might not be possible as it might violate invariants (e.g., local stack and heap growing towards each other)—the to-space is immediately copied back to the original from-space and released after the copying phase. The copy-back is usually fast, and this method results in a memory usage that is in practice smaller than the factor two usually ascribed to copying collectors.

The experimental evaluation of all garbage collection schemes presented in this paper was performed on a Pentium III 866MHz with 256Mb RAM and timings are given in milliseconds. All memory sizes are given in number of cells: each cell is 4 bytes in this case. The timings include the gathering and printing of some statistics needed for producing the tables, but their impact is negligible.

2.1   The Method: Preserving the Segment Order by Counting during Marking

We make further use of the marking phase by *counting* the number of marked cells *in each segment*. To this end, before marking, we construct a list of segment counters with one counter for each segment, that are initialized to zero and a *segment list* of the heap addresses that delimit the heap segments: these addresses can be found in the choice points. Any time a heap cell is marked, a *lookup* in the segment list takes place in order to determine which segment counter needs incrementing. Thus, at the end of the marking phase, we know exactly how many surviving cells each segment contains. We can therefore allocate for each segment exactly the amount of space needed and during the copy phase copy each surviving cell to its corresponding to-space, possibly at the cost of another lookup. At the end, all *to-segments* are copied back to the original heap in the correct order.

We use a Cheney-like algorithm for copying; see [7]. This algorithm originally uses two pointers, named *scan* and *next*, which both point into the to-space. After the root set is forwarded, the copying continues until scan has caught up with next. The algorithm is easily adapted to copy segments to their corresponding to-space: each segment has now its own scan and next pointer. They are both

---

[1] No experimental evaluation of the extent to which this is a problem in practice exists.

initialized to the start of their to-space. After the root set has been forwarded, the scan pointer of each segment is made to catch up with its corresponding next pointer, at which point the copy is complete.

Compared to traditional mark&copy, the overhead of preserving the segment order in the above method comes from looking up which segment a cell belongs to. The lookup function can become a bottleneck if there are many segments. By organizing the segment list as an ordered list, the cost is $O(log(n))$ where n is the number of segments. However, note that the lookup function is called once for each live cell during marking, but during copying, it is not called for every live cell: as explained in [5], contiguous blocks of marked cells are forwarded together, so the algorithm needs to call the lookup function only once for each contiguous block of marked cells during the copying. We have experimentally confirmed that one can observe this in practice. On the programs of our benchmark set, whose characteristics are presented in detail in Section 2.3, the number of lookups during copying is typically below 7% of the number of lookups during marking; being less than 1% quite often (in **browse**, **dnamatch**, **tsp**, and **muta**) and 19% only once (in **serial**).

Preserving the order of segments allows instant reclamation of heap upon backtracking. Losing this ability can in principle lead to a considerably larger number of calls to the garbage collector. Indeed, while the segment order preserving collector might allow enough instant reclaiming to avoid a future heap overflow, the non-preserving collector blocks garbage in an older segment and a later heap overflow can be provoked. The following artificial Prolog program shows this:

```
go :- mklist(650000,L1), cp(L1).

cp(_) :- mklist(320000,_), mklist(80000,L2), use(L2), fail.
cp(_) :- mklist(340000,L3), use(L3), fail.

use(_).

mklist(N,L) :-
     ( N =:= 0 -> L = [] ; M is N - 1, L = [N|R], mklist(M,R) ).
```

Starting ilProlog with an initial heap size of 2M, triggers copying garbage collection twice when segment order is not preserved and only once when it is. Garbage collection figures are shown in Table 1. For comparison, we also give figures for performing garbage collection in SICStus 3.8.6 and Yap 4.3.0, just to show that our collectors are generally speaking of similar quality. Both SICStus and Yap are based on a sliding algorithm and started with initial heap such that they perform only one garbage collection during this small program.

Table 1. Effect of recovery on backtracking on garbage collection time

	$m\&c\_gc$	sop_gc	SICStus	Yap
total gc time	370	260	250	390
heap recovered	142147	2140138		

However note that the effect of loss of instant reclaiming is countered partly by garbage collection itself: garbage trapped in a segment by not preserving the segment order during garbage collection, will be freed in the next (major) collection. In a copying collector, this comes virtually for free, as garbage is not looked at.

2.2 An Optimization: Collapsing Segments

If there are many segments at the moment of the garbage collection, it might not be worthwhile to preserve all of them: when some small segments are collapsed into one segment, the loss of instant reclaiming is expected to be small as well. Since by collapsing segments the number of effective segments in the segment list decreases, the lookup function becomes faster. Collapsing segments can be implemented in several ways, but it is most easily visualized by merging two consecutive entries in the segment list when their combined size is less than a certain threshold.

Our implementation allows to specify this threshold at runtime or to opt for the default collapsing strategy which puts the threshold at the (initial) heap size divided by 64.

In [16] we describe another method for collapsing segments and in [18] evaluate its usefulness experimentally; more information can be found there.

2.3 Experimental Evaluation

With the experimental evaluation of this section we aim at measuring the benefits and drawbacks of preserving the segment order and with that of Section 3.6 of different schemes for generational garbage collection. In this paper, we seek neither to compare our collectors with those of other Prolog systems, nor compare collection algorithms (e.g. sliding versus copying). The system chosen to implement our new garbage collection schemes is ilProlog, a Prolog system that is heavily used for machine learning applications; see e.g. [6]. ilProlog is WAM-based; see [19,1]. Its main deviation from the WAM is that free variables are always put on the heap; see for instance [10]. Another deviation, like in many other Prolog systems, is to have separate stacks for the environments and the choice points. So we expect that our experimental results will also hold in other WAM-based systems. The advantage in doing all the experiments in the same system is that for sure the results cannot be affected by abstract machine differences, like for example term representation.

Prior to this research, ilProlog had a copying collector *ála* [5] which is not segment order preserving; we refer to it as *m&c_gc*. All other collectors we implemented are based on *m&c_gc*, in that they use basically the same marking and copying algorithm. The ilProlog compiler generates live variable maps, so the collector has precise information about which environment slots are live. No extra initialization of environment variables (as in SICStus for instance) is done nor needed. In fact, one of our starting principles was that we would not change the underlying Prolog engine to cater for garbage collection. In Section 3.4 we will deviate, albeit only slightly, from this principle.

Also, in this paper we will refrain from investigating garbage collection *policy* issues, and we will therefore *a priori* fix a (reasonable) policy: In all experiments, the ilProlog system was started with its default heap size (which is 256K cells, K = 1024) and with the size of the other stacks set high enough so that they do not need expansion. In several benchmarks the heap needs expanding: the heap size at the end of the run, together with the number of heap expansions, is indicated in the tables just below the name of the benchmark. The heap expansion policy doubles the heap size whenever more than 70% of the heap consists of live data after garbage collection. The policy must of course also take into account the amount of heap space that the caller of the collector requests to be free after the collection: this is relevant for built-in predicates like `findall/3`.[2] Expansion based on the requested amount of heap space only occurs in the **muta** benchmark. The *m&c_gc* collector collapses all segments, i.e., after a collection, there is only one non-empty segment. All other collectors are approximately segment order preserving, in that they collapse by default segments smaller than 4K cells with enough neighbouring segments so as to make the collapsed segments just larger than the threshold, but the order of the (collapsed) segments is preserved.

The small benchmarks are taken from [13].[3] The **muta** benchmark is much larger than the others and performs a typical run of an inductive learning tool written in ilProlog: without garbage collection, this application would not be able to run (this can also be seen by the number of collected garbage cells). The program uses abstract machine extensions that efficiently support query packs (see [6], also for more detail on this application) and thus does not run without changes in standard Prolog systems.

The first new collector we evaluate is referred to as *sop_gc* and implements the segment order preserving schema as described above. Table 2 shows data about *m&c_gc* and *sop_gc*, in particular for each benchmark, we show: the total number of heap cells marked during the run of the benchmark, the number of heap cells reclaimed instantly on backtracking, the number of collected heap cells; the number of collections, the total marking time, the total garbage collection time, and the total runtime of the benchmark. As mentioned, the heap size at the end of the run is also shown: it indicates the extent to which heap expansion was needed.

From the figures in Table 2 we observe the following:

- The number of collections is the same in *m&c_gc* and *sop_gc*: the potential increase in the number of garbage collections in *m&c_gc* seems not to occur in this benchmark set.

---

[2] The size of the answer list to be copied back to the heap is known before the copying starts.

[3] Some benchmarks used there are excluded because their memory usage makes them uninteresting; see [18].

Table 2. Segment order preserving vs. non-segment preserving garbage collection

benchmark		$m\&c\_gc$	sop_gc
boyer	total marked	72155851	72155851
8190K/5	heap recovered	7180443	11259478
	heap collected	67955085	67955085
	num collections	68	68
	total mark time	4470	5990
	total gc time	13630	16780
	total run time	29880	33070
browse	total marked	1380517	1380517
510K/1	heap recovered	14605833	14885921
	heap collected	968767	968767
	num collections	5	5
	total mark time	70	90
	total gc time	270	330
	total run time	9070	9160
dnamatch	total marked	4302012	4302012
254K/0	heap recovered	196609	198429
	heap collected	26915147	26915147
	num collections	120	120
	total mark time	230	330
	total gc time	710	770
	total run time	6140	6290
qsort	total marked	5308921	5308921
510K/1	heap recovered	1950205	2246796
	heap collected	5657071	5657071
	num collections	22	22
	total mark time	460	490
	total gc time	1110	1280
	total run time	2130	2340
serial	total marked	18209426	18209424
16382K/6	heap recovered	20272313	21720525
	heap collected	32104202	32104205
	num collections	9	9
	total mark time	1650	1830
	total gc time	3850	4310
	total run time	21730	22210
tsp	total marked	26909982	26909982
254K/0	heap recovered	236075	259553
	heap collected	271212807	271212807
	num collections	1146	1146
	total mark time	1210	1800
	total gc time	2690	3890
	total run time	65600	66810
muta	total marked	217118144	217120159
8190K/4	heap recovered	325879486	325879485
	heap collected	817187753	817187404
	num collections	267	267
	total mark time	14760	21490
	total gc time	46840	56340
	total run time	665060	672100

– The number of collected cells is most often the same; when it is different, the difference is small. Since garbage collections do not need to occur at the same moment during the execution of the program, such differences are difficult to predict or reason about. The total number of marked cells shows the same behaviour.
– The amount of heap recovered by instant reclaiming varies widely from 40% to 1% and is always larger for *sop_gc* in the small benchmarks; surprisingly, in the large benchmark, it is slightly smaller for *sop_gc*. One should not draw general conclusions from these figures, as the amount of heap which is recovered by instant reclaiming is highly dependent on the initial heap size and the exact backtracking behaviour of the program.
– The mark time in *m&c_gc* is always smaller than in *sop_gc*: this is caused by the overhead of the segment lookup and the counting per segment.
– The total garbage collection time in *m&c_gc* is always smaller than in *sop_gc* and the difference shows that this is not only due to the lookup cost. Indeed, we have measured for **boyer** for instance that the lookup function is called about 27 times as often during the marking phase than during copying, while the marking phase is responsible for only half of the speed loss of *sop_gc* compared to *m&c_gc*. The extra overhead is in the set up of the segment lists at each garbage collection and the maintenance of and switching between the scan and next pointers for the different to-spaces.

Additionally, we note that in *m&c_gc*, there is potentially more trailing, because segments are effectively made as old as the oldest one. However, we have hardly noticed this in the benchmark set used here; see also [18].

We can conclude that our segment order preserving method shows a varying, but non-negligible overhead over a plain mark&copy garbage collector. Preliminary attempts to speed up the lookup function further by applying heuristics show already good results, but given the philosophy of the method, counting per segment, we cannot hope for zero overhead. Still, the price is worth paying because preserving the segment order is the basis for a good generational schema that will be the subject of Section 3.

2.4   Comparison with other Methods

As far as we know, there is only one other garbage collection method for the WAM heap that preserves the segment order during major collections: it was implemented in the BinProlog system [9]. The method starts by marking in the usual way from new to old. Then the copying phase visits segments in the root set from older to younger: in this way heap segments are copied also from old to new. The algorithm delays copying recursively a heap cell that points to a newer segment, until the moment it is encountered on the trail: it will necessarily appear there because of the trailing mechanism of the WAM. It is possible that the algorithm copies a heap cell that is not reachable from an older segment, but reachable from a newer segment, to a newer segment than it belonged to originally. This makes the method of [9] only approximately segment order preserving, but this phenomenon called *rejuvenation of data* is considered good: at no extra cost, the collector manages to make some data available for instant reclaiming sooner than normally. In the context of generational garbage collection however, the same algorithm might also move data from an older to a newer *generation* and thereby make the data subject to more frequent collections, which is exactly what generational garbage collection tries to avoid. Especially in view of the fact that this rejuvenating behaviour of [9] cannot be avoided without a high cost, it is not completely clear whether it is an asset in the generational context.

Our segment order preserving collector on the other hand, does not move data from one segment to another: in fact, the traversal from older to newer segments is essential for rejuvenation. Also our method depends crucially on knowledge of the amount of live data in each segment (or generation) before the actual copying starts. Acquiring this information in a rejuvenating collector would require an extra counting pass between the marking and the copying phase, and thus impose overhead.

3   Generational Garbage Collection

Generational garbage collection [14] exploits the dynamic property exhibited by many programs that most objects die young while a small percentage lives much longer. The heap is divided into a number of areas, called *generations*, with each area containing objects of a particular range of ages. The generations are collected independently with the younger generations being collected more often. The frequent young generation (or *minor*) collections reclaim the space of the many short-lived objects without incurring the execution cost of collecting the entire heap which contains all the long-lived data (which is likely to be still useful). In addition, as reported in the literature, minor garbage collections have a much smaller working set and result in less paging. Objects which survive long enough are *promoted* (or *advanced*) to an older generation, thus avoiding the cost of repeatedly rescuing them during minor collections.

In order for generational garbage collection schemes to properly work, it should be possible to find all references from objects in old generations (those areas that are not collected) to objects in the collected ones *without* visiting the old generations. This can be achieved by the introduction of a *write-barrier*[4] which records the creation of inter-generational pointers on an *exception list* so that these pointers can be used as part of the root set during each minor collection. In imperative or functional programming languages, this results in a non-negligible additional runtime cost for supporting generational scavengers. See for instance [12] for more details about generational garbage collection.

---

[4] Also *read-barrier* methods exist.

3.1   Generational Garbage Collection in Prolog

The most commonly used virtual machine for Prolog execution, the WAM, already caters for these concepts in the form of *conditional trailing* and there is no extra cost associated with generational garbage collection provided that generations consist of a set of heap segments (as delimited by the choice points). This makes generational garbage collection well-suited for WAM-based Prolog and this property has been exploited in the form of *segmented garbage collection* (i.e., where each generation coincides with a heap segment) in the mark&slide collector of SICStus Prolog [3] which is two-generational.

Despite being well-suited for the WAM, besides segmented collection, only simple variants of generational copying garbage collection have been studied before: Touati and Hama [17] use a copying collector when the new generation consists of the topmost heap segment (i.e., when no choice point is present in the new generation), while Bevemyr and Lindgren use a two-generational scheme with an immediate promotion policy which performs well on a set of three small benchmarks [5]. The experience from another two-generational scheme, having the additional constraint that the region to collect must fit in the cache, is similar; see [13].

The introduction of a two-generational garbage collection scheme to an existing Prolog collector is attractive and, especially in the context of a sliding collector, at first sight seems easy: one just has to be able to distinguish between the old and new generation. It has been noted already in [3] and later in [5] that the most recent choice point at the moment of garbage collection can be used as a barrier between generations. In such a scheme, the trail naturally acts as an exception list and the barrier is in fact a write-barrier. This is the scheme implemented in SICStus and we will henceforth refer to this scheme of delimiting generations as *last_cp*.

3.2   A Problem with This Scheme: Determinism

Note that in a segment preserving collector, the *last_cp* scheme is imprecise in remembering generations: after a collection, the heap possibly contains data on the top segment that will be subject to collection again in the next minor collection. The problem is potentially severe in the case where a heap-allocating deterministic computation follows after garbage collection: in this case no choice point is created and data in the new generation is repeatedly collected.

This can be very simply illustrated with a program that calls the garbage collector explicitly, as in:

```
go(N) :- mklist(N,L), b(L), use(L).
b([_|R]) :- garbage_collect, b(R).
use(_).
mklist(N,L) :-
    ( N =:= 0 ->
        L = []
    ;   Term = f(1,2,3,4,5,6,7,8,9,10),
        L = [Term|R], M is N - 1, mklist(M,R)
    ).
```

All collections are now major collections, and the total running time (including garbage collection time of course) of queries ?- go(N) is $O(N^2)$, while without garbage collection, the execution of this program would be $O(N)$.

Although the above example is artificial, it clearly shows the inefficiency of *last_cp*. This inefficiency has been identified as a real problem in practice. The example also shows that without a modification, *last_cp* cannot perform what we consider proper generational collection: data is repeatedly collected and never promoted to the old generation.

A simple-minded approach to avoid this phenomenon is to set the H pointer of the most recent choice point and the **HB** register to point to the top of heap after each minor garbage collection, and perform a similar action for the environment stack. The correctness of doing so is based on the fact that any choice point can be used as a generation delimiter: in the WAM it is correct to have a topmost sequence of choice points protect the local stack and heap after garbage collection. This solution results in increased trailing, but that is acceptable as it is a necessity in any generational scheme. However, it also over-approximates segments (the topmost segments are collapsed) and consequently, when non-determinism enters the picture, some opportunity for instant reclaiming is lost. A better way to deal with this inefficiency of *last_cp* is inspired by the following observation: the above example would run in linear time even with *last_cp* if the definition of b/1 were slightly adapted to:

```
b([_|R]) :- ( garbage_collect ; fail ), b(R).
```

That is, remembering the last choice point at the moment of collection, gives precise information about the corresponding generation line. The next section exploits this idea further.

3.3 An Initial Solution: Naive Pushing of Generational Choice Points

If one is interested in preserving instant reclaiming, another scheme that avoids multiple minor collections of the same generation is to always push a *generation delimiter choice point* after each garbage collection. For the current purpose, the alternative field (the failure continuation) of the generational choice point can be set to a special instruction that on backtracking just removes the choice point and fails, but which is distinguishable from any other possible alternative.

Because of this property, one can easily avoid pushing more than one such choice point immediately after each other at the cost of collapsing collected generations; this is not an issue in a two-generational garbage collector. From the choice point chain at the moment of the next collection, it is now easy to recognize the choice point(s) which delimit consecutive generations. We will refer to this scheme of delimiting generations as *push_cp*.

We note that this solution to the determinism problem of generational garbage collection is folklore and used to be implemented in ECLiPSe but was later switched off because it seemed to cause problems.[5] It has recently been adopted in SICStus Prolog (introduced in version 3.8.5). To the best of our knowledge, the *push_cp* technique has nowhere been described nor systematically investigated. Our aim was to fill this gap and in doing so, we indeed identified some problems. We begin by describing them below; their solutions are then presented in the following sections.

In a straightforward implementation, the *push_cp* scheme of delimiting generations potentially has the following problems: A generational choice point blocks the environment that is current at the moment of garbage collection— even if this environment belongs to an otherwise deterministic clause that would be deallocated by last-call optimization—and keeps variables in this clause alive. We have observed that in such a naive implementation, these effects can result in a much larger local stack and can also worsen marking time as environments will be repeatedly traversed during the marking phase; see [18] for an example. A solution that avoids this problem is presented in Section 3.5. A second problem is that when garbage collections occur frequently (e.g. in a long-running application), a long chain of generational choice points might be created. Besides increased choice point stack consumption, it is crucial that these choice points do not result in additional complexity problems. The issue is also discussed further in Section 3.5. The last problem is related to generational choice points disappearing due to backtracking or the Prolog cut; this introduces impreciseness in remembering collected generations and subtly undermines the *push_cp* scheme. We address this issue first.

3.4   Precise Schemes of Maintaining Generation Lines

In order to have all information about which segments have been collected and how often, we maintain a *generation line list*. In practice this means that we keep a list of the contents of the pushed generational choice points together with their survival rate. This list also contains the topmost choice point at the moment of garbage collection. Based on this list, we can make a decision on which part of the heap to collect at the next garbage collection. This generation line list is also maintained on a major collection even though we do not yet exploit it for multi-generational garbage collection. As mentioned previously, backtracking (through execution of a trust instruction or one of its variants) can remove a generational choice point from the choice point stack. Instead of forgetting completely the

---

[5] Note by J. Schimpf in comp.lang.prolog, October 1999.

generation delimited by this choice point, at the moment of executing the trust, we replace the corresponding information in the generation line list, by the choice point that now becomes the topmost. This means that trust must:

> check whether the backtracked over choice point is indeed at the tail of the generation line list and if so:
> - replace the generation line list tail by the new topmost choice point information, or
> - if now the two most recent remembered generation lines are the same, pop one.

Another way to deal with disappearing generation delimiters is to employ an alternative stealing method similar in spirit to the *CHAT*-trick [11] or the actions performed in Muse [2]. More specifically, on backtracking over a generational choice point, we can promote the now top (Prolog) choice point to a generational choice point by stealing its failure continuation. We make it point to a new instruction (called gen_gc) that contains as argument the old failure continuation and an indication on where to find the generation and linking information in the list. The situation is slightly different from that in e.g. [11] because the execution of the gen_gc instruction must adapt its own operand to reflect the change of alternative of the original choice point, instead of filling a new alternative in the choice point. Also, depending on whether the stolen Prolog alternative was a retry or a trust, the action is different, which means that in a native code implementation, this solution is slightly more complicated than in an emulator.

As mentioned, the execution of a Prolog cut (!/0) can also remove a generational choice point from the choice point stack. We consequently decided to make the cut operation check the generation line list and adapt it appropriately.

Note that both changes to the implementation of the WAM—the change of the trust instruction and of cut—put a small overhead on the abstract machine which is moreover at most linear in the number of created choice points and executed cuts, thereby not changing the complexity of any execution.

Two more methods for maintaining precise generation lines seem also attractive; both must be combined with pushing a generational choice point:

1. Define choice points to have an extra field, named e.g. *gc_info*; in this field, one can store the information on whether the segment just younger than the choice point, has been collected and how often. At garbage collection time, one then just scans the choice point stack to find which is the most recent generation delimiter. This scanning imposes only a constant overhead to the collection.
2. Keep in each heap segment 1 or 2 words for similar information; these two words should be the last two of a segment and can be installed easily only for collected segments. This method is easy in a copying collector; it is slightly more complex in a sliding context.

Both methods are quite simple, but the first one increases the size of all choice points. The second one is attractive because the price is only paid at garbage collection time—except for the small space overhead in each collected heap segment.

We have implemented the methods that change the implementation of trust and cut: their combined overhead is reported in Table 4. The garbage collector using this scheme is referred to as *precise_cp*. Its implementation (as well as those of all other generational schemes) takes into account the issues described in the next section.

3.5 Refinements: Careful Handling of Generational Choice Points

Pushing generational choice points can introduce significant overheads when repeated collections make a chain of generational choice points, which delimit very small segments. The problem with such behaviour is that the choice point stack can grow very large and at each garbage collection it gets traversed three times (during marking, reversing choice point pointers, copying). Several things can be done to reduce or solve this problem. A first point to note is that there is little use in pushing a generational choice point, if the segment that it will create is smaller than a minimum segment size. In the next garbage collection cycle, such a segment would be collapsed with another segment anyway. A second point is that there is no use for a chain of generational choice points (pushed by the garbage collector), on the condition that the segments they delimit have already reached tenuring age. One could then decide to *update* an existing generational choice point after collection, instead of pushing a new one. Updating is done by replacing the heap pointer in the choice point. This prevents the building up of a chain of generational choice points. A more complex solution could allow a maximum number of chained pushed generational choice points. Currently, all our collectors that push a generational choice point, do this unconditionally, but as mentioned before, too small segments are collapsed.

In Section 3.3 we mentioned problems with a naive implementation of pushing generational choice points w.r.t. marking from the environment stack. However, one can observe that a generational choice point has no forward continuation. This means that the environment and continuation pointer in a generational choice point will never be used during execution, so it is correct to also *ignore* the generational choice points during garbage collection. During the marking phase this fits in quite easily and during the copying phase, it is also possible. However, the environments remain blocked, thereby enlarging the memory footprint of the program. However, since a generational choice point does not need to protect environments, it is sufficient to let it protect the same environments as the previous choice point. This is achieved by putting in the generational choice point as top-of-local-stack (tops) pointer the same tops as in the previous choice point. In this way, the check for last-call optimization in the deallocate instruction, which looks at the tops in the current choice point, will not fail unnecessarily. This solution does not introduce any extra problems and in ilProlog is implemented in all collectors that push generational choice points (i.e., both in *push_cp* and in *precise_cp*). However, note that in a traditional WAM with a combined environment and choice point stack, this solution will not work: environments are not only logically but also physically blocked by the generational choice point.

3.6   Experimental Evaluation

The experimental setting is as in Section 2.3 with the following additions. All generational collectors have been implemented to be multi-generational; i.e., they preserve generation information even after a major collection. The policy is kept fixed: data which has survived two collections is promoted to the part of the heap that is not collected during minor collections. This policy avoids tenuring cells that are too young at the point of a minor collection and were not yet given a proper chance to die. Thus, the collectors effectively operate in a three-generational mode. The expansion policy after a major collection is unchanged (i.e., as in the non-generational collectors). If a minor collection has recovered enough heap space for execution to continue, expansion does not occur. However, if the live data in the collected heap after a minor collection is more than 70%, the next collection will be a major one. This is done so as to avoid the case where a minor collection which does not recover enough heap space is immediately (i.e., in the same call to the collector) followed by a major collection; a scheme that visits data in the new generation twice. An alternative to forcing a major collection in the next cycle is to take advantage of the information about multiple generations and make an (informed) decision on the part of heap to collect at runtime. However, this is a policy issue, and not what we seek to investigate here.

Table 3 contains the obtained results. The measured items are as in Table 2 with the exception that heap reclaimed instantly is not shown as it is not interesting here, the number of collections is shown in the form Major+Minor, and we also present the maximum size of the choice point stack because extra choice points are pushed in some of the collectors. From the figures we observe that:

- The *last_cp* scheme indeed suffers from the problems mentioned in Section 3.2; the number of collected cells is almost always similar and the marked data is more than those marked by *sop_gc* (**boyer** is the only exception). This is partly explained by programs being mostly deterministic, but the lesson learned is that the use of an extra generational choice point is almost a necessity so as to get the behaviour expected from a generational garbage collector.
- Despite having the bigger number of collections, the *push_cp* and *precise_cp* schemes have the smaller mark and total garbage collection times and often the difference with those of *last_cp* is significant (cf. **qsort**, **tsp**, and especially **dnamatch** where the difference of marked cells is striking). Observe that this is the same set of benchmarks where these schemes result in increased choice point consumption.
- Disregarding increased choice point consumption, *precise_cp* is the overall winner. Compared with *push_cp*, it manages to lower the number of major collections and the time needed for them (cf. **boyer** and **muta**). Although the figures do not show a uniform improvement of *precise_cp* over *push_cp*, we definitely prefer *precise_cp* because it has better properties and an improved implementation of the same idea—perhaps using the alternative schemes suggested in Section 3.4—will probably beat *push_cp* consistently. Maintaining generational information precisely pays off.

Table 3. Comparison of different generational copying garbage collectors

benchmark			sop_gc	last_cp	push_cp	precise_cp
				generational collectors		
boyer	totalmarked		72155851	39053376	39053376	29020524
8190K/5	heapcollected		67955085	65710207	65710207	65710207
	maxcp		235	235	235	235
	numcollections		68+0	15+57	15+57	7+65
	totalmarktime		5990	3310	3300	2570
	totalgctime		16780	9300	9060	7080
	totalruntime		33070	25540	25410	23880
browse	totalmarked		1380517	1380496	854528	854528
510K/1	heapcollected		968767	968767	955002	955002
	maxcp		86	86	96	96
	numcollections		5+0	2+3	2+3	2+3
	totalmarktime		90	110	70	80
	totalgctime		330	350	200	210
	totalruntime		9160	9140	8990	9270
dnamatch	totalmarked		4302012	4301186	278518	278518
254K/0	heapcollected		26915147	26915147	26965789	26965789
	maxcp		68	68	1082	1082
	numcollections		120+0	2+118	2+144	2+144
	totalmarktime		330	310	10	30
	totalgctime		770	780	70	80
	totalruntime		6290	6270	5590	5690
qsort	totalmarked		5308921	5308781	3424126	3424126
510K/0	heapcollected		5657071	5657071	5602942	5602942
	maxcp		68	68	257	257
	numcollections		22+0	2+20	5+23	5+23
	totalmarktime		490	480	280	280
	totalgctime		1280	1270	820	760
	totalruntime		2340	2350	1930	1880
serial	totalmarked		18209424	29955995	29338655	29338655
16382K/6	heapcollected		32104205	36600502	31395072	31395072
	maxcp		68	68	138	138
	numcollections		9+0	7+7	7+7	7+7
	totalmarktime		1830	2750	2740	2720
	totalgctime		4310	6900	6970	6770
	totalruntime		22210	24630	25290	25890
tsp	totalmarked		26909982	26901974	635085	635085
254K/0	heapcollected		271212807	271212807	271249819	271249819
	maxcp		68	68	9544	9544
	numcollections		1146+0	2+1144	2+1352	2+1352
	totalmarktime		1800	1880	440	400
	totalgctime		3890	3980	580	580
	totalruntime		66810	66990	63720	63470
muta	totalmarked		217120159	220557488	215405117	215103780
8190K/4	heapcollected		817187404	823263687	823263644	823185989
	maxcp		7495	7495	7495	7495
	numcollections		267+0	22+250	22+250	7+265
	totalmarktime		21490	21850	21390	21190
	totalgctime		56340	58220	56780	56530
	totalruntime		672100	675640	674980	668680

Table 4. Overhead of maintaining precise generational information

benchmark	*sop_gc*	*precise_cp*
boyer	2000	2040
browse	1590	1540
dnamatch	2100	2140
qsort	1010	1010
serial	1850	1820
tsp	3020	3170

- One benchmark, **serial**, reacts differently to the series of garbage collectors than the other benchmarks: *sop_gc* is faster than the generational schemes. The reason is twofold: First of all, **serial** is deterministic,[6] but this determinacy is obtained through cuts in the split/4 predicate. Secondly, these cuts cut away almost all generational choice points as well as the last choice point that could have been used by *last_cp*. This means that the generational schemes cannot lower the number of major collections. Indeed alternating minor and major collections take place that do not recover enough garbage; note the number of collections, expansions, and the final heap size. Since we have already put some overhead in the cut operation, a possible improvement here might be to make cut preserve any pushed generational choice points. This needs further investigation.
  The same phenomenon does not occur in **qsort** because the partition/4 predicate does not provoke a garbage collection just before the cut.
- **muta** does not benefit significantly from the generational schemes. The reason is that **muta** has very small old generations, namely in the order of 1% of the total heap or even less, meaning that most effort put in maintaining generations and in performing a generational collection is wasted.

Finally, to get an idea of the overhead in the mutator due to maintaining the generation lines precisely, the six small benchmarks were run with enough initial heap so as not to trigger garbage collection (and some of them with a smaller input so as to achieve this) in *sop_gc* and *precise_cp*. Results are shown in Table 4. The difference in execution time ranges from -3% to +5% which is close to noise level. However, it is safe to conclude that the overhead of maintaining precise generational information is small and in any case acceptable in practice.

4   Conclusion

We presented a new algorithm for preserving the order of heap segments in a copying garbage collector. Within the same context, we showed how a collector can be made generational and how pushing generational choice points and maintaining precise generational information is necessary for proper generational

---

[6] **serial** is actually a version of the quick sort algorithm transforming a list into a binary search tree.

collection and leads to good performance. Most of these techniques are new and even the rare one (**push_cp**) which is folklore has not, to the best of our knowledge, been investigated systematically. It is clear that alternative schemes are possible: For example, by devoting a new field in every choice point just for garbage collection, we can associate with each segment its survival count and in this way maintain precise generation information even more easily, at the cost of increased choice point stack usage and a slightly more costly choice point creation. Whichever method is chosen, it does not seem reasonable to expect that it incurs no overhead during the execution of the mutator if one wants optimal performance. Also a formal model of generational garbage collection in the presence of backtracking seems needed, in order to provide a basis for adaptive garbage collection policies. We intend to investigate these issues.

References

1. H. Aït-Kaci. *Warren's Abstract Machine: A Tutorial Reconstruction.* The MIT Press, 1991. See also: http://www.isg.sfu.ca/~hak/documents/wam.html. 303
2. K. A. M. Ali and R. Karlsson. The Muse approach to OR-parallel Prolog. *International Journal of Parallel Programming*, 19(2):129–162, Apr. 1990. 311
3. K. Appleby, M. Carlsson, S. Haridi, and D. Sahlin. Garbage collection for Prolog based on WAM. *Communications of the ACM*, 31(6):719–741, June 1988. 299, 300, 308
4. Y. Bekkers, O. Ridoux, and L. Ungaro. Dynamic memory management for sequential logic programming languages. In Y. Bekkers and J. Cohen, editors, *Proceedings of IWMM'92: International Workshop on Memory Management*, number 637 in LNCS, pages 82–102. Springer-Verlag, Sept. 1992. 299
5. J. Bevemyr and T. Lindgren. A simple and efficient copying garbage collector for Prolog. In M. Hermenegildo and J. Penjam, editors, *Proceedings of the Sixth International Symposium on Programming Language Implementation and Logic Programming*, number 844 in LNCS, pages 88–101. Springer-Verlag, Sept. 1994. 299, 301, 302, 303, 308
6. H. Blockeel, L. Dehaspe, B. Demoen, G. Janssens, J. Ramon, and H. Vandecasteele. Executing query packs in ILP. In J. Cussens and A. Frisch, editors, *Proceedings of the 10th International Conference on Inductive Logic Programming*, number 1866 in LNAI, pages 60–77, Springer, July 2000. 303, 304
7. C. J. Cheney. A nonrecursive list compacting algorithm. *Communications of the ACM*, 13(11):677–678, Nov. 1970. 300, 301
8. Yoo C. Chung, Soo-Mook Moon, Kemal Ebcioglu, and Dan Sahlin. Reducing sweep time for a nearly empty heap. In *Proceedings of the ACM SIGPLAN Symposium on Principles of Programming Languages*, pages 378–389. ACM Press, Jan. 2000. 300
9. B. Demoen, G. Engels, and P. Tarau. Segment order preserving copying garbage collection for WAM based Prolog. In *Proceedings of the 1996 ACM Symposium on Applied Computing*, pages 380–386. ACM Press, Feb. 1996. 299, 301, 306, 307
10. B. Demoen, P.-L. Nguyen. So many WAM variations, so little time. In J. Lloyd, editor, *Proceedings of Computational Logic - CL2000, First International Conference*, number 1861 in LNAI, pages 1240–1254, Springer, July 2000. 303

11. B. Demoen and K. Sagonas. CHAT is Θ(SLG-WAM). In H. Ganzinger, D. McAllester, and A. Voronkov, editors, *Proceedings of the 6th International Conference on Logic for Programming and Automated Reasoning*, number 1705 in LNAI, pages 337–357. Springer, Sept. 1999. 311

12. R. Jones and R. Lins. *Garbage Collection: Algorithms for automatic memory management*. John Wiley, 1996. 307

13. X. Li. Efficient memory management in a merged heap/stack Prolog machine. In *Proceedings of the 2nd ACM SIGPLAN Conference on Principles and Practice of Declarative Programming (PPDP'00)*, pages 245–256. ACM Press, Sept. 2000. 304, 308

14. H. Lieberman and C. Hewitt. A real-time garbage collector based on the lifetimes of objects. *Communications of the ACM*, 26(8):419–429, June 1983. 307

15. F. L. Morris. A time- and space-efficient garbage compaction algorithm. *Communications of the ACM*, 21(8):662–665, Aug. 1978. 299, 300

16. K. Sagonas and B. Demoen. From (multi-)generational to segment order preserving copying garbage collection for the WAM. K. U. Leuven CW report 303, October 2000. See
http://www.cs.kuleuven.ac.be/publicaties/rapporten/cw/CW303.abs.html
300, 303

17. H. Touati and T. Hama. A light-weight Prolog garbage collector. In *Proceedings of the International Conference on Fifth Generation Computer Systems (FGCS'88)*, pages 922–930. OHMSHA Ltd. Tokyo and Springer-Verlag, Nov./Dec. 1988. 308

18. R. Vandeginste and B. Demoen. The implementation of a new segment preserving and/or (multi-)generational copying garbage collection for the WAM and its approximation. K. U. Leuven CW report 319, July 2001. See also:
http://www.cs.kuleuven.ac.be/publicaties/rapporten/cw/CW319.abs.html
303, 304, 306, 310

19. D. H. D. Warren. An abstract Prolog instruction set. Technical Report 309, SRI International, Menlo Park, U. S. A., Oct. 1983. 303

Exploiting Efficient Control and Data Structures in Logic Programs

Rong Yang[1] and Steve Gregory[2]

[1] School of Computer Science, University of the West of England, UK
Rong.Yang@uwe.ac.uk
[2] Department of Computer Science, University of Bristol, UK
steve@cs.bris.ac.uk

Abstract. One of the distinguishing features of declarative languages is the separation of control and logic. Ideally, this allows us to improve the efficiency of an algorithm by changing only the control but not the logic. In this work, we investigate new control strategies and data structures in logic programs. Our main focus is on logic programs which contain dependent non-determinate computation.

We propose a new type of finite domain variables, which allow any kind of compound terms in their domain. A compound term in the domain may contain unbound variables which can also become domain variables, leading to *nested domain variables*. With nested domain variables, we can represent the Cartesian product of several domains as a tree structure. That is, disjunctive constraints stores can be constructed as a nested domain. The consistency of a nested domain can then be checked simultaneously by different parts of computations. Two forms of lookahead are used to perform the consistency checking: deep lookahead and shallow lookahead. It is hoped that, with our lookahead techniques and nested domains, many unnecessary or-branches can be pruned at an early stage. We have tested our ideas by an experimental implementation under SICStus Prolog, and obtained very encouraging results.

Keywords: logic programming, constraints satisfaction, sequence comparison

1 Introduction

The starting point of this work was when we were tackling some unsolved problems left in the Extended Andorra Model [3,15]. A very simple example given by David Warren [5,15] attracted our attention.

The example used a Prolog program sublist(S,L) listed below, which holds if S is a sublist of the given list L.

```
sublist([],[]).
sublist([X|L],[X|L1]):- sublist(L,L1).
sublist(L,[_|L1]):- sublist(L,L1).
```

S. Krishnamurthi, C. R. Ramakrishnan (Eds.): PADL 2002, LNCS 2257, pp. 318–331, 2002.
© Springer-Verlag Berlin Heidelberg 2002

It is a typical list manipulation program which can be found in many Prolog textbooks. Why is it interesting? Consider the following query:

```
?- sublist(L,[c,a,t,s]), sublist(L,[l,a,s,t]).
```

The query returns all common sublists between the two input lists, `[c,a,t,s]` and `[l,a,s,t]`.

It is well known that finding the longest common subsequence of N sequences is a very important problem with many applications such as molecular biology and speech processing, and many algorithms have been studied [10].

With the above Prolog program, we can extract the common subsequence of any number of sequences, such as,

$s_{11}, s_{12}, \dots s_{1n},$
$s_{21}, s_{22}, \dots s_{2n},$
......
$s_{m1}, s_{m2}, \dots s_{mn},$
by simply joining `sublist/2` goals. That is,
```
?- sublist(L,[s11,s12,...s1n]),
   sublist(L,[s21,s22,...s2n]),
   ...
   sublist(L,[sm1,sm2,...smn]).
```
This is a pure declarative way to describe the problem of finding common subsequences, simple and concise. Unfortunately, it is a very inefficient Prolog program.

One of the distinguishing features of declarative languages is the separation of control and logic. Ideally, this allows us to improve the efficiency of an algorithm by changing only the control but not the logic. Can we really achieve this? What is the new control needed for this particular type of program?

If these sound rather narrow questions, generally speaking, the programs which contain dependent non-determinate computations are our major concern. *Non-determinate* computation is the opposite of *determinate* computation. A computation is determinate if it can terminate without making any choicepoint. Otherwise, the computation is non-determinate. The `sublist/2` is a typical example of a non-determinate computation. The word *dependent* refers to the fact that there are some variables shared between computations.

For dependent non-determinate computations, Prolog's left-to-right and depth-first control faces a serious problem. That is, the chronological backtracking used in Prolog often leads to much unnecessary repeated computation. For instance, in the above `sublist` example, the goal `sublist(L,[c,a,t,s])` produces the sublist in the following order: L=`[]`, `[c]`, `[c,a]`, `[c,a,t]`, ... Although we know that, if `[c]` is not a sublist of `[l,a,s,t]`, then any list beginning with c, i.e. `[c|_]`, cannot be a sublist of `[l,a,s,t]`, Prolog cannot "see" this. Therefore, `sublist([c,a],[l,a,s,t])`, `sublist([c,a,t],[l,a,s,t])` etc. all have to be tested.

There are other logic programming systems which provides more sophisticated control than Prolog. In constraint logic programming systems, checking the consistency of constraints is always done before each labeling (i.e. choice point making). In the Andorra-I system [2,12,11,17], determinate goals are always eagerly executed before creating a choice point. In those systems, Prolog's left-to-right execution order no longer exists between determinate computations. However, non-determinate computations are still executed in a traditional fashion, i.e. left-to-right, depth-first with chronological backtracking.

In this work, we investigate new control strategies and data structures in logic programs. Our main focus is on logic programs which contain dependent non-determinate computation.

We propose a new type of finite domain variables, which allow any kind of compound terms in their domain. A compound term in the domain may contain unbound variables which can also become domain variables, leading to *nested domain variables*.

With nested domain variables, we can represent the Cartesian product of several domains as a tree structure. Note that, unlike computation trees, this is a tree of data, not a tree recording the states of execution, choice points, etc. Why and when do we need this kind of data tree? It is especially useful when there are several non-determinate computations that share a set of variables. Having a tree to represent the solution space of shared variables, several non-determinate computations can construct the tree together. The consistency of these variables can be checked simultaneously by different part of computations. Therefore, many unnecessary or-branches can be pruned at an early stage.

We have tested our idea by an experimental implementation under SICStus Prolog. The result is encouraging.

The rest of the paper is organized as follows. Section 2 is the longest section. It defines and explains nested domain variables. It also presents our lookahead procedure. In Section 3, implementation issues are discussed. Section 4 presents some test results. Related work is discussed in the following section, while the final section gives some conclusions.

2   Nested Domain Variables

2.1   Definitions

Definition 1. A *nested domain variable* X is a variable with a finite domain D, in which both constants and structures are allowed. That is,

D = $\{v_1, ..., v_n\}$ where v_i can be either a number, an atom, or a structure.

As with the traditional finite domain variables of CLP system, the semantics of X with a domain D is that all possible solutions of X must be in D. As you can see from the definition, nested domain variables are just the same as CLP's finite domain variables except that CLP's domain variables only allow integers.

Definition 2. A finite domain D is *nested* if there is at least an open-structure (i.e. a structure with unbound variables) $v_i \in$ D and at least one of the variables in v_i is a domain variable.

For example, when D1 = $\{p(a),q(X)\}$, and X is a nested domain variable with a domain D2 = $\{a,b\}$, we say D1 is a nested domain. It actually represents the domain {p(a),q(a),q(b)}. In order to clearly show how the nested domain grows, we use a functor "dvar" to indicate a layer of a domain. That is, in the above example, the variable D1 can be represented as

D1 = dvar(p(a), q(dvar(a,b))).

Having defined our new domain variable, we discuss how to initially generate them and how to perform consistency checking. As we know, domain variables are statically declared in CLP. We can use the same approach to declare our domain variables. However, in addition to using static declarations, we want domain variables to be dynamically created. For example, if there is a program

int(0). int(1). int(2). int(3).

then evaluating the goal ?- int(X) could make X a domain variable with the domain {0,1,2,3}. The idea of dynamically changing an unbound variable to a domain variable was originally suggested by R. Bahgat [1]. The focus in [1] was to use compile-time analysis techniques to extract domain information. The technique relied on the data appearing in the heads of clauses. Here we take this idea further. It is not only based on head unification, but also uses local computation to collect domain information. For example, we want

?- member(X, [a,b,c]).

to return X a domain {a,b,c}. Another important development is that our domain variables have the unique feature that a domain can be nested inside another domain.

We apply a run-time procedure to collect the domain information for a given variable. If the variable is unbound, it will become a domain variable. If the variable is already a domain variable, then consistency checking will be performed. The idea is similar to the lookahead technique [14] except that lookahead is used to reduce the existing domain of a variable while we also use it to generate a domain for an unbound variable.

Here we borrow the term *lookahead* to name our run-time checking procedure as they are very similar to each other. But, with nested domain variables, we need to further distinguish two different kinds of lookahead. They are defined as the following.

Definition 3. When a domain contains structures, a *deep lookahead* looks down to all levels of structures.

Definition 4. A *shallow lookahead* only checks one level of structures.

To explain the difference between deep and shallow lookahead, we use the following program. It defines the relation between a list L and a list which is the same as L expect that one element is removed.

```
delete_1_element([H|R], R).
delete_1_element([H|R], [H|T]):- delete_1_element(R,T).
```

A deep lookahead on ?- delete_1_element([1,2,3,4],X) returns X a domain {[2,3,4],[1,3,4],[1,2,4],[1,2,3]}. A shallow lookahead on the same goal returns X a much smaller domain {[2,3,4],[1|_]}.

Of course, if a domain only contains constants, there is no difference between deep and shallow lookahead.

2.2   How Nested Domain Variables Work

We now go back to the `sublist` example. Using this example, we explain how nested domain variables help us to improve efficiency.

Recall that the goal list is

`?- sublist(L,[c,a,t,s]), sublist(L,[l,a,s,t]).`

Under Prolog's left-right and depth-first execution order, the first goal generates a sublist of a given list, and the second goal tests whether the sublist is also a sublist of another given list. The number of possible sublists of a given list L is 2^n where n is the length of L. Therefore, the time complexity of the above query is $O(2^n)$ under Prolog's control strategy.

Back to the classical question: can we improve the efficiency of an algorithm by changing only the control but not the logic? In the above example, if two goals can be executed concurrently (or in a coroutined way), then the test goal (i.e., the second `sublist`) can run eagerly to prevent unwanted sublists at an early stage.

Our solution is to apply shallow lookahead on both goals. In this way, the first goal, `sublist(L,[c,a,t,s])` only searches sublists with the first element filled. That is it only looks for possible bindings to the head of the sublist. As a result of shallow lookahead on goal `sublist(L,[c,a,t,s])`, it returns L a domain $\{[], [c|\_], [a|\_], [t|\_], [s|\_]\}$. That is,

`L = dvar([],[c|_],[a|_],[t|_],[s|_])`

During the shallow lookahead, the consistency checking on the second clause

`(i.e., sublist([X|L],[X|L1]):- sublist(L,L1))`

stops after the head unification because the body goal no longer contributes to the first element of the list.

Now we have a domain which contains some open-ended lists. This is a good place to explain our notion of nested domain variables in more detail. A nested domain variable has incomplete structures in its domain and these incomplete structures may contain domain variables. Going back to the example, all tail variables in the domain can become domain variables. This happens if a new shallow lookahead is applied again, but targeted on the next element of the list. The domain of L would be updated to

```
L = dvar([],[c|dvar([],[a|_],[t|_],[s|_])],
            [a|dvar([],[t|_],[s|_])],
            [t|dvar([],[s|_])],
            [s])
```

So far, we have ignored the second `sublist` goal in the query. Its shallow lookahead should be performed "simultaneously" with the first goal. Assuming that the lookahead switches between the two goals, the solutions for the variable L is produced in the following steps:

Step 1   shallow lookahead on the first goal at the first element

`L = dvar([],[c|_],[a|_],[t|_],[s|_])`

Step 2. shallow lookahead on the second goal at the first element

L's domain obtained from step 1 is immediately visible from the second goal. Thus, this lookahead is actually to test existing domain values and remove inconsistent ones, if any. The following is L's newly reduced domain:

```
L = dvar([],[a|_],[t|_],[s|_])
```

Step 3. shallow lookahead on the first goal at the second element

```
L = dvar([], [a|dvar([],[t|_],[s|_])], [t|dvar([],[s|_])], [s])
```

Step 4. shallow lookahead on the second goal at the second element

```
L = dvar([], [a|dvar([],[t|_],[s|_])], [t], [s])
```

Step 5. shallow lookahead on the first goal at the third element

```
L = dvar([], [a|dvar([],[t|dvar([],[s|_])],[s])], [t], [s])
```

Step 6. shallow lookahead on the second goal at the third element

```
L = dvar([], [a|dvar([],[t],[s])], [t], [s])
```

This represents the final solution for L. That is,

L can be either [], [a], [a,t], [a,s], [t], or [s].

From this example, we have shown how a nested domain variable is used as a communication channel between non-determinate computations.

2.3   Relation to Consistency Techniques

Consistency techniques are contsraint algorithms that reduce the search space by removing impossible values from variable domains. It is based on notions of arc consistency and path consistency [7], where a constraint satisfaction problem is represented as a network of binary relations. A relation, i.e., an arc in the network, arc(X,Y) is consistent if and only if, for any value x in X's domain, there is a value y in Y's domain such that arc(x,y) holds. A network is arc-consistent if and only if every arc in the network is consistent. Many algorithms to remove arc inconsistent values have been studied [4,6].

Although arc consistency checking can remove many values from variable domains, it cannot guarantee that the whole network is consistent. As an example consider the network of Fig. 1. When we check every "$\neq$" relation, all values are satisfied, but the network actually has no solution. This is a typical example of a network with arc consistency but not *path consistency*

A path through arc(X1,X2), arc(X2,X3), ..., arc(Xn-1,Xn) is consistent if and only if, for any value x_1 in X1's domain, there is a sequence of values x_2, x_3, ..., x_n in the domains of X2, X3, ... Xn, respectively such that arc(x_1,x_2), arc(x_2,x_3), ... arc(x_{n-1},x_n) are simultaneously satisfied. A network is path consistent if and only if every path in the network is consistent. Obviously, the path consistency checking is much more expensive than arc consistency checking [8]. Therefore, it has not been implemented in CLP systems.

We believe that nested domain variables can be effectively used to implement path consistency algorithms. Instead of keeping domain information for each variable separately, we can group a set of variables together as a single structure.

For instance, in the above example (Fig. 1), we can put variables X, Y, and Z into a list L, i.e., L = [X,Y,Z]. Now assume that a program all_different(L) is already defined, which makes sure every pair of elements in the list L are

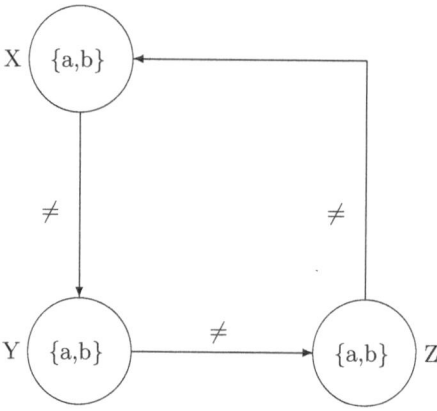

Fig. 1. A network showing path inconsistency

different. Then, we can perform a path consistency checking by applying a deep lookahead on ?- all_different(L). This lookahead will of course return an empty domain for L, indicating that the goal is not solvable.

If we make a change to the network in Fig. 1, letting X, Y, and Z have a bigger domain {a,b,c}, then the network is path consistent. Using an original path consistency algorithm we would obtain a "yes" answer. But, using our nested domains, we do not only have a "yes" answer, but also receive a solution tree as below:

```
        /-- b -- c         i.e. L = dvar(
      a
     / \-- c -- b                   [a|dvar([b,c],
    /                                       [c,b])],
   /     /-- a -- c
  L =   -- b                         [b|dvar([a,c],
  ~    \-- c -- a                           [c,a])],
  ~
  ~ /-- a -- b                   [c|dvar([a,b],
    c                                   [b,a])]
     \-- b -- a                  )
```

2.4   Another Example: Job Scheduling

We believe that the nested domain variable is a useful data structure not only for Prolog-type programs but also for finite domain constraint programs. We use a simple job scheduling example to explain this in more detail.

Suppose that two jobs need to be scheduled. Finite domain variables St1 and St2 represent the start times (non-negative integers) of job1 and job2. We know that job1's duration is 5 hours and job2's duration is 2 hours. Assume that the two jobs have to be done within a maximum duration of 7 hours. These can be expressed by the inequalities:

St1+5 =< 7 and St2+2 =< 7.

At this point, after evaluating these inequalities, we have two reduced domains:

St1 $\in$ {0,1,2} and St2 $\in$ {0,1,2,3,4,5}.

If we further assume that the two jobs have to share the same resource, this can be expressed by a **non_overlap** constraint:

non_overlap(St1, St2):- St1+5 =< St2; St2+2 =< St1.

That is, we either do not start job2 until job1 has finished or do not start job1 until job2 has finished.

The **non_overlap** constraint consists of two disjunctive inequalities, so it cannot be checked determinately. With current constraint programming techniques, this can be handled by an arc consistency algorithm [7,14], which enumerates the domain values of St1 and St2 and removes impossible values from the two domains. In our example, after we test **non_overlap** constraints using lookahead, we can discover that there are only two possible pairs:

(St1 = 0, St2 = 5), or

(St1 = 2, St2 = 0).

In current constraint programming systems, the result from the arc consistency algorithm reduces each domain individually. Therefore, we now have

St1 $\in$ {0,2} and St2 $\in$ {0,5}.

Although this has greatly reduced both domains, a much tighter constraint,

(St1,St2) $\in$ {(0,5), (2,0)}

has been lost.

By introducing nested domain variables, we can represent several domains together as a tuple: St1 and St2 can be paired as S = (St1,St2). Then, after the local search on the **non_overlap** constraint, we will obtain:

S = dvar((0,5),(2,0)).

No information is lost. non_overlap(St1,St2) will terminate, whereas with two separate domains the goal non_overlap(St1,St2) would have to suspend.

One might question whether it is really necessary to maintain this kind of relation between several domains. To further demonstrate its advantage, let us assume that in the above example a new constraint, St1 =< St2, is imposed later on. If the system knows

St1 $\in$ {0,2} and St2 $\in$ {0,5},

the constraint St1 =< St2 cannot discover any impossible values. However, if the system knows

(St1,St2) $\in$ {(0,5), (2,0)}

it can immediately remove the impossible pair (2,0) and produce determinate bindings for St1 and St2.

Another question is whether it is practical to use a nested domain variable combining many variables together. A nested domain might grow exponentially. During our experiment (Section 4), we tested a program which produces a deeply nested domain whose size is greater than 2^{16}. It did increase the running time, but did not run of memory.

3 Implementation

We are interested to see whether our idea is feasible. As a first experiment, we decided to use SICStus Prolog, a well established Prolog system, rather than develop a low-level implementation. SICStus Prolog has a powerful coroutine facility and provides a special library, the attribute variable library [13], which allows us to define destructively assigned variables.

3.1 Program Transformation

For programs which require lookahead, two different sets of code are needed: the original Prolog code for non-determinate execution (when necessary) and the new code for lookahead. That is, we need to transform an ordinary Prolog program into different code such that the lookahead can be performed.

First of all, some kind of declarations are introduced to let user to indicate which program can be executed as a lookahead procedure and in what conditions. For example,

```
:- deep_lookahead p(X,g) with target(X).
```

declares that the program p/2 can be executed in a deep lookahead fashion when its second argument is a ground term, and the variable needed to be looked ahead is the first argument of the goal. Another example is

```
:- shallow_lookahead p(d,X) with target(X).
```

It says that the program p/2 can be executed in a shallow lookahead fashion as long as its first argument is a domain variable, and the variable needed to be looked ahead is the second argument of the goal.

We now discuss how to compile a program into its lookahead form. For the deep lookahead, it is rather straightforward. All we need to do is check whether the lookahead condition is met and, if so, we check whether the targeted variable is already a domain variable or still a free variable. This leads to two different types of code: in the first case we do consistency checking, while in the second case we simply use **findall** or **bagof** to collect all solutions and return them as a domain.

For shallow lookahead, we need to generate special code which performs lookahead incrementally. Going back to our **sublist** example, provided the compiler knows that the first element in the first argument is the target, it can identify that the body goal in the second clause should be stopped. Similarly, it can also identify that the recursive goal in the third clause must be carried on because the head unification does not produce any output on the first argument. The following is the transformed **sublist/2** used for shallow lookahead:

```
sublist_s_lk([],[], true).
sublist_s_lk([X|L],[X|L1], sublist_s_lk(L,L1,_)).
```

```
sublist_s_lk(L,[_|L1], SusGoal):-
        sublist_s_lk(L,L1, SusGoal).
```

Comparing this code with the original code, we can see that they are almost identical except for the following two changes. First, we added an extra argument (the third argument) which returns the suspended goals, if any. In other words, the new argument indicates where the computation should continue when the next local search is performed. Another change is that the recursion in the second clause is removed but is returned as a suspended goal.

3.2 Implementing Domain Variables

Domain variables are implemented by using attributed variables [13] provided in SICStus Prolog. An attributed variable can be associated with arbitrary attributes. Moreover, these attributes can not only be updated but also are backtrackable.

We have already shown how nested domain variables are structured in the sublist example. As well as a set of values, our domain variable can also be associated with some suspended goals, so we have an extra slot to store this. The actual domain variable in our implementation has the following structure:

```
dvar((Value1,GoalList1),(Value2,GoalList1), ...)
```

Another issue is how to deal with unification after introducing nested domain variables. Unification between two nested domain variables is carried out by performing an intersect operation recursively along the nested structure. Unification between a nested domain variable and a ground term is also very easy. We simply follow the ground term to trim out all incorrect values in the nested domain. The tedious part is to unify a nested domain with a non-ground structure. For example, consider a domain variable

```
L = dvar([2+dvar([4,5]),3+dvar([6,7])]),
```

which represents four possible expressions:

```
2+4, 2+5, 3+6, and 3+7
```

When L is unified with X+Y, we can produce

```
X = dvar([2,3]) and Y = dvar([4,5,6,7]).
```

but we cannot terminate this unification at this point because, if either X, Y, or L changes its domain, we need to check it again. That is, we have to keep L=X+Y suspended and resume it when the domain of any of the variables is reduced.

4 Some Results

4.1 Tested Programs

We have developed code to support nested domain variables, and tested it with a few simple programs: three database examples and three string comparison examples. At this stage, our compiler is not yet implemented. Therefore, the transformation is actually done by hand.

The database examples are from the world geography database. database1 (in Fig. 2) is the query

```
?- ocean(X), borders(X,C1), country(C1), in(C1,africa),
   borders(X,C2), country(C2), in(C2,asia).
```

We assume that the following lookahead declarations are used:
```
:- deep_lookahead borders(X,g) with target(X).
:- deep_lookahead borders(g,X) with target(X).
:- deep_lookahead in(X,g) with target(X).
:- deep_lookahead in(g,X) with target(X).
```
This a typical example where intelligent backtracking is needed. With chronological backtracking, much unnecessary computation takes place. A "Prolog solution" [16] is to annotate the query into the following form:

```
?- ocean(X),
   {borders(X,C1), country(C1), in(C1,africa)},
   {borders(X,C2), country(C2), in(C2,asia)}.
```

where "{...}" means commit to the first solution found. This version would lead to a much smaller number of computation steps. Here, we took the constraint programming approach. That is, we use finite domain variables and consistency checking techniques to avoid unnecessary backtracking.

The other two database examples are similar to database1. Note that, in our testing, the comparison is done between our approach and the original Prolog program.

Three string comparison benchmarks are all based on the sublist/2 program. protein_seq takes three protein sequences and searches for common subsequences between them. reverse_list is to find common sublists between two reversed list, while same_list is a query which looks for all common sublists between two identical lists.

4.2 Results

The machine used for testing is a Pentium II PC. All programs were compiled and run under SICStus 3.6 (Linux version). As database queries are quite fast, we tested them by repeating 10 runs as well as by a single run.

The results are summarized in Fig. 2.

As the above table shows, apart from the last one, all transformed programs are much faster than the original programs. We know that for the first five programs the search space (i.e., the number of inferences) is greatly reduced under our approach. However, we were not sure whether the overhead for supporting our consistency technique and nested domain variables is too big to make it feasible. The above results are very encouraging.

We deliberately chose the last example, same_list, because it is a special case where our approach cannot provide any advantage. In its original program, all possible sublists (a total of 2^{16}) are generated and tested one by one through backtracking. Under our approach, a nested domain variable has to be constructed, comprising a tree with 2^{16} nodes. This requires huge memory space,

	Prolog	our approach
database1	110	30
same prog. 10-run	580	150
database2	20	10
same prog. 10-run	120	55
database3	50	20
same prog. 10-run	310	135
protein_seq	13510	1910
reversed_list	2780	20
same_list	10370	29500

Fig. 2. Test Results (time in millisecond)

which is why its run time ends up about 3 times slower. Programs like same_list are very rare, so we believe that the result here does not really represent a draw-back.

5 Related Work

The idea of using consistency techniques has a long history and has been applied in many areas. Within the logic (and constraint) programming discipline, a widely applied form of consistency technique is *lookahead* [14], based on the classic idea of arc consistency [7]. The work presented here is similar to traditional lookahead in all but a few respects. Under constraint programming, lookahead is used to reduce existing domains. In our case, we also use it to generate a domain for an unbound logical variable as well as to restrict a domain. Most importantly, we aim to achieve a general form of lookahead which can not only check arc consistency but also incrementally check path consistency.

In AKL implementations [5,9], a form of local search is provided, which is similar to our proposed deep lookahead in many respects. Perhaps the main difference is at the language level: AKL's local search has to be explicitly defined by using deep guards, while we aimed to make it more flexible.

In our proposal, a variable can be dynamically changed to a domain variable. A similar idea has also been proposed in the past [1]. However, our domain variables have the unique feature that a domain can be nested inside another domain.

6 Conclusion and Future Work

This work has investigated issues of how to provide better control for logic programs such that the efficiency of programs can be improved. We proposed two forms of lookahead: deep lookahead and shallow lookahead. They are designed for both CLP and Prolog type programs. Another important outcome from this work is the notion of nested domain variables. We introduced a special domain which can contain non-ground compound terms, i.e., open structures. Variables within these open structures can become domain variables. A nested domain can keep information on the Cartesian product of several domains. With our current implementation, the Cartesian product is represented as a tree structure. Nested domains can be exploited not only in Prolog-type programs but also in finite domain constraint programs. From our experimental results, it seems that our approach is beneficial for applications which contain dependent non-determinate computations. With our lookahead techniques, more than two non-determinate computation can be executed simultaneously. The communication between non-determinate computations is done through nested domain variables, which can represent disjunctive constraint stores.

We have tested our idea by an experimental implementation under SICStus Prolog. Nested domain variables are implemented by using the attributed variables of SICStus Prolog. The experimental results confirm the expected benefits.

Our work is still at an early stage of development. As future work, we would like to investigate the following issues:

- We need to study in more detail how nested domain variables can be applied to finite domain constraint programs. For instance, we may need some clear rules to select which variables should be grouped as a tuple, i.e., represented as a nested domain.
- Although we have proposed two forms of lookahead: deep and shallow lookahead, it might not be very clear from a programmer's point of view in what situations which forms of lookahead should be applied. We will have to carry out a wider study of various types of programs to answer these questions.
- The program transformation part is still not implemented. More technical details needed to be addressed.

Acknowledgements

We would like to thank all anonymous reviewers for their useful and encouraging comments. We also would like to thank David Warren for his invaluable feedback on the paper.

References

1. R. Bahgat, V. Santos Costa, and R. Yang. ARCH: A Parallel Execution Model that Minimises the Search Space of Logic Programs. *Egyptian Computer Journal*, 23(2), 1996. 321, 329
2. I. Dutra. A Flexible Scheduler for Andorra-I. In A. Beaumont and G. Gupta, editors, *Lecture Notes in Computer Science 569, Parallel Execution of Logic Programs*, pages 70–82. Springer-Verlag, June 1991. 320
3. G. Gupta and D. H. D. Warren. An Interpreter for the Extended Andorra Model. Presented at ICLP'90 Workshop on Parallel Logic Programming, Eilat, Israel, June 1990. 318

4. P. V. Hentenryck, Y. Deville, and C.-M. Teng. A generic arc-consistency algorithm and its specialization. *Artificial Intelligence*, 57, 1992. 323
5. S. Janson and S. Haridi. Programming Paradigms of the Andorra Kernel Language. In *Logic Programming: Proceedings of the International Logic Programming Symposium*, pages 167–186. MIT Press, October 1991. 318, 329
6. A. Mackworth and E. C. Freuder. The Complexity of Constraint Satisfaction Revisited. *Artificial Intelligence*, 59(1,2):57–62, 1993. 323
7. A. K. Mackworth. Consistency in Networks of Relations. *Artificial Intelligence*, 8(1):99–118, 1977. 323, 325, 329
8. R. Mohr and T. C. Henderson. Arc and Path Consistency Revisited. *Artificial Intelligence*, 28:225–233, 1986. 323
9. R. Moolenaar and B. Demoen. Hybrid Tree Search in the Andorra Model. In *Proceedings of the 8th International Conference on Logic Programming*, pages 110–123. MIT Press, June 1994. 329
10. D. Sanoff and J. B. Kruskal, editors. *Time Warps, String Edit and Macromolecules: the Theory and Practice of Sequence Comparision*. CSLI Publications, Reissueed edition, 1999. 319
11. V. Santos Costa, D. H. D. Warren, and R. Yang. The Andorra-I Engine: A parallel implementation of the Basic Andorra model. In *Logic Programming: Proceedings of the 8th International Conference*. MIT Press, 1991. 320
12. V. Santos Costa, D. H. D. Warren, and R. Yang. The Andorra-I Preprocessor: Supporting full Prolog on the Basic Andorra model. In *Logic Programming: Proceedings of the 8th International Conference*. MIT Press, 1991. 320
13. The Intelligent Systems Laboratory, Swedish Institute of Computer Science. SICStus Prolog User's Manual. www.sics.se/sicstus/docs/3.7.1/html/sicstus_toc.html, 1998. 326, 327
14. P. Van Hentenryck. *Constraint Satisfaction in Logic Programming*. MIT Press, 1989. 321, 325, 329
15. D. H. D. Warren. The Extended Andorra Model with Implicit Control. Presented at ICLP'90 Workshop on Parallel Logic Programming, Eilat, Israel, June 1990. 318
16. D. H. D. Warren. Personal communication, October 2001. 328
17. R. Yang et al. Performance of the Compiler-based Andorra-I System. In *Logic Programming: Proceedings of the 10th International Conference*. MIT Press, 1993. 320

Suspending and Resuming Computations
in Engines for SLG Evaluation

Luís F. Castro, Terrance Swift, and David S. Warren

Department of Computer Science SUNY Stony Brook
{luis,tswift,warren}@cs.sunysb.edu

Abstract. SLD resolution, the evaluation mechanism for Prolog programs, is modeled as a sequence of SLD trees. Since only one branch of an SLD tree needs to be active at any time, SLD can be implemented via engines whose memory management is stack-based, as the WAM. Tabling, and more specifically SLG resolution, is modeled as a sequence of forests of trees in which several computation paths may need to be active at any time. This reflects the fact that a computation path that consumes answers may need to be suspended and resumed multiple times as answers are derived.

The SLGWAM architecture defines instructions to implement SLG resolution. Implementations of the SLGWAM architecture have so far shown a great deal of similarity in table access methods, high-level scheduling strategies, and support for incremental completion. However they have made different choices in what may be termed *environment management*: how to store suspended environments and how to check whether these environments need to be resumed. This paper describes the environment management techniques of different implementations of the SLGWAM architecture and analyzes their performance.

1 Introduction

Prolog implements SLD resolution using a depth-first search algorithm over an SLD search tree. This evaluation strategy allows for simple and efficient implementations of SLD via stack-based architectures, like the Warren Abstract Machine (WAM)[17]. However, SLD suffers from well-known deficiencies that stem from the fact that SLD trees may contain infinite paths, (i.e. loops), even for finite propositional programs. These infinite paths mean that many Prolog programs don't terminate that should; in addition, the inability to detect infinite paths causes semantic limitations when negation as finite failure is added to SLD. Tabling, or memoing, can avoid repetitive computations and allow programs to terminate in many cases where Prolog does not. Tabling can also recognize infinite loops in a derivation, and determine whether negative calls are involved in these paths. This allows tabling to detect *unfounded sets* and thereby form a basis for implementing the well-founded semantics [15]. Indeed, many implementations of the well-founded semantics, such as SLG [2] use tabling.

S. Krishnamurthi, C. R. Ramakrishnan (Eds.): PADL 2002, LNCS 2257, pp. 332–349, 2002.
© Springer-Verlag Berlin Heidelberg 2002

SLG evaluations are modeled as a sequence of forests of SLG trees. In any forest, several different computation paths may be active and awaiting the production of answers from other computation paths. The need to maintain several active computation paths requires memory management and scheduling techniques more flexible than those used by the WAM. In order to fully implement SLG resolution, a Prolog system has to support suspension of computations (e.g. when these computations await answers), and their later resumption (e.g. when an answer is derived). Suspended computations are represented by portions of the stacks. There exist several alternatives for the management of these stacks — for instance, suspended computations can share stack space with an active computation, or they can be copied out into a memory area separate from an active computation. The need to suspend and resume computations also means that simple stack-based scheduling may not be efficient for practical programs. The SLGWAM architecture [11] was designed as an extension to the WAM to support SLG resolution, while still retaining the efficient implementation techniques developed for traditional Prolog systems.

One may speak of an *SLGWAM architecture* as the instruction set presented in the SLGWAM definition of [11]. In that sense, the SLGWAM implementation in [11], which we refer to as $SLGWAM_{98}$, was the first instantiation of the SLGWAM architecture. Other implementations of the SLGWAM architecture have been developed, notably CAT [3], CHAT [5], and Síntese (the Portuguese word for "synthesis") which is a combination of $SLGWAM_{98}$ and CHAT. These implementations show a great deal of similarity overall, but differ in what we term *environment management*, which consists of how information for suspended computations is managed, and in what algorithms are used to determine that suspended computations need to be resumed. In addition, YapTab [10] has recently implemented the SLGWAM architecture in an Or-parallel framework. For sequential evaluation, the management of suspended environments in YapTab closely resembles that of $SLGWAM_{98}$, but YapTab differs in how it performs the incremental completion of mutually dependent sets of tabled subgoals.

These different implementations have arisen in part because of different goals for using tabling in program evaluation. The goal of $SLGWAM_{98}$ was to create an efficient tabling engine by distributing the overhead of modifications for tabling among different WAM and SLGWAM instructions. The primary goal of CHAT was to ensure that overheads of tabling were incurred almost exclusively by tabling instructions. The goal of Síntese was to explore whether a hybrid of $SLGWAM_{98}$ and CHAT might provide performance superior to both. And finally, the goal of YapTab was to provide an engine with good sequential performance that could be fit into the environment-copying Or-parallel engine of YAP. Recently so-called Linear Tabling Methods [19,13,7] have been proposed and implemented. These methods do not suspend computations, but restore the necessary earlier states by recomputing them. This recomputation causes them to have worse complexity than SLG on some programs. Since these are not implementations of the SLG architecture, they are not further considered here.

In this paper we describe in detail the differences in environment management between four engines that have been implemented for the SLGWAM architecture: SLGWAM$_{98}$, CHAT, Síntese, and YapTab [1]. Using a suite of Prolog and tabled programs, we compare and analyze time and space performance of all engines.

2   SLG Evaluation

In this section we review informally those aspects of SLG Resolution [2], that are relevant to the discussions that follow. An SLG evaluation can be modeled as a (possibly transfinite) sequence of forests of trees – that is, the state of an SLG evaluation can be modeled as a forest in which each subgoal encountered by an evaluation is represented by the root of a tree and the tree itself represents the actions performed in solving the subgoal (see e.g. [14] for a formal treatment using the forest of trees model) [2].

Example 1. We introduce relevant aspects of SLG via the evaluation of a simple double transitive closure.

```
:- table p/2.
p(X,Y) :- p(X,Z), p(Z,Y).
p(X,Y) :- a(X,Y).
a(1,2). a(1,3). a(2,3).
```

Figure 1 shows a forest at the end of the evaluation of the query ?- p(1,X) to this program. A node in an SLG evaluation is either the atom *fail* or has a clausal form:

$$Answer\_template <\text{-} Delay\_set | Goal\_list$$

In the clausal form, *Answer_template* maintains the relevant bindings to a sub-query that have been accumulated along a computation path, and *Goal_list* is a sequence of unresolved literals for the clause. Without loss of generality, we assume a left-to-right selection rule for literals in *Goal_list*. The *Delay_set* is a set of literals whose evaluation has been delayed, as discussed below.

Restricted to definite programs, SLG resembles other tabling methods. The first time a subgoal is encountered in an evaluation, a new tree with a single node is created via a NEW SUBGOAL operation. In Figure 1 nodes 1, 6, and 12 are created in this manner. Each immediate child of the root of a tree is created via a PROGRAM CLAUSE RESOLUTION step, as are nodes 2, 3, 7, 8, 13, and 14 in Figure 1. A non-root node N whose *Goal_list* is non-empty may have a selected literal whose atom is a tabled predicate (as is p/2) or a *non-tabled* predicate, (as a/2). We slightly abuse terminology by referring to each as tabled and non-tabled literals respectively. If N has a selected non-tabled literal, its children are

---

[1] We note that development of CAT was superceded by that of CHAT due to the poor performance of the former engine on tabled evaluations.

[2] The following discussion omits the SLG ANSWER COMPLETION which is not considered in this paper.

produced via PROGRAM CLAUSE RESOLUTION as in Prolog. However, if N has a selected tabled literal L, N is called a *consuming node*. If L is tabled and positive, the children of N are created through ANSWER RESOLUTION operations. If L is tabled and negative, a child of N may be produced in one of two ways. L may be evaluated directly, via a NEGATION RETURN operation if its truth value follows from the interpretation of the current forest (as explained below). Otherwise, if L is involved in a loop through negation or if there is a conditional answer for L, a DELAYING operation creates a child of N in which L is moved from the *Goal_list* to the *Delay_set*. If the truth value of L becomes known in a future forest a SIMPLIFICATION operation can be performed on any leaf node N_L that contains L in its *Delay_set*. This SIMPLIFICATION operation can either remove L from N_L or add a child $fail$ of N_L. A leaf node, *Ans*, in clausal form that has all literals in its *Goal_list* resolved away or delayed is called an *answer*; if the *Delay_set* of *Ans* is empty, *Ans* is *unconditional*. In Figure 1, nodes 4, 9, 10, and 20 are all unconditional answers. Intuitively a subgoal S has been *completely evaluated*, in a forest $\mathcal{F}$, if there can be no further answers produced in $\mathcal{F}$ (although answers for S may be simplified). Such a subgoal can be marked as completed via a COMPLETION operation. A node may become completely evaluated in one of two ways. First, the tree for S may contain an unconditional answer identical to S, so that no further information can be gained by evaluating S, a condition sometimes called *early completion*. Alternately, it may become completely evaluated if all SLG operations other than SIMPLIFICATION have been performed for S and for all other subgoals that S depends on.

Finally, we note that each forest $\mathcal{F}$ induces an interpretation $I_{\mathcal{F}}$ as follows. Any ground atom subsumed by an unconditional answer in $I_{\mathcal{F}}$ is *true* in $I_{\mathcal{F}}$; a ground atom subsumed by a completely evaluated subgoal S but not by *any* answer for S is *false* in $I_{\mathcal{F}}$; all other atoms are *undefined* in $I_{\mathcal{F}}$. In the interpretation induced by the forest of Figure 1 the atoms $\{p(1,2), p(1,3), p(2,3)\}$ are true, while all other atoms are false. Completeness stems from the fact that, given a forest $\mathcal{F}$ in which no further operations are possible, $I_{\mathcal{F}}$ corresponds to the well-founded model restricted to the subgoals in $\mathcal{F}$.

Operational Aspects of SLG Example 1 illustrates several important operational aspects of tabling. First is the need to *suspend* and *resume* computation paths: the computation path to node 2 is suspended immediately after it is created to allow the evaluation to produce node 3 and the answer p(1,2)<- at node 4. Once this answer is derived the path to node 2 is resumed and node 5 is produced. A similar sequence of events occurs at node 7. At an operational level a tabling engine must maintain environments for all consuming nodes against which further ANSWER RESOLUTION or NEGATIVE RETURN operations may lead to new answers. Furthermore, consumer nodes must continue to be resumed as new answers are derived or as subgoals are determined to be completely evaluated — i.e. until a *fixed point* is reached. And finally, a practical engine must perform *incremental completion* when (sets of) subgoals have become completely evaluated so that NEGATION RETURN operations can be scheduled, and so that

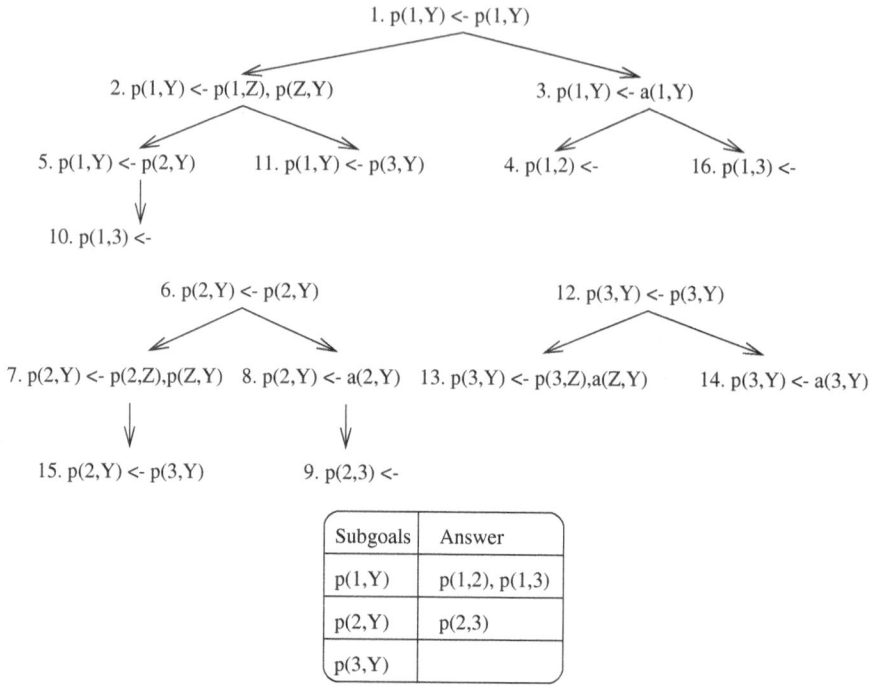

Fig. 1. An SLG Forest

memory can be reclaimed that is used by paths to consumer nodes in the trees of completed subgoals.

Incremental completion can be performed by maintaining an approximation of a *Subgoal Dependency Graph* for a forest $\mathcal{F}$ (SDG($\mathcal{F}$)) . Briefly, SDG($\mathcal{F}$) is a directed graph whose vertices are the non-completed subgoals of $\mathcal{F}$. Given a non-completed subgoal S_1, there is an edge from S_1 to all non-completed subgoals S_2 such that S_2 or *not* S_2 is a selected literal in some node in the tree for S_1. In Example 1 there are thus links from p(1,Y) to p(1,Y),p(2,Y), and p(3,Y); from p(2,Y) to p(2,Y) and p(3,Y); and from p(3,Y) to p(3,Y).

3   Environment Managing and Scheduling

In this section we present aspects of environment management that are relevant to the implementation descriptions and performance evaluations that follow, along with a brief description of scheduling strategies for tabled evaluations.

The Need for Management of Suspended Environments Before considering management of suspended environments, consider the management of environments in Prolog, under a 4-stack model. The Heap maintains long-lived structures and variables. The Local stack maintains the environments for clause-local variables, much like activation records in imperative languages. The `Control` and `Trail` stacks store information required to perform backtracking. Backtracking support requires that computation states be saved in order to be reinstalled later. For this, two kinds of information have to be stored: the value of registers, and the state of the `Heap` and `Local` stacks. The registers are kept in *choice-points*, stored in the `Control` stack. The state of the other stacks is kept by maintaining a log of conditional bindings in the `Trail`. In (pure) Prolog, variables may be bound only once during forward execution, and unbound during backtracking. Since no destructive update to variables is allowed, there is no need for the `Trail` to keep old values of variables that are bound. Thus the `Trail` requires only the addresses of variables that may become unbound upon backtracking.

For non-tabled predicates, the SLGWAM behaves as the WAM, using backtracking to perform a depth-first search of the state space. Each time a choice is made during execution, a *choice-point* is laid down in the `Control` stack. When backtracking is necessary, the topmost choice-point in the `Control` stack is used. When a choice-point is exhausted it can be discarded and its predecessor taken as the next source of alternatives. So a depth-first search is realized by using a stack-based evaluation on the computation states stored in the `Control` stack.

As noted above, SLG evaluation may require that a computation be suspended and other alternatives be executed, before it may be resumed, as with nodes 2 and 7 in Example 1. The choice-point for a call to such a node has to be taken off of the list of choice-points considered during backtracking. Moreover, a suspended computation may have to be resumed multiple times before it is completely evaluated, and a fixed point is reached.

Suspended computations are represented by portions of the execution stacks but implementations vary in how these sections are maintained. Sections can be either protected and kept in the execution stacks, or copied to an outside area. Notice that to recreate the state of a suspended computation, the system may need to redo bindings undone by backtracking while this computation was suspended. Thus, the `Trail` must be augmented to keep the values to which (conditional) variables are bound [16], so that the engine can traverse the trail not just backwards, but also forwards, rebinding variables needed to reconstruct a suspended state.

Fixpoint Scheduling The SLGWAM architecture extends the WAM stack-based scheduling with a second, fixpoint scheduler. In order to perform incremental completion, the SLGWAM architecture maintains, for each forest $\mathcal{F}$, safe over-approximations of SCCs of SDG($\mathcal{F}$), called *Approximate* or *Scheduling SCCs* or *ASCCs*. Within an *ASCC*, the first subgoal encountered by an evaluation is called a *leader*. At various times during a tabled evaluation, such as backtracking to a leader's choice-point, a fixpoint scheduler may be called. This scheduler is responsible for determining whether any suspended goals within the SCC require resumption. Conceptually, suspended goals that have answers to consume are reintroduced in the stacks, so that the WAM-style scheduler will subsequently run them. The fixpoint scheduler is thus responsible for performing a fixpoint algorithm that ensures that each answer of a non-completed subgoal is returned to each consuming node once and only once. The interface between the WAM and fixpoint schedulers is performed by the *suspension* and *resumption* operations. Upon backtracking to the choice-point of a consumer node of a non-completed subgoal, the consumer may be *suspended* if there are no further answers to return to the node. In addition a *resumption* operation for a consumer node may require both unbinding of variables and restoration of bindings using a forward trail.

Implementations of a fixpoint scheduler mainly differ in how suspended nodes are scheduled for resumption. Upon executing a fixpoint check, one or more suspended goals may be scheduled for resumption each time the fixpoint scheduler is activated. We say that a given engine implements a single- (resp. multiple-) dispatching scheduler if it resumes one (several) goal(s) at a time. In Example 1, when the answer in node 9 is derived, either node 5 or node 7 would be scheduled for resumption in a single-dispatch scheduler, while both would be scheduled in a multiple-dispatch scheduler. In the latter case, the resumed computations are set up so that backtracking will be responsible for resuming them when appropriate. For certain applications, multiple-dispatch fixpoint scheduling may be faster than single-dispatch. Given an ASCC with N consumer nodes that have unresolved answers, single-dispatch scheduling will require N traversals of the consumer nodes of the ASCC to return the answers, while multiple-dispatch may only require one traversal of the ASCC.

High-Level Scheduling Different algorithms for scheduling the return of answers to consuming nodes may be implemented by calling the fixpoint scheduler at different times, by parameterizing the fixpoint scheduler, and by altering the actions that occur when an answer is derived. Two high-level scheduling algorithms have emerged for implementations of the SLGWAM architecture [6]. *Batched* evaluation aims at computing the first answer to a given subgoal as soon as possible. To this end, answers are returned to their first call as they are computed. Conversely, *Local* evaluation aims at completing goals as soon as possible. Its basic principle is that answers should not be returned to subgoals outside of an ASCC until that ASCC is completely evaluated. The name "Local" is derived from the fact that the engine works only on a single independent *ASCC* in the subgoal dependency graph of an evaluation. Both types of evaluations have important properties. For applications like model-based diagnosis, in which finding a single diagnosis is of interest and may take substantially less time than finding all diagnoses, Batched evaluation is of interest. For applications in non-monotonic reasoning in which some answers are weaker than others [14], Local evaluation can have better complexity than Batched evaluation. Beyond such classes of programs, the choice of Batched or Local evaluation can have a large effect on the performance of various engines, as shown in Section 5.

4   SLGWAM Implementations

This section describes five implementations of the SLGWAM architecture that have been presented in the literature. CAT, CHAT, and Síntese are all based on the SLGWAM$_{98}$ code of XSB, while YapTab is based on Yap's Or-parallel engine. All of the implementations support Batched and Local evaluation (Section 3), incremental completion, and table access mechanisms based on tries [9].

SLGWAM$_{98}$ SLGWAM$_{98}$ ([11]) was the first implementation of the SLGWAM architecture, and its main goal was to provide an efficient engine for tabled logic programs, with overheads distributed among tabled and non-tabled instructions.

Suspended computations, in SLGWAM$_{98}$, are *frozen* in the execution stacks. The freezing process involves maintaining the portions of the stacks that represent the suspended computations in their original places. In order to protect these portions of the stacks from being overwritten, *freeze registers* are used. Freeze registers are new registers in the virtual machine architecture, one for each stack, that always point to the latest frozen computation. These registers protect against space being recovered for any computation that is older than the youngest suspended goal in the stacks, until the subgoal is incrementally completed. The use of *freeze registers* incurs an overhead in evaluation, even for non-tabled Prolog programs, since they have to be checked in several operations of the WAM — for instance, the `Heap` and/or `Local` freeze register must be checked when deciding if a binding is conditional, and the `Local` freeze register must be checked upon the WAM `allocate` instruction. Furthermore, since suspended computations are maintained in execution stacks, there is no guarantee that a stack frame is a child of its predecessor in the stack. To maintain information of the parent of a given frame, parent pointers are added to trail frames and choice-points (WAM `Local` stack environments already contain such a parent pointer). Thus `Trail` frames for SLGWAM$_{98}$ contain 3 cells: the address of the trailed variable, the value to which the variable was bound, and a parent pointer. In terms of managing suspended environments, SLGWAM$_{98}$ has the advantage that it is efficient to suspend and resume consumer nodes, by simply untrailing and following a forward trail. On the other hand, Prolog choice-points may be trapped beneath a *freeze register*. As a result their space may not be reclaimed upon a `trust` operation, but may need to wait until all space used to compute the fixed point for the *ASCC* is reclaimed.

In SLGWAM$_{98}$, the fixpoint scheduler uses parent pointers of choice-points to maintain *scheduling chains* of choice-points. It suspends computations by removing choice-points from the current chain. Conversely, it implements a multiple-dispatch *resumption* operation at fixed point check for an *ASCC S* by determining which consumer nodes for subgoals in *S* have operations that should be scheduled, and then inserting the appropriate choice-points for these consumer nodes into the scheduling chain [6]. We note in passing that to implement incremental completion efficiently SLGWAM$_{98}$ maintains a *completion stack* with a frame for each non-completed tabled subgoal in an evaluation. The completion stack is also used by CAT, CHAT, and Síntese, which descend from SLGWAM$_{98}$.

CAT The goal of CAT [3] is to add tabling to the WAM, without changing engine performance for non-tabled code. To accomplish this, CAT copies all relevant portions of the stacks to a separate area, instead of keeping suspended computations in the stacks as does SLGWAM$_{98}$. Copying of the stack sections corresponding to a computation is performed at suspension time. These areas are copied back to the top of the stacks when the computation is resumed.

Since the execution stacks don't have to support multiple branches of execution simultaneously, they can be implemented as in the WAM. As a result, *freeze registers* are not necessary, which makes non-tabled Prolog execution faster than SLGWAM$_{98}$. In terms of space, `Trail` cells in the execution stacks require only one word rather than the 3 words for the SLGWAM$_{98}$ [3], while no unused memory is ever trapped in execution stacks as in SLGWAM$_{98}$. However, the cost of suspending and resuming goals may be arbitrarily worse than SLGWAM$_{98}$, due to the copying involved [3].

CHAT The goal of CHAT [5] is to keep the overhead on non-tabled Prolog execution as low as possible, while having a better behavior for tabled programs than CAT. CHAT, like SLGWAM, uses the *freezing* technique to conserve suspended portions of the `Heap` and `Local` stacks; like CAT, it copies suspended computation states out of the `Trail` and the `Control` stacks

Within CHAT, Prolog choice-points in the `Control` stack are identical to the WAM: they do not require parent pointers; and freezing of the `Control` stack is not required. CHAT has other sophisticated techniques to reduce overhead of Prolog computations. First, while in the execution stack, `Trail` cells require 1 word, as in the WAM; their forward values are collected at suspension time, when the actual copying is done. Thus, only those portions of the `Trail` that are copied outside of the stack keep forward values. This allows CHAT to approximate the resumption of SLGWAM$_{98}$, while executing trailing as does the WAM. In addition, *freeze* variables for the `Local` stack and `Heap` are simulated by traversing frames of the `Control` stack whenever *freeze registers* would need to be maintained in the SLGWAM$_{98}$, a technique we term *simulated freezing*.

A characteristic that arises from CHAT's copying of the `Trail` is its single-dispatch fixpoint scheduler. Since the `Trail` does not keep forward `Trail` values in execution stacks, the resumption process would have to be split into two phases in order to support a multiple-dispatching scheduler. That is, multiple choice-points of suspended goals could be scheduled for resumption by the fixpoint scheduler, but their corresponding `Trail` sections would have to be copied into the stacks upon backtracking.

As discussed in [4], the techniques used in CHAT to optimize behavior of Prolog code incur complexity for tabled code. First, arbitrarily many Prolog choice-points may have to be traversed by any new (consumer) tabled subgoal in order to perform *simulated freezing*. In order to attack this, a modification of the *simulated freezing* operation is suggested that involves identifying special choice-points in the `Control` stack to be place-holders for the simulated freeze registers, as well as other modifications. Second, not all bindings common to two suspended environments are shared between computation paths. `Trail` sec-

---

[3] In engines that use a pre-image trail to implement attributed variables, CAT requires 2 words per trail element, while SLGWAM$_{98}$ requires 4 words.

tions for suspended computations have the form of a tree, and are maintained as such in both SLGWAM$_{98}$ and CHAT. However, CHAT considers sharing only up to tabled choice-points. If the oldest common choice-point between two suspended computations is a non-tabled choice-point, CHAT will create two copies of this (and possibly other) choice-points if these environments are suspended. Besides the potential memory overhead, non-incremental resumption also affects the amount of bindings and unbindings performed when switching environments. For example, suppose two suspended computations A and B share a common ancestor in the non-tabled Prolog choice-point P. In reality, the copied `Trail` sections for A and B will be shared only up to C, the youngest tabled Prolog choice-point older than P. In order to switch from A to B, the engine has to unbind variables trailed between P and C when removing A from the stacks, only to rebind them to the same values again when installing B. We say that an engine supports *incremental resumption* if it shares all bindings common to computation paths. [4] proposes an extension to the CHAT suspension operation that would support incremental resumption. If extended according to the proposals in [4], CHAT can attain the same time complexity as SLGWAM$_{98}$. However, to the best of our knowledge these extensions, which we denote as ΘCHAT, have not been implemented.

For Prolog programs CHAT is more efficient in terms of space than the SLGWAM$_{98}$. However, for tabled programs CHAT has tradeoffs with respect to the SLGWAM$_{98}$. In one sense, CHAT manages memory more efficiently than SLGWAM$_{98}$, since obsolete Prolog environments will not need to be maintained in the `Control` and `Trail` stacks. On the other hand, CHAT requires an overhead for maintaining suspended environments, and the lack of incremental resumption can lead to a large amount of memory consumption due to duplication of trail information. These tradeoffs are examined further in Section 5.3.

Síntese Síntese was designed with the goal of optimizing performance across a spectrum of tabled and non-tabled programs. Síntese adopts the SLGWAM *freezing* technique for the `Heap`, `Local` and `Trail` stacks. The `Control` stack is copied, as in CHAT. As discussed in Section 3, and demonstrated on practical programs in Section 5, the *simulated freezing* technique may incur an arbitrary overheads due to repeated updates to the top portions of the `Control` stack. In order to avoid this, Síntese uses *freeze registers* to freeze the stacks. The motivation for freezing the `Trail` is twofold. First, it addresses the lack of incremental resumption of CHAT, since in Síntese common `Trail` sections are always implicitly shared in the stack. Second, it provides an environment that better supports multiple-dispatching scheduling. Resumption can be implemented simply by copying the choice-points to the `Control` stack, since all `Trail` sections are always available in the stack. Section 5.2 demonstrates practical programs in which multiple-dispatch is responsible for huge savings in execution times.

YapTab YapTab is a partial implementation of the SLGWAM architecture within the Or-parallel engine of YAP [10]. YapTab supports tabling of definite clauses, but does not implement tabled negation or deletion of answers. In terms of environment management it closely resembles SLGWAM$_{98}$: suspended computations reside in execution stacks and freeze registers are used. However the trailing mechanism of YapTab is optimized for Prolog execution. Trail cells contain addresses and their bound values, but no parent pointers. Rather, special cells are put onto the trail when the parent for cell T_1 is not contiguous to T_1. In addition, YapTab is implemented on a 3-stack WAM architecture, in which control information is kept on the Local stack.

The fixpoint scheduling of YapTab is quite different from the previous engines. Because of its support of the Or-parallel paradigm, YapTab supports both public choice points — those whose alternatives may be executed by different workers — and choice points that are private to a worker. Within an Or-parallel execution the least common public ancestor of two consumer nodes, C_1 and C_2, may be a Prolog choice point C_P, a fact that has two implications. First, it is convenient in such a case to make the non-tabled choice point C_P the (potential) leader of the ASCC to which C_1 and C_2 belong. And second, it may be difficult to schedule a fixpoint check from such a node if incremental resumption is not supported in the engine [4].

The fixpoint scheduler of YapTab can be characterized as multiple-dispatch. For sequential execution, it has the following behavior. Rather than creating a scheduling chain during fixpoint check, as with SLGWAM$_{98}$, the leader backtracks into the first consumer node for which there are unresolved answers. That node in turn backtracks through its answer and then determines the next consumer node with unresolved answers, if any, and backtracks to it. YapTab can thus execute a multiple-dispatch fixpoint scheduling operation in one traversal of the consumer nodes in an ASCC. By contrast, SLGWAM$_{98}$ requires one traversal to determine which consumer choice points belong in a scheduling chain, and then another to actually return the answers to the choice points.

Summary of Implementations In Table 1, we summarize the preceding implementations with regard to their memory layouts for various execution stacks (shared or copied), their choice of freeze registers (actual or simulated), and their choice of scheduling dispatch (single or multiple).

5   Experimental Evaluation

In this section we compare performance of SLGWAM$_{98}$, CHAT, Síntese, and YapTab. Both SLGWAM$_{98}$ and CHAT were obtained through configuration options of XSB 2.4. Separately, Síntese was implemented starting from XSB 2.4 system code. A pre-release of YapTab was obtained from R. Rocha and compiled to use tabling but not Or-parallelism.

---

[4] To support incremental completion of ASCCs that belong to more than one worker, YapTab replaces the completion stack of SLGWAM$_{98}$ with data structures that reside in a shared dependency space [10].

Table 1. Summary of Implementation Choices

	SLGWAM₉₈	CAT	CHAT	Síntese	YapTab
`Heap`	shared	copied	shared	shared	shared
`Heap` Freeze	actual	none	simulated	actual	actual
`Local` Stack	shared	copied	shared	shared	shared
`Local` Freeze	actual	none	simulated	actual	actual
`Trail`	shared	copied	copied	shared	shared
`Trail` Freeze	actual	none	none	actual	none
`Control` Stack	shared	copied	copied	copied	n/a
`Control` Freeze	actual	none	none	none	n/a
Scheduling Dispatch	multiple	single	single	multiple	multiple

5.1 Methodology

The Prolog benchmarks consist of traditional Prolog programs: `deriv`, a symbolic derivative benchmark; `nrev`, an implementation of the naïve reverse algorithm; `qsort`, the quicksort algorithm; `query`, a search program for countries of approximately equal population density; `serialize`, a program that itemizes a list of integers; `ack`, a predicate to compute the Ackerman function and `compiler`, part of the XSB compiler on a program consisting of 222 clauses. The first five programs were written by David H. D. Warren, `ack` by C. R. Ramakrishnan, and `compiler` by the XSB Group.

Both synthetic and applications benchmarks were used to test tabled evaluation. The synthetic benchmarks include a left-recursive ancestor predicate `lanc`; `ranc`, a right-recursive ancestor, and the benchmark `win - not win`, implementing the stalemate game. All programs are executed over chains and cycles. Applications benchmarks `leader`, `sieve4(a)` and `sieve4(b)` are concurrent verification benchmarks as executed using the XMC model-checker (both XMC and the benchmarks used are explained in [8]). The `flora` benchmark reasons about objects and their attributes over a sophisticated inheritance network using the FLORA system [18]. Finally, the `diag` system diagnoses multiple faults in a 16-bit multiplier [1].

All timing numbers shown are the smallest execution time over 11 runs, each with a different memory size configuration, in an attempt to minimize spurious cache effects. Timing figures are in seconds, and represent the amount of CPU time used to run the programs. Garbage collection has been disabled for all runs. The benchmarking platform is a Sun workstation with two UltraSPARC-II processors at 336MHz, and 3Gb of core memory. All configurations were compiled using `gcc` version 2.95.1. The benchmarks are available via the XSB test suite, `http://xsb.sourceforge.net/`.

5.2 Comparing Engine Times

Table 2 shows a comparison of execution times for Local evaluation for the three engines currently implemented in the XSB System.

Table 2. Comparing Performance of Different Engines under Local Evaluation

Programs	Slgwam$_{98}$	CHAT	Síntese
compiler	3.80	3.54	3.82
deriv	1.44	1.27	1.44
nrev	1.70	1.55	1.62
qsort	1.17	0.97	1.08
query	1.69	1.49	1.56
serialise	2.79	2.49	2.74
ack	4.92	4.69	5.22
lanc(1k,chain)	2.21	2.58	2.11
lanc(1k,cycle)	2.22	2.64	2.15
lanc(2k,chain)	4.44	5.21	4.29
lanc(2k,cycle)	4.42	5.29	4.44
ranc(1k,chain)	1.35	1.40	1.09
ranc(1k,cycle)	4.20	4.19	3.27
win(2k,chain)	5.29	5.41	5.46
win(2k,cycle)	6.18	275.11	8.91
leader5	2.89	2.74	2.88
sieve4(a)	7.20	12.03	12.77
sieve4(b)	5.66	5.31	5.66
flora	3.17	73.98	5.15
diag	61.83	63.59	67.08

Table 2 shows that CHAT is fastest of the three engines for Prolog programs – having an arithmetic mean that is about 9% better than either SLGWAM$_{98}$ or Síntese. The tabled benchmarks show more variance. For left and right ancestor, Síntese is faster than both SLGWAM$_{98}$ and CHAT. It is not yet clear why this is so, since this was not one of the expectations for Síntese. Note that CHAT is much slower than SLGWAM$_{98}$ and Síntese for the win(2k,cycle) and the flora benchmarks, while Síntese is also about 62% slower than SLGWAM$_{98}$ on the flora benchmark. We analyze the reasons for this behavior below.

Measuring the Impact of Freeze Registers and Fixpoint Schedulers To understand the anomalies in Table 2 for the win(2k,cycle) and flora benchmarks, two separate versions of Síntese were constructed to model aspects of CHAT. SínteseNF implemented simulated *freeze registers*; and SínteseSD replaced its multiple-dispatch fixpoint scheduler with a single-dispatch scheduler.

As expected, non-tabled Prolog programs run faster without freeze registers: SínteseNF is about 3% slower than CHAT, due mostly to its use of the 3-cell SLGWAM$_{98}$ trail. A speedup for SínteseNF is also observed in some of the *Applications* benchmarks, where non-tabled execution is significant. However, simulated freeze registers incur a large overhead on the flora benchmark for which SínteseNF is more than 6 times slower than Síntese.

In terms of fixpoint scheduling, the synthetic benchmarks show a small slow-down for most programs in SínteseSD due to the greater number of times

Table 3. Freeze Register and Fixpoint Scheduler Variations for Local Evaluation

Programs	Síntese	SínteseNF	SínteseSD
compiler	3.82	3.55	3.70
deriv	1.44	1.38	1.43
nrev	1.62	1.62	1.62
qsort	1.08	1.03	1.10
query	1.56	1.63	1.56
serialise	2.74	2.66	2.72
ack	5.22	4.68	4.92
lanc(1k,chain)	2.11	2.10	2.15
lanc(1k,cycle)	2.15	2.13	2.16
lanc(2k,chain)	4.29	4.22	4.41
lanc(2k,cycle)	4.44	4.22	4.47
ranc(1k,chain)	1.09	1.13	1.12
ranc(1k,cycle)	3.27	3.20	49.34
win(2k,chain)	5.46	4.98	5.40
win(2k,cycle)	8.91	8.10	68.51
leader5	2.88	2.80	2.87
sieve4(a)	12.77	12.37	12.76
sieve4(b)	5.66	5.46	5.60
flora	5.15	37.94	84.34
diag	67.08	63.26	66.78

the single-dispatch scheduler has to be activated. This is most evident in `ranc(1k,cycle)`, `win(2k,cycle)` and especially `flora`. These programs create large ASCCs which benefit from multiple-dispatch scheduling. Profiling shows that most of the subgoals created during `flora` benchmark evaluation are in a single large ASCC containing 9314 subgoals, and 119354 consumers. As a result, savings from a multiple-dispatch scheduler are large in this case.

Comparing Times for Local and Batched Evaluation As noted in Section 3, Local and Batched evaluation can be implemented using either single or multiple dispatch scheduling, and both types of evaluations have been implemented in both XSB and YAP. Table 4 compares running times for the `Applications` benchmarks between Local and Batched scheduling. The results are for multiple-dispatch Síntese with actual freeze registers. The times suggest that the algorithms are comparable for the XMC programs. On the other hand, `diag` performs slightly worse and `flora` is an order of magnitude slower in Batched.

Comparing Times with YapTab Comparisons of YapTab indicate that it is about 2.5 times faster than XSB compiled for CHAT for Prolog evaluation [10]. Some of the difference in speed can be attributed to the different designs of XSB and YAP: for instance XSB checks for a debugger interrupt at every WAM `call` and `execute` instruction. However, it is likely that most of the speed of YAP

Table 4. Benchmarking Batched vs. Local Evaluation

Programs	Síntese	
	Local	Batched
`leader5`	2.88	2.86
`sieve4(a)`	12.77	12.77
`sieve4(b)`	5.66	5.61
`flora`	5.15	52.55
`diag`	67.08	72.34

is due to coding optimizations of the YAP bytecode emulator [12]. Surprisingly, despite the speed of sequential YAP, YapTab incurs an overhead of about 5% over sequential Yap [10] — less than the overhead for SLGWAM$_{98}$ over CHAT. This low overhead perhaps indicates that the handling of freeze registers is amenable to the same optimization techniques as other parts of the WAM emulator.

[10] also indicates that YapTab is about 2 times faster than CHAT (XSB 2.4) for left ancestor, right ancestor, `sieve` and `leader`. It should be stressed that these results are preliminary. It remains an open question how much of this speedup is due to YapTab's restricted tabling functionality (Section 3); how much is due to YAP's faster evaluation of Prolog code; how much is due to the coding of features that it shares with SLGWAM$_{98}$; and how much is due to YapTab's fixpoint scheduler

5.3   Comparisons of Memory Consumption

For Prolog evaluation, the main difference between the engines in space consumption lies in how they handle the trail. SLGWAM$_{98}$ and Síntese both require an address, a binding value, and a parent pointer for each trail cell; YapTab requires an address and a binding value, while CHAT requires only an address. For tabled evaluations memory consumption may be critical to whether a query can terminate. Tradeoffs among the engines are less clear cut, however, as memory consumption depends not only on aspects of engine design, but also on whether Batched or Local evaluation is used. Table 5 compares space consumption for Local and Batched evaluation for a number of queries and engines. The table records the maximum space used for the WAM stacks, the completion stack, and external enviornment space. This last space contains copying space for the trail and control stack for CHAT; and for the control space in Síntese. In addition the total table space is also recorded, although it should be noted that the table space persists after a query is evaluated unless it is explicitly reclaimed, while space is automatically reclaimed for the other memory areas.

From Table 5, it can be seen that for `leader` and `sieve(a)`, Local evaluation is significantly more efficient than Batched evaluation. Indeed, Local evaluation can be expected to save space in an evaluation with many ASCCs. However, in evaluations for which there are few ASCCs – such as the ancestor predicate over a chain or `flora` (Section 5.2) – Local evaluation does not save space. It can also

Table 5. Memory Consumption of Different Engines and Evaluation Strategies

		SLGWAM$_{98}$ (Local)	CHAT (Local)	Síntese (Local)	SLGWAM$_{98}$ (Batched)	CHAT (Batched)	Síntese (Batched)
Flora	Max Heap	403936	431116	431064	238068	210460	210344
	Max Local Stack	543124	512432	512688	484996	494736	494492
	Max Trail	1683160	1268	1677580	168260	120	1622596
	Max Control Stack	7293860	29408	723488	8014380	6160	81872
	Ext. Env. Space	0	78364904	12094384	0	26057248	12476540
	Max Compl. Stack	149088	298176	298176	235176	392200	392080
	Table Space	3357916	3269176	3269432	3588116	3516104	3500232
Left anc.	Max Heap	604	604	604	604	604	648
2k cycle	Max Local Stack	844	844	844	844	844	844
	Max Trail	244	44	244	244	84	124
	Max Control Stack	712	668	820	676	712	676
	Ext. Env. Space	0	152	108	0	152	108
	Max Compl. Stack	16	32	32	24	40	40
	Table Space	61604	61600	61600	61604	61600	61572
Right anc.	Max Heap	604	8716	8716	4604	12796	8512
1k cycle	Max Local Stack	20792	20732	20972	20792	20792	20768
	Max Trail	244	44	244	244	84	124
	Max Control Stack	86400	53588	61824	74112	53632	61768
	Ext. Env. Space	0	155648	110582	0	41072	108
	Max Compl. Stack	16384	32768	32768	24576	40960	40960
	Table Space	31606828	31602732	31602732	31606828	31602732	31602732
Leader	Max Heap	47252	47404	47388	2345060	3060824	2022824
	Max Local Stack	2824	2764	11776	90000	87996	91192
	Max Trail	1084	264	11368	44212	14588	43636
	Max Control Stack	5468	5956	12752	230812	212060	351924
	Ext. Env. Space	0	0	0	0	472312	205468
	Max Compl. Stack	608	1216	1216	23328	38800	38880
	Table Space	7534488	7522840	7522840	7542248	7530600	7530060
Sieve(a)	Max Heap	152312	151120	151104	5308656	5699292	4831468
	Max Local Stack	35104	35044	35044	812024	812024	884652
	Max Trail	30052	9944	29800	712384	237468	712180
	Max Control Stack	71044	87764	74968	1807948	176756	2098860
	Ext. Env. Space	0	0	0	0	0	0
	Max Compl. Stack	1696	3392	3392	60504	100840	100840
	Table Space	13829468	13809308	13809308	13849620	13839460	13829460

be seen from these benchmarks that the space savings in the CHAT execution trail is usually outweighed by the cost of storing the trail in external environment space. Furthermore, while SLGWAM$_{98}$ generally has a larger control stack than the other engines, due to its freezing of suspended environments, maintaining copied consumer nodes in the external environment space does not usually save space overall, as can be seen by comparing the SLGWAM$_{98}$ and Síntese space.

As mentioned in Section 4, SLGWAM$_{98}$ shares choice points for active and suspended environments on the `Control` stack; as a result Prolog choice points may be trapped in the `Control` stack, so that they cannot be deallocated upon a WAM `trust` operation. If such a case is common, then the `Control` stack size of SLGWAM$_{98}$ can be reduced by garbage collecting exhausted Prolog choice points from frozen memory. Such a garbage collector would be relatively easy to implement as the trapped choice points can be marked via the `trust` operation. While this should be useful in principle, trapped choice points do not account for a large portion of `Control` stack memory in SLGWAM$_{98}$: 143688 bytes for `flora` under both Local and Batched evaluation; 154720 bytes for `leader` under Batched evaluation; and 0 bytes for all other evaluations in Table 5.

6   Conclusion

This paper discussed designs and performance of 4 engines that implement the SLGWAM instruction architecture. All four engines use tries for table access; support Local and Batched Evaluation; and maintain approximate SCCs for incremental completion. For the latter feature, the three XSB engines, SLGWAM$_{98}$, CHAT, and Síntese use a completion stack, while YapTab uses other dependency structures. Otherwise, the implementations differ in whether they share or copy suspended environments, in whether they use freeze registers, and in their scheduling dispatch.

All of the engines have undergone a sustained implementation effort and can support large applications. Determining which engine is best depends on the type of queries one wishes to evaluate. If an application mix is weighted heavily towards Prolog, CHAT requires the least memory, while YapTab is fastest. For tabled queries, SLGWAM$_{98}$, and Síntese avoid the problems of simulated freeze registers and single-dispatch fixpoint scheduling, while SLGWAM$_{98}$ is suprisingly efficient in terms of memory. Detailed time and space comparisons with YapTab for tabled queries that do not involve negation are not yet available. However given its design, it is expected that YapTab would most resemble SLGWAM$_{98}$ in terms of space consumption and comparative query speed.

Of course, each of these implementations can be improved. As mentioned in Section 3, ΘCHAT proposes a solution to the problems of simulated freeze registers and to CHAT's lack of incremental resumption. It is also possible that memory management of the external environment space can be improved in CHAT and in Síntese. And finally, Section 5.3 discussed how memory consumption of SLGWAM$_{98}$ could be improved by garbage collecting trapped Prolog choice points. It is hoped that detailed comparisons of the various engines will lead to overall improvements in all of the systems they support.

Acknowledgements

This work was partially supported by NSF grants CCR-9702581, EIA-97-5998, and INT-96-00598.

References

1. J. J. Alferes, F. Azevedo, P. Barahona, C. Damásio, and T. Swift. Logic programming techniques for solving circuit diagnosis. Technical report, Universidade Nova de Lisboa, 2001. 343
2. W. Chen and D. S. Warren. Tabled Evaluation with Delaying for General Logic Programs. *Journal of the ACM*, 43(1):20–74, January 1996. 332, 334
3. B. Demoen and K. Sagonas. CAT: A copying approach to tabling. In *PLILP*, pages 21–35, 1998. 333, 339, 340
4. B. Demoen and K. Sagonas. Chat is θ(slg-wam). In *Proceedings of the 6th International Conference on Logic for Programming and Automated Reasoning*, pages 337–357, 1999. 340, 341
5. B. Demoen and K. Sagonas. CHAT: the Copy-Hybrid Approach to Tabling. In *Practical Aspects of Declarative Languages: First International Workshop*, 1999. 333, 340
6. J. Freire, T. Swift, and D. S. Warren. Beyond depth-first: Improving tabled logic programs through alternative scheduling strategies. *Journal of Functional and Logic Programming*, 1998(3), 1998. 338, 339
7. Haifeng Guo and Gopal Gupta. A new tabling scheme with dynamic reordering of alternatives. In *Workshop on Parallelism and Implementation Technology for (Constraint) Logic Languages*, July 2000. 333
8. Y. S. Ramakrishna, C. R. Ramakrishnan, I. V. Ramakrishnan, S. Smolka, T. Swift, and D. S. Warren. Efficient model checking using tabled resolution. In *Proceedings on the Conference on Automated Verification*, pages 143–154, 1997. 343
9. I. V. Ramakrishnan, P. Rao, K. Sagonas, T. Swift, and D. S. Warren. Efficient access mechanisms for tabled logic programs. *Journal of Logic Programming*, 38(1):31–55, January 1999. 339
10. R. Rocha. *On applying Or-parallelism and tabling to logic programs*. PhD thesis, Universidade do Porto, 2001. 333, 341, 342, 345, 346
11. K. Sagonas and T. Swift. An abstract machine for tabled execution of fixed-order stratified logic programs. *ACM TOPLAS*, 20(3):586 – 635, May 1998. 333, 339
12. Vítor Santos Costa. Optimising bytecode emulation for prolog. In *LNCS 1702, Proceedings of PPDP'99*, pages 261–267. Springer-Verlag, September 1999. 346
13. Yi-Dong Shen, Li-Yan Yuan, Jia-Huai You, and Neng-Fa Zhou. Linear tabulated resolution based on Prolog control strategy. *Journal of Theory and Practice of Logic Programming*, 1(1):71–122, 2001. 333
14. T. Swift. Tabling for non-monotonic programming. *Annals of Mathematics and Artificial Intelligence*, 25(3-4):201–240, 1999. 334, 338
15. A. van Gelder, K. A. Ross, and J. S. Schlipf. Unfounded sets and well-founded semantics for general logic programs. *Journal of the ACM*, 38(3):620–650, 1991. 332
16. D. S. Warren. Efficient Prolog memory management for flexible control. In *ILPS*, pages 198–202, 1984. 337
17. D. H. D. Warren. An abstract Prolog instruction set. Technical Report 309, SRI, 1983. 332
18. G. Yang and M. Kifer. Flora: Implementing an efficient DOOD system using a tabling logic engine. In *DOOD'2000: 6th International Conference on Rules and Objects in Databases*, 2000. 343
19. Neng-Fa Zhou, Yi-Dong Shen, Li-Yan Yuan, and Jia-Huai You. Implementation of a linear tabling mechanism. In *Proceedings of PADL 2000*, pages 109–123, 2000. 333

Author Index

Boyer, Robert S. 9
Bunus, Peter 280
Burnett, Margaret 173

Castro, Luís F. 332

Dahl, Veronica 3
Datta, Nayana 82
Demoen, Bart 299

El Khatib, Omar 82
Erwig, Martin 173

Fritzson, Peter 280

Gallagher, John P. 243
Gregory, Steve 318
Guo, Hai-Feng 82
Gupta, Gopal 82

Hudak, Paul 155

Iglesias, Juan Raymundo 82

Jayaraman, Bharat 28
Johansson, Erik 101

Karczmarczuk, Jerzy 225
Karshmer, Arthur I. 82
Kiselyov, Oleg 209

Lämmel, Ralf 137
Liang, Chuck C. 47

Meadows, Catherine 1
Milligan, Brook 82
Moore, J. Strother 9

Noamany, Mohammed 82
Novello, Stefano 262

Pontelli, Enrico 82
Puebla, Germán 243

Ranjan, Desh 82
Rhiger, Morten 120

Sagonas, Konstantinos 101, 299
Schimpf, Joachim 262
Shen, Kish 262
Singer, Josh 262
Swift, Terrance 332

Taha, Walid 155
Tambay, Pallavi 28
Thiemann, Peter 192
Torgersson, Olof 64

Vandeginste, Ruben 299
Visser, Joost 137

Wan, Zhanyong 155
Warren, David S. 332

Yang, Rong 318

Zhou, Xinhong 82

Lecture Notes in Computer Science

For information about Vols. 1–2179
please contact your bookseller or Springer-Verlag

Vol. 2180: J. Welch (Ed.), Distributed Computing. Proceedings, 2001. X, 343 pages. 2001.

Vol. 2181: C. Y. Westort (Ed.), Digital Earth Moving. Proceedings, 2001. XII, 117 pages. 2001.

Vol. 2182: M. Klusch, F. Zambonelli (Eds.), Cooperative Information Agents V. Proceedings, 2001. XII, 288 pages. 2001. (Subseries LNAI).

Vol. 2183: R. Kahle, P. Schroeder-Heister, R. Stärk (Eds.), Proof Theory in Computer Science. Proceedings, 2001. IX, 239 pages. 2001.

Vol. 2184: M. Tucci (Ed.), Multimedia Databases and Image Communication. Proceedings, 2001. X, 225 pages. 2001.

Vol. 2185: M. Gogolla, C. Kobryn (Eds.), «UML» 2001 – The Unified Modeling Language. Proceedings, 2001. XIV, 510 pages. 2001.

Vol. 2186: J. Bosch (Ed.), Generative and Component-Based Software Engineering. Proceedings, 2001. VIII, 177 pages. 2001.

Vol. 2187: U. Voges (Ed.), Computer Safety, Reliability and Security. Proceedings, 2001. XVI, 249 pages. 2001.

Vol. 2188: F. Bomarius, S. Komi-Sirviö (Eds.), Product Focused Software Process Improvement. Proceedings, 2001. XI, 382 pages. 2001.

Vol. 2189: F. Hoffmann, D.J. Hand, N. Adams, D. Fisher, G. Guimaraes (Eds.), Advances in Intelligent Data Analysis. Proceedings, 2001. XII, 384 pages. 2001.

Vol. 2190: A. de Antonio, R. Aylett, D. Ballin (Eds.), Intelligent Virtual Agents. Proceedings, 2001. VIII, 245 pages. 2001. (Subseries LNAI).

Vol. 2191: B. Radig, S. Florczyk (Eds.), Pattern Recognition. Proceedings, 2001. XVI, 452 pages. 2001.

Vol. 2192: A. Yonezawa, S. Matsuoka (Eds.), Metalevel Architectures and Separation of Crosscutting Concerns. Proceedings, 2001. XI, 283 pages. 2001.

Vol. 2193: F. Casati, D. Georgakopoulos, M.-C. Shan (Eds.), Technologies for E-Services. Proceedings, 2001. X, 213 pages. 2001.

Vol. 2194: A.K. Datta, T. Herman (Eds.), Self-Stabilizing Systems. Proceedings, 2001. VII, 229 pages. 2001.

Vol. 2195: H.-Y. Shum, M. Liao, S.-F. Chang (Eds.), Advances in Multimedia Information Processing – PCM 2001. Proceedings, 2001. XX, 1149 pages. 2001.

Vol. 2196: W. Taha (Ed.), Semantics, Applications, and Implementation of Program Generation. Proceedings, 2001. X, 219 pages. 2001.

Vol. 2197: O. Balet, G. Subsol, P. Torguet (Eds.), Virtual Storytelling. Proceedings, 2001. XI, 213 pages. 2001.

Vol. 2198: N. Zhong, Y. Yao, J. Liu, S. Ohsuga (Eds.), Web Intelligence: Research and Development. Proceedings, 2001. XVI, 615 pages. 2001. (Subseries LNAI).

Vol. 2199: J. Crespo, V. Maojo, F. Martin (Eds.), Medical Data Analysis. Proceedings, 2001. X, 311 pages. 2001.

Vol. 2200: G.I. Davida, Y. Frankel (Eds.), Information Security. Proceedings, 2001. XIII, 554 pages. 2001.

Vol. 2201: G.D. Abowd, B. Brumitt, S. Shafer (Eds.), Ubicomp 2001: Ubiquitous Computing. Proceedings, 2001. XIII, 372 pages. 2001.

Vol. 2202: A. Restivo, S. Ronchi Della Rocca, L. Roversi (Eds.), Theoretical Computer Science. Proceedings, 2001. XI, 440 pages. 2001.

Vol. 2203: A. Omicini, P. Petta, R. Tolksdorf (Eds.), Engineering Societies in the Agents World II. Proceedings, 2001. XI, 195 pages. 2001. (Subseries LNAI).

Vol. 2204: A. Brandstädt, V.B. Le (Eds.), Graph-Theoretic Concepts in Computer Science. Proceedings, 2001. X, 329 pages. 2001.

Vol. 2205: D.R. Montello (Ed.), Spatial Information Theory. Proceedings, 2001. XIV, 503 pages. 2001.

Vol. 2206: B. Reusch (Ed.), Computational Intelligence. Proceedings, 2001. XVII, 1003 pages. 2001.

Vol. 2207: I.W. Marshall, S. Nettles, N. Wakamiya (Eds.), Active Networks. Proceedings, 2001. IX, 165 pages. 2001.

Vol. 2208: W.J. Niessen, M.A. Viergever (Eds.), Medical Image Computing and Computer-Assisted Intervention – MICCAI 2001. Proceedings, 2001. XXXV, 1446 pages. 2001.

Vol. 2209: W. Jonker (Ed.), Databases in Telecommunications II. Proceedings, 2001. VII, 179 pages. 2001.

Vol. 2210: Y. Liu, K. Tanaka, M. Iwata, T. Higuchi, M. Yasunaga (Eds.), Evolvable Systems: From Biology to Hardware. Proceedings, 2001. XI, 341 pages. 2001.

Vol. 2211: T.A. Henzinger, C.M. Kirsch (Eds.), Embedded Software. Proceedings, 2001. IX, 504 pages. 2001.

Vol. 2212: W. Lee, L. Mé, A. Wespi (Eds.), Recent Advances in Intrusion Detection. Proceedings, 2001. X, 205 pages. 2001.

Vol. 2213: M.J. van Sinderen, L.J.M. Nieuwenhuis (Eds.), Protocols for Multimedia Systems. Proceedings, 2001. XII, 239 pages. 2001.

Vol. 2214: O. Boldt, H. Jürgensen (Eds.), Automata Implementation. Proceedings, 1999. VIII, 183 pages. 2001.

Vol. 2215: N. Kobayashi, B.C. Pierce (Eds.), Theoretical Aspects of Computer Software. Proceedings, 2001. XV, 561 pages. 2001.

Vol. 2216: E.S. Al-Shaer, G. Pacifici (Eds.), Management of Multimedia on the Internet. Proceedings, 2001. XIV, 373 pages. 2001.

Vol. 2217: T. Gomi (Ed.), Evolutionary Robotics. Proceedings, 2001. XI, 139 pages. 2001.

Vol. 2218: R. Guerraoui (Ed.), Middleware 2001. Proceedings, 2001. XIII, 395 pages. 2001.

Vol. 2219: S.T. Taft, R.A. Duff, R.L. Brukardt, E. Ploedereder (Eds.), Consolidated Ada Reference Manual. XXV, 560 pages. 2001.

Vol. 2220: C. Johnson (Ed.), Interactive Systems. Proceedings, 2001. XII, 219 pages. 2001.

Vol. 2221: D.G. Feitelson, L. Rudolph (Eds.), Job Scheduling Strategies for Parallel Processing. Proceedings, 2001. VII, 207 pages. 2001.

Vol. 2223: P. Eades, T. Takaoka (Eds.), Algorithms and Computation. Proceedings, 2001. XIV, 780 pages. 2001.

Vol. 2224: H.S. Kunii, S. Jajodia, A. Sølvberg (Eds.), Conceptual Modeling – ER 2001. Proceedings, 2001. XIX, 614 pages. 2001.

Vol. 2225: N. Abe, R. Khardon, T. Zeugmann (Eds.), Algorithmic Learning Theory. Proceedings, 2001. XI, 379 pages. 2001. (Subseries LNAI).

Vol. 2226: K.P. Jantke, A. Shinohara (Eds.), Discovery Science. Proceedings, 2001. XII, 494 pages. 2001. (Subseries LNAI).

Vol. 2227: S. Boztaş, I.E. Shparlinski (Eds.), Applied Algebra, Algebraic Algorithms and Error-Correcting Codes. Proceedings, 2001. XII, 398 pages. 2001.

Vol. 2228: B. Monien, V.K. Prasanna, S. Vajapeyam (Eds.), High Performance Computing – HiPC 2001. Proceedings, 2001. XVIII, 438 pages. 2001.

Vol. 2229: S. Qing, T. Okamoto, J. Zhou (Eds.), Information and Communications Security. Proceedings, 2001. XIV, 504 pages. 2001.

Vol. 2230: T. Katila, I.E. Magnin, P. Clarysse, J. Montagnat, J. Nenonen (Eds.), Functional Imaging and Modeling of the Heart. Proceedings, 2001. XI, 158 pages. 2001.

Vol. 2232: L. Fiege, G. Mühl, U. Wilhelm (Eds.), Electronic Commerce. Proceedings, 2001. X, 233 pages. 2001.

Vol. 2233: J. Crowcroft, M. Hofmann (Eds.), Networked Group Communication. Proceedings, 2001. X, 205 pages. 2001.

Vol. 2234: L. Pacholski, P. Ružička (Eds.), SOFSEM 2001: Theory and Practice of Informatics. Proceedings, 2001. XI, 347 pages. 2001.

Vol. 2235: C.S. Calude, G. Păun, G. Rozenberg, A. Salomaa (Eds.), Multiset Processing. VIII, 359 pages. 2001.

Vol. 2236: K. Drira, A. Martelli, T. Villemur (Eds.), Cooperative Environments for Distributed Systems Engineering. IX, 281 pages. 2001.

Vol. 2237: P. Codognet (Ed.), Logic Programming. Proceedings, 2001. XI, 365 pages. 2001.

Vol. 2239: T. Walsh (Ed.), Principles and Practice of Constraint Programming – CP 2001. Proceedings, 2001. XIV, 788 pages. 2001.

Vol. 2240: G.P. Picco (Ed.), Mobile Agents. Proceedings, 2001. XIII, 277 pages. 2001.

Vol. 2241: M. Jünger, D. Naddef (Eds.), Computational Combinatorial Optimization. IX, 305 pages. 2001.

Vol. 2242: C.A. Lee (Ed.), Grid Computing – GRID 2001. Proceedings, 2001. XII, 185 pages. 2001.

Vol. 2243: G. Bertrand, A. Imiya, R. Klette (Eds.), Digital and Image Geometry. VII, 455 pages. 2001.

Vol. 2244: D. Bjørner, M. Broy, A.V. Zamulin (Eds.), Perspectives of System Informatics. Proceedings, 2001. XIII, 548 pages. 2001.

Vol. 2245: R. Hariharan, M. Mukund, V. Vinay (Eds.), FST TCS 2001: Foundations of Software Technology and Theoretical Computer Science. Proceedings, 2001. XI, 347 pages. 2001.

Vol. 2246: R. Falcone, M. Singh, Y.-H. Tan (Eds.), Trust in Cyber-societies. VIII, 195 pages. 2001. (Subseries LNAI).

Vol. 2247: C. P. Rangan, C. Ding (Eds.), Progress in Cryptology – INDOCRYPT 2001. Proceedings, 2001. XIII, 351 pages. 2001.

Vol. 2248: C. Boyd (Ed.), Advances in Cryptology – ASIACRYPT 2001. Proceedings, 2001. XI, 603 pages. 2001.

Vol. 2249: K. Nagi, Transactional Agents. XVI, 205 pages. 2001.

Vol. 2250: R. Nieuwenhuis, A. Voronkov (Eds.), Logic for Programming, Artificial Intelligence, and Reasoning. Proceedings, 2001. XV, 738 pages. 2001. (Subseries LNAI).

Vol. 2251: Y.Y. Tang, V. Wickerhauser, P.C. Yuen, C.Li (Eds.), Wavelet Analysis and Its Applications. Proceedings, 2001. XIII, 450 pages. 2001.

Vol. 2252: J. Liu, P.C. Yuen, C. Li, J. Ng, T. Ishida (Eds.), Active Media Technology. Proceedings, 2001. XII, 402 pages. 2001.

Vol. 2253: T. Terano, T. Nishida, A. Namatame, S. Tsumoto, Y. Ohsawa, T. Washio (Eds.), New Frontiers in Artificial Intelligence. Proceedings, 2001. XXVII, 553 pages. 2001. (Subseries LNAI).

Vol. 2254: M.R. Little, L. Nigay (Eds.), Engineering for Human-Computer Interaction. Proceedings, 2001. XI, 359 pages. 2001.

Vol. 2255: J. Dean, A. Gravel (Eds.), COTS-Based Software Systems. Proceedings, 2002. XIV, 257 pages. 2002.

Vol. 2256: M. Stumptner, D. Corbett, M. Brooks (Eds.), AI 2001: Advances in Artificial Intelligence. Proceedings, 2001. XII, 666 pages. 2001. (Subseries LNAI).

Vol. 2257: S. Krishnamurthi, C.R. Ramakrishnan (Eds.), Practical Aspects of Declarative Languages. Proceedings, 2002. VIII, 351 pages. 2002.

Vol. 2258: P. Brazdil, A. Jorge (Eds.), Progress in Artificial Intelligence. Proceedings, 2001. XII, 418 pages. 2001. (Subseries LNAI).

Vol. 2259: S. Vaudenay, A.M. Youssef (Eds.), Selected Areas in Cryptography. Proceedings, 2001. XI, 359 pages. 2001.

Vol. 2260: B. Honary (Ed.), Cryptography and Coding. Proceedings, 2001. IX, 416 pages. 2001.

Vol. 2264: K. Steinhöfel (Ed.), Stochastic Algorithms: Foundations and Applications. Proceedings, 2001. VIII, 203 pages. 2001.